Cain and Abel

The Cain and Abel story may be the first in the Western canon where the temptation to burrow in self-pity appears, where a man who spills blood thinks *himself* the victim. Rather than take responsibility for his actions, Cain chooses envy and somewhere deep inside swears that the reminder of his failure—Abel, his own brother—must be wiped from the earth. Thus, in Cain, we glimpse the mindset of a self-professed victim all of us have encountered: a friend, relative, or colleague, actually injured by someone else or just life, or wrongly believe themselves a victim. Either way, they invite additional misery with their response, a chronic "looking back" and blame of others, which sacrifices the future to the past.

Canada's blame culture

There are significant challenges for First Nations in particular as average educational levels are lower, with unemployment rates higher and incomes lower as a result. But education and one's own location are both "correctable." The statistics that show where and how higher incomes are obtained—off-reserve and with more education—make it clear that aboriginal Canadians are succeeding given an urban location and higher education. That hardly endorses the radical and false claim that Canada is akin to a genocidal state. There is instead much room for reasoned optimism.

On the rise of the Pacific class

According to proponents of the notion that past egregious actions pose an almost eternal barrier to success, the result should have been failure: in education, family, economic outcomes, and in the broader communities. Chinese and Japanese Americans continued to experience informal discrimination for years after formal, legal equality was granted. Those two communities *should* have foundered on the hard rocks of prejudice and discrimination. That was the theory. Reality would turn out very different.

vic•tim: *a person who suffers from destructive or injurious action or agency*

cult: *a group or sect bound together by devotion or veneration of the same thing, person, ideal, etc.*

ALSO BY MARK MILKE

THE
VICTIM
CULT

**How the culture of blame hurts
everyone and wrecks civilizations**

MARK MILKE

FOREWORD BY ELLIS ROSS

Thomas & Black

Published by Thomas & Black. Copyright © 2019 by Mark Milke

ISBN: 978-0-9687915-7-8
eISBN: 978-0-9687915-8-5

Photos used on cover by Jan Krnc (Pexels) and
Keystone Archives (Age Fotostock, used under license)

Definitions of 'victim' and 'cult' care of dictionary.com

Printed in Canada. Book distribution by Sandhill Book Marketing
www.sandhillbooks.com

Contents

Foreword by Ellis Ross

In 2004, as an elected councillor for my small First Nations village on the west coast of British Columbia, I began to realize that I had fallen into a narrative that prevents First Nations people from a better life as full participants in Canadian society and the economy.

I was born and raised in Kitamaat Village; got married and had two children; ran a crew boat, hunted, and fished.

But I didn't really know much about our issues and problems until I joined Council, and started to see the reality we faced.

Government funding formulas for programs didn't offer much for our issues. After looking at the Indian Act in the context of our village and our people, I concluded that "the Indian Act" was an imaginary hurdle and not the source of our band's problems, as so many aboriginal activists claimed it to be. It was pretty clear that fighting to change "the Indian Act" was a distraction, and a waste of our limited resources.

I remember a discussion at our council table where I was the only one arguing that my own personal problems were *not* the result of residential schools but was a result of my own decision-making. This is still my position, even though both my parents went to residential school and taught me to be a hardworking, honest, and independent person.

In looking for alternative solutions, I ended up reading up on two specific subjects: Haisla history from our archives, and aboriginal rights and title case law.

In reading our own history I was shocked, saddened, and angered at the treatment of my ancestors to the point of wanting revenge. I put that aside when I read about what we are experiencing today as aboriginals in terms of imprisonment, our children in care, our suicide rates, poverty, lack of education, and other social issues that demanded immediate attention.

It became clear that aboriginal rights and title was key to helping our people *today*, which in turn would set the stage for future generations. I didn't know exactly how it would be done, but I knew there were no limits on how far we could take it if we were smart and thoughtful.

It was definitely a long-term project, but what kept me going were the personal stories of success and rebirth. The single mom who complained that she was only working five days a week instead of seven. The ex-convict (a friend of mine) who, after given a chance at a real job, turned his life around and is flourishing. My community has gone from begging for jobs and government money to determining our own priorities and paying for it ourselves.

It's been an incredible journey, and every day I'm seeing and hearing more success stories coming from ordinary people who just want an opportunity to build a good life. To positively affect peoples' lives is why I agreed to take on public office and is what keeps me going.

In meeting Mark Milke, and reading this book, I saw what I had learned put in print for the first time. The false narratives or ideologies—the Indian Act, residential schools, etc.—that convince people that they are doomed to fail and that someone else or something else is to blame. There is plenty of blame to go around, but I prefer finding solutions.

I try to fight the idea that individuals are destined to fail, especially when I see political leaders using this to their own advantage instead of finding a way out for people who are stuck.

The First Nations story in Canada is not always a positive one. We have serious issues to address, and serious work to do.

I believe in Canada. I do believe that every Canadian, aboriginal or non-aboriginal, has an opportunity to build a good life and contribute to our society. It starts with accepting responsibility for our own decisions and facing reality, no matter how ugly or challenging that may be.

False narratives will only produce false solutions that will fall apart as soon as they are tested.

—ELLIS ROSS, former elected chief councillor, Haisla First Nation

There is nothing more fragile than civilization.

—HAVELOCK ELLIS

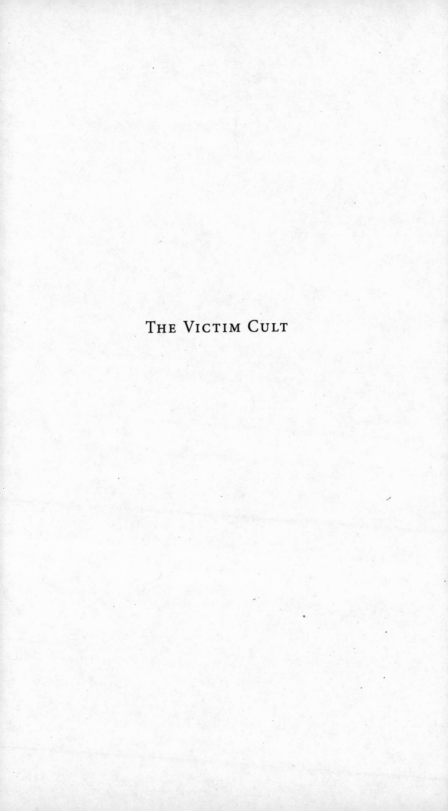

THE VICTIM CULT

PART I

The Eternal Temptation

One of the most striking traits of the inner life of a crowd is the feeling of being persecuted, a peculiar angry sensitiveness and irritability directed against those it has once and forever nominated as enemies.

—Elias Canetti, 1960, in *Masse un Macht (Crowds and Power)*

INTRODUCTION

Ultimately, claiming victim status does not itself bring sound ethical choices. Stalin and Hitler both claimed throughout their political careers to be victims. They persuaded millions of other people that they, too, were victims: of an international capitalist or Jewish conspiracy.... No major act of war or mass killing in the twentieth century began without the aggressors or perpetrators first claiming innocence and victimhood.

—TIMOTHY SNYDER, *Bloodlands: Europe Between Hitler and Stalin*

Actual victims vs. real victims

Ever since our distant ancestors stopped crawling on four feet and stood aright on two, people of every colour and creed mostly lived a Hobbesian nasty, brutish, and short life. They often did so in societies where tyrants, "neighbours," and life could be utterly cruel. A Jew in Spain in 1491? One year later, you were expelled and cast across the sea to North Africa. In Africa between the 16th and 19th centuries? Your life might end as a slave in the American south. A merchant in Russia in 1917, or an educated worker under Mao and Pol Pot, or a Tutsi with a Hutu neighbour in 1994? One would be fortunate to survive. Many did not.

Black Americans endured slavery and then post–Civil War lynching, prejudice, and discrimination. If one was of Asian descent at any time between 1850 and 1950 in Canada and the United States, governments in both countries made life difficult—to understate it, with severe institutional discrimination including withholding civil rights, and then for those of Japanese ancestry, internment camps. Native Americans and native Canadians faced similar and even more institutionalized prejudice and harm for over a century, with the added insult that it was their ancestors who arrived in the Americas first. Women in much of history faced challenges unknown to men. A few examples: subjected to foot-binding in China; expected to throw oneself on a funeral pyre upon the death of a husband in India; and refused the right to hold property and vote even in Western liberal democracies until the late-19th and early-20th centuries.

Men of every colour and creed too have been actual victims, though this is out of fashion to note in an age of identity politics. Today, presumed and past victimhood claims alike are tallied up with men ostensibly at the top of any privilege scale and at the bottom of any well of sympathy. Except the facts of biology and life meant that, for much of history, most women were ensconced in home and hearth, voluntarily or otherwise; such realities also meant that men were, until very recently, the ones in the forests, factories, and mines. It was mainly male lungs breathing poisonous air in the shafts and tunnels, and men's limbs shredded by machinery in industrial accidents. Men also fought the wars and suffered. In the Second World War—a just quest for survival and freedom from tyranny—men from Canada, the United Kingdom, the United States, India, and other Allied countries moved Nationalist Socialist Germany and imperial Japan off the world map by dying: The military death toll was 45,400, 450,700, 418,500, and 87,000, respectively, for those four countries alone. Millions of others who came home were wounded and forever hobbled physically and psychologically. Most of the dead and injured were men.

The problem with tallying up victim counts, even as just done, is how in history can we actually compare and weigh suffering as if an impartial scale exists? While mostly men were killed and wounded in war, wives and children on the home front lost husbands and fathers. An industrial accident that maimed a man also hurt his family. All we can say with any accuracy is all of the foregoing and millions more over the millennia were actual victims.

Now consider the 21st century's healthier and longer lives; more food than our ancestors could have imagined; more money, choices, and comforts for billions and improvements in diets, health, and lifespans even for the poorest; rights previously unknown for many with expanded choices for women and others long discriminated against. The world has mostly prospered and progressed in the last two centuries and especially in the last seventy years. This has not been without exception and the world is not now perfect: The

Syrian civil war, mass shootings in the United States, and terrorist attacks demonstrate that new victims are created daily. But compared with 1900, or 1800, and certainly with any other "zero" year in history, never has so much of humanity been better off. Despite such flourishing conditions for many, the rise of grievances and constellations of people that obsess over them—victim cults—has proceeded apace. Examples can be found that range from the mild to the murderous.

Start with the former: On American campuses, selected millennials routinely worry about "microaggression," words that might hurt or imply they are less than already accomplished. In New York City and Washington, D.C., a self-proclaimed billionaire managed to win his way to the White House by claiming to be a victim: of the media, other Republicans, and a judge. The now-president even complained of a rigged American election system until he won the White House. Those are the mild examples. What I will label as "moderate" assertions to victimhood also exist, where someone may have been victimized and thus should not be casually dismissed. They include past generations of indigenous Canadians and American minorities. The question here becomes what if anything can be done to ameliorate past harm. There are sober arguments for and against, and I explore both possibilities.

The third type of grievance narrative is of a different variety, not in degree but of kind: These are the victim cults that turn murderous. They include terrorists who claim to fight for others. Examples include atheists and theists with extreme interpretations of ideologies and faith alike. After Timothy McVeigh detonated 5,000 pounds of explosives at the Alfred P. Murrah Federal Building in Oklahoma City in 1995, he went to the execution chamber claiming he acted to protect Americans from their own federal government. In 2009, when Army Major Nidal Hasan, a U.S. Army psychiatrist, gunned down thirteen colleagues at the Fort Hood, Texas, army base, Hasan claimed he was protecting Muslims from Americans. The murderous victim-cult can also include a regime and an entire population. This happened in Rwanda where the Hutu majority that came to power after independence relentlessly propagandized against the Tutsi minority for three decades. State discrimination and revenge for alleged previous Tutsi privilege was accompanied by hatred pushed through schools, universities, the army, and in state-controlled media. A tinder-keg of deep resentment was created that needed only a spark to light. That happened in 1994, and the result was genocide. Marinating in blame for an extended period of time can and has led to mass murder.

The victim cult defined

Here is how the victim cult is defined in this book: Any person or group focused on the past over the present and at the expense of the future; whose imagined or real victimization dominates their vision and their interactions with others; who pathologically obsess over others whom they believe responsible for their condition, or that of their ancestors, or their tribe. In short, think of victim cultists as perennial stalkers, roaming to and fro, looking ravenously for someone to blame. Sometimes they are even in charge of nations.

On the mild side, one can charge erstwhile victims of overstating cause-and-effect links, of exaggerated or fake claims, of dredging up tragedies for monetary or political gain. Or they simply do not know their history. Depending on the example, one or more charges might stick. But if members of the victim cult were restricted only to sensitive college students or a developer/television celebrity-turned-president, the phenomenon would be of temporary interest only to sociologists and academics. Instead, the victim assertion when combined with potential touchstones for conflict (race, religion, ethnicity, and nationalism) and linked to a justification for some action (compensation, preferential treatment, revenge) risks nitroglycerine-like misfortune for all. The Hutus in Rwanda pre-1994 just noted is one example. There are others: Josef Stalin, Mao Tse-tung, Fidel Castro, and Pol Pot blamed their societies' economic troubles on entrepreneurial capitalists rather than on their own economic illiteracy and tyranny. The permanent revolutionary Yasser Arafat's self-pitying, murderous career was premised on the partial reality of some Palestinians' displacement in 1948, but his repeated rejection of opportunities for peace harmed Palestinians more than any Israeli politician ever could.

The common link: An intense focus on the past, which sacrifices the future

The common link in victim cults is not a particular creed, one's view of the state, racism, or even a destructive ideology. All can play a part, but they are not its drivers. Instead, the shared DNA in victim cultists across the centuries is a focus on actual or perceived wrongs, which then turns pathological. It becomes a way of defining oneself vis-à-vis others: I and my tribe are the victims and you are the oppressor. For some, the victim cult goes further and also becomes an ideological narrative.

This belief in the inherent unfairness of others is why Yasser Arafat blamed Israelis for Palestinian suffering. It is why he never agreed to a deal for a permanent Palestinian state. Arafat's uncompromised grievance-stance murdered children and every peace dove that flew across his life's journey. This mindset existed in Rwanda when Hutu leaders attached themselves to statistical perfection and to a permanent policy of blaming Tutsis, a single-mindedness that led to nearly a million massacred Tutsis and others in 1994. The victim cult was obvious in Germany in the 19th and early-20th centuries when nascent nationalism held that France, Western liberalism, and Jews were at fault for any and all national ills. Germany's victim cult sought to first restrict and then expunge all such "undesirables" from a narrowly defined collective. It was a belief that predated Adolf Hitler but was crystalized in his rise to power. The consequence was the fall of Germany, the destruction of much of Europe, the mass murder of European Jewry, and war that spread worldwide over six years. Perhaps the best symbol of this beyond the human bloodshed is St. Paul's Cathedral in London, part of the image for the cover of this book. St. Paul's, in various forms existed for 1,400 years. The latest iteration was built in the late-17th century by Christopher Wren. Bombed during the German "blitz" in the Second World War, the attack on St. Paul's was symbolic of the attack on civilization itself. Most victim narratives never reach such extremes, but the ones that do are existential threats to civilizations.

Victim cults, even when anchored in actual, past tragedies and legitimate grievances stare into the abyss. The relentless focus on the past, imagined or real, sacrifices progress in the present as entirely dependent on the correction of past sins. It is an impossible and fruitless quest. The result is that any conception of a future, any light, is submerged in the ever-deeper dark tunnel of fear, hate, and blame. The result is a nihilism that traps all who are near it, the innocent included. Such grievance narratives can infect leaders, a small cohort or entire societies; it can and does paralyze whole countries from moving forward due to a relentless focus on the past.

The dead end of victim cults and the outline of this book

Pause to consider what inspires all such ruin. The claim that one has been victimized, sometimes horribly so, may be accurate. There has never been a shortage of hate, cruelty, prejudice, and intended injury directed at others. The difference between victims in every age and members of the victim cult is not the lack of a past or present injury—everyone or some distant ancestor could fit that description—but also by the belief that those alive today must right past wrongs and to the satisfaction of the present, to engage in what economist Thomas Sowell characterized as the belief in a program of "cosmic justice."

Blame of others is a perennial temptation, and my initial chapters trace humanity's history and also victim-claims from American college students and President Donald Trump. The first is overwrought and the second offers a substandard example of leadership, but both the students and the president can at least be partly defused with analysis and derision. They are not equal to claims with some historical justifications for their existence. In a look at Canada's apology culture, I show how successive prime ministers from Brian Mulroney to Justin Trudeau made it their mission to express multiple regrets for multiple past actions of multiple past governments. It is not clear that this has added to the sum total of human compassion. Still, legitimate issues are raised, and the "apology" chapter sorts through such matters, as does the following one, which ponders the current obsession with ostensible privilege, defined by race and gender. Drawing on the work of Sowell, who has spent a lifetime analyzing such claims, and with new data from statistical agencies in the United States and Canada, I show (as did Sowell) how race and gender and outcomes are not as connected as many people assert. The better explanations are linked to education, geography, and culture, among other—better—causal explanations.

I then profile three historical examples of grievance narratives, which have been world-consequential. The first is from the 19th century, when Germans were actual victims of France's partial occupation. But Germans, in an attempt to recreate a cohesive national identity, became enamoured with cultural authenticity and race purity. Most people know about the last influence; they forget or do not know that German romanticism and a drive for pure German culture preceded it. That led to the wrong type of nationalism, an obsessive focus on one minority, blame, a fixation with cultural and then, only later, with race "purity." All of it was swathed in mystical, romantic worship of medieval emperors. The century-long victim cult was deepened later with post–World War One accusations of betrayal by Germany's leaders and blame of everyone else: the war's victors at Versailles and, of course, Jews. (Bizarrely, even Adolf Hitler, whom I profile in a separate chapter, thought himself a victim.) The various influences intensified the culture of blame; once that deepened, that culture was never to be dislodged absent some severe psychological shock. That only arrived with the necessary destruction of the land of Luther, Bach, and Beethoven in 1945. Germany serves as a warning to others tempted to dabble in cultural isolationism, blame, and self-pity for extended periods of time.

Rwanda's victim cult is profiled next. I examine its origins and then education system and political rhetoric as causal in the lead-up to the Rwandan genocide in 1994. Hutu complaints originated in real-world events: There was some discrimination by Tutsis and Belgian colonialists against the Hutu population, but there were also other factors that explained some statistical disparities between the more successful Tutsis and the Hutus. Regardless of the exact proportion of blame to be assigned, after Rwandan independence in 1961 and with the numerically dominant Hutu population in charge, they yet claimed to be under continual threat from the tiny Tutsi cohort. Obsessed with statistics they believed resulted from past prejudice, the Hutu-dominated government began its own discrimination campaign against Tutsis. For over three decades, state-sponsored discrimination and propagandic campaign of blame in Rwanda's schools, universities, and media exacerbated Rwanda's divisions. When the perfect storm of blame, fear, civil war, and opportunity arose in the early 1990s, the result was one million dead Rwandans, mostly Tutsis. It was another victim cult that ran its destructive course to a murderous end.

The last historical example is not a nation or a regime but Yasser Arafat, whose terrorism and revolutionary politics erupted from his fierce, unrelenting attachment to a grievance tied to the notion that the Palestinians' woes should command the world's attention. Arafat believed and proclaimed that Palestinians were always victims and never aggressors, a worldview born and wrapped in swaddling self-pity. That focus allowed Arafat to avoid responsibility, including a chronic refusal to come to a permanent peace treaty with Israel. The last offer, in 2000, was telling. It was offered on a platter from Israeli Prime Minister Ehud Barak and served up by President Bill Clinton. Arafat declined the peace offer in a fit of adolescent unreality, demanding more than the 97% deal already offered. At that juncture, Palestinians needed a statesman. In Arafat, they received a perpetual revolutionary, the Peter Pan of international politics. Arafat's psychological *refusenik* stance thus had consequences not only for Jews, Israel, and other victims of his worldwide terror activities over the decades but ultimately for Palestinians themselves.

Questions to answer and the standard explanations

How does an entrenched grievance culture arise? A variety of explanations are offered up by others. One is that victim thinking becomes entrenched, given the obvious fact that many people have been victimized. In this explanation, victims are just that and grievance narratives are a natural outgrowth of past harms and injustices. Another supplementary answer widely assumed in much of academia, media, and politics is similar: Past European imperialism and British colonialism disrupted pre-contact societies and are largely to blame for any ensuing troubles. Yet a third explanation: Elites in pursuit of power divide people and lead populations down this path because it serves their own agenda. Adolf Hitler, Rwanda's Hutu elite, and Yasser Arafat are all examples.

The explanations possess partial elucidative power, but none fully capture the phenomenon. That some people, tribes, countries, and civilizations have been damaged by others is true but banal. It does not explain why those in similar or worse circumstances never subscribe to the psychology of a permanent victim: Japanese Americans and Japanese Canadians after internment; Palestinians who took a contrarian view of Arafat's destructive agenda and created a life outside of the West Bank and Gaza; Jews the world over who have suffered time and again, yet repeatedly carve out an existence beyond the tragedies. Nor can the standard explanations account for leaders who move entire populations beyond tragic histories to forgiveness and societal peace, the late Nelson Mandela being recent history's most poignant example. Historical broad brushes are also of little help if one civilization, the West for some, is assumed to be the main drive for disruption and for the pathologies in others.

The third notion, where leaders exacerbate a prejudice and posit their society as a victim vis-à-vis another country or group is likewise inadequate to understanding the "why" of victim cults and their durability. That political explanation only takes us partway to understanding how grievance cultures become entrenched. It fails to explain the existing assumptions, the "raw material" used by demagogues. Politicians, monarchs, and dictators almost never invent a nation's culture. They instead work with the available "clay" and exploit mass cultural beliefs anchored in the raw material that predate them. Hitler capitalized on cultural assumptions and prejudices that Jews were too wealthy, unfairly advantaged, and foreign. He exploited that and the Versailles Treaty on his way to conquering and genocide. We are then still left with the question of how significant portions of a population become deeply aggrieved, so much so that they spot a weak, isolated entity and blame it for their own failures.

My explanations: perfectionism, romanticism, and Western self-loathing

Each standard theory has some explanatory power—explains part of the "why." But they fail to fully account for the phenomenon from the ancient world to the present day. To grasp the link between disparate cultures over time requires that we go below the historical tragedies that produce victims and beyond the blame of empires that have long since crumbled into Ozymandias-like sand. I offer three "spurs," which go beyond transitory events. The first arrives from philosophy and the damnable perfectionist fantasy first concocted by Plato. In his theory of how we should govern ourselves, the ancient Greek philosopher mused that a just society was possible if only we followed our imagination, the one which allows for perfectionist musings. For Plato, if we could imagine perfection, it followed that we should try and recreate it in our world, no matter the on-the-ground realities. (Think of Plato as the John Lennon of ancient Greece.) This belief in man's perfectibility has plagued the human race ever since.

Rousseau is the second problem. It was he who popularized the notion of pre-modern societies as more natural and authentic and thus more desirable. Rousseau thought civilization was the reason for humanity's wounds. In that sense, he had a naïve view of pre-modern societies, ones that were never quite the refuge for the beautiful lives he assumed. That much should be clear with the briefest historical review: Pre-modern societies untouched by contact with others have rarely been bastions of Woodstock-like freedom, populated by free-love flower children. They were also never London or New York City in diversity and opportunity. Instead, in the more untouched and culturally pure societies, men mostly ruled; women were mostly subservient and second-class citizens; slaves were ubiquitous; most people warred; and almost everyone met an early, unpleasant, and painful end. This was life for most, whether one lived in medieval Europe, indigenous America pre-Columbus, or on a Viking settlement on the edge of the north Atlantic.

The combination of Plato's perfectionism and Rousseau's romanticism has now led us back to the dark recognition from Thomas Hobbes, that tribalism is inevitable between men. In our case, the perfectionism and romanticism has led to renewed tribalism spurred by identity politics—let us call them identity isolationists. They retreat to the shell of a mythically pure culture where one's race or ethnicity or gender is assumed to determine views, opportunities, and incomes, especially vis-à-vis other "identities" assumed to have power. Such identity isolationists ensconced in victim cults see human beings not as individuals but as trapped or benefitting from some category: black, white, African, European, Asian, man, woman, indigenous, or immigrant, this or that religion, gay or straight, one nationality or another. The identity isolationists see people and their tribe, in history or now, as conquerors or victims but never both, which is simplified cartoonish history.

In addition to Plato and Rousseau, but touched on in my overview of today's victim cults, is a modern and new third influence. It is the suicidal self-loathing of a mainly Western class of intellectuals and academics (and others who follow them), who breathe in assumptions of Western guilt. This class is, in the best Western tradition, fine with self-criticism of their own civilization but too often negate the unique benefits of the last five Western centuries, faults notwithstanding. They loathe the West, or, more precisely, the Anglo-Saxon West, which, for all its faults, was in various iterations the civilization that ripped out institutional discrimination against women and minorities and, in its most significant accomplishment, ended the trade in human flesh—slavery—and then pressed other civilizations to do the same. Historic victim-cults engaged in a narrative of blame against the outside; but the modern Western victim-cults are deeply critical of their own civilization. Ironically and tragically as I write, just as protesters in Hong Kong desperately try to retain the best elements of the British legacy that made Hong Kong what it is, some in the West are self-critical to the point of civilizational suicide.

The problem is that even in mild or moderate grievance narratives, victim-cult claimants proceed while fixated on the past and possessed by the belief that history is a once-and-for-all deterministic force that blasts away choice in the present. Victim cultists are not satisfied with the arrival of a liberal society where individuals are, finally, treated as just that in law and policy and not as members of some collective. For victim cultists, present equality of opportunity and liberalism is never enough; they insist that some extraordinary effort be made today to correct for multiple ancient "yesterdays," for wrongs of a century or a millennium ago. It is an attempt to put history in the dock, to try long-dead peoples, and somehow balance the scales of justice across the ages. Such advocates remove moral choice and responsibility from those alive today. Both the individual and liberalism are sacrificed to the collective, to the tribe, yet again. Ominously and unbeknownst to their own narrow sensitivities, the victim-cult tribalists have invented nothing new. They have instead copied the culture worship enunciated by German philosophers, students, and nationalist groups at the turn of the late-18th and early-19th centuries. That fomented a disastrous narrow nationalism for 150 years. Today's victim cult is thus born courtesy of those who are blind to how they borrow heavily from German romantic nationalism with all its disastrous assumptions and results. Let us recall its murderous train-wreck ending in 1945.

Moving beyond grievances to hope

After explanations, I then turn to why the newest victim-cults are mistaken to use history as a cudgel against the present: because almost everyone's ancestors were less than ideal by our modern standards. The best example is slavery. I trace how few in anyone's tribe were innocent of that evil but also how it was abolished: due to evangelical Christians and colonials. This chapter exists to make clear this point: Whatever the sins of Western civilization and past British imperialists, if anti-Western critics wish to begin tabulations of intergenerational and intercultural guilt, honest accounting not only measures one civilization but all cultures and also both sides of the harm/help ledger.

This analysis is connected to a real question alive in Canada and in the United States: When should today's citizens compensate for past harm? When should one generation should make restitution for the sins of another? My answer: rarely, within reason, and carefully circumscribed. Finally, continuing on that theme, I offer five arguments against using the past forever against the present—the *modus operandi* of many victim cults. We need a statute of limitations against any eternal grievance.

In the last part of the book and positively to move beyond blame narratives, I examine a minority harassed and persecuted for a century, Asian Americans—specifically, those of Chinese and Japanese heritage. Their earliest struggles are chronicled. However, critically and as an antidote to the victim narrative, it is clear that Asian Americans (now a flourishing cohort by almost any measurement) showed evidence of success earlier than previously thought. They did so in spite of massive, harmful discrimination.

Four factors explain the achievements of both groups: relentless pushback against discrimination, an integrationist aim, entrepreneurship, and education. The flowering of one priority, education, was evident as early as the 1920s when Americans of Asian ancestry trumped white Americans on measurements such as high-school and college attendance, a legacy that continues today when Taiwanese Americans, for example, are among the most highly educated and highest income-earners in the United States. Their success is all the more remarkable given how prejudice was so ingrained in the first part of the last century that the American federal government could, without consequence, ban all Asian immigration starting in 1924. Despite that, those whose families emigrated from China, Japan, and, later, from other parts of Asia soon rose above other Americans on multiple measurements including education and incomes.

Critically, vis-à-vis grievance narratives, early Asian Americans rejected the tendency, prevalent today, to churn through the discriminatory past in an attempt to explain away poor choices and results in the present. Instead, Asian Americans consistently refused to define themselves as permanent victims.

This section in *The Victim Cult* is thus a hopeful accounting of how America's Asian immigrants from the mid-19th century onward renewed the American republic and its civilization.

We are all alike

Back to today's victim cults. A core animating drive is the presumption of permanent innocence ("us") and permanent guilt ("them") based on one's tribe. For some, surface divisions—colour, ethnicity, gender, or faith and politics—are assumed as *the* division among humanity, instead of the deeper, more intractable divide in each one of us: All have hearts with good and evil. Some understand the danger in thinking fault always lays elsewhere, in some other heart or some other civilization. In his account of life in Soviet labor camps, Alexander Solzhenitsyn pointed to this temptation to see each other in stark terms, to believe harm results from someone *else* who is depraved: "If only there were evil people somewhere insidiously committing evil deeds and it were necessary only to separate them from the rest of us and destroy them," wrote Solzhenitsyn in *The Gulag Archipelago*. With more insight than a thousand college graduate seminars could ever produce, Solzhenitsyn points to the actual source of humanity's woes: "But the line dividing good and evil cuts through the heart of every human being."

Solzhenitsyn's observation was that a wiser understanding of history starts with a wider understanding of human beings: We are all the problem. It is why a case can be made for optimism: Men and women are sentient beings with choices about which part of their divided hearts they will emphasize. Importantly, whether harmed or not, no one is forced to think of themselves as a permanent victim, without any options on how we think and live. The history of men and women is also one of individual choices: We can choose our own attitudes and actions; we can recognize our own—and our own tribe's—divided heart and blemished history; and then we can concentrate on a better project, the creation of a flourishing future for all.

—MARK MILKE, August 2019, Calgary

CHAPTER 1

From Cain and Abel to Donald Trump:
A journey through blame

---

*Here is the deeper truth: Blindness of superstition, old
stories embellished, retold, and then made more bitter in the
retelling, lie at the heart of these journeys through history.*

—ANDREW WHEATCROFT, *Infidels*

The first family of blame

"What have you done?!"[1] demands the deity of one brother as he inquires after the fate of the other.

God, who well knows what just transpired, still requires an accounting: "Your brother's blood cries out to me from the ground!"[2] he exclaims to Cain, soon to be marked as the world's first murderer.

Cain and Abel are part of the Genesis creation narrative where the sons of the first family of Eden offer sacrifices to God. The youngest, Abel, presents the fattest and firstborn sheep from his herd. Cain, the oldest, tills the ground and offers up vegetables. God accepts Abel's offering and rejects his brother's. That makes Cain angry—*very*, according to the story. To add to the rejection, God then lectures the supplicant: "Why are you angry?"[3] the Lord asks of a sullen Cain. "If you do what is right, will you not be accepted?"[4] The celestial dialogue then ends with the deity's warning to Cain to not succumb to resentment, to an evil that can corrupt the soul, but to instead master and defeat it. But the caution goes unheeded. Instead, Cain lures his brother to a field and in a simmering rage murders his brother.

The Cain and Abel story may be the first in the Western canon where the temptation to burrow in self-pity appears, where a man who spills blood thinks *himself* the victim. Rather than take responsibility for his actions, Cain chooses envy and somewhere deep inside swears that the reminder of his failure—Abel, his own brother—must be wiped from the earth. Thus, in Cain, we glimpse the mindset of a self-professed victim all of us have encountered: a friend, relative, or colleague, actually injured by someone else or just life, or wrongly believe themselves a victim. Either way, they invite additional misery with their response, a chronic "looking back" and blame of others, which sacrifices the future to the past.

Cain illustrates the ambiguity of claims to victimhood and which we should approach with initial openness because, perhaps, fate *was* unkind. While a traditional reading of Cain and Abel is the moral lesson taught to generations of Sunday school students—avoid resentment because that nourishes a bitter seed—there is another way to view Cain, God, and the slaughter of a brother: Maybe Cain, at least pre-bloodshed, should be pitied. After all, in the Genesis story there is no hint that God instructs Cain on the finer details of acceptable sacrifices. Abel was a shepherd and Cain a farmer and both offered gifts from their own labour. In this alternate reading, God seems less the Old Testament rock of consistency and more akin to a capricious Greek deity, one who toys with men on the field of life absent any markers to navigate the uneven ground. Let us then side with Cain for a moment: He was set up to fail. It was unfair for the Divine to demand that a mere mortal grasp God's wishes and then lecture him when he fails to properly guess them.

Even if sympathetic to this reading, Cain yet had a choice. Even if the object of divine unfairness, Cain skirts a direct confrontation with the source of his woe. Cain does not plead or contend with the deity as will other Old Testament figures such as Noah, Moses, Lot, and Jonah. They all debate the Divine on instructions they think harsh. (They even occasionally win an argument: Recall how Jonah convinces God to not destroy Nineveh.) Instead, Cain marinates in his anger and lashes out at the nearest, weakest target, Abel, who never suspects he will become a conduit for his brother's grudge-match against God.

But the destruction of others is not a remedy to our own real or imagined tragedies, and Cain's response signals the chronic human temptation to blame others and, just as often, to lash out at the wrong target. And it is right there where we re-enter Cain's story: When God first asks after Abel, we can almost see Cain's narrowing eyes, curling lip, and sneer in his evasive response: "Am I my brother's keeper?"[5] The response reveals a man who thinks not even the Creator is owed an account for the taking of human life. And then, in mixing red blood and black soil—"Your brother's blood cries out to me from the ground!"[6]—Cain's divine prosecutor creates a haunting, eternal image of unchained bitterness: It turns murderous with the virgin earth stained by the death of an innocent man, and another man, Cain, soon condemned to extract a living from the same patch of earth he himself poisoned.

Cain is thus the archetype of the victim psyche we encounter repeatedly in our own lives, or in grievance narratives we will encounter in the chapters to come: those harmed in the past or who merely imagine it but who become obsessed with blame and lash out with rage.

And that is the *other* lesson in the Genesis story: An intense focus on the past, and a refusal to consider one's own attitudes and actions at least partly at fault for life's woes, leads to new victims and new blood spilt.

Cain thinks of himself only as a victim. It is all he can see.

Sound familiar?

A short history of blame

Blaming others is a perennial human temptation and one demonstrated by more than a creation myth. Time-travel back to the Roman Empire and observe the Carthaginian historian, Tertullian, who recounts how the pagan Romans of his age reacted to natural calamities: By reflexively targeting a new religious sect—his: "If the Tiber comes down in flood to the walls, if the Nile fails to rise up to flood the fields, if the sky stands still, if the earth moves, if there is famine or pestilence," wrote Tertullian, "the cry goes up 'To the lions with the Christians.'" Pagans were the majority of Rome's population until the twilight of the empire, so it was odd that they saw themselves as victims of a small, breakaway Jewish sect and this because of lousy weather at harvest time. But fear of the unknown, and belief that Roman gods would be angered by this new sect's obstinate belief in another deity, helps explain the propensity to blame Christians for nature's capriciousness—that, and the human tendency to explain tragedies as more understandable if someone nearby can be targeted as responsible.

Past victimization can lead to a temptation to exact revenge or merely repeat the shifting of blame when one is in power. When Christians became a majority in the empire, the formerly oppressed tribe persecuted their previous oppressors, including pagans and Jews.[7] In Alexandria, once home to the ancient world's great libraries and a centre for astronomy, philosophy, mathematics, and scientific inquiry, Christians harassed pagans, tore down their temples, and burned their books and libraries.[8] They did so in part because they blamed pagans for leading Alexandrians away from what was for Christians the true faith. In another part of the empire, blame was directed at Jews by Christians who saw themselves or their flock as potential victims. In the early-fifth century at Antioch, the Archbishop of Constantinople, John Chrysostom (A.D. 354–407) gave a series of eight sermons where he engaged in a counter-theological blame of Jews for the death of Christ. "They [the Jews] crucified the Christ whom you adore as God," argued the Archbishop to his flock in his fourth homily.[9] The Archbishop's reasoning was off: Traditional Christian theology did not hold Jews responsible for Christ's death; it saw *all* men as fallen and responsible for Christ's necessary crucifixion. Jews on the pathway to Golgotha were mere human instruments in the Divine Plan that must take place if the Christian narrative—all have committed evil; man requires a sacrifice to be redeemed—was to make any sense. Nonetheless, Chrysostom, with a faith now in ascendancy, saw himself and his flock as threatened. The blame that flowed from such assumed victimhood was to become a noxious poison that deeply infected strains of Christianity over the coming centuries. It would on occasion turn deadly with massacres and pogroms.

Victim thinking and blame: There's always a reason…

These early examples are pagan, religious, and ancient. But history contains similar narratives that are ideological, secular, and modern. Put aside, for now, the question of whether a victim claim and cult accurately targets *who* or *what* is at fault. Instead consider more recent examples of how often men and women think of themselves as victims and blame others even in the most implausible ways.

In the 19th-century American South, victimhood was routinely claimed not by the people who *were* victims—slaves—but by slave-owners. The South's attachment to a victim narrative arose in part because it was anchored in a reflex and an idea, tribalism and nationalism, both of which feed on stories of unfairness. The stories can be accurate, exaggerated, or false—deserved or not—but it matters little once widely believed. The tribalism of the South was a tyrannical, racist variety that assumed the superiority of whites and the non-personhood of blacks. Nonetheless, any opposition to the same, no matter how mild or ineffectual, became a reason for southerners to blame northerners for the South's ostensible victimization. For example, and morally indefensible as it was, one southern pre-Civil-War complaint was that the North ignored its constitutional obligation to send back escaped slaves, part of the awful pre-Civil-War political "deal" between the slaveholding South and the rest of the country. As historian Harry Jaffa has written, the South was largely in error—the North, to its shame, did send back some slaves who escaped from the South, but "No grievance loomed larger in the rhetoric of secession than the alleged refusal of the free states to comply with the Fugitive Slave Law of 1850."[10]

In addition, the South's victim cult, a double narrative of narcissism given the region's trafficking in other human beings and complaints of victimization, was even reinforced by the U.S. Supreme Court in its infamous 1857 Dred Scott decision.[11] There, the majority of the court ruled that Dred Scott, a slave who resided in a free state but whose slaveholding "owner" voluntarily brought him to Illinois, could not be a citizen and was thus not entitled to presumptions of freedom in free states. That flew in the face of practice and settled law in multiple northern states where some black Americans already possessed full citizenship including voting rights. But the court's decision, which southerners welcomed, would yet become part of the South's grievance culture when northern states mostly ignored the high court. Maine's state Supreme Court, for example, issued an advisory opinion that African Americans were full citizens and could vote in state and federal elections. The Ohio Supreme Court ruled that any slave who entered Ohio with his slave-owner's permission was free and should not be returned to a slaveholding state. Other free states began to enact laws explicitly clarifying that any slaves residing in their states were henceforth free men and women.[12]

All such events and responses reinforced what historian Paul Quigley writes were the notions of victimhood that predate the Civil War and served as part of the foundation for the South's self-created grievance narrative. "Southern nationalists had long portrayed the South as a victim and an underdog, and whipping up resentment of apparent northern oppression had long fuelled southern nationalism."[13] Thus in 1860, outgoing President James Buchanan argued that "the long continued and intemperate interference of the northern people with the question of slavery in the southern States has now at length produced its natural effects,"[14] by which Buchanan meant division and a war to come and which he blamed in advance on the North. Quigley again: "The sense of shared victimhood that had always been so important was intensified by the passions of war... [a]nd war's suffering, interpreted through a religious lens, sanctified that sense of shared victimhood...."[15] It would continue even into the next century. After the First World War, when half a million black Americans left the South for northern opportunities and for what they hoped would be a less prejudiced society, the Georgia Bankers Association complained of their loss of cheap labour. The bankers compared the mass emigration as "comparable only to Sherman's march to the sea in its damage to agriculture in the state."[16] It demonstrated a narcissism common in those who, wrongly, think themselves the victim, only to overlook obvious, actual victims in their midst.

Victim thinking courtesy of faulty ideas

Victim thinking can, obviously, result from actual harms. But errant ideas and theories of victimization also drive ahead such narratives, especially when combined with human impulses such as envy. The anti-reality economic theories that originated with the 19th-century German philosopher, Karl Marx, about capital and labour are illustrative. Marx, convinced that the economy was a zero-sum equation, thought that capital was merely "stored-up labour"[17] and selfishly hoarded. Thus, a farmer who owns land and hires others to work on it or a landlord who owned a flat and charges rent were, according to Marx, usurping the labour of the worker or the renter. They were blamed as sources of poverty and inequality, with inequality always an assumed evil.[18] Expressed differently, for Marx, the poor *were poor* because others added to their incomes through something else other than manual labour.

Marxist theory overlooked the labour necessary to construct a home and the transaction of cash needed to pay for it, which also resulted from labour from the owner. More generally, Marx and his followers were in error in their basic assumptions about human beings and also how markets work.[a] Nonetheless, it was a short walk from the view of populations as victimized by anyone with property to the 20th century's communist revolutions where blame was stirred to attack those with property or seen as privileged in some fashion. Thus Vladimir Lenin, the Bolshevik revolutionary and first leader of the Soviet Union, translating Marx's ideology into practice urged his revolutionary comrades to show no mercy in purging Russia of such people. "For as long as we fail to treat speculators the way they deserve—with a bullet in the head—we will not get anywhere at all," wrote Lenin in November 1917.[19] Lenin was the first in a cascading 20th-century cult of utopian communists who saw citizens as victims of structural forces that were to be routed and revolutionized out of existence, including anyone part of such "structures."

The list would include peasant farmers targeted by the Bolsheviks and, even before the October revolution, forced to hand over machinery, land, and animals where Lenin's forces had control. They were labelled as "blood-sucking kulaks" and "money-grubbing peasants."[20] In China, in the 1920s, early communist revolutionaries distinguished between peasants with land and those without, with the former targeted by early communist revolutionaries.[21] Mao Tse-tung's 1927 book, *Report on the Peasant Movement in the Human*, was a lengthy rant against landlords and feudalism and which blamed the former for the latter.[22] Similarly, in North Vietnam in the early 1950s, communist village activists urged poorer peasants to attack richer peasants. In the 1970s in Cambodia, Pol Pot and the Khmer Rouge claimed to be victims of not only enemy soldiers but their children, travellers, intellectuals, those of Chinese ancestry (especially near the borders where they might be classified as "historical enemies"), merchants, traders, and anyone else the Khmer Rouge thought insufficiently Cambodian in spirit, including even monks.[23]

The attempt to divide people based by economic class was not always

---

[a] Marx, who never visited a factory floor, was profoundly in error on nearly everything he analyzed: He believed that the economy and trade were mere imposed constructions when human beings had long engaged in commercial activity since the first Mesopotamian fishermen and farmers traded fish for grain. He also believed that the economy could be organized from the top down and human nature was malleable and thus men and women could be molded into servants of a super-state where incentives and price signals did not matter (e.g., that one would work to produce food at a loss or work for the same pay as a lazy colleague). Such notions were unworkable even in early communism as when even Vladimir Lenin was forced to back away from full communism in the 1920s if Russians were to be fed by farmers who rebelled against early attempts at collectivization.

successful, in part because the Marxist assumption that economic divisions drove societal fracturing was often inaccurate. As historian Robert Conquest points out, Marx's class analysis, the notion that divisions in societies were mainly economic, was not a new idea and often not true. In the English Civil War, "entire villages from rich peasants to laborers and ploughman were united together against outsiders, not divided internally against each other."[24] This was why in some instances Marxist leaders had to provoke the belief that one was a victim through manufactured hatred. Le Duc Tho, the Vietnamese general who directed much of North Vietnam's forces as Ho Chi Minh's health declined, understood this conundrum for his ideology: "If one wishes to convince the peasants to take up arms, first of all you have to fill them with hatred for the enemy."[25]

Thus, over eight decades in the 20th century, dozens of other similarly ideologically inspired movements, regimes, and tyrants in Latin America, eastern and central Europe, Africa, and Asia would target landowners, landlords, entrepreneurs, the nobility, farmers, and shopkeepers for blame. If Marxist disciples were to gain power and keep it, they had to continually make the case, flawed as it was, that the poor were poor because someone else had more. The ideological focus on inequality as proof *de facto* of victimhood produced history's largest body count of actual victims. The practitioners of economic envy and blame in power in communist states would end up responsible for nearly 95 million deaths in the 20th century.[b] Among other examples: the dead came care of state policy that starved farmers in Ukraine in the 1930s and in China in the 1960s; they included political prisoners that perished in Russian *gulags*; and there were those that were directly murdered—shot as traitors to the revolution or because they tried to escape from East Berlin to West Berlin.

Taking offense on behalf of the tribe

Twentieth-century Marxists were wrong about the cause of poverty and injustices but they gained traction by believing—or pretending to believe—that they spoke for the disadvantaged, the world's actual victims. A modern victim-cult has also arisen on this basis, the claim to represent the oppressed,

---

[b] See Stéphane Courtois, Nicolas Werth, Jean-Louis Panné et al., *The Black Book of Communism*, 1999.

from the unlikeliest of claimants: terrorists. After Timothy McVeigh detonated a Ryder truck with nearly 5,000 pounds of explosives on April 19, 1995, at the Alfred P. Murrah Federal Building bombing in Oklahoma City,[26] the FBI would later describe McVeigh, a decorated army veteran from the first Gulf War, as possessed by a deep anger that "hardened" after Waco. The reference was to the April 19, 1993, conflagration at the Branch Davidian compound where cult leader David Koresh and 76 men, women, and children died during the 51-day standoff with federal agents in Waco, Texas. Some, including McVeigh, watched it unfold on television and thought the fire that engulfed the compound had been set by FBI agents.

In later letters to a friend, Bob Papovich, released to a journalist shortly before McVeigh's execution in 2001, McVeigh made clear his motivation, for which he showed no remorse. He justified his bombing "as a pre-emptive (or pro-active) strike" and referenced FBI raids and actions. It included the Ruby Ridge incident in August 1992, near Naples, Idaho, where the agency shot and killed 14-year-old Sammy Weaver and later his mother, Vicki Weaver.[c] Waco and Ruby Ridge were tragic events that never had to happen had federal agencies been smarter and less focused on their own interpretation of what was unfolding, especially at Ruby Ridge. However, McVeigh took it upon himself to pronounce his own verdict and sentence. His letters indicate he saw those who died at Waco and Ruby Ridge as victims and that he was their avenger. "It was in this climate then," he writes, "that I reached the decision to go on the offensive—to put a check on government abuse of power where others had failed in stopping the federal juggernaut run amok."[27] McVeigh would arrive at the execution chamber and leave it believing he had avenged victims. The reality was he only added to history's total of real victims. When McVeigh's explosives tore through the Oklahoma City federal building, the death toll was double that of Waco—168 people, including 19 children and toddlers in daycare.

McVeigh was not the only terrorist to claim his actions were justified with a reference to other victims, imagined or real. In November 2009, Army Major Nidal Hasan, a U.S. Army psychiatrist, killed thirteen people at an army base at

---

[c] A later federal investigation into both deaths and the agency's use of force concluded the agency was overly focused on their own theory that the Weavers were white supremacists and also a threat, instead of the reality of the situation: They were not the first and they merely wanted to be left alone.

Fort Hood, Texas. As with McVeigh, Hasan was born in the United States, but, in the six months leading up to the Fort Hood massacre, Hasan felt isolated from his fellow citizens because of an allegiance to another tribe. According to colleagues, Hasan complained of ongoing discrimination, telling them "he was being treated like a Muslim, like an Arab, rather than an American." It was never clear why he could not argue for his rights as both, as have other Muslim Americans, but Hasan's former army colleagues think his radicalism might have started soon after 9/11, as he began blogging favourably about the motivations of the 19 suicide bombers, comparing them to soldiers who throw themselves on a grenade for a comrade.[28]

Later, in prison, Hasan would demonstrate another trait common to those who believe themselves or their cohort victims: ire and blame directed at those in the tribe who reject their narrative. For Hasan, other Muslims were thus disloyal after they rejected his terrorism. In a 2017 hunger strike at his Fort Leavenworth death row prison cell, Hasan said he was refusing food in part to protest "America's hatred for (Shariah) laws." More telling, he then shifted blame to Muslims; Hasan accused other Muslims of weakness in the struggle he presumed to lead: "I hope this will also serve as a reminder of how weak the Muslim Ummah [community] is."[29] As with others enmeshed in the belief that they serve a righteous cause, after failure, or near the end of their life, they will blame even their own tribe for not following them into the abyss. Hasan's actual tribe, though, was neither Muslim nor American but the same as McVeigh's, that of self-proclaimed avengers.

McVeigh's and Hasan's notion of avenging past or imagined future victims was also evident in the tribalism of Norwegian terrorist Anders Breivik who murdered 77 people, mostly children, with a bomb in Oslo and a shooting at Utoya island in 2011. Breivik justified his own killing of innocents with reference to NATO'S war on Serbia in the 1990s, which included bombing Serbia to stop its military from ethnically cleansing Muslims. For Breivik, this was a betrayal of his European tribe: "It was completely unacceptable how the U.S. and Western European regimes bombed our Serbian brothers," wrote Breivik in his 1,500-page manifesto, released after his terror attack. "All they [the Serbs] wanted was to drive out Islam by deporting the Albanian Muslims back to Albania."[30] As with other self-appointed advocates for others, Breivik justified his murders with reference to his own tribe and used the language that shows up in other victim narratives, the notion that culture is akin to a flesh-and-blood human being and thus harm or changes to it are akin to mass murder. "I'm driven by my love for Europe, European culture and all Europeans," wrote Breivik. "This does not mean that I oppose diversity. But appreciating diversity does not mean that you support genocide of your own culture and people."[31] Breivik, as with other terrorists, leapt from claimed past victims to prophesied future ones. He saw himself as their avenger and also that of imagined future victims. The outcome was more dead Europeans, mostly children.

The abdication of moral agency

The most extreme victim cults produce new casualties, but also evident is the abdication of any moral responsibility. To such men an act is not only justified but called into reality by some *other* prior event, person, or force. In the extreme, in murderous victim-cults, the actual person who pulls the trigger or detonates the explosive is thus self-excused from moral responsibility. Blame is instead placed on the FBI, NATO, Jews, Muslims, imperialists, Europeans, or Americans. But in apportioning blame to others, they place a double responsibility on everyone else: Others are deemed more responsible for their actions while they are responsible for nothing. Others are the first movers while the terrorist is only an automaton without a free will. The assumption is that human beings are mere Pavlovian animals who respond only to stimuli in a reflexive manner and never to reason, and to sympathy. It is an abdication of agency, of moral responsibility.

Also, to see how reflexive the desire to blame has become in such men, consider how possible grievances could arise even if different historical choices were made by others. Osama bin Laden objected to American interference in the Arab and Muslim world. He could just as easily have created a grievance out of alternate actions or their absence: for example, had Americans never funded and provided weapons to the anti-Soviet Mujahedeen in Afghanistan in the 1980s (of which bin Laden was a part), or had the George H. Bush administration never assembled a coalition to eject Iraq from Kuwait in 1991, or had NATO never bombed Serbia in the 1990s to protect European Muslims. The bin Ladens of the world who excoriated Western involvement in mainly Muslim lands could as easily have offered up a reverse narrative:

that America and her allies abandoned Muslims in Afghanistan who faced a brutal, atheist superpower; that when a tiny mainly Muslim nation of Kuwait was strangled, the U.S. and the United Nations did nothing; or that NATO's historically Christian nations turned a blind eye to the ethnic cleansing of Muslims by Orthodox Serbia.

This was in fact the exact complaint from Middle Eastern scholar Edward Said. Said, a Palestinian émigré to the United States who died in 2003, made a career of arguing that the West has been "massively and calculated aggressive" in its ostensible "attack on the contemporary societies of the Arab and Muslim world,"[32] to quote from Said's most famous book, *Orientalism*. Yet in another book, one that criticized Western media for how they covered Islam or mainly Muslim societies, Said wrote of how he was sympathetic to the notion from "[m]any Muslims… that had the Bosnian, Palestinian, and Chechnyan victims not been Muslim, and had 'terrorism' not emanated from 'Islam,' the Western powers would have done more."[33] For Said, the West was always at fault. Its nations were wrong when they were colonial powers and missing in action when they were not. To wit, proponents of victim narratives are endlessly creative in asserting a claim to victimhood. What matters for such propagandists is the raw material of a possible grievance. Using rhetorical tongs and a hammer, they can pound any event or past tragedy, or an absence of action, into a story of the inexcusable guilt of others. Blame of others is a siren song that never ceases.

From deep to shallow victim-claims: The power of victim tales

The call to victimhood powers demagogues, be they 20th-century revolutionaries, terrorists, or, as Paul Quigley observed about the South and its erstwhile philosophers, pastors, and politicians before and after the Civil War, those who saw themselves as victims of northern Yankees: "They realized that when it comes to justifying claims to national independence, victimhood confers power."[34] Indeed, victimhood narratives feed on stories of unfairness, false or true; but even in the latter case they would have faded into the mists of time, absent determined efforts to keep wounds fresh for a new generation.

Beyond ancient and modern grievances, it would be remiss to leave the initial survey of grievance narratives without reference to an obvious recent, albeit very mild, claim to victimhood, which stands out because the assertion is so unlikely: a Manhattan developer/self-proclaimed billionaire, now president, Donald Trump. In his race for the Republican nomination in 2015 and 2016 and in the general campaign that followed, Trump loudly and repeatedly proclaimed his victimhood while rhetorically attacking those that disagreed with him or, worse, those that could not fight back. Recall how Trump became (politically) known for his insults to Mexican immigrants, women, the disabled, and the parents of a soldier killed in Iraq. The candidate lashed "the mainstream media," the Republican "establishment," primary opponent Ted Cruz, and a judge presiding over a lawsuit involving Trump University. Trump, as it was disclosed during the election, also once bragged about sexually assaulting women—the Access Hollywood recordings. For all that, Trump routinely claimed to be the one ill-treated by others. It was *he* who was a victim. During the August 2015 Republican debate when then-Fox-news-anchor Megyn Kelly pressed Trump about the billionaire's disparaging comments about the fairer sex, the would-be politician then offered up an adjective to describe Kelly's line of questioning: "unfair." "Kelly," Trump asserted, "didn't ask those questions of anybody else.... I thought it was an unfair question." The after-debate response from a man in a metropolis not known for indulging complainers: "Megyn behaved very nasty to me."[35]

The charge of unfairness was one Trump would repeat often. In his business life, the developer and reality-TV-show personality drew attention to himself and emblazoned his name on skyscrapers. But in pursuit of votes, Trump's chronic grievance was that too much attention was paid to him; he complained of being analyzed and critiqued too often,[36] including during a CNN debate: "I thought it was very unfair that virtually the entire early portion of the debate was 'Trump this,' 'Trump that,' in order to get ratings, I guess," groused Trump in December 2015.[37] In early 2016, after losing the Iowa delegate contest to Ted Cruz,[38] Trump again leaned on a familiar crutch. In February he tweeted that coverage of his loss was "unfair."[39] One month later, thinking ahead to what was once considered a routine gauntlet for a candidate to run if no winner emerges early, Trump said a contested Republican convention would be "pretty unfair."[40] In April the billionaire claimed that another one of the few victories by Cruz, this time in Colorado, was the result of a process that was "totally unfair."[41] Trump even complained about Fox News,[42] where he regularly received gentle treatment from hosts Bill O'Reilly and Sean Hannity.

With reference to California Judge Gonzalo Curiel, who presided over a class-action lawsuit against Trump University, Trump's response in June 2016: "I have had horrible rulings: I have been treated very unfairly by this judge."[43] The same month Trump again grumbled about the media coverage of his campaign as "dishonest and unfair."[44] After protests erupted over police shootings of blacks that summer, Trump compared his own struggle with those of black Americans: "Even against me the system is rigged,"[45] he told Fox News's Bill O'Reilly. The self-professed Manhattan billionaire who bashed *other* American businesses for running Chinese factories then carped when the *Wall Street Journal* outed Trump for his China investments.[46] Trump even complained of a rigged American election system, until he won the White House. In spring 2016, the *Daily Wire* ran a piece called "7 Times Donald Trump Whined Life Was Unfair."[47] The *Washington Post* produced its own tally: Eighteen.[48]

The problem with the president's victimhood

There is no equivalence between Trump's chronic claim to be a victim and history's consequential, murderous narratives. The president's cry of victimhood matters for a different reason: because it reflects the *zeitgeist* of our age and is a departure from the traditional American ethos of Harry Truman's "the buck stops here" declaration of responsibility. However unfairly treated, previous White House occupants, from George Washington to Barack Obama, would never deign to publicly complain. That was due both to respect for the office but also to personal experiences, cultural norms, and the context of the nation at the time. Dwight Eisenhower, John F. Kennedy, and George H. Bush all served in the Second World War. They saw its horrors and actual, innocent victims. To publicly complain about their peacetime treatment by scribblers or fellow politicians would be unthinkable in that historical context. Even Richard Nixon, who lost the California gubernatorial race to Democrat Pat Brown in November 1962 and famously complained about negative coverage, avoided overindulging in blame. Even his famous self-pitying remark to the assembled media after his loss—"You won't have Nixon to kick around anymore, because gentlemen, this is my last press conference...."—was followed by a circumscribed complaint: "... and it will be the one in which I have welcomed the opportunity to test wits with you. I have always respected you. I have sometimes disagreed with you. But unlike some people, I've never cancelled a subscription to a paper, and also, I never will."[49]

Trump's grievance narratives are a departure even from Nixon, to say nothing of other presidents, but they are unlikely to catch fire in a way that an ideological or racial narrative might, examples of which are explored in subsequent chapters. Personal victim narratives can only metastasize if connected to a deeper societal concern. Marx's victim narrative multiplied because poverty, repression, and inequality of the sort that really was harmful was a reality for much of the world's population. His theories to alleviate such ills and later communist calls to revolution naturally gained a hearing even if wrong in diagnosis and proposed remedies. Southerners could play off Yankees because northerners, quite properly, really did think southerners who supported slavery evil, and abolitionists in particular, worked to undermine the trade; southern whites could use such northern antipathy to shore up their own narrative of victimization. Terrorists draw on grievances in the tribe with whom they identify, even when they are supported by few in their tribe.

In contrast, Trump's victim cries are anchored in narcissism, irrationality, and political ploys. It is not clear that he even takes his own assertions of victimization seriously. "I am the most fabulous whiner. I do whine because I want to win... I keep whining and whining until I win," Trump told CNN in the summer of 2015.[50] The lapse into victim language by Trump matters for another, more critical reason: Because men and women are remarkably adept in slithering away from responsibility for their own choices and the consequences for the same. The problem with the president's self-referencing grievance language, beyond its corrosive example and thus effect on respect for the office, is that just as the public and the Western world need leaders to counter the self-indulgent, ill-advised, and over-the-top claims of victimization embedded in popular culture, politics, and academia, the American president reinforces the victim culture and its first impulse: Others are to blame for my imperfect world.

Trump's example will not help us weaken the victim cults that have now developed be they murderous or mild: the "avengers" who, Cain-like, kill on the justification that they or their tribe have been treated unfairly; or the grievance culture on campuses where equality of statistical outcomes are demanded lest the charge of racism be flung; or where a glance, the wrong word, or so-called appropriation now regularly leads to claims one has been victimized; or the widespread notion that past harm to one's ancestors largely explains one's own status today.

Let us now turn to one of those new victim cults, on campus, where extreme sensitivity has been twinned with a narcissism that parallels Trump, elevated to a virtue, and where the most privileged now think of themselves as among history's victims while they busily shred civility.

PART II

Siren songs of blame

You will come to the Sirens who enchant all who come near them. If any one unwarily draws in too close and hears the singing of the Sirens, his wife and children will never welcome him home again, for they sit in a green field and warble him to death with the sweetness of their song. There is a great heap of dead men's bones lying all around, with the flesh still rotting off them. Therefore, pass these Sirens by, and stop your men's ears with wax that none of them may hear...

—The goddess Circe, to Ulysses, in Homer's *Odyssey*

CHAPTER 2

The fake victimhood of 20-something totalitarians

———

The key to social and intellectual legitimacy is to be a victim, or, if one has little or no concrete personal experience of being a victim, to be a member of a recognised victim group.

—ROBERT MARTIN, *Orthodoxy and Research*

Microaggression monsters under the bed

The young are always susceptible to tales of woe, followed by pied pipers who sell easy answers on how to view and "fix" the world. It is not, initially, their fault—youth by description have not lived long enough. But mix knowledge of some historic wrong, a modern statistic that implies injustice and self-righteousness—the young see an imperfect world and wonder why their elders did not "fix" everything already—and a perfect storm exists for discontent.

Problematically, an initial faulty analysis plus the response can lead to new harms, including what is best described as mini-totalitarian impulses. An additional problem: Previous Westerners were so successful at demolishing actual injustices and diluting personal prejudice—this anathema to those who believe they live in a racist, sexist dystopia—that a newer generation in search of dragons to slay will often focus, wrongly, on minutiae they think support a claim to victimhood. That combined with a culture of sensitivity on campuses has led to a belief in microaggressions everywhere as if, with a journey back to childhood, multiple monsters exist under their student beds. But let us be more precise.

Oppression in English Grammar 101

In the autumn of 2013, a student petition at the University of California, Los Angeles, claimed that its classrooms had become "hostile" and "toxic," that "white supremacy, patriarchy, heteronormativity" and "other forms of institutionalized oppression" had derided the students' "intellectual capacity, methodological rigor, and ideological legitimacy."[1] The students claimed that administration responses to their previous complaints of "bias, discrimination, and intolerance" had been inadequate. The various classroom experiences, from which the petitioners demanded relief, were described as "traumatic."[2] In one class, some students described the professor as having wreaked "havoc" on their "psychophysiological health."[3]

The claims were remarkable, as if a university in the multi-racial, multi-ethnic metropolis of Los Angeles had suddenly been taken over by David Duke, the 1990s-era Louisiana politician who once belonged to the Ku Klux Klan. In fact, the professor at the centre of the alleged toxicity was Val Rust, with four decades in the field of comparative education, who specialized in education reform, leadership, and ethnic issues, and possessed awards for the same.[4] The complaints originated in his graduate faculty of education classroom earlier that fall. But Rust had not suddenly become a spokesman for white nationalism akin to Boers in 20th-century South Africa before Nelson Mandela. Instead, Rust's sin was to do what supervisory professors are in part paid to do: correct graduate students' grammar and spelling in essays, theses, and dissertations. Later, in a letter, Rust described what led to the accusations: "I have attempted to be rather thorough on the papers and am particularly concerned that they do a good job with their bibliographies and citations, and these students apparently don't feel that is appropriate."[5] Rust also insisted that students use *The Chicago Manual of Style* in their assignments and doctoral dissertations; the professor also allowed a debate between two students to continue including the notion that not everyone who claims to be oppressed, is. That offended a few other students who thought such self-proclaimed victimization should be accepted at first blush.

A few students—in particular, one student, Kenjus Watson, who founded "Students of Color" to fight back against "microaggressions"—thought such duties, permitted debates, and Rust's class and approach were inherently colonial and racist.[6] In a rambling note resembling a 1970s communiqué from a European revolutionary cell, the student group complained of how "our epistemological and methodological commitments have been repeatedly questioned by our classmates and our instructor." They wrote how the distress endured by the "barrage of questions by white colleagues and the grammar 'lessons' by the professor have contributed to a hostile class climate."[7] The Students of Color continued, objecting about the correction of "perceived grammatical choices that in actuality reflect ideologies."[8] Additional hurts included how one student was surprised that a fellow student, of Hispanic origin, lacked an accent, and how when one student wrote 'Indigenous' with an upper-case 'I,' Rust changed it to lowercase.[9]

Before long, the erstwhile victims were soon criticized by other graduate students of colour who objected to the collective "we." The skeptics may have suspected some who claimed to suffer from apostrophes and conjunctions might merely have preferred to skip the hard work necessary to master the structure of the English language, even though those with a grievance concurrently managed to master the campus protest-culture. However, undeterred by their more skeptical fellow students, and to combat their own alleged victimization, two dozen students staged a "teach-in" one afternoon in Rust's class. Their said hope was to address such discrimination and also other UCLA microaggressions. The protestors surrounded Rust and five students (two Europeans, two Asians, and one American) and told them they were racists and then read aloud their "Day of Action" statement.[10]

The situation descended from there, in part due to the administration's earnest response. After the initial complaints, sit-in, and a petition, Marcelo Suárez-Orozco, UCLA's Dean of Graduate School of Education, wrote the students to explain how he was "aware of the last of a series of troubling racial climate incidents at UCLA." It was a reference not only to complaints about Rust but a just-released 2013 UCLA report on discrimination on campus. Except even that report found little evidence of it, noting just one 2009 grievance from staff at the David Geffen School of Medicine to the Associate Dean for Diversity Affairs. However, 30 staff members did complain to another campus agency, the "Ombud," where six complaints involved "general incivility," four concerned "discrimination," and three were filed for "bullying." The report noted that almost all complainants had achieved tenure and other markers of professional academic success yet felt aggrieved in some fashion. There were a few allegations of actual racist language—one complainant reported he had been called a "spic"—otherwise much of the UCLA report offered up the language of perceived bias.[11] More than a few complaints mentioned irritation with Proposition 209, a 1996 referendum that banned the illiberal practice that involves hiring quotas based on ethnicity, race, or gender—affirmative action—and was spearheaded by businessman Ward Connerly, then a University of California regent. As a black American, Connerly disliked racial preferences of any sort because they might lead to suspicions of unearned success due to skin colour. That proposition was endorsed by 55% of California voters.

Despite little hard evidence of racial discrimination in hiring or promotion, the report anyway advocated additions to UCLA's diversity bureaucracy and new procedures for dealing with grievances. Suárez-Orozco said that he took it all "extremely seriously" and looked forward to "listening and to learning" so that "together, we shall heal."[12] The dean then placed three other professors, with backgrounds in race and ethnic studies,[13] in the classroom with Rust, this to oversee the remainder of the course.[14] The protesters, still unsatisfied, found new examples of victimization. It included the new format for Rust's course, where mock examinations meant students would be invited at specific times to present. Without irony about the historical discrimination to which he would now compare classroom life at UCLA, Watson complained that the new format "amounted to a kind of segregation.[15] Weeks later, after a town hall requested by Rust upon his return from intercultural education work in China, the professor touched Watson's arm as a friendly gesture to begin a conversation. As one account of the incident later noted, Kenjus Watson, "a large and robust young man, erupted in anger and eventually filed a criminal charge of battery against the 79-year-old professor."[16]

Google "Val Rust" and your screen will turn up a picture of a kindly, smiling octogenarian who could double for Henry Reagan in the television series, Blue Bloods. Reagan, played by Winnipeg-born actor, Len Cariou, is the grandfather of the Reagan clan, a family of cops; Henry Reagan most often has an inviting disposition and a twinkle in his eye even as he remonstrates over dinner with his grandchildren and son, Frank, played by Tom Selleck. Surface resemblances to a television grandfather aside, Rust was the most unlikely target for the accusations. In the age of victimhood, that mattered little.

Contra the self-proclaimed victims, the professor had long been a favourite of students, local and international. One graduate student who knew Rust for ten years said she thought all the accusations were unjust, especially given Rust supported intercultural learning and collaboration: "It is disturbing that students would make such unfounded accusations based on misperceptions of what they believe as racism," said Emily Le to a student newspaper. Another graduate student who worked with Rust on her master's thesis, Weiling Deng, said she had once been "innocent in thinking that all students in the department are friendly." Deng wrote of how the professor always supported students of colour throughout his time as a professor. Another student also defended Rust: "As a woman of color," wrote Stephanie Kim in a column, "I am deeply saddened that my adviser and mentor for the last five years, Rust, was unjustly demonized as the symbol of white male oppression as a cheap way of arousing public support." Kim wrote that while she agreed that racism was deeply embedded within the institutions that made up UCLA, the Students of Color's approach was a "clumsy and disingenuous act." She took dead-aim at the students at their sit-in: "[It] was a deliberately mean-spirited circus that creates exactly the hostile and toxic environment split along unsettling racial lines that the demonstrators claim to be fighting against."[17]

The general consensus about Rust and the testimony of other students might be why the late autumn petition to remove Rust, with a goal of 1,000 sign-ups, managed to attract only 133 online supporters.[18] Despite the absurdity of the accusations, more *mea culpas* came from the administration and more self-abnegation from the dean. They both surrendered and made a deal: UCLA would drop the pending disciplinary charges against the 79-year-old professor—if he stayed off campus for a semester. After Rust agreed to stay away (he soon retired), Suárez-Orozco then informed students that the campus would now be less dangerous given the octogenarian was gone. UCLA's administration then appointed Rust's accuser, Watson, and other complainants—but not anyone who supported Rust—to a committee to examine "all aspects" of UCLA's "operations and culture from the perspective of race and ethnic relations."[19] The graduate students—who thought punctuation, grammar, and *The Chicago Manual of Style* were racist, oppressive, and ideological and wreaked "havoc" on the "psychophysiological health" of students—won. Kenjus Watson was later hired by Occidental College in Los

Angeles as an instructor. As of 2019, six years after his complaints about Rust's direction on ellipsis and citations, Watson was still a doctoral candidate[20] with just one academic paper solely in his name.[21]

Halloween and costumed cultural appropriation: Yale circa 2015

UCLA was not alone in producing victim claims. Another high-profile example occurred at one of America's most prestigious universities and over a basic human activity—dressing up—in this case, for Halloween. Four days before the festivity, Yale University's Intercultural Affairs Committee sent an email to students already of age to drink, marry, and make war, about what not to wear: "Halloween," wrote the committee, is "unfortunately a time when the normal thoughtfulness and sensitivity of most Yale students can sometimes be forgotten." The email admonition then listed what it thought in poor dress-up taste for October 31: "Feathered headdresses, turbans, wearing 'war paint' or modifying skin tone or wearing blackface or redface." It then offered an additional caution that "these same issues and examples of cultural appropriation and/or misrepresentation are increasingly surfacing with representations of Asians and Latinos."[22]

After some students complained to Erika Christakis, an associate master at Yale's Silliman College, about the Committee's *in loco parentis* email, Christakis sent her own, more adult-recognizing thoughts to her charges. She pointed out that Halloween, actually, was traditionally "a day of subversion for children and young people."[23] But that never stopped adults from trying to exert control. Christakis wrote of how when she was young, adults "were freaked out by the specter of Halloween candy poisoned by lunatics, or spiked with razor blades," even though there was no record of any such deeds. She opined on how Yale's Intercultural Affairs Committee "seem afraid that college students are unable to decide how to dress themselves on Halloween." Christakis, likely aware of the hypersensitivities of her university in the manner scientists in the medieval world or in Islamic-devout countries now offer up paeans so as not offend the religious establishment, expressed the usual caveat common to academics in such situations: She had no wish to "trivialize genuine concerns about cultural and personal representation." She acknowledged "complex issues" about identities, free expression, cultural appropriation, and virtue signalling.

"But," she wrote, as someone who once taught kindergarten, it was hard to "give credence to a claim that there is something objectionably 'appropriative' about a blonde-haired child's wanting to be Mulan for a day." Christakis pointed out that pretending and playing is what kids *do*. She then posed a reasonable rhetorical query: Was it perhaps okay for an eight-year-old to imagine, but not wear, Tiana the Frog Princess dresses "if you aren't a black girl from New Orleans?" Or was it "okay if you are eight, but not 18?" In full confession mode in the hopes of introducing sense, honesty, context, and reason into cultural appropriation debates, Christakis wrote of how, when she lived in Bangladesh, she once bought a sari "because it was beautiful, even though I looked stupid in it and never wore it once." Was she "fetishizing and appropriating others' cultural experiences?" Her honest answer: "Probably, but I really, really like them too."

Christakis and her husband Nicholas, a master at Yale's Silliman College, had no idea what would hit them next.

Attacks in emails, petitions, and demands by a student group to have them removed from the college;[24] a class walk-out and march of over 1,000 undergraduate Yale students—one-fifth of the undergraduate student body;[25] and death threats that forced Erika Christakis to flee New Haven.[26] A few days later, Nicholas Christakis engaged with a crowd of students about his wife's email. In one exchange, a former student, Michaela, tells Christakis that before his wife's email she loved her college; "but I can't say that any more, it's no longer a safe space for me." His former student explained that the couple had not provided "an appropriate response... our opinion has been dismissed you guys did not said [sic] 'I hear you; I hear that you are hurting and I am sorry I have caused you pain.'" In the video, Michaela is sincere, which highlights the problem: A twenty-something Yale student with a near-guaranteed privilege-ticket to the good life believes that wearing clothing from another culture on Halloween, awkwardly or properly carried off, is harmful and creates an unsafe environment.

When Christakis attempts to respond, another student interrupts in impatient frustration to say that the "core" of the issue was that he did not apologize: "Are you going to give an apology... that's all I want.... We just want an acknowledgment of hurt.... Are you going to say that or not?"[27] The discussion, with more students now gathering, descends when Christakis, in

Socratic fashion, tries to draw out the interrupting student. He queries why, if he owes an apology to Michaela, perhaps this newest interjector should apologize to *him*. After all, she is delaying his obligations to other students. At that point, the crowd murmurs in dismissiveness. Christakis tries again, noting that to sincerely apologize, one must first consider for what one is asked to apologize.

The video is interrupted briefly; but when it resumes, yet another student, Jerelyn Luther, joins in to yell at Christakis: "Be quiet!" she shouts at an adult at least twice her age, who has already shown the patience of Job. "It's your *job* to create a place of comfort, a home for the students who live in Silliman. You have not done that!" At this point, the student is quivering with rage and nearly crying: "By sending out that email, it goes against your position as master. Do you understand that!?" yells Luther. As Christakis replies "I don't agree with that"—he is again interrupted by an even-angrier Luther: "Then why the f**k did you accept the position!? Who hired you!? If that's what you think you should step down!" When Christakis calmly replies, "I have a different vision than you," the newest aggrieved student responds—"Step down! If that is what you think of being a master, you should step down! It is *not* about creating an intellectual space! It is *not*! *Do you understand that*!?" screams Luther at the professor. "It is about creating a home here! You are not doing that!" continues Luther, who now asserts students will leave Yale University because of Christakis and his wife. "You are a poor excuse; you should not sleep at night! You are disgusting!"

The student, having performed the role of a 21st-century cultural inquisitor, then walks away.

It would be a mistake to think the majority of students supported the treatment of the Christakises, though it is impossible to know for sure. The couple received encouraging emails and calls from fellow academics, and Yale's administrators expressed support for the Christakises, reaffirming their employment. But the university administration also turtled. It catered to students who created a controversy out of what Nicholas later noted was the "extraordinary and shameful vilification" of his wife by students who either did not understand or intentionally overlooked "the subtlety in her email and the confidence it actually had in Yalies."[28]

Regrettably but understandably given the inquisition, even the Christakises retreated somewhat, sending a joint, follow-up email acknowledging the "pain" caused to some students. But as with anyone in full victim mode encouraged by the sacrificial offerings of others, the peace offering only invited more demands. The march of the 20-something totalitarians continued, literally. On November 12, 2015, just after midnight, roughly 200 students calling themselves "Next Yale" marched on the home of President Peter Salovey. Their demands included that ethnic and gender courses be made mandatory for all students, $8 million in new funding be given to campus cultural centres, and that the Christakises be fired.[29]

The Yalies demanded a response by November 18.[30]

On November 17, Salovey announced multiple new initiatives: a new centre for race and ethnicity studies and $50 million for diversification efforts, multiculturalism, and anti-racism training for all Yale senior staff. Salovey wrote of how the previous weeks demonstrated the Yale community's "steadfast devotion to full freedom of expression" given no one was "silenced or punished for speaking their minds, nor will they be." Yale's president wrote of how he had been "moved" and "encouraged" by the events of the previous two weeks.[31] As it happened, the president of the Foundation for Individual Rights in Education, an organization founded to defend campus free-speech rights among other liberties, filmed Yale's "shrieking student" episode. As he later wrote, the Yale students' demands for the resignations and punishment of faculty amounted to "freedom *from* speech rather than freedom *of* speech."[32] Indeed, and thus students at a prestigious university and among the most fortunate human beings alive in history, claimed to be victims, or at least to represent them. As it happened, the student who yelled and swore at Nicholas Christakis, Jerelyn Luther, was not the product of some tragic upbringing—though that would still not excuse her behaviour—she came from a middle-class background. Her parents, both educated, owned a home valued at $760,000,[33] yet Luther played the victim.

After Yale weakly reaffirmed its support for the Christakises, one student, Michael Fitzgerald, said he "personally loved that [the Christakes] are staying."[34] Seven hundred people also signed a petition asking the couple to stay and for Nicholas Christakis to remain a master.[35] The couple themselves thanked the Yale administration for their support. In December, Erika quit teaching, "to return to her work with young children and families"; Nicholas took a sabbatical for the following semester.[36] Seven months after Halloween, in May 2016, the couple announced their resignation from Silliman.[37]

Lost in all the trauma over appropriation was the original issue, Halloween itself, and fears of cultural appropriation. The festival originated with pagan Celts and the Samhain festival, where animal skins and masks were worn at bonfires and where animal and agricultural sacrifices were offered to pagan gods; Samhain was later fused with Roman and Christian festivals including Feralia, Pomona, and All Saints Day and the night that preceded it, All-Hallows Eve, from where we derive Halloween. The festival itself was thus a perfect example of appropriation over the ages, and one which cultural purists at Yale should have avoided celebrating at all—unless they were Celtic and pagan.

The victim revolution eats its young, and old

Perhaps the most notorious example of the victim culture on campus took place at Evergreen State College in Olympia, Washington, in 2017. There a left-wing professor at a left-wing college would be harassed, mobbed, chased off the grounds, and pushed to quit for refusing to obey a student diktat that would turn the Martin Luther King–Rosa Parks struggle wrong-side down. Evergreen's Bret Weinstein, an evolutionary biologist with progressive credentials that included opposing both Gulf Wars, objected to a demand from a student organization that all white students and staff leave Evergreen for a day.[38] The demand came after a change to an Evergreen tradition in play since the 1970s, a Day of Absence, was flipped on its head by a student committee.[39]

Originally, black students and staff of colour would meet off-campus on that day, which, as Weinstein explained, mimicked "a symbolic act based on the Douglas Turner Ward play in which all the black residents of a Southern town fail to show up one morning."[40] In the play and in Evergreen's imitation, the absence of blacks was meant to highlight their importance to the community. But, as the campus newspaper reported, in 2017, the First Peoples Multicultural Advising Committee decided on a new approach: "White students, staff and faculty will be invited to leave the campus for the day's activities." The campus newspaper straightforwardly reported the diktat and how the theme for 2017 was "Revolution is not a one-time event; your silence will not protect you."[41]

That theme turned out to be eerily prophetic. Weinstein, who voted for Bernie Sanders in the 2016 Democratic primaries, objected to banishment by race and put it in writing to the college's director of First Peoples Multicultural Advising Services. The professor argued that it was one thing for people to voluntarily leave campus to highlight an issue—that was tradition—and quite another to be "asked" to leave because of skin colour. The latter "is a show of force, and an act of oppression in and of itself," wrote Weinstein. His objection led to 50 protesters confronting the professor outside his classroom. That descended into a verbal melee-turned-swarming. In the video, some students tell Weinstein he is a racist. Others yell that his objection to a ban on whites means he supports white supremacy.[42] The crowd is soon hysterical and one student lobs the "long bomb" of non-sequiturs: "Stop telling people of color they're f***** useless—*you're* useless, get the f** out of here!"[43] The students, in full mob behaviour at this point, continue with more cursing, chanting, screaming, and demands.[44] Weinstein was soon advised by the administration that his safety could not be guaranteed, though that was the fault of Evergreen's president, George Bridges, who ordered campus police to stand down as a larger crowd of about 200 took control of college grounds. Weinstein then moved his students to a nearby park for the scheduled class; but, later, photographs of Weinstein's students were posted online with harassment following. Weinstein was again asked to avoid campus for his own safety.

Weeks after the initial confrontation, Evergreen's president offered a grovelling half-explanation/half-apology to the student mob but not Weinstein, who along with his wife (also an Evergreen professor) never returned to Evergreen and later settled out of court.[45] Weinstein later described the student insurgency at his classroom door that day as reminiscent of what happened in Cambodia under the Khmer Rouge in 1975.[46] There cultural regime enforcers and the Khmer Rouge regime systematically harassed, imprisoned, banished, and later murdered the educated classes whenever they refused to apologize for being enemies of the revolution.

Real victims

When campus administrators fail to reinforce a right to civil debate by expelling students who swear at and mob a professor, all that remains are street battles between who can shout the loudest and who is more accomplished at organizing mass rallies at midnight. (All that the Yalies on a midnight march to the president's home lacked were torches and pitchforks.) Beyond the class of campus victims who posit grammar and costumes as injustices, the various claims highlight the new academic-inspired definition of victimization. Racism, as most people think of it, is close to the dictionary definition: "a belief that race is the primary determinant of human traits and capacities and that racial differences produce an inherent superiority of a particular race."[47] It is likely the way most people still define the term. But the college notion of racism and harm differs from an actual liberal conception in previous decades, which centred upon the individual and her treatment. In the past, progress on combatting racism could be measured by breaking down institutional barriers to opportunity—i.e., ending a neighbourhood ban on those of Chinese origin, outlawing the practice of banning African-Americans from "white" restaurants and restrooms; and reversing Ivy League discrimination against Jews, among other identifiable, institutional, concrete discrimination in the past and obliteration of the same. At UCLA, Yale, and Evergreen, racism is now claimed if one is forced to follow *The Chicago Manual of Style*, write in full sentences, take Halloween less seriously, and treat professors as individuals and not part of some predetermined colour caste.

If the described charges of racism from UCLA, Yale, Evergreen, and the others—white supremacy, institutionalized oppression, bias, discrimination, and intolerance—had arisen in early- or mid-century America, the petitioners would have had a point. In 1905 several white parents at San Francisco's Washington Grammar School insisted that four high-scoring Chinese children were regularly cheating, this by allegedly exchanging answers in Chinese during tests. When separated during the next exam, the four students still trumped the results of their white classmates. The Board of Education anyway removed the students from the mostly white school.[48] In the 1920s, Jews made up an increasing proportion of students at Harvard University, reaching nearly 28% in 1925. At that point, Harvard changed its admissions policy to emphasize new factors, an "holistic" approach beyond just academic scores. That helped limit the percentage of Jews accepted to Harvard's incoming undergraduate class, and the proportion of Jewish enrollees dropped to 15%, where it remained until after the Second World War and the Holocaust, when anti-Semitism was no longer fashionable.[49] Or ponder American economist

Shelby Steele, who tells of how he received a rhetorical "punch in the gut" on his first day back in school in the early 1960s. A friend on his swimming team, of which Steele was captain, innocently exulted in how the entire team spent three weeks at the coach's summerhouse on Lake Michigan. His friend offered up how it was too bad that Steele had to work, but that was not the reason: Steele was never informed or invited by the swim coach. Steele was black and his coach's mother did not like blacks.[50] Steele confronted the coach and then quit the club.

Personal prejudice in Western societies has not been eliminated—any survey of online comments on any racially charged topic will regrettably reveal that—but the difference between the 1960s and the second decade of the 21st century is the abolition of institutional racial discrimination, once widespread, and an improvement in attitudes.[a] One example: Until the mid-20th century, 30 states prohibited marriage between blacks and whites.[b] California was the first in the 20th century to repeal its ban (in 1948), with another 13 states to follow by 1967. And it was only in 1967, in Loving v. Virginia, where the U.S. Supreme Court ruled that marriage across racial lines was legal and which overturned a Virginia law banning the practice,[51] also nullifying the remaining 16 states' laws that forbade mixed-race marriages.[52] Attitudes have changed as well. In 1958 just four percent of Americans approved of marriage between blacks and whites; in 2013, 87% favoured the practice.[53] For all but a tiny minority in the 21st century, Americans no longer cared. All of it and more constituted progress.

This dramatic change in laws and attitudes is why those who argue that racism is yet endemic increasingly resort to theories apart from human experience to assert that racism is structural, hidden, and invisible to our consciousness and evident in glances, costumes, microaggressions, and cultural appropriation. Unlike such actual institutional discrimination in decades past, or the personal prejudice where a teacher would disinvite his own student to a summer retreat because he was black, today's acts of alleged prejudice are a stretch: staring, insensitive jokes, so-called appropriation, or the

---

[a] The obvious exception is in affirmative-action race and gender quotas, which do take into account race, ethnicity, or, in some cases, gender.

[b] Only nine states never prohibited interracial marriage; and another 11 states repealed their bans before the end of the 19th century.

reverse—the mere feeling one has been excluded. "Despite increased diversity efforts, stigmatized targets report frequent experiences with discrimination, particularly in its subtle, everyday forms," wrote one author in the 2013 report cited by UCLA's administration in the same year they asked Val Rust to stay off campus. The nebulousness of such alleged subtle discrimination means that academics and organizations must use analytical microscopes to find the victimized and, if not discovered, persuade those unaware that they really are victims. In one academic paper cited by UCLA's Equity, Diversion and Inclusion department,[54] the authors note how the apparently sinned-against are often unaware: "Stigmatized targets sometimes have difficulty detecting discrimination," they write, noting that "many are low in stigma sensitivity."[55] In other words, those who take no offence and see no offence must be educated into knowing they are victims.

The new version of racism also resurrects discrimination against individuals using old-fashioned racism: discrimination based on looks, exactly why Ward Connerly drove ahead California's Proposition 209 in 1996, a measure that banned race, ethnic, and gender quotas at California's universities. That became an issue because Asian Americans were increasingly denied admission to California colleges and universities vis-à-vis other minority applicants. This new-old racism is also more recently on display at Harvard University, where the university again limits successful applicants from one cohort just as it did one century ago with Jews. In their 2018 filing against Harvard University alleging racial bias—the old-fashioned kind against applicants because of their ethnicity—Students for Fair Admissions allege that if Harvard was not so busy "balancing" out minorities through the use of a "personal rating" that dilutes academic scoring, Asian Americans would make up between 43% and 50% of admissions to Harvard instead of 19%. That proportion flatlined for a decade despite 27% growth in the Asian cohort of 14- to 17-year-olds, i.e., the cohort most relevant to college admissions.[56] Harvard introduced its personal rating system to try to promote minority inclusion, except East Asians are not considered the right minority. Thus, Harvard's policy is an example of today's lazy definition of racism, which wraps itself in an historically illiberal contradiction. Martin Luther King and Rosa Parks spoke, demanded, marched, and sat for the right of black Americans to join white Americans at any lunch counter and in any bus seat in the nation. But that liberal vision of a colour-blind America was already passé in academic theorizing by the time of UCLA's grammar complaints, Evergreen's reverse racism, and Harvard's admissions policy. The new version of racism, as with the old version, again suppresses and hurts individuals as individuals.

Lastly, the newest victim cult, with its misplaced obsession on race, has arisen in an age and where Western liberal democracies are as colour-blind, non-prejudiced, tolerant, and opportunity based for all, as any that have ever existed. Also, American students at prestigious universities are not victims, and never will be. Graduate from UCLA and your mid-career pay will be $124,100 every year; "for Yalies"— the students who marched at midnight on the Yale president's home—$146,300 is what they shall soon earn. Leave the campus with a Harvard degree and halfway into your professional life, average alumni will earn $151,600 annually.[57]

The cultural revolution 2.0: The 20-something victim cult meets the demand culture

Claims to victimhood on campus are problematic enough as they reveal a significant gap in awareness of history's real victims banned from attending college based on their race or ethnicity. In contrast, whereas actual victims in the past were direct victims of institutionalized prejudice, today's erstwhile victims expend much energy seeking proof that fellow students, professors, or the wider world are ever-ready to harm and hurt them. The enormity of the grievance culture on campus might be best seen through one national group, WeTheProtesters, self-described and self-flattering as a "national collaborative of activists fighting to end racism and police violence in America."[58] The group listed 80 American and Canadian universities with a panoply of demands,[59] rife with assumptions that America in the second decade of the 21st century is the antebellum south in 1865.

The various demands included: guaranteeing black students and faculty are represented in proportion to their percentage of the general population (multiple colleges and universities) or even greater, such as 20% to 30%; an anonymous student reporting system for bias, "including microaggressions, perpetrated by faculty and staff" (Wesleyan University); a 16% decrease in tuition (Webster); mutually agreed-upon commissioned artwork (St. Louis University); that 30% of the faculty should be black (St. Louis Christian College and Simmons College); that "faculty and staff be put through rigorous diversity training that emphasizes the requirement that they address microaggressions and misinformation" (Simmons College); that the Office of Diversity and Inclusion "maintain the list of acceptable events" (Santa Clara University); "sweeping curriculum reform, departing from the westernized and outdated form of art and design education that are inclusive only to some" (Rhode Island School of Design); freedom from hostility (Purdue University); that funding increase so year-round courses on "Hip Hop Nation" could be offered (California State University, East Bay).

Two Canadian universities were represented on the demand list. At the University of Ottawa, student demands included a therapist of color (Ottawa students used the American spelling), free tuition for "all black and indigenous students," and a "racialized students centre." University of Guelph students wrote of how they were troubled that the university used pictures of black students in advertising to portray the university as diverse, "even as we find ourselves excluded and alienated in concrete ways as a minority population." Students at St. Louis Christian College made a similar demand. Neither Guelph nor St. Louis students considered what their response might be if their universities actually stopped multi-race advertising to use whites-only pictures in their public relation efforts.

Meanwhile, Cultural Revolution–like behaviour from both the attacked and the victim cultists has now multiplied. Recall Yale president Peter Salovey, whose home 200 students marched on near midnight to give him a list of demands. In reporting on the incident at the time, *Yale News* reported that "he considers the manner by which the students delivered the demands entirely acceptable and in compliance with University policy." *Yale News* then quoted Salovey directly: "This was a peaceful group of students visiting me at my home at a somewhat late hour, completely consistent with University protest policy."[60] Evergreen's president, George Bridges, the one who allowed protesters to take over his campus, responded to the activist uproar in the spring of 2017 with a fulsome response. In an appearance in May that year, Bridges began by signalling, lest someone take offence at the antiquated notion of binary gender, that "I use he/him pronouns." He then said he was "grateful to the courageous students who have voiced their concerns." Students in attendance tell Bridge not to raise his hands as that constitutes microaggression, a demand to which he complied.[61] As if a prisoner of war in Hanoi in 1970 reading from a script provided by his captors, Bridges then responded, point by point, to the protesters' eleven demands.[62]

Submissions to WeTheProtesters also show how the victim culture "hooked up" with the student demand-culture. Students at the Rhode Island School of Design wanted cultural and identity-based sensitivity training and punishment for those professors "who fail to abide by basic principles established in training or who develop a record of repeated offenses." They "MUST be held accountable" wrote the demanders. University of Missouri students wanted president Tim Wolf to write a hand-written letter and hold a press conference "reading the letter" and that "In the letter and at the press conference, Tim Wolfe must acknowledge his white privilege, recognize that systems of oppression exits [sic]." Over at New York University, the students demanded a veto on staff hires. The Black Students Union at California State Los Angeles was particularly emphatic, writing demands in capital letters along with multiple demands as if a ransom note. "WE DEMAND," wrote the California students 15 times and with monetary demands ranging from $20,000 for the Black Students Union itself to $30 million for additional financial assistance for students. The president was warned to pay heed and attend a meeting "on Monday, November 23, 2015 at 3:00 p.m." where "we will discuss the fulfillment and implementation of each demand."

It all read like an excerpt from Tom Wolfe's mocking 1970s recounting of revolutionary protest culture in New York City and also in the Bay area. In *Radical Chic & Mau-Mauing the Flak-Catchers*, Wolfe portrays self-proclaimed activists as both earnestly serious and over-the-top in their demands—except that fawning society-figures, bureaucrats, and politicians almost always respond with self-abnegation and lucrative peace offerings. The self-recriminations often had a resemblance to self-confessing, Soviet-era, enemies-of-the-people rhetoric.

The priorities of the various student groups were evident from a search of the submissions and of which words turned up most often: "Sensitivity"—racial cultural or otherwise—showed up 28 times; "white," including attached to men, males, women, supremacy, or privilege, tallied up to 44; "bias" was mentioned 67 times; "training," i.e., for staff and others, totalled 140; instances of "black" appeared 470 times; while the most frequent word in the submissions was "demand," at 640. Some were more polite: "request" showed up 20 times, though two-thirds of the kinder and nicer approach came from just one college (Babson, in Wellesley, Massachusetts). Some submissions were short and others extended. Georgia Southern University students were brief in their six demands (98 words), including one for a campus climate-survey. Harvard University's submission clocked in at 2,838 words but was edged out for verbosity by Providence College students. They filled up 12 pages with 2,881 words.

Describing modern victimhood on campus is an exhaustive process. In total, the demands from 80 mostly American colleges and universities at Demand.org filled up 212 pages and amounted to 58,934 words. In contrast, the manifesto from the Unabomber, convicted in 1998 of killing three people and injuring 23 others with letter bombs between 1978 and 1995, was comparatively brief at 34,540 words.[63]

CHAPTER 3

Blinded by blame:
Apologies and missed opportunities

Have we reached the ultimate stage of absurdity where some people are held responsible for things that happened before they were born, while other people are not held responsible for what they themselves are doing today?

—THOMAS SOWELL

The culture of political apologies

Canadian politicians agree on virtually nothing except that apologies are owed.

In recent decades, the first high-profile regret for history came from Prime Minister Brian Mulroney, in 1988, for the internment of Japanese Canadians and the government's theft of their property during the Second World War. Next was a 1990 apology for how the government declared Italian Canadians "enemy aliens" in that same war (after Italy joined the Axis against Canada and her allies). In 2001, the Veteran's Affairs minister in the Jean Chretien government, Ron Duhamel, expressed official regret for the army's execution of 23 soldiers during the First World War. In 2008, Prime Minister Stephen Harper apologized for residential schools, where native Canadian children attended (sometimes by force, and sometimes at the request of parents) between the 1880s and 1990s and where sexual and physical abuses occurred.[1] Harper also offered apologies for the 1885–1923 Chinese head-tax; to Ukrainians for internment during the First World War; and also for how the federal government denied entry in 1914 to the Komagata Maru, a Japanese ship with 376 southeast Asian people on board including those who were Sikh, Hindu, and Muslim.

Shortly after coming to office, Prime Minister Justin Trudeau again apologized for the Komagata Maru. (Harper's apology was given in British Columbia, not in the House of Commons, was the cited reason.) The denial was "a stain on Canada's past," said Trudeau in early 2016.[2] Later, in 2017, Trudeau reiterated the Conservative government's apology for residential schools but for the Newfoundland and Labrador versions.[3] Speaking in Goose Bay, Trudeau used the language of therapy, telling the crowd that it was "not a burden you have to carry alone anymore." The prime minister told the audience it was his hope that they could "begin to heal—that you can finally put your inner child to rest."[4]

In November 2018, Trudeau issued three apologies in rapid succession: For the actions of British Columbia's first chief justice, Judge Matthew Baillie Begbie, who convicted and sentenced five Tsilhqot'in chiefs in 1864 and another in 1865 to death by hanging;[5] for the 1939 rejection of an asylum request from 900 German Jews, 254 of whom later died in the Holocaust;[6] and to gay and lesbian Canadians for past laws but also for the federal government's practice of outing and firing them from the civil service until the 1990s.[7] In March 2019, the prime minister apologized for how the Inuit in northern Canada were treated for tuberculosis in the mid-20th century[8] and in May 2019 for the imprisonment of Saskatchewan's Chief Poundmaker, convicted of treason-felony and imprisoned during the 1885 North-West Rebellion.[9] Since Brian Mulroney's first apology in 1988, at just the federal level, at least 15 apologies have been issued, with eight from the Trudeau government in four years.[10] Justin Trudeau's apologies were so numerous that even the BBC headlined a news report with the question, "Does Justin Trudeau apologise too much?"[11]

Thinking through regrets

Mixing politics, history, and an apology is often a mistake. There were always nuances in the various regrets, which could support or alternately undermine them. The six Tsilhqot'in chiefs sentenced to the gallows by Judge Begbie faced that fate after they murdered twenty-one men building a road through Tsilhqot'in territory.[12] Some would defend the six chiefs on the grounds that the killing was a battle in a war against invaders—this was the Trudeau government's reasoning. Alternately, some of the attackers who murdered the workers (there were 24 and not all were executed) were "singing and merry-making" with the road builders the night before. They also killed more than just the road crew but also those on a pack train along with a lone settler.[13] The issue is further complicated by how Chief Justice Begbie was not unsympathetic to First Nations and others discriminated against by white settlers. As left-wing journalist Stephen Hume wrote in 2017, Begbie spoke Secwepmc and Tsilhqot'in; favoured notions of aboriginal title; opposed settler efforts to displace First Nations by force; ruled against provincial legislation to ensure First Nations women received an equitable share of the estates of their white husbands; and sided with Chinese communities against racist laws. Justice Begbie also often "commuted the expected death sentences for First Nations—something he never did for a non-aboriginal offender."[14] History is not as simple as politicians would have us believe.

Governments sometimes offer apologies with more caution. When offering the Liberal government's 2001 regret for the execution of the 23 soldiers during the Great War, Jean Chretien's government deliberately did not also pardon the soldiers. That would have cast doubt on the judgement of the commanders at the time in the war who ordered the executions, in part to prevent desertions. (One such commander was Capt. George Vanier who served as Canada's governor-general between 1959 and 1967.) In a 2006 interview, military historian Desmond Morton argued that even the 2001 statement of regret "turned fact into fiction" and unfairly tarnished commanders. "They did it to encourage people to behave," he remarked. "If everyone who decided to flee, fled, where would the army be?"[15]

The possible gradations left out of most political apologies are purposeful. The point of the numerous *mea culpas* is to morally preen and take issue with the dead who cannot argue back. It is often excellent politics, at least in the short term. It also leads to hollowed-out, incomplete history, and a simplistic caricature of events. It is the "Disneyfication" of often difficult decisions from another era. Also, while personal apologies are valuable in that they take the "sting" out of a personal offence, it is not clear that government regrets add much to the overall stock of human compassion. In most instances, the apologies are given in place of dead men who harmed other dead men. But if everyone today agrees that some act committed long ago was morally beyond the pale, then progress as a species is already evident, at least until the next injury we commit in supreme self-confidence that we, as with every generation, have arrived at peak morality. If there is division on a matter— some think Judge Begbie was wrong to sentence six chiefs to death while others argue road-building without permission on territorial land did not give the chiefs a right to premediated murder—then an apology changes no one's mind. And the hung men and Judge Begbie are still dead and beyond the reach of our present, political morality plays.

Apologies vs. progress

Beyond the political apology culture, now routine, it is not clear that official regrets satisfy the more extreme critics in the community that, historically, possessed the most legitimate claims of injury, those whose ancestry is aboriginal. It is not clear such apologies even satisfy the specific First Nations to whom an apology has been given: In the spring and summer of 2019, the Tsilhqot'in First Nation set up a blockade to prevent the development of a mine in their traditional territory despite a Supreme Court of Canada ruling that rebuffed the Tsilhqot'in attempt to have the courts strike down a provincial drilling permit.[16] Still, to be aboriginal in Canada is to potentially have an historical memory of actual institutional prejudice, never mind personal racism that can linger given that laws cannot change hearts. Thus an 80-year-old aboriginal person alive today will recall that the right to vote was only returned in 1960, care of a civil rights advocate—a lawyer who also happened to be Prime Minister John Diefenbaker. Or ponder the betrayal of soldiers who volunteered in each world war as members of Canada's armed forces: Three thousand of our fellow citizens fought tyranny in Europe, only to be denied equality in law, policy, and even veterans' benefits upon their return.[17] It was because they were aboriginal. There is a reason why voluminous work has been done on the mistreatment of native North Americans: because both the sins and errors of some in the past were real, cruel, and sometimes deadly. Even well-meaning policy often went awry because it was not anchored in the equality and dignity of the individual or an understanding of how economies work.

More broadly, today, average socioeconomic indicators ("average" being an important qualifier) for aboriginal populations are not, in isolation, encouraging. However, as we will see, there are increasingly positive and more numerous exceptions and models worth emulating. In the main, though, for now, from First Nation homes twice as likely to be unsuitable for habitation compared with non-aboriginal peoples to employment rates and incomes on average lower than other Canadians, and where unemployment rates and poverty rates higher, outcomes for aboriginal Canadians lag that of the general population.[18] The problem with the apology culture is that it has overwhelmed other reasons why average indicators are poor in some cases: the remote location of many reserves, for example. The intense focus on apologies has also removed media attention from the problem of corruption and, worse, of sexual abuse on reserves in favour of easy explanations for any troubling social and economic issues: Most everything is the fault of colonialists and other Canadians today. However, before considering tighter cause-and-effect links and these other matters, first the accusations and the blame.

European blame and a belief in pure culture

Three reports in the last quarter-century best illustrate the culture of blame that is now ubiquitous in Canada. The first was the 1996 Royal Commission on Aboriginal Peoples, the second the 2015 Truth and Reconciliation Commission of Canada, and the third the 2019 report released by the National Inquiry into Missing and Murdered Indigenous Women and Girls. All resulted from legitimate concerns and tragic events: poorer outcomes for aboriginal Canadians as a cohort vis-à-vis other Canadians and also specific tragedies; sexual and physical abuse in now-closed residential schools; and missing and murdered aboriginal women, among others. The various reports were right to investigate past racist treatment in Canada's institutions, laws, policies, and practices. Where they erred was to take a broad-brush approach to both aboriginal and "European" culture, romanticizing the first and wholly condemning the second. They were also in error to offer up generalized correlation–causation links. That matters because if the wrong cause is linked to some observed effect, with a mistaken remedy following, progress on solving a particular problem will not happen. Thus, scathing condemnation of Canada's British inheritance and a race to cultural "silos" was evident in all three reports. It was also wildly off the mark.

The 1996 Royal Commission on Aboriginal Peoples properly chronicled the wrongs, the past policy intended to "remove Aboriginal people from their homelands... suppress Aboriginal nations and their governments... undermine Aboriginal cultures... [and] stifle Aboriginal identity."[19] It also noted what almost everyone would think a wrongheaded tragedy: the Indian Act, which not only treated aboriginal peoples as inferior but induced permanent separation through the reserve system—"designed to protect Aboriginal people and preserve their ways, but operated instead to isolate and impoverish them."[20] The report then painted an idealized view of Aboriginal life before other settlers arrived in the Americas, referencing aboriginal peoples pre-contact, as if harmony prevailed with no mention made of wars, slavery, or human sacrifices, also the reality of life in the Americas before contact.[a]

Similarly, in the 2015 report from the Truth and Reconciliation Commission of Canada, tasked to consider the record and legacy of residential schools, the authors were proper to catalogue the sexual and physical abuses in residential schools. Their particular error was to always link poor socioeconomic outcomes for a multitude of aboriginal Canadians today to selected residential school abuses in the past. This was always an overreach. For example, even by the commission's own estimate, when the proportion of registered First Nations children in residential schools was at its peak, in 1944/45, the proportion was 31%.[21] Thus even though that was the high watermark for attendance, and even if one accepts the Commission's narrative that all residential schools made victims of all students (beyond those subject to sexual and physical abuse), it is yet a leap to attribute modern-day social and economic outcomes for all aboriginal Canadians to an education model where less than one-third attended at its peak. Even if the link between attendance at a residential school and poor economic and social outcomes in the 21st century was inextricably tight for every single attendee, that link would still not explain economic and social outcomes for the vast majority of aboriginal Canadians who never attended such schools and nor did their ancestors.

---

[a] Among others, see Donald Leland, Aboriginal Slavery on the Northwest Coast of North America (Berkeley: University of California Press, 1997), 177; Thomas Sowell, Conquests and Cultures: An International History, (New York: Basic Books, 1998), 276.

The charge of genocide

More extreme accusations continued in the 2019 report released by the National Inquiry into Missing and Murdered Indigenous Women and Girls. The report was an overdue focus on some of the most marginalized members of Canadian society, in part spurred by revelations that Aboriginal women disappeared from the streets of Vancouver and elsewhere, with some murdered and others never found. That happened despite early pleas from relatives to the police that were routinely ignored—aboriginal women fell "through the cracks," to use a cliché that was horrific and true. The tragedy was investigated and chronicled in a 2012 report in British Columbia by former B.C. Attorney General Wally Oppal.[22] Oppal's report was comprehensive. It recognized the distrust by many in the aboriginal community, including wariness of the police and others due to ignoring cultural differences between mainstream society and aboriginal communities. It also contained clear, practical recommendations: a metro Vancouver police force, for example, so investigations would no longer be lost in jurisdictional "gaps." In contrast, the national report on missing and murdered women veered into creation myths; romanticized pre-contact aboriginal culture as pure, ever-peaceful, and harmonious with the environment; argued any notion of two genders for most people was merely a result of "colonization and Christianity;"[23] disdained the liberalism of Pierre Trudeau's 1969 White Paper;[24] defended shamans as equivalent to science-based medicine;[25] and treated culture as static.[26]

Pure culture worship

The core approach and error in all three national reports on aboriginal issues was a tendency to treat culture not as an amorphous, ever-changing set of beliefs and practices, but as akin to a living, breathing human being. The initial focus on culture was useful both to illustrate the intentional harm to aboriginal cultures by some in the past (though the authors also took a broad-brush approach here) and because assumptions which animate a society matter, including a conception of what constitutes the good life. But the authors of the 2015 and 2019 reports leapt far beyond routine, sensible treatment of culture as a real living "muscle" to be understood as one also capable of adaptation. They instead treated injuries to culture as akin to mass murder: "Physical genocide is the mass killing of the members of a targeted group, and biological genocide is the destruction of the group's reproductive capacity. Cultural genocide is the destruction of those structures and practices that allow the group to continue as a group,"[27] argued the 2015 report's authors.

In parallel, the 2019 report compared past real harms and alleged present maltreatment of aboriginal Canadians as akin to deliberate massacres in Germany under Adolf Hitler: "The truth is that we live in a country whose laws and institutions perpetuate violations of basic human and Indigenous rights. These violations amount to nothing less than the deliberate, often covert campaign of genocide…."[28] The use of the present tense was intentional. In the separate appendix on genocide, the national inquiry's authors justified using the term genocide with an argument that "colonial policies in Canada have often been rooted in lethal but also non-lethal measures, aimed at assimilating and obliterating Indigenous populations."[29] It cited the Holocaust, the Armenian genocide, and the Rwandan genocide. The inquiry saw those three and the treatment of aboriginal peoples as a quibble only about time. The Nazi, Armenian, and Rwandan massacres were rapid in comparison to Canada's "colonial genocide [which] is also a slow-moving process,"[30] wrote the authors.

The actual effect of cultural isolationism: Cultural vulnerability

The attempt to make past colonial or present Canadian policy akin to genocide by equating culture—critical as it is—to a human being, failed but not because culture is irrelevant. Human beings operate in a sea of assumptions, customs, and institutions, which when disrupted can create chaos in daily life but also affect the trajectory of an entire society. The authors missed the mark because they were possessed by the notion that the strongest cultures are those uncontaminated by outsiders—a false and dangerous assumption. It assumes human beings should live in cultural silos untouched by others' ideas and encounters, except perhaps in only carefully controlled environments where outsiders are thought quite literally as contaminants.

This is folly. Pure, "authentic" cultures weaken themselves and are dangerous for the most vulnerable societies because, eventually, another nation that has busily borrowed, stolen, and appropriated influences from others will show up on the "doorstep" of those who have remained static. The most compelling example is Japan, which shut itself off from most contact with the outside world between 1633 and 1853. The general lack of a continual transfer of ideas, technology, most trade, and critical developments in weaponry meant that in 1853, after Commodore Mathew Perry's four American ships sailed into Tokyo harbour, Japan had no choice but to open up anyway—but on another nation's terms. Japan had neither the economic nor military resources to do otherwise.

The same unbalanced encounter was of course what occurred between France, Great Britain, and the original settlers in Canada. Those two countries along with the rest of Europe had long been adapting, because they had no choice: The European continent with its coasts, inland waterways and roads, along with the Mediterranean "lake," meant territories were conquered, lost, and reconquered for the entirety of human settlement in Europe, with both forced and adopted cultural transfers. Whether conquered or conquering, princes, emperors, and nation-states alike appropriated the most advantageous parts of what others possessed, be it improvements in arms, technology, and trade over a millennium and more, and from wherever they encountered others. It included a superior numbering system (Hindu-Arabic numerals), gunpowder (created in Asia), trigonometry (Egypt), and ships steered by rudders (invented in China).[31] Such transfers did not make Europeans morally superior when they arrived in the Americas in 1492 and beyond, any more than Americans were ethically above the civilization of Japan in 1853. It just made such forces unbeatable because of a lack of adaption, often but not always unintentional, in the peoples they encountered. The authors of the three reports ignored the role of transfers in favour of an assumed authentic and morally pure aboriginal culture in ages past. It is how they could define cultural changes—forced and repressed in some cases and voluntary and negotiated in others—with genocide.

A ten-fold increase in real spending per person is not genocide

Mass murder was never British policy or later federal government policy, and the latter two reports on aboriginal life in Canada in particular overreached and undermined their useful work in offering such a comparison. Beyond error in equating injury to beliefs and practices to actual genocides around the world, the broader charge that Canada was yet still a racist haven as per mainstream views in 1867 ignored policy that has been pro- and not anti-aboriginal. In Canada, a plethora of constitutional carve-outs exist that include traditional hunting and fishing rights despite the reality of a population that could not be sustained on such a basis; tax-free status on most reserves; "citizen plus" rights and—there is no other word for it—privileges for registered First Nations peoples that have developed, especially since the 1980s. Those include affirmative action programs at every level of government and universities.

The charge of genocide is also exactly opposite the reality, given such attempts to mitigate and remedy poor outcomes with more government spending, especially for reserve populations. In data I tracked from the mid-1940s to the early part of this decade, federal increases in spending on Canada's aboriginal peoples has been significant. In inflation-adjusted numbers, both in total dollars spent but also per person every year, spending increased from $79 million annually in the late 1940s to almost $7.9 billion in 2012—for just one department (then titled Aboriginal Affairs and Northern Development Canada).[b] The per-person rate of increase rose from $922 per registered First Nation individual in 1950 to $9,056 by 2012, or a ten-fold increase in real, inflation-adjusted terms per person. That was not spending on aboriginal Canadians in place of other federal spending available to them but in addition to it. On that, and by comparison, federal government spending on all Canadians (with inflation accounted for) grew five-fold between 1950 at $1,504 per person then to $7,316 by 2012.[32] In other words, spending within that envelope specific to aboriginal Canadians rose even more dramatically than spending on all Canadians. In an updated version of my study, it turns out that an analysis of only two federal departments, and provincial government spending, $263 billion has been spent on Canada's aboriginal peoples. That includes the federal department of Indigenous and Northern Affairs Canada since the mid-1940s, and Health Canada spending and provincial government spending since the mid-1990s, and runs at $12.7 billion annually for those three entities.[33]

Not all that spending was required by treaty or the constitution—funding aboriginal television networks, for example—while some is mandated.

---

[b] Multiple other federal departments and also provinces spend on Aboriginal peoples as well, such as Health Canada on benefits and housing not included in the above figures. I also found that provincial spending on Aboriginal Canadians also soared. See my 2013 report on the matter: "Ever-Higher: Government Spending on Canada's Aboriginals Since 1947."

Regardless, what is clear is that aboriginal Canadians do benefit from federal spending that other Canadians must incur out of pocket, through insurance plans, and for which their employer must pay. For example, federal government health-care policy specific to First Nations peoples includes dental, pharmacare, and eye-care benefits worth more than $1.1 billion annually, or about $1,200 per person.[34] One can argue for some measures as helpful to settling historical grievances, against others on equality grounds, and some specific policy as treaty-obligated. But whatever one thinks of the list and spending, the various policy measures such as affirmative action or dramatically increased government spending have been of a pro-aboriginal variety and not designed to harm. Such realities do not support the claim of a genocidal nation-state on the northern half of the North American continent. The conclusion should rather be the opposite.

Lastly, in a moral contradiction no one noticed, both the 2015 and 2019 reports appealed to British norms and the rule of law, in specific the British monarchy and the 1763 Royal Proclamation. That proclamation from King George III set the parameters for how colonial governments in British North America were to conduct themselves, including a requirement to negotiate treaties. The authors of both the 2015 residential school report and the 2019 missing and murdered women report appealed to 1763 and the Crown as a source of authority, including moral, yet then equated the Crown and its agents with German National Socialists who sent six million Jews and others to their deaths, Hutus who massacred one million Tutsis and other Rwandans, and to the Turkish state that murdered one-and-a-half-million Christian Armenians.

Apartheid, not genocide

Unlike the 2015 and 2019 reports, an accurate description of the historic harm to First Nations comes from Calvin Helin, son of a Tsimshian chief and also a lawyer and entrepreneur. In his 2011 book, *Dances with Dependency, Out of Poverty through Self-Reliance*, Helin accurately and with more precision characterizes the harm done to native Canadians in the past: It was apartheid akin to what black South Africans experienced under the Boers until the 1990s. Helin's own family history is illustrative: "In Tsimshian society, my grandmother was an aristocrat from the royal house of Gitchiis," wrote

Helin, who then describes not the evil of genocide but the sin of apartheid. "Throughout most of her life, she could not vote in federal or provincial elections. Indians—along with Chinese and some other minorities—were forced to sit in separate areas from whites in movie theatres, could not go into bars, and were effectively barred from becoming doctors or lawyers,"[35] writes Helin, who described "Aboriginal people of her generation [as] treated like second-class citizens," which is exactly correct. Helin then also notes how land and resources were "simply removed," with aboriginal culture and language effectively outlawed, and that what "was instituted to replace self-sufficient Aboriginal societies was an incompetent and patronizing bureaucracy whose prescription amounted to a heavy dose of welfare."[36]

Other explanations for present disparities

Moving past the effects of apartheid requires not only the institutional removal of discriminatory laws and policies; it also requires correct cause-and-effect links. But we are not there yet in terms of political understanding. One significant factor in First Nations poverty is the location of reserves: in rural areas, far from major urban centres—a significant barrier to better educational and economic opportunities. A university with options for careers that range from music to engineering cannot be provided in most rural areas with any degree of comprehensiveness. Nor can a government offer a fully functioning hospital in a hamlet. And while some reserves will rightly capitalize on a nearby resource (Fort MacKay in Alberta with oil or the Haisla Nation on the coast of British Columbia with natural gas) or on a spectacular setting (the Westbank and Osoyoos First Nations in the Okanagan's wine-belt), location greatly matters to a First Nation's success or failure. Unlike MacKay, the Haisla, or First Nations in the Okanagan in wine country, most reserves are located in isolated parts of the country where opportunities are few.

To grasp the enormity of the problem and the geographic disadvantage, in 2016, 39% of aboriginal peoples lived in a village of fewer than 1,000 people, and another 20% in a town between 1,000 and 30,000 people.[37] That compares with 19% and 13% for the general population.[38] In other words, nearly 60% of aboriginal Canadians (First Nations, Métis, Inuit) lived in a community smaller than 30,000 people compared to 32% of the general population.[c] This matters, as the 2016 census showed that First Nations people living

---

[c] Recall as well that registered First Nations, the cohort that used to be labelled as registered "Indians," are proportionally even more concentrated on reserves, including those in remote locations.

off-reserve were twice as likely to possess a bachelor's degree than those on-reserve (11.4% and 5.4%, respectively) and they were also more likely to have an apprenticeship certificate (4.9% versus 3.9%).[39] That additional education helps with incomes: In 1981, those living off-reserve recorded incomes 92% higher than on-reserve; while the proportion 35 years later, in 2016, was still 81% more than on-reserve income. Living where opportunity exists matters, positively, to one's income.

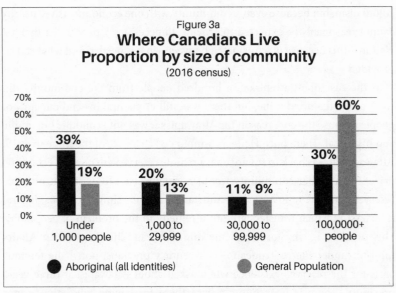

Figure 3a
**Where Canadians Live
Proportion by size of community**
(2016 census)

Sources: Statistics Canada, 2016 census. Population Centre and Focus on Geography Series; Distribution of the Aboriginal population by population centre size.

The issue of geography is critical to claims that Canadians—consciously or not—or their governments are somehow still racist in intent and policy, or that significant legacy effects yet exist from previous government policy. The fact that nearly 60% of aboriginal Canadians (and a higher proportion of First Nations) live in rural Canada offers a tighter cause-and-effect link for the continuing gaps between aboriginal peoples and other Canadians. A clear, tragic example is the Attawapiskat reserve in northern Ontario, located near the southern tip of Hudson's Bay, which became famous in the last decade for poor living conditions and substandard housing, among other issues.

Normally those who live in remote areas do so because their skills match nearby opportunities or they are retired or they can simply afford to live in a rural area they like. Communities that exist because of a nearby opportunity (a mine or a sawmill or a refinery) attract those who can work in such industries and have the qualifications to do just that. When industries or economies change, some workers move away and new people move in if other opportunities appear. In contrast, even Attawapiskat, with a diamond mine nearby, was at a disadvantage, not because of racism or the effects of colonialism, but because even a community with one economic driver nearby cannot reasonably be expected to provide all necessary jobs to a nearby First Nation—this because of a mismatch between what is needed and what can be provided.

In the case of Attawapiskat, a hundred people from the community did work at the diamond mine, but there was still no natural in- and out-flow of people because the core reason for Attawapiskat was not economic but ethnic and historical. Then, once DeBeers announced a closure of the mine in 2019, Attawapiskat was back to square one: a remote reserve with one less economic driver.[40] Any other community would normally cease to exist. But multiple reserves continue in just such circumstances and for similar reasons, federal transfers. But such transfers are not a remedy to the problem of geography. This problem is why former prime minister Jean Chretien, Indian Affairs minister under Pierre Trudeau a half-century previous, noted the tenuous basis for the reserve's existence when asked about Attawapiskat three years previous: "There is no economic base there for having jobs," the former prime minister said, "and sometimes they have to move, like anybody else."[41] Chretien was not being cruel; he was acknowledging the obvious: Worldwide, men and women have shifted from rural areas for two centuries, ever since the agricultural economy could no longer support a growing population.

The original sin: Separation and isolation

There is indeed a significant legacy effect from past colonial actions, but one about which few are willing to be as blunt as Chretien: reserves. The original sin of John A. MacDonald and early politicians in Canada is not, as is commonly assumed, the creation of residential schools—that was a consequence and not the prime mover—but two others: the assumption of the inferiority of native

Canadians and the decision to create reserves. The assumption of inferiority was illiberal and racist; the creation of reserves, even where well intended to preserve communities and culture, locked many native Canadians into a permanent rural location and poverty. The poverty exceptions turned out to be only specific reserves that were lucky enough to be near major urban centres (then or now) or mines, forests they could harvest, fishing, and other economic opportunities. In contrast, all other Canadians could move as the rural economy declined, as indeed all in the world have done since the start of the Industrial Revolution. As the Haisla Nation described in their 2015 primer on reconciliation, "There are lots of places where our forefathers had their habitation from different places where we were born."[42]

The creation of reserves was akin to a government in 1925 ordering all who had arrived in the dry Palliser Triangle in Alberta to continue to farm—i.e., to stay put—even when it was clear such land was more suitable to ranching than producing bountiful crops. Or if the federal government in 1945 had, instead of shutting down internment camps for Japanese, kept them open and required internees to remain in them for time immemorial. In both cases, rural Canadians and the Japanese would have been circumscribed to a postage-stamp existence, with most opportunities for education, work, and self and familiar actualization out of reach by virtue of location. And poverty and social pathologies would have inevitably followed just as they have for many First Nations reserves for a century and a half.[d]

---

[d] I have deliberately avoided policy prescriptions, including alternatives to the reserve system, to focus on the grievance cultures. One option, albeit with constitutional and legal changes and with First Nations leaders choosing such an option themselves, has been to turn reserves into private property. However, that was rejected by many First Nations leaders in 1969 with the release of "The Statement of the Government of Canada on Indian Policy," or the "White paper," as it was known, from Pierre Trudeau's government and in which Jean Chretien was Indian Affairs minister. However, the Westbank First Nation, across from Kelowna, B.C., where I grew up, and selected others, have made the most possible of collectively owned property by treating much of it as parcels that can be leased. While still collectively owned by the Crown, significant parts of Westbank First Nation land are leased out for homes, offices, and commercial real estate with long-term leases. It is akin to treating reserve property as a corporate entity with the Westbank First Nation as the de facto shareholder. Westbank is fortunate in that is has a unique location in the Okanagan. However, the model—treat reserves as corporate entities with some income thus derived and its First Nations members living elsewhere—may be the only way to square the circle of continued Crown and collective ownership and yet see First Nations people thrive in other locales that offer opportunity specific to each individual. Another option is to encourage much more natural resource development in rural areas near reserves. That too should be considered but, as per Attawapiskat, it is not a permanent remedy for everyone or every reserve. The problem of geographic isolation will still linger.

Location and hope off-reserve

The challenge of geography was overlooked when blame was assigned in all three major aboriginal reports in 1996, 2015, and 2019. For our purposes—thinking through the extreme rhetoric—when apple-to-apple statistics are available, aboriginal Canadians demonstrate incomes near, equal to, or greater than that of other Canadians. And that offers hope. In 2016, the median income for non-aboriginal Canadians who worked full-time all year was $53,648. The same statistic for all aboriginal Canadians was $47,596 and ranged from $43,812 for First Nations, $51,789 for Métis, and $57, 276 for Inuk/Inuit. (The Inuit are an outlier, given the northern location of most Inuit and higher salaries in the north for most residents.) The most telling statistic is that Métis' median annual income is within $2,000 of other Canadians. That matters because two-thirds of Métis live in a metropolitan area, the highest proportion of any aboriginal group.[43] It is possible that discrimination yet explains that gap, except that the average age and education levels of each group help explain the differences (the older a cohort, the greater its median earnings): the median age for First Nations is just over 27 years, for Métis it's 33, and for the non-aboriginal population it's 41.[44] In terms of education,[e] 43% of First Nations have never finished high school compared to 30% of Métis and 20% of non-aboriginal Canadians.

An even more useful comparison is a nearly exact one: How do similarly educated people at a similar station in life fare? Here the results are stark and encouraging: For those aged 25 to 34 years old, aboriginal Canadians with a bachelor's degree had nearly the same median income as non-aboriginal Canadians with a bachelor's degree ($42,603 versus $43,110). Of note, aboriginal Canadians with education beyond a bachelor's degree earned over $3,000 more than non-aboriginal peoples in that same educational cohort ($47,115 and $44,100, respectively).[45]

---

[e] Over the age of 15.

	No certificate, diploma or degree	High school diploma	Certificate of Apprenticeship	University certificate or diploma below bachelor level	University certificate, diploma or degree at bachelor level or above	Bachelor's degree	Diploma or degree above bachelor level
Figure 3b **Income in 2015 for full-year full-time workers,** **ages 25-34, Aboriginal and non-Aboriginal**							
Median employment income ($) 2016 census							
Aboriginal	15,675	25,407	46,091	31,062	**43,445**	42,603	**47,115**
Non-Aboriginal	**24,912**	**30,039**	**50,948**	**33,866**	43,346	**43,110**	44,100

Statistics Canada - 2016 Census, Catalogue Number 98-400-X2016178, highest median income in bold.

At lower levels of education, wide gaps remain; but that is again related to location. Those with degrees are more likely to live off-reserve and in cities. In addition, while the $500 gap between aboriginal and non-aboriginal Canadians with a bachelor's degree could yet be taken as evidence of discrimination, there are other reasons, including the type of education earned. One example: Of all aboriginal Canadians with post-secondary education, just 1.3% possessed a lucrative engineering degree compared to 5.1% of non-aboriginal peoples with such a degree.[46] Or expressed another way, it appears that aboriginal and other Canadians of similar age and education earn roughly the same, with education choices influencing incomes. There are significant challenges for First Nations in particular as average educational levels are lower, with unemployment rates higher and incomes lower as a result. But education and one's own location are both "correctable." However, the statistics that show where and how higher incomes are obtained—off-reserve and with more education—make it clear that aboriginal Canadians are succeeding given an urban location and higher education. That hardly endorses the radical and false claim that Canada is akin to a genocidal state. There is instead much room for reasoned optimism.

A missed opportunity for aboriginal women

The two reports in 2015 and 2019 blamed the poor social and economic indicators for aboriginal Canadians on past government policy and discrimination, including residential schools and selected colonial attempts to repress native culture in the 19th and 20th centuries, along with institutional and personal discrimination. However, the shortest distance between an observed effect and a recent action is often the most likely cause, a cause-and-effect link known as "Occam's Razor." The National Inquiry into Missing and Murdered Indigenous Women and Girls ignored this approach in favour of every other possible explanation, and did so even with the cohort meant to be its focus, aboriginal women.

The final report consisted of two volumes in English with supplementary reports on Quebec and genocide; it totalled over 1,300 pages. The report only addressed the actual murdered and missing women two-thirds into the first volume on page 508 (of 728 pages). There the authors discuss the sexual and physical abuse of aboriginal women.[47] As per other reports, blame is placed on past colonial policy and practices, including residential schools, but also day schools and child welfare placements in the 1960s.[48] A discussion of who actually murdered aboriginal women appears only in the second volume, near the end, and where the authors attempt to disagree with RCMP statistics. Here, some background is helpful. The Department of Justice and the Royal Canadian Mounted Police both report the following:[49]

- Between 1984 and 2014, 6,849 women were murdered, and 16% were aboriginal women.

- In 2013 and 2014, 26 of 32 cases (81%) involving homicides of aboriginal women were solved, and in all solved cases, 100% of those who killed the women knew the victim: They were current and former spouses, family members, or an acquaintance.[50]

- For non-aboriginal homicides involving women, the solve rate was 83%; 93% of the killers were known to the women, a rate and proportion of known killers not far off the percentages for aboriginal women.

- As of 2014, of the 1,750 women reported missing in Canada, 10% (174) were of aboriginal ancestry.

The National Inquiry report took issue with the RCMP report, arguing that the data was "inaccurate" and "misleading" because the 100% figure was based on the years 2013 and 2014.[51] As the RCMP note, the statistics are consistent with the previous decade. In addition, as even the inquiry report acknowledges, the RCMP polices 40% of Canada's aboriginal population compared to 20% of the general population. As a result, RCMP statistics on the murders of aboriginal women are at least as comprehensive as other police departments whose data would be more fragmented and less indicative of a trend. The murder of women, aboriginal and not, is most often an act by someone who knows them. It is a depressingly similar statistic for all women, aboriginal and otherwise.

Abuse on reserves

The two recent reports on aboriginal life in Canada erred in another way, this time by omission. In 2014, *Atlantic Monthly* delved into the subject of the rape culture in the Alaskan wilderness,[52] a frank piece about the horrific rate of sexual assault on Alaska's native-American reserves. That same year, Statistics Canada reported similarly disproportionate data for First Nations girls and women in Canada and based on self-reporting by females who live on and off reserves.[53] This issue has generally been underreported in Canadian media. When I asked editors and publishers at nearly every major magazine and newspaper in Canada about this in 2015—i.e., if they would investigate the issue more deeply—all demurred, noting the controversial nature of such a topic, or that it was best left to aboriginal media themselves to investigate and cover.

Neither position was one most media outlets would take if the subject matter was abuse by Catholic priests or a Hollywood mogul such as Harvey Weinstein. Editors would be unlikely to respond that only Catholic newspapers or the entertainment media should cover such stories. I found a few exceptions: In 2016, the *Toronto Star* reported that the Ontario Federation of Friendship Centres estimated that 75% to 80% of girls under 18 on reserves may have been victims of sexual assault.[54] In 2016, CBC Radio interviewed "Deborah" from Vanderhoof, B.C. (Her last name was not provided.) She told the CBC that her mother, sister, and other female relatives had died of alcohol and drug abuse as a result of the sexual abuse they had suffered as children. Their abusers got away with it, she said, because "there's a really strong no-talk culture on First Nations reserves where people know things are going on." It's actually dangerous to speak out, she noted, recalling that when she tried to obtain legal help for two young girls who were being sexually abused, someone tried to burn down her on-reserve house.[55] A few women have also gone public with their stories. One of the rare ones to do so was Freda Ens, who was 59 when she told a reporter in 2016 that she had been repeatedly raped by male relatives while growing up in Old Masset Village, a Haida community in British Columbia. Ens urged other victims to come forward; otherwise, she said, "We are covering it up."[56] The rural location of many reserves is part of the problem. Los Angeles reporters will cover Hollywood scandals, and the political media in Canada will cover developments in provincial capitals and Ottawa. But an investigative story about possible sexual assaults on remote reserves requires time, resources, contacts on the ground, and people willing to tell their stories. That is often the weak link between newsrooms in urban centres and rural areas in general, but it might be especially problematic for reserves.

However, none of that explains why First Nations bodies such as the Assembly of First Nations have not called for a full inquiry as per the other issues such as residential schools or murdered aboriginal women, or why politicians eager to look at the colonial record are not just as diligent to investigate contemporary abuses on reserve and draw direct links where they exist. The National Inquiry into Missing and Murdered Indigenous Women and Girls was a $92-million exercise. On the very subject the inquiry was tasked to investigate, it had an opportunity to be frank about who murdered most aboriginal women—their spouses, boyfriends, and acquaintances—but chose not to, in favour of blaming dead colonialists and accusing the living of genocide. Also, the 2019 inquiry, media, and politicians overlooked a major issue on reserves—sexual assault—and thus ignored the nearly 250,000 aboriginal women who live in such communities.[57]

CHAPTER 4

Victims of identities and arguments over privilege

I have unfairly benefitted from the colour of my skin.
White privilege is not acceptable.

—Gold River, British Columbia, School District
Superintendent THERESA DOWNS

My first reaction to people like this is always the same: Where were you when
I needed you? I had grown up in the rigid segregation of 1950s Chicago,
where my life had been entirely circumscribed by white racism.

—SHELBY STEELE, *Shame: How America's Past Sins*
Have Polarized Our Country

Progress undone

There have never been societies as tolerant, with as much opportunity for many including tens of millions of immigrants, as prosperous, and as uninterested in someone's colour and ancestry as those that now exist in Canada and the United States. Both countries are also where economic class and one's family history matter less than anywhere else in the world and in history.

This was not always the case. In the 1940s, those of Japanese ethnicity *because they had Japanese ancestry* were herded into war-time internment camps and had their property stolen by governments in Canada and the United States. In 1950, just before Ontario began to pass a raft of bills banning the practices, minorities could be denied housing and motels based on their skin colour. In the 1960s, Martin Luther King, Rosa Parks, and other black

Americans braved dogs, water cannons, braying racists, and police to exercise basic civil rights and to choose their own bus seats and lunch counters.

That was then.

By the 1980s, black married couples with college educations already earned slightly *more* than white college-educated married couples in the United States.[1] In 1981, in Canada, earnings for those with Japanese ancestry were 13% higher than those of European ancestry. By the late 2000s, Americans elected a president who was half black and half white.

That was progress. And it is still unequalled in the rest of the world, slow to catch up. Americans killed each other to end slavery in 1865 while Mauritania waited another 116 years, until 1981, to make slavery illegal, and only criminalized it in 2007. But the latter regime's heart is not in the fight. As of 2018, there were an estimated 90,000 slaves in the country,[2] and *The Economist* published an article on how Mauritania's government ignored slavery and instead jailed those who protested against it.[3]

Regression on race and reawakening of oppression?

Modern-day Americans and Canadians, or newer immigrants who arrive in the same, could be forgiven for thinking their countries are unredeemed bastions of prejudice. Plenty of academics, politicians, and headline writers seem to think so, especially with the notion of "white privilege," the idea that skin colour—race[a]—is quasi-deterministic for employment, incomes, and much else, as if little had changed since in the middle of the last century.

"White privilege" was an academic theory that originated in the mid-1980s with a then-unknown Massachusetts academic who had an awakening of sorts. Peggy McIntosh, a professor at Wellesley College, later wrote of how her encounters with men unaware they possessed privilege based on their gender, led to her subsequent discovery: "After I realized the extent to which men work from a base of unacknowledged privilege, I understood that much of their oppressiveness was unconscious," she wrote in a short essay in 1989

---

[a] For multiple reasons, the concept of "race" is problematic, and I prefer not to use it. Ethnicity is often better as a descriptor; but even there, it is problematic for analysis. One might be of British origin and black and thus ethnicity is of limited use in describing the problem: A racist act against someone of a different skin colour. Also, the notion of race—"white" and" black"—is still used by statistical agencies for select cohorts; thus, to analyze their data one is, for now, stuck with it.

titled "White Privilege: Unpacking the Invisible Knapsack."[4] As McIntosh described it, she then realized her own blind spot: race. "Then I remembered the frequent charges from women of color that white women whom they encounter are oppressive. My schooling gave me no training in seeing myself as an oppressor, as an unfairly advantaged person, or as a participant in a damaged culture."

McIntosh's essay listed 26 "effects" of white privilege; i.e., attitudes or actions that she argued were proof of privilege. They included: "I can if I wish arrange to be in the company of people of my race most of the time"; "I can turn on the television or open to the front page of the paper and see people of my race widely represented"; "I am never asked to speak for all the people of my racial group"; "I can be pretty sure that if I ask to talk to 'the person in charge,' I will be facing a person of my race"; "I can take a job with an affirmative action employer without having co-workers on the job suspect that I got it because of race"; "I can choose blemish cover or bandages in 'flesh' color and have them more [or] less match my skin." Of note, McIntosh said that "Whiteness protected me from many kinds of hostility, distress and violence, which I was being subtly trained to visit, in turn, upon people of color."

The theory has since grown into a corporate, cottage industry in academic, media, business, and political circles. In a 2013 column published in Yale University's divinity school magazine, Melanie Morris wrote of how it was important to confront "racism and white privilege where [we] live, work, study, and worship."[5] In 2016 two *Harvard Business Review* authors opined that "subtle bias is often worse than blatant discrimination." Eden King and Kristin Jones wrote how "Our research shows that the new kinds of bias can be even worse than the older kinds,"—an odd claim given that the "older kinds" included the denial of bus seats, lunch counters, and motel rooms to black Americans.[6] That same year, Princeton University's Imani Perry, a professor in the Center for African American Studies, argued that "Identity is a marker of how resources and opportunities are distributed in our society."[7] Note Perry's assumption—chronic in identity-politics practitioners—that the economy is zero-sum and "distributed," common among those who assert that past discrimination explains the modern economy.

The notion of white privilege is now deep in public consciousness. A Google search will turn up over five million results. Wikipedia defines the concept as "the societal privilege that in some countries benefits white people over non-white people, particularly if they are otherwise under the same social, political, or economic circumstances."[8] In 2019, Kirsten Gillibrand, a Democratic senator from New York running for president, was asked by a young mother at a town hall meeting in Youngstown, Ohio—where the economy has never recovered from rust-belt layoffs decades ago—if using that term was any less divisive than Donald Trump's un-subtle baiting, or smart politics. "This is an area that across all demographics has been depressed because of the loss of its industry and the opioids crisis," said the mother, who then queried, "So what do you have to say to people in this area about so-called white privilege?"[9] Gillibrand answered that white privilege was real, reflected in differing arrest rates for young black males versus white males, in jobs denied for blacks, and in high maternal mortality-rates. The senator said privilege was indeed white and that it was "institutionalized racism."[10]

The concept is now part of a 21st-century victim narrative with identity politics at its core: You are a beneficiary or a victim of your race. Your identity, most often defined by race, but also gender or ethnicity, is thus deterministic in its effect upon income and wealth. As with other illiberal theories, Canadian academics follow American leads and the theory is now standard fare north of the 49th parallel. In 2018, Toronto's Ryerson University hosted a "white privilege" conference and defined the concept as a "socio-political system that distributes power, privilege and benefits unequally among groups in societies and countries in our world."[11] (Note again the academic notion that economies are static and "distributed.") Those wishing to study, lecture, and write on the subject can choose from multiple websites, analytic "tools," seed projects, and annual conferences dedicated to exploring the phenomenon. They can ponder white privilege at conferences that align with their preferred academic getaway: mountain towns such as Colorado Springs or desert cities such as Mesa, Arizona; historic Philadelphia or St. Louis, Missouri; or one abutting the Great Lakes' location of Cedar Rapids, Michigan. At one conference, written about later by a participant sympathetic to the notion that white privilege in the 21st century is real, he admitted to cringing, this after one seminar leader at a white privilege conference declared that "Racism is a white creation."[12] Even the sympathetic attendee understood history is full of racists of every pigmentation.

Unpacking identity politics and privilege theory

White privilege is now more than a theory; it is also an accusation and a justification for racial and ethnic quotas. It undergirds calls for compensation based on past prejudice or from the era of slavery. As with all compelling theories, there is some truth in the assertion; but specifics matter. The older the example, at least in Western countries, the stronger the case that whites were privileged, which led to wealth that was unjust. The obvious example is slavery. Until emancipation in 1865, southern blacks in slavery contributed directly to southern-white wealth. A version of the privilege theory is also obvious in arguments for reparations—called for in a famous 2014 essay by Ta-Nehisi Coates in *The Atlantic* magazine—based in the notion that some statistical disparities in income, crime, or maternal mortality rates prove a legacy effect from slavery or past institutional prejudice (or personal bigotry today).

The privilege theory is relevant because both the United States and Canada offer programs explicit in racial, ethnic, and gender consciousness, which assume privilege and ongoing harm from past or present prejudice in employment and income. In Canada, the federal government is explicit that this is why racial, ethnic, and gender quotas exist. The reasoning is enunciated in its Employment Equity Act, which dates back to the mid-1980s: Women, aboriginal peoples, members of visible minorities, and the disabled are preferred in government hiring.[b] The federal justification of preferential hiring is that it "corrects the conditions of disadvantage in employment."[13]

Beyond earlier historical examples, the privilege theory is analytically weak, based as it is in assumed correlation–causation links now confounded by massive wealth creation and immigration that has washed previous effects of privilege out to sea, and brought in subsequent data on incomes that often contradict what McIntosh and Coates claim: That skin colour matters in the modern economy. The theory also ignores earlier, already-underway improvements and, critically, other data that defeat the claim: socioeconomic outcomes for black Americans already rising before the civil rights era, and data for comparable family units that show an absence of any legacy effect.

---

[b] For our purposes the federal government defines minorities as "non-Caucasian in race or non-white in colour." Of note, I would agree with government programs that favour the disabled given that equal opportunity is impossible in such cases, precisely due to the disability.

Dealing with the American reality first, economist Thomas Sowell notes how some claims that tightly link even America's slaveholding past to economic outcomes today[c] are not supported by the historical data. If the charge is that institutionalized racism from slavery's era yet has economic consequences a century and a half later, there are apple-to-apple comparisons that contradict that assumed link. They include intact two-parent families and vastly improved educational outcomes *before* institutional denials of civil rights were substantively dealt with and removed starting in the 1960s, and a decline in such measurements after the civil rights movement was successful.

In one example, 31% of black children were born to unmarried women in the early 1930s, but that proportion rose to 77% by the early 1990s. "If unwed childbirth was a 'legacy of slavery,'" wrote Sowell in 2011, "why was it so much less common among blacks who were two generations closer to the era of slavery?"[14] Another example: In 1899, just one generation after the abolition of slavery, three of four public schools in Washington, D.C., were white and one was black. In standardized tests, "students in the black school averaged higher test scores than students in two of the three white schools."[15] The same school showed similar, superior results until the early 1950s, when newer educational reforms, and not racism, hollowed out the school's unique advantages. As Sowell points out, black children in that successful D.C. school came not from self-selecting privileged families but the opposite. In the 1892–93 school year, of known occupations of the parents, 51 were labourers, 25 were messengers, and 12 were janitors. Just one parent was a doctor.[16] Other measures of past success: While the rise of the civil rights era was positive in ending daily discrimination and worse for black Americans, the number of blacks in white-collar occupations doubled between 1940 and 1960 and also almost doubled in professional occupations.[17] Sowell credits education as key to lifting African Americans out of poverty. In 1940, 87% of all black families lived below the poverty line, a figure that dropped to 47% in 1960 and 30% by 1970.[18]

In other words, poverty reduction was well underway even before deserved civil rights were finally in play and enforced by a federal government upon recalcitrant states and a significant number of Americans. Sowell writes of how, even by 1969, barely after the modern civil rights era began, young

---

[c] See the 2014 essay, *The Case for Reparations,* by American essayist Ta-Nehisi Coates.

black males with newspapers, magazines, and library cards at home were as statistically likely to pursue as much schooling as white children whose homes consisted of the same elements. Those same children would also go on to record "the same income as their white counterparts."[19] Writing in 1978, Sowell pointed out one problem in comparing average black and white incomes nationally was that American blacks were still more heavily concentrated in the South, where incomes for everyone were lower than the national average. That skewed average incomes downward in national statistics. (A far-smaller proportion of white Americans resided in the South.) With a tighter comparison—dual-income couples outside the South—young black families earned "virtually the same incomes in 1970 as young white families of the same description," wrote Thomas.[20] Or another apple-to-apple comparison: By the 1980s, black married couples with college educations already earned slightly *more* than white college-educated married couples.[21] In other words, when considering surface claims about privilege, other factors should be explored, ones especially critical to addressing root causes to current poverty.

Family and cultural breakdown

An early example of other factors that influence economic outcomes appeared courtesy of Daniel Patrick Moynihan in 1965, then a sociologist and an assistant secretary at the U.S. Department of Labor. Later a Democratic senator from New York state, Moynihan authored a now-famous report on the state of black Americans, where he discussed the state of economic inequality and black families in the context of family structure. Controversial for some, the report warned that "the family structure of lower class [American blacks] is highly unstable, and in many urban centers is approaching complete breakdown."[22] He further noted that the rise of the black middle-class would only temporarily mask some of these trends in the statistics; they would not, in real life, shield black Americans—the children in particular—from the effects of family breakdown. For example, Moynihan pointed out how, in 1964, 25% of black women in the American northeast were "either divorced, separated, or have their husbands absent" and that the figure in New York City was above 30%. The report pointed to how 36% of black children were "living in broken homes *at any specific moment* [and] it is likely that a far higher proportion of [black] children find themselves in that situation at one time or another in their lives."[23]

The Moynihan report, one of the first to broach the subject of non-material causes for poor economic outcomes, was followed up by additional work over the decades. They include the importance of:

- social capital, as pointed to by Francis Fukuyama in two books in 1995[24] and 1999;[25]

- the lessening of community, mentioned by Robert Putnam (*Bowling Alone, 2000*[26]);

- economics' inability to explain the modern world, addressed by Deirdre McCloskey (*Bourgeois Dignity: Why Economics Can't Explain the Modern World,* 2010[27]) and the ability of ideas and culture to do just that (by Deirdre McCloskey in *Bourgeois Equality: How Ideas, Not Capital or Institutions, Enriched the World,* 2016[28]); and

- economic and social decline for white America post–1960, by Charles Murray in his 2012 book, *Coming Apart.* The reasons were similar in what leads any community to fray socially and economically: The decline in marriage, industriousness, honesty, and religiosity.[29]

Or consider a positive example of an obvious non-economic cause that influences outcomes—family—a point made by J.D. Vance in his 2016 book, *Hillbilly Elegy:* "Mom was never much of a math person, but she took me to the public library before I could read, got me a library card, showed me how to use it, and always made sure I had access to kids' books at home," wrote Vance.[30] The premise of *Hillbilly,* the same as *Coming Apart,* was that culture— beliefs, assumptions about what is right and wrong, a focus on education (or lack of), how success is defined—matters in considering why some people and communities fail and others succeed. And culture can be at the family level or outside the front door. (As evidence that victimhood-claims know no skin colour, consider that Vance points to the growing tendency in the white working-class to blame their problems on society or government, and that "that movement gains adherents by the day," he writes.[31]) In describing the counterbalance to the anti-success culture in the Ozarks and his mostly chaotic family life, including a drug-addicted mother, Vance credited his mother's inculcation of reading and his grandparents solidity and shelter for him among chaos: "In other words, despite all the [negative] environmental pressures from my neighbourhood and community, I received a different message at home. And that just might have saved me."[32]

Moynihan and the others were onto something, but critics argued his work impugned those who were actually victims; i.e. black Americans who only recently had a federal government willing to enforce civil rights. William Ryan, writing in 1971, popularized the term "blaming the victim" in his book of the same name and targeted Moynihan and his 1965 report. Ryan labelled the sociologist's report and another, similar study as "ideological artillery." He said they were the opening salvo in "range-finding shots" that were to become "more varied, more primitive, more openly repressive," asserting that Moynihan and others invented a "generic formula" to justify inequality by finding "defects" that allowed poor, black, or working people in general to be blamed. These "blame the victim" sorties allowed such authors to "slow down progress towards equality," wrote Ryan in the book's revised 1976 introduction.[33] Ryan's language betrayed his priority: He cared more about income equality than poverty,[d] and he also defined victims quite broadly: "The victims in American society are not simply the 10 per cent who are Black, the 15 per cent or so who are officially below 'poverty line,'" wrote Ryan, who went on to describe everyone not among the wealthiest, as victims. "The real issue," wrote Ryan, in expanding his initial analysis, "is inequality as a characteristic that pervades American society."[34] For Ryan, everyone except the wealthy were victims *of* the wealthy.[e]

Ryan and other critics missed or deliberately overlooked the critical Moynihan point: Not every poor outcome is due to economic causes, or racism and discrimination. Single-parent families are highly correlated with

---

[d] Complete income equality is a chimera given different individuals and groups have differing priorities. One employee may wish to become a CEO and will work 70 hours a week for two decades and endure two divorces to reach the corporate top. Another may prefer to stay with her husband and instead work 40 hours a week. All else being equal, they will never be equal in salaried outcomes, and of such individual choices are inequality statistics derived. Another matter to consider when it comes to inequality statistics: There is less inequality during a recession because everyone's incomes and stock portfolios (such as in pension plans) are lowered and compressed. When economies recover, and incomes and asset values rise, those with more assets than the average person—more property or stocks, thus "take off," and that shows up as more inequality. But given that recessions create high unemployment, especially for the most vulnerable, few would wish for a recession simply so inequality is lessened.

[e] This is a similar refrain now for the white-privilege theorists that assume zero-sum economics; they often refer to income as "redistributed," as if an unseen prejudicial hand was cutting an income "pie" that never grows.

poverty while two-parent families are not. In 1970, most black children were still in two-parent families; but that dropped to one-third by 1995, exactly what Moynihan feared would happen. That had consequences for poverty rates and social pathologies given the absence of fathers for ever-more black children. Two-parent families make a difference: At the end of the 20th century, a majority of black single-parent families lived in poverty while the poverty rate for two-parent black families was just 10%.[35] Family matters—it always mattered. All Moynihan did was point that out.

Numbers versus privilege claims: U.S. census data from 2014

Beyond social causes for some economic outcomes, the other problem with assuming race influences incomes in a straight line in our century in Western liberal democracies with market economies and low unemployment is the fallacy of the sole cause. Level of education, average age of a cohort, whether immigrant or native-born, the particular cultural emphases of one group or another: all make simplistic comparisons less than useful. To be sure, local disparities exist. The median income of black Americans is less than white Americans; native Canadians, even off-reserve, earn less than non-native Canadians. However, not all or even most of the income disparity is necessarily attributable to discrimination, explicit or hidden. As Sowell points out as an example, disparities that show up in averages often disappear when comparable cohorts are on offer. Consider the earnings of native-American men: "In the United States, for example, by the 1980s American Indian males earned incomes quite comparable to those of white males, when various language, demographic, and other factors were held constant, even though American Indian males as a whole were still earning markedly less than white males as a whole."[36] The relentless focus on race as responsible for poverty or inequality is thus simplistic. It leaves out multiple other causal possibilities and nuances in the statistics.

Consider census data from 2014: In the United States, per-capita black income that year was $19,297 while for whites the figure was $31,752. At first glance, the statistics seem to support the claim that white privilege existed in 2014 and led to higher median incomes. But such simple claims are confounded once broken down because of other per-capita incomes for other non-white Americans: those whose ethnic origins are Korean ($31,790), Japanese

($43,132), (mainland) Chinese ($35,235), and Taiwanese ($45,084). Thus, Americans of other, non-white ancestries demonstrated per-capita median incomes in 2014 slightly above whites (e.g., Koreans) with the other three East Asian cohorts higher by 11%, 36%, and 42%, respectively.[37] One reason for the differences in median incomes is education, itself a predictor of higher income along with family structure. In the 2014 data, only 20% of blacks possessed an undergraduate degree or a graduate level degree, compared to 31% of whites. The rates were dramatically higher for East Asian ancestry: Japanese (50%), Korean (54%), Chinese (53%), and Taiwanese (74%).[38] One might still claim that racism is a factor, except that with reference to much-earlier data (from the 1969 U.S. census) and profiled by Sowell in a 1978 book on ethnic incomes, incomes of black immigrants from the West Indies were higher than American-born blacks. Also, the children of immigrants from the West Indies would not only earn more than American-born blacks, but second-generation West Indians would also record higher incomes than Anglo-Saxons, i.e., American whites.[39] Education once again made a difference. West Indian and American-born blacks showed a divergence on: median years of education (10.7 versus 10.0 years), children (2.4 and 1.8 per family, respectively), and also location; West Indians were concentrated around New York City where incomes and employment opportunities were always higher when compared to the American South where a greater proportion of American-born blacks resided.[40] As Sowell pointed out, the difference was not slavery. It existed in both the United States and in the British West Indies and "by all indications, the treatment and conditions of slaves were harsher in the West Indies than in the United States."[41]

Four decades later, this same pattern was still evident in median household income data. In 2013, immigrant blacks earned $43,800 (from all locations), $10,300 more than American-born blacks at $33,500. The "input" differences included how immigrant blacks were more likely to have a college degree and twice as likely to be married; their median age was also older. Depending on origin, immigrant median household incomes for those who self-identified as black ranged from $41,400 (if from Central America) to $55,000 (from South America), with other black immigrants within that range. The median household income that year for all Americans was $52,000,[42] so some immigrant blacks were below and above that median, with American-born blacks below.

Canadian incomes: Jewish and Japanese ancestry at the top

The same dynamics are at play in Canada, and the same factors matter to arguments of privilege. The evidence for an open, dynamic society with prejudice and discrimination having little effect upon incomes now goes back decades. In his 1998 book *The Pursuit of Division: Race, Gender and Preferential Hiring in Canada*, Martin Loney noted how the original impetus for employment equity—race and gender quotas—was Justice Rosalie Abella's 1984 royal commission on equality of employment report.[43] As Loney wrote two decades ago, "the disadvantages of visible minorities in the labour market were never documented, though a casual reader could have been excused for assuming the learned judge had seen overwhelming evidence."[44] In fact, as Loney found when he examined the census data and other income and labour statistics, there was no "generalized trend for visible minorities to be concentrated at the bottom of the labour market."[45] Even an advocate for preferential hiring, Monica Boyd, reviewed census data in 1986 and found, as Loney paraphrases it, "scant evidence of discrimination against racial minorities in Canada. Instead, visible minority women born in Canada actually displayed mean employment income 13 per cent higher in 1985 than their white female counterparts."

The data from that period supports what Loney and Boyd both found. The 1981 census shows that those not in a visible minority with a median employment income of $11,565 per capita, with the median for visible minorities at $10,953—a $600 five-percent difference. Incomes for specific races or ethnicities as defined by Statistics Canada in 1981: Black ($10,946), Korean ($10,037), Chinese ($10,032), Latin American ($9,680), and southeast Asian ($6,528). At first glance, there seems to be some potential for discrimination, e.g., median employment income for blacks at just over five percent less than white Canadians. Except that visible minorities were all over the income map. Median employment incomes for other visible minorities were *higher* than whites: Pacific Islanders ($11,565), West Asians and Arabs ($11,574), South Asians ($11,975), Filipinos ($12,557), and those of Japanese ethnicity at the top: $13,034.[f]

---

[f] The statistics are not an anomaly. In every year covered by the census thereafter, Japanese Canadians out-earned white Canadians until 2010, where they lagged slightly behind those not in a visible minority. The erosion in the income advantage for Canadians of Japanese ancestry was not due to some uptick in racism and discriminatory state policy against those of Japanese ancestry in the 21st century: The average age in the cohort of Japanese Canadians was getting older, with peak earnings declining, which led to a decline in the median employment income number.

If the assertion is that white privilege was and is rampant, especially when Canada was more "white," then privilege works in mysterious ways. In 1981 it worked against Southeast Asians but somehow had no effect on West Asians or Arabs or Filipinos who recorded *higher* median employment incomes than whites. Also, while white Canadians recorded a $1,528 advantage over the incomes of Koreans, they earned $1,469 *less* than those of Japanese ancestry. Privilege somehow led white Canadians to gain a 13% advantage over those whose family origins were Korean, but resulted in a 13% *disadvantage* relative to those of Japanese ancestry. The problem for the claim of prejudice—not its existence in the hearts and heads of some, or the existence of an occasional bigoted employer today who tries to skirt anti-discrimination laws—but for its assumed deep "structural" existence and any noticeable impact on income, is that Japanese Canadians were the second-most discriminated-against group in Canadian history (after aboriginal Canadians). Their homes and property were confiscated in the Second World War with only a portion in compensation paid (about one-third of the estimated value of the property taken). It is an example of where past harms are clearly provable and for which victims should have been fully compensated.[46] And yet by 1980, just three-and-a-half decades later, their employment incomes were the highest in the country.[g]

Management and assumed prejudice

The Abella report was flawed in other ways: Consider how it looked at minorities as a percentage of management positions using percentages provided by Crown corporations and census data from 1971 and 1981. Abella argued that males, white at that, made up the vast proportion of those in management categories, though female participation was increasing.[47] Oddly, despite noting that male immigrants were more likely to end up in management positions than Canadian-born males,[48] the problem for Abella

---

[g] Data from 1971 is also telling. That census shows that another group severely discriminated against institutionally by the state before the mid-20th century nevertheless managed to out-earn others in later decades. In 1971, median employment income was $4,509 for all Canadians, but $4,593 for those of British origin and $4,490 for the French. Poles ($4,499), Germans ($4,508), the Dutch ($4,743), and Italians ($4,847) all out-earned French Canadians. Jews showed per-capita median employment income of $5,020.

was that such immigrants tended to be British. Despite that, some immigrant cohorts were doing well anyway, even though they were neither British nor white. More than half of "Indo-Pakistani" males, as Abella characterized that cohort, were in white-collar or professional occupations. The key to their success was that their education and degrees matched labour-market needs.[49] Of note, many were earlier arrivals, in the 1950s and 1960s, before much non-white immigration, and they anyway succeeded despite being a visible minority in the 1960s and 1970s.

Indo-Chinese males did less well and were found in lower-income jobs; but as the Abella report noted, they were mostly recent arrivals to Canada.[50] Black Canadians too were concentrated in blue-collar jobs and with lower incomes, but then a significant proportion were not Canadian-born. Their education levels were also low (compared to those from India and Pakistan who were more successful) and significant numbers arrived from Haiti who only knew French. That further limited their ability to earn significant income given their ability to function daily was limited mostly to Quebec and Nova Scotia. Of note, native-born black women did better than native-born black men. For example, Canadian-born black men earned 79% and 77% of average-male income in Ontario and Nova Scotia. In distinct contrast, Canadian-born black women earned as much as did other females in Ontario and 4% more than the average female income in Nova Scotia.[51] This again undercuts a clear claim that skin colour and personal prejudice encountered was definitive in it's effect upon incomes. Black females, unlike black males, matched or exceeded average female incomes depending on the province. The data was all there in the Abella report, but the reverse conclusions were drawn. Lastly, as with all other data sets, Japanese Canadians were doing well, "generally represented" throughout a range of occupations and with high incomes, according to the report.[52]

Beyond any clear lack of discrimination on income—black males earned less in Nova Scotia and black females earned *more* compared with others' incomes, while those of Japanese ancestry earned more than everyone—the claim of management discrimination vis-à-vis minorities missed important context: Unless one is an entrepreneur, it takes decades to reach the top of any organization, especially corporations and governments with significant numbers of employees in the queue. Further, this mattered if one tries to use 1971 and 1981 data to make claims of discrimination. To argue privilege existed in the 1970s for the purposes of 1980s-era race and ethnic quotas in the civil service was to ask the question vis-à-vis whom? In 1971, 95% of Canada's population still listed their ethnic origin as European.[53] Even by 1981, two-thirds of foreign-born immigrants still emigrated from Europe.[54] To expect, in 1971 or even a decade later, that newer immigrants would suddenly appear in management positions proportionate to their most recent share in the general population was mistaken. It was to assume that a new cohort could be diffused upward through corporations and the civil service practically overnight. The Abella report again wrongly attributed discrimination when a simpler factor was in play: time in the country and time served in an organization.

All of this would be consistent with what social scientist Conrad Winn found and published in 1985 with regards to immigrants and income, and offered in testimony before Parliament on the then-bill on employment equity: that the initial low incomes of immigrants were not due to racism. Immigrants often arrive with "different language abilities, job skills and capital" and thus "fewer of the requisites for occupational achievement that become available to their Canadian-born children." Winn pointed out the difference between the first and second generation in an example from Montreal, where native-born Asian Montréalers earned 56% more than those who were foreign-born.[55] Winn's study, "Affirmative Action and Visible Minorities: Eight Premises in Quest of Evidence," also found that intra-group differences were sometimes as significant as inter-group differences. For example, similar to the U.S. data that showed blacks of West Indian origin earning more than American-born blacks, Winn found—contrary to the normal pattern of immigrants earnings less than the native-born population—that when comparing "apple to apple" on education, black immigrants from the West Indies with a college degree earned $2,000 more annually than Canadian-born black with a college degree.[56] If discrimination, racism, and prejudice were rife in the 1980s, somehow it worked in favour of recent black immigrants from the West Indies over Canadian-born blacks.

Averaging down or up: Immigration inflows and income

The same rainbow variety shows up in recent census data from 2016, with the same confounding of an easy claim of a racist Canada. With a focus now on those who worked full-time, all year, the 2016 census shows that a variety of ethnicities were clustered at the bottom, from $35,000 to $50,000; here is a sampling: Somali ($36,773), Punjabi ($40,878), Congolese ($40,911), Korean ($42,018), Peruvian ($44,974), Mexican ($45,894), Albanian ($46,017), Chilean ($46,962), Ghanaian (48,010), West Indian ($49,196), and Syrian ($49,364).[57]

Now consider higher median-incomes for full-year, full-time work from $50,000 to $65,000. Again, there exists a rainbow of ethnic origins at every income level: Taiwanese ($50,934), East Indian ($50,948), Nigerian ($52,226), Barbadian ($53,004), Métis ($53,053), Chinese ($53,777), Bulgarian ($53,191), Trinadadian/Tobagonian ($54,314), French ($54,728), Swiss ($56,964), Irish $57,623), Israeli ($58,217), English ($58,253), Japanese ($58,298), Scottish ($58,485), Egyptian ($59,745), British Isles not in other categories ($60,576), Slovak, ($63,541), Slovenian ($64,137), and Jewish ($64,283).[58]

As per other data, if one hopes for a pattern to prove prejudice, it becomes a challenge. If we assume the usual surface characteristic many people employ in arguments about discrimination (race and ethnicity), minority-status Egyptians earn more than majority-status Swiss, Irish, and English. Meanwhile, Ghanaians, West Indians, and Syrians—mostly non-white and Arab, respectively—earned more than Taiwanese, Chileans, and Albanians, the latter two which fall into the "white" category. Those of Japanese, Slovak, Slovenian, and Jewish ancestry earned more than everyone else.[59] As with all the other data, differences can be explained by a variety of factors: average age and education levels and the proportion of an ethnic group recently arrived. For example, 7.5 million Canadians are immigrants, and the decades in which proportions of diverse groups arrived vary. For those who list the British Isles as their heritage (median income of $60,576), 70% immigrated before 1981 compared to just three percent of those who arrived from Iran ($51,328) before that year. Eighty percent of Dutch immigrants made their way to Canada before 1981 ($56,581) compared to four percent from Congo ($40,911) and one percent of Albanians ($46,017). Twenty-one percent of Japanese immigrants came to Canada before 1981 ($58,298) compared to only ten percent of South Korean immigrants ($42,018).[60] Racism is an unhelpful and incorrect explanation if we are to assume it has somehow negatively affected Korean incomes but not those of Japanese ancestry. As with other statistics, Ockham's Razor applies here: Given two competing theories, the simpler explanation for an outcome is preferred. In this case, all else being equal, the larger the proportion of a cohort new to a country, the lower their incomes relative to other groups with few recent arrivals. That helps explain some statistical differences.

The problem with identity politics: Which identity?

There is another problem with identifying people as part of a collective and based on obvious characteristics such as colour, as opposed to some other way people might self-identify. It is that the assumed characteristic may not mean anything to others. For example, ponder someone whose mother is British, aristocratic, and white and whose father is black, whose background was Ghanaian, and anti-colonial, was raised as a devout Christian, attended a British boarding school, later moved to the United States, and is gay and married. That describes Kwame Anthony Appiah, a British-Ghanaian philosopher and cultural theorist. If one were to ask what his primary identity should be, one stumbles if the assumption is that he is black, or white. He may primarily think of himself as gay, a lapsed Christian, Ghanaian, or British. As for race, as the *Guardian* reported when it interviewed Appiah in 2016, he never even considered racial categories until as a student at Yale "others began to define him entirely by his race. They even questioned whether having a white mother made Appiah 'really black.'"[61]

Such existing diversity within one person, never mind in society, complicates the stark, "black-and-white" narrative to which some subscribe. There is another problem with identity politics: The notion of race is invalid, as Appiah himself noted in 2016 when then British Prime Minister Theresa May was dismissive of cosmopolitans. The controversy is not germane here; but, as Appiah pointed out, "biologically [race is] nonsense. If you try to say what the whiteness of a white person or the blackness of a black person actually means in scientific terms, there's almost nothing you can say that is true or even remotely plausible. Yet socially, we use these things all the time as if there's a solidity to them."[62]

Personal prejudice: Not the same as lasting harm or institutional discrimination

Appiah was correct that there is no scientifically defensible conception of race.[63] We use such constructs because, insofar as governments and others care to measure people, they assign such categories to obvious differences that we use to parse through assertions; but they are not scientifically valid. In all this, the central argument is not that all bigotry has been banished from all human hearts but that the dragon is no longer fed by the state in either the United States or Canada. Since the 1950s, successive governments instead slashed at the dragon's tendons and arteries by enacting policies that forswore race as a basis for government or public discrimination. In 1951 in Ontario, discrimination in the workplace or in the buying or selling of property based on religion or race was outlawed under the Fair Employment Practices Act. That was followed up by the Female Employees Fair Remuneration Act that ensured equal pay for equal work for women was protected; the 1954 Fair Accommodation Practices Act also prevented discrimination in lodging and other services based on race or religion.[64] To be sure, some present-day policies are illiberal and imperfect now in their own right: preferential race and gender hiring preferences, for examples. But those are anyway the opposite of anti-minority racism and prejudice given that their very purpose, right or wrong, is to ameliorate the effects of past discrimination upon minorities.

The argument against the chronic victim-cult assumptions found in race and ethnic issues is thus what Shelby Steele points out: It is not that America (or Canada, for Canadians) is perfect. Instead, what a country owes its citizens are not guaranteed outcomes but instead liberalism and a free society. Steele thinks it impossible for the state to guarantee a nation free of all bigotry, but the state can certainly be "free of all illegal discrimination."[65] That has now been delivered with legal reforms in the 1950s and 1960s. For Steele, the problem is guilt over the past, which prevents a clear view of how far America advanced. Steele regularly encounters this notion that the United States is "structurally" racist and possessed of hidden discrimination.

Steele was exposed to just such a view at the Aspen Institute mid-decade. There, Steele argued in a speech that in the 1950s and 1960s, equality of opportunity for the individual was the needed critical advance, and it had been, and that modern race preferences were illiberal. For good measure,

Steele opined that the post-1960s proliferation of identity politics had created a grievance culture just as America was "at last beginning to free up minorities as individual citizens who could pursue their own happiness to the limits of their abilities."[66] One day later, the moderator approached him along with a fidgety, young white man who wanted to speak to the audience about Steele's speech the previous day. In the spirit of debate, Steele said "yes," whereupon the young graduate student proceeded to warn the audience against Steele's "false consolation," that "racism, discrimination and inequality were still alive—still great barriers to black advancement."

A young white college student with little experience thus warned the audience against a black professional who faced severe racism and discrimination decades before. Steele's response: "My first reaction to people like this is always the same: Where were you when I needed you? I had grown up in the rigid segregation of 1950s Chicago, where my life had been entirely circumscribed by white racism. Residential segregation was nearly absolute. My elementary school triggered the first desegregation lawsuit in the North. My family was afraid to cross the threshold of any restaurant until I was twenty years old." For Steele, the young man he encountered that day offered no serious ideas or a coherent rebuttal but instead attempted to make Steele "an untouchable—someone from a dark realm of ideas who was at once seductive and evil." Except the young man was a poseur, "pretending to the heroism of those 'good whites' who back in the civil rights era, had actually 'spoken truth to power'—whites who had risked their careers, their families, their standing in their communities and even their lives."[67] In contrast, here was a young white in Aspen who was a moral redundancy, "a man protesting racism to people for whom it was already anathema," wrote Steele—and, one might add, saying such things in the very privileged surroundings of a conference resort in Colorado.

CHAPTER 5

New victims and the false
lure of pure culture

It is a sordid business, this divvying us up by race.

— U.S. SUPREME COURT CHIEF JUSTICE JOHN ROBERTS

Baby Veronica, cultural purity, and modern-day collectives

Imagine that after years of trying and seven in vitro fertilization attempts you accept that having your own children will never be a reality, and only after working though a laborious adoption process are you given the gift of a baby girl.[1] Also, the young woman who gives you parenthood does so only after making her own multiple, difficult choices: She refuses a "shotgun" offer of marriage and the financial security, and gives up her unborn child—after the ex-fiancé, via a text, abandons his parental rights rather than pay child support. Consider how privileged you feel when the mother invites you into her life, to the birth, and asks your husband to cut the umbilical cord. All of you now have a treasure, but each of you will weep and for very different reasons: the birth mother because of the daughter she gives up, and you and your husband four months later, after you bring your adopted daughter home, because the father now wants his daughter—your daughter—after all.

Or imagine you are the father and discover your ex-fiancée's plan to give your girl up for adoption only one day before your deployment to Iraq. Also, as you later find out, it appears your ex-girlfriend made only a half-hearted attempt to notify you (and the Cherokee Nation to whom you belong) of your daughter's partial native-American status—your name was misspelt and incorrect birth information filed, possibly on purpose. That meant you could not, until the last moment, exercise your rights under the U.S. Indian Child Welfare Act,[2] a 1978 federal law designed, as the National Indian Child Welfare Association characterizes it, to "keep American Indian children with American Indian families."[3] That law was created to end the 1970s-era practice and before, where native American children were sometimes separated from their parents without justifiable cause.

Those are the two distinct ways in which the story of Baby Veronica might be told: one from the birth mother and the parents she chose for her child, the other from the father. Beyond either version, here are the facts that are not in dispute: In early 2009, when Christine Maldonado found out she was pregnant, her fiancé Dusten Brown pressured her to marry earlier than planned. Any financial support for the child was conditional on saying "yes." Instead, after their relationship soured, Maldonado broke off the engagement and sent a text to ask Brown if he preferred to pay child support or to relinquish his parental rights. Brown chose the latter. After that, Maldonado worked with an adoption placement agency to give up her daughter, meeting the adoptees, Matt and Melanie Capobianco, in the process. They supported the young Hispanic woman in the final months of her pregnancy and soon after the birth, with permission from the state of Oklahoma, the Capobiancos took their baby daughter home to Charleston, South Carolina. It was four months after that—after Brown's application to stop the adoption—when a multi-year legal battle began that put Baby Veronica in the middle of two families' claims. Thus in 2011, a South Carolina family judge ruled that a federal law designed to keep Indian families together was relevant. When the Capobiancos appealed, the state Supreme Court agreed with the lower court ruling—that the Indian Child Welfare Act applied, because Veronica was 1.2% Cherokee Indian (3/256th). The other 98.8% heritage, that was at least half-Hispanic, was irrelevant. But it was that other sliver of heritage that made the difference: On New Year's Eve 2011, Veronica, 27 months old, was handed over along with clothes and toys by the Capobiancos to Dusten Brown, a man whom Veronica had never met.

Understandably, for all involved, it was not to end there.

In October 2012, the Capobiancos appealed to the U.S. Supreme Court to hear the case and, in 2013, five justices determined that the lower courts were mistaken: The Indian Child Welfare Act did not apply because that law was intended to prevent the unnecessary *breakup* of Indian families. That did not apply to Brown who had "abandoned the Indian child before birth and never had custody of the child,"[4] wrote Justice Samuel Alito for the majority. Nor did the father ever apply to adopt his baby girl and nor did the Cherokee Nation. As a result, the U.S. Supreme Court redirected the case back to lower courts where the South Carolina trial court finalized the initial adoption, a decision then temporarily stayed by the Oklahoma Supreme Court, but which finally lifted it in August 2013 and ordered Brown to return Veronica to her adoptive parents. When Brown refused, more legal action and judgments ensued, including the arrest of Brown[5] until four weeks later[6] he returned Veronica to Matt and Melanie Capobianco. In just over four years, Veronica spent half her life with each family.

The Solomon-like dilemma that never had to happen

The battle between a birth mother, adopted parents, and the natural father placed a baby girl where she never should have been, between duelling lawyers and families. The affair illustrated the problem with viewing the present and people in it through the tinted glass of past wrongs, in this case against native Americans. There are sensible reasons for policy and laws that preserve individual rights in law and policy—among them, how the opposite was done, including and especially to indigenous peoples who were of the "wrong" race in the minds of some colonialists—but also because collectives do not cry, bleed, and die; only real children, women, and men within them do. But the notion that politicians and courts must now make up for past injustices by permitting the collective control of children or their parents by a community consciously ethnic-based and, with that, protected in law and policy, is creating new, actual victims. It is not akin to a province or a state where governments rightly interfere if danger exists or abuse is occurring; that routinely occurs without institutional preferences based on race or ethnicity in play. But that focus on the collective and culture—the belief that ever-purer culture will save or restore or help aboriginal communities prosper—is what mistakenly animates much academic, policy, political work, and media reporting on the subject.

There are understandable reasons why this temptation exists. When the

Baby Veronica case first arose, the original author of the 1978 law, former South Dakota senator Jim Abourezk, pointed back to the harms against native Americans that were recently routine. Dating back decades, "Indian" children were sometimes separated from their parents without justifiable cause. When family problems arose among native Americans, state social services agencies sometimes placed their children in foster homes and after that soon up for adoption without attempts to first preserve their families.[7] When children were taken away without due cause or process, it was a government-directed attack on native American families. The statistics from that era convey the magnitude of the potential problem: In the late 1960s and early 1970s in the State of Minnesota, for example, one in eight native American children under the age of 18 was in an adoptive home. In one year alone (between 1971 and 1972) in that state, nearly one in every four infants of native ancestry and under one year of age was placed up for adoption; nationally, between 1969 and 1974, between 25% and 35% of all native American children were separated from their families, placed in foster care, or adopted, or ended up in institutions.[8] In addition, native American children were adopted out at a rate "eight times that of non-Indian children," with 90% of those placed in non-Indian homes.[9]

Abourezk's remedy to this was the Indian Child Welfare Act,[10] a well-intentioned law that meant to reverse government and agencies' assumptions about and practices vis-à-vis native American families. Congressional testimony in 1978 was clear about the intent to reinforce tribal life: "There is no resource that is more vital to the continued existence and integrity of Indian tribes than their children" and that "an alarmingly high percentage of Indian families are broken up by the removal, often unwarranted...."[11] Moreover, the House of Representatives' reasoning was evident when, in its 1970s-era report on his proposed law noted that "An Indian child may have scores of, perhaps more than a hundred, relatives who are counted as close, responsible members of the family. Many social workers, untutored in the ways of Indian family life or assuming them to be socially irresponsible, consider leaving the child with persons outside the nuclear family as neglect, and thus as grounds for terminating parental rights."[12]

The proper focus on preserving families was thus twinned with the larger government and tribal goal of promoting a specific collective *for the sake of* the collective, i.e., the tribal community. That position, a problem when the collective is based in racial lineage, presumes race should trump the right of every child, woman, and man to be treated as belonging to themselves and no one else. It assumed tribal sovereignty over both the child and parents. It flew in the face of an historic liberalism that favours organic communities and culture that should flourish through voluntary association, especially with the wishes of the parents paramount, absent any danger to the child. But the contrary assumption produced another example of how a flawed response to past victimization can create new tragedy, this time 1,800 miles away from South Carolina, in Alberta, to another four-year-old girl whose life was shattered forever by the idea that purer culture and collectives are *de facto* desirable.

Serenity, the "most beautiful angel"

"Marie," as the government named her but whose real name was Serenity, was a four-year-old native girl who in 2014 was admitted to a central Alberta hospital with dilated pupils, hypothermia, and a head injury. But Serenity had been a potential tragedy long before that day. Before she was born, two older half-siblings were removed from her mother's home given her dependency on drugs, abuse of alcohol, and her live-in boyfriend's violence. (Serenity's father, "Wyatt," was not normally involved with the family.) After Serenity came into the world, the provincial child welfare agency allowed her mother to keep her for a time; but after Wyatt appeared and beat Serenity's mother in front of her, Serenity was placed in foster care at seven months of age.

Described later in a government report as a "a shy little girl" with "dark hair and big brown eyes,"[13] her mother and social workers visited Serenity at her foster home and, by all accounts, found her healthy, thriving, and of normal weight. Also, the later review of her shortened life acknowledged that all three children were better off in foster care and likely grieved when moved from those families back to kin.[14] But Serenity and her siblings were transferred back to the extended family (and presumably the reserve, though only alluded to in the government report) for reasons similar to Veronica's two-year fate: the defensible impulse to protect families as families, except with the add-on policy preference that applies to no other ethnicity, to also support culture and the local community, i.e., the collective that is a First Nations reserve and where Serenity's tragedy began.

Adoption policy in Alberta mandates identification of the father and mother if First Nation or Métis with the same information to be provided by those who wish to adopt and not for mere statistical purposes.[15] Since at least the 1990s, Alberta policy preferred that where a child is assumed a resident of a First Nations reserve, or of that cultural background, the reserve government or its agents should approve or deny a child's non-native adoption.[16] While not always followed in practice and thus criticized by some,[17] this preference for kinship placement,[18] as it is known, refers not only to direct relatives but also to the wider community, i.e., friends, neighbours, and institutionally to the reserve government and its agencies. In practice, the policy means First Nations politicians and civil servants hold actual institutional power over registered First Nations children. In 2014[19] and 2018, the Alberta government reaffirmed those policy preferences. A 2018 committee appointed to review child care intervention,[20] along with the government response, both assumed that culture should play a larger role in foster care and adoption, that collective control based on ancestry was desirable, and that "colonization" explained much of the disparity between aboriginal and other Canadians.[21]

In Serenity's case, her grandparents volunteered to care for her and passed the usual checks, including past criminal activity and any record of past child intervention in the home. However, as the provincial report on Serenity's death would later obliquely note, the grandparents' other adult children living in the household were never vetted. That omission was contrary to policy, but it mattered less than one might hope. In Serenity's case, just two months after the grandparents were given guardianship, someone in the community complained to Child Intervention Services. During the subsequent investigation, "unexplained" marks, bruises, and scratches were found on Serenity and her half-siblings; they also appeared malnourished. The grandmother told the caseworker that Serenity had fallen and bruised her cheek and forehead. Serenity's mother, who regularly visited her three children, told Child Intervention Services she was concerned that they were being hit and not given enough to eat, and that Serenity was left alone some nights in the basement. The mother told the caseworker that she wanted her three children moved back to a foster home. The response from the caseworker: "The situation is being assessed."

After the investigation turned up nothing official, the matter was closed and the grandparents obtained private guardianship, a move supported by the Band designate.[a] Alberta's child services agency had no contact with the grandparents or Serenity for eight months, until shortly after Serenity's fourth birthday when someone again reported the children appeared malnourished (and, as it turned out, had tapeworms) and were roaming about the community unsupervised.[22] Three months later, Serenity was admitted to hospital with an extensive brain injury and multiple bruises. The grandparents initially claimed Serenity fell from a swing. The next day, after questioning from the social worker and the police, they admitted that they often hit Serenity "because she was bad, did not listen and stole food."[23] At the time Serenity was admitted to the hospital, her weight was equal to that of a one-year-old child, just 19 pounds. Serenity's half-siblings, also underweight, were apprehended that same day and returned to a foster home. Serenity died from her injuries six days later.

Assigning blame: Not the adults but colonialism

In reviewing Serenity's death, a later provincial government report noted that the grandparents may have had a more challenging time with all three children given the domestic abuse they had witnessed (while with their mother). The report also blamed colonial-era history, with the Office of the Child and Youth Advocate explaining cause-and-effect this way: "Aboriginal kinship caregivers may be resistant to getting involved with Child Intervention Services due to historical experiences of oppressive and culturally inappropriate services."[24] The report also referenced an Australian academic paper that complained of how standard approaches "to Indigenous kinship care do not take into account culturally specific customs, such as communication styles, parenting practices, physical environment, community relationships and household composition."[25] In other words, when asked who was to blame for Children Services' decision to place three native children with grandparents in a household with other adults not properly vetted, this to buttress the indigenous culture, the answer was anyone except the adults present with Serenity or provincial social workers or the Band designate. Instead, non-

---

[a] The person designated by band council to work with social services to ensure band children in the care of the province are "connected to family, community and their culture."

native social workers were blamed for their lack of cultural understanding, and a general notion of European-induced harm along with colonial history. This has now become a standard response for those who see present tragedies but not present causes. Modern-day harms are instead often traced back to colonialism, Europeans, the British and their progeny, policy, laws, and actions of 50 or 150 years ago. Responsibility assigned to adults in the present is thus foregone.

Medical notes were kept out of the official provincial review of Serenity's short life but were later leaked to the media: They describe much else beyond the dyspeptic account given in the official report. While the official Child Services report summarized Serenity's injuries as "unexplained," the leaked notes reported bruising around Serenity's pelvic area and that her hymen was gone. To anyone not writing an official report or attempting to shift blame, such injuries were not inexplicable but obvious, and disturbing: A four-year-old native girl had been abused, starved, and raped by someone who was either family or part of the larger collective because of a policy preference for maintaining cultural continuity via the collective that is the reserve. The proponents of such policy assumed that governments and others should support such collectives with the force of law and concurrent policy as opposed to the possibility of voluntary attachment to a culture. That preference led to decisions to give Serenity over to marginal caregivers, including her grandparents, merely because they shared the bloodline and/or the same community. No matter how well intentioned, Serenity's placement back on or near the reserve was exactly what advocates of the notion of a purer culture wanted for aboriginal children: collective power over individuals based on a bloodline. The desire for the collective and an ostensible stronger aboriginal culture trumped other possibilities for Serenity's care, including her own mother's earlier wishes for the same.

History, collectives, and culture as justifications

This notion that a village raises a child, now assumed as *de facto* desirable for aboriginal policy in Canada and the United States, was cited decades ago in explaining the unique cultural aspect of native Americans, in particular, American tribes, in the lead-up to the 1978 Indian Child Welfare Act. In 1974 testimony, Calvin Isaac, Tribal Chief of the Mississippi Band of Choctaw

Indians and representative of the National Tribal Chairmen's Association, remarked that "Culturally, the chances of Indian survival are significantly reduced if our children, the only real means for the transmission of the tribal heritage, are to be raised in non-Indian homes and denied exposure to the ways of their People."[26] The senator driving ahead the legislation, Jim Abourezk, spoke at the conclusion of the 1974 senate hearings and made the same point as the house report, that friends and other non-relatives were merely extended families who also cared for children: "We've had testimony here that, in Indian communities throughout the Nation, there is no such thing as an abandoned child, because, when a child does have a need for parents for one reason or another, a relative or a friend will take that child in. It's the extended family concept."[27]

In Canada, the stories, statistics, and assumed remedies for past harm have been similar to the prompts for the American legislation. In Canada in 1977, for example, 15,500 aboriginal children were under the protection of child welfare officials. Fully 20% of all children in care were aboriginal, even though aboriginal children made up just five percent of all children in the general population. Similar to American statistics on adopted-out children, in Canada, between 1969 and 1979, 78% of children then known as "status Indian" were adopted into non-native homes.[28] As with American practice, in some cases, real abuse and danger necessitated removal in past decades just as it would now. Patrick Johnston, whose 1983 book on native children taken into the child welfare system in the 1960s came up with the term "Sixties Scoop," noted just this reality when he writes that "no doubt that some of the children removed during the Sixties Scoop needed protection."[29] Johnston never cites a percentage—it is impossible to know given that paper records of individual cases from half a century ago are long discarded. Also, as Johnston notes, "As was the case with Indian Residential Schools, not all children apprehended during the Sixties Scoop were adversely affected by the experience. Some were placed with loving and supportive adoptive families and have gone on to lead happy, productive lives. But for many Indigenous children... the outcome was far from positive."[30] Johnston never rationalises the claim of "many," which is a problem given we do not know how many children needed protection versus those who were unjustly removed. To be clear about Johnston's views, though, he sees the "scoops" as "a terrible blot on Canada's history."[31]

Given the history, calls for First Nations children to be subject to First Nations government preferences and for a restoration of culture through law and policy are now routine. The 1996 Royal Commission on Aboriginal Peoples objected to "cross-cultural foster placement and adoption," blaming it as the "second major cause of family disruption" (after residential schools). It also blamed "migration to cities and towns," which the report said "also disrupts families."[32] Culture was also tagged as critical as when the royal commission wrote of how "Aboriginal people face an enormous struggle to maintain culture and identity in urban settings—let alone pass them on to their children," noting that city life, "with its myriad cultures and lifestyles, does not necessarily validate theirs."[33] The 1996 royal commission argued that "the Aboriginal family must be restored to its traditional role as nurturer of the young and protector of the old, guardian of the culture and safety net for the vulnerable."[34] It is a sentiment with which no reasonable person would disagree. The problem is the leap beyond the family to arguing that the larger collective—tribal/First Nations governments and agencies associated with them—are entitled to control over individuals because of their ancestry and not just in the interim but permanently. "Child welfare is one of the services that Aboriginal people want most to control for themselves"[35] is how the 1996 royal commission described the priority. In the 2015 Truth and Reconciliation Commission of Canada report, which concentrated on the stories of abuse in residential schools, it widened its scope to recommend that the federal government require that "placements of Aboriginal children into temporary and permanent care be culturally appropriate," i.e., for foster care and adoption.[36] The National Collaborating Centre for Aboriginal Health was more specific. It also implied that the notion of kinship protection was somehow inherently aboriginal, as opposed to a common practice in any culture where grandparents, aunts, and uncles step in to raise children when one or both parents are absent: "Despite diverse languages, cultures and traditions," argued the centre's authors in the 2017 bulletin, "the Indigenous Peoples share a high value for children, with a community-centred approach to caring for children."[37]

Across Canada, policy, practice, and laws vary but all tilt to a native veto in law or in practice over provincial practices and laws vis-à-vis native children and/or direct services to children by First Nations agencies, or a call for more. In British Columbia, for example, a 2016 report from Grand Chief Ed John recommended that First Nations governments be given "full jurisdiction" over indigenous child welfare, which would include adoption policy.[38] He was frustrated with "existing limitations" on the ability of "Indigenous governments to be assigned guardianship of children once they are removed"[39] from First Nations families and the reserve. He complained that existing British Columbia law "only allow[s] for custody to be assigned to an individual person, and do not allow for custody to be transferred to a collective, such as to an Indigenous government."[40] In other words, aboriginal politicians via the collective of a reserve government should be allowed control over a child *as a collective* because of aboriginal ancestry and for her full 18 years, and then her children and grandchildren and beyond. It would be akin to a city council in Akron, Ohio, or Toronto demanding involvement in and a veto over foster care and adoption practices over any child who ever had a connection to such cities. The difference is that, except with native North American children, the demand is linked to ethnicity, that "one drop" or one percent of indigenous blood.

New victims care of cultural purity

Baby Veronica and Serenity suffered because of policies and laws that were an understandable but flawed response to past victimization of native populations in the Americas—that and the revived notion of collective and cultural protectionism. But Baby Veronica and Serenity were not the only examples of how a preference for cultural continuity can potentially harm children and where the collective demands control for the sake of control. Consider another example that again illustrates the problem. In 2003 two teenage aboriginal girls in British Columbia had to petition the courts to allow them to stay with their foster parents, the only parents they had known since 1990 when they were first placed with them. Dawn and Lisa, two sisters whose Vancouver Island mother had seven children in total, all from a different father, but whose alcoholism and drug use meant she could not capably care for any of them, were the subject of another attempt to think about the collective first and the girls second. Soon after the foster placement, the Sto:lo Nation in Chilliwack began to demand that the foster parents move near to the Fraser Valley so the girls could be more immersed in local aboriginal culture. The parents, who lived in the interior, refused, at which point Sto:lo Nation Child and Family Services began actions to transfer the girls to a single foster care parent who lived near the reserve and already cared for three of Dawn and Lisa's half-siblings.

Given that the foster parents, both the couple and the single mother, were white, the issue was all about culture, and it was only after a long battle, including to the B.C. Supreme Court in 2003, that the girls were allowed to stay with the foster couple that both have always called Mom and Dad. As one media report noted, Ernie Crey, a Sto:lo himself, who has written of the abuse suffered by Canada's indigenous peoples, filed an affidavit to support the girls' desire to stay with their foster parents. Crey argued that his own band's arguments that culture needed to be inculcated was wrongheaded given the girls already made regular trips to Sto:lo reserve. It was "all about a powerful, misguided, and punitive aboriginal child welfare agency determined to trash the lives of a pair of foster parents and impose its will on a couple of scared Indian kids,"[41] he remarked to reporters after his court filing. "It's as if we are going to do to our own kids what we accused those misguided whites of doing with the residential schools."[42] But as the reporter who covered the hearing noted in 2003, full control of such children was due to be transferred to just such First Nations agencies two years later.[43] It is not clear that the judgment rendered in 2003 would recur later in similar circumstances once First Nations agencies were given full jurisdiction over First Nations children. As with the American preferences endorsed by the U.S. Supreme Court, the preference for culture and the collective often trump individual wishes.

Practical effects: The reserve collective vs. parents

For advocates of cultural purity, the remedies to past abuse are assumed to be two-fold: a return to the collective and thus control over children based on bloodlines and purer aboriginal culture. In the United States, the Cherokee Nation that appealed the adoption of Baby Veronica straightforwardly wants Cherokee children placed with family first or, absent that possibility, with a member of the tribe.[44] How this preference for purer culture, the collective, and lineage plays out in practice is clear from a U.S. Supreme Court judgment, the 1989 *Mississippi Band of Choctaw Indians v. Holyfield*[45] case that reinforced this collective "village" understanding of 1970s-era legislation. The case involved twin babies born out of wedlock in December 1985 and whose parents were both enrolled members of Mississippi Band of Choctaw Indians and the Choctaw Reservation in Neshoba County, Mississippi. The mother, "J.B.," purposely gave birth 200 miles from the reservation in Gulfport, Mississippi; the children were then placed with the adoptive parents two days after birth.[46] Two weeks later, in early 1986, the mother signed a consent-to-adoption form before the Chancery Court of Harrison. A later Supreme Court of Mississippi judgment, siding with an earlier lower court ruling, made clear that "the Indian twins… were voluntarily surrendered and legally abandoned by the natural parents to the adoptive parents." The courts made clear that "it is undisputed that the parents went to some efforts to prevent the children from being placed on the reservation as the mother arranged for their birth and adoption in Gulfport Memorial Hospital, Harrison County, Mississippi."[47]

However, despite the choice of the parents to have their children off-reserve and to put them up for adoption to non-Indian parents, when the case reached the U.S. Supreme Court, six justices ruled that the two children were nonetheless subject to the Indian Child Welfare Act and thus to the Choctaw tribal government, not to state adoption laws and policies. The court majority led by Justice William J. Brennan ruled that it mattered little what parents intended or wanted. What mattered was the collective, the tribe, a point made multiple times by the justices: "[O]ur inquiry into that child's best interests must also account for his or her status as an Indian, and… based on the fundamental assumption that it is in the Indian child's best interest that its relationship to the tribe be protected,"[48] wrote Brennan. He also dismissed the notion that the ultimate choice on the children's adoptive future was up to the parents: "Nor can the result be any different simply because the twins were 'voluntarily surrendered' by their mother,"[49] he wrote. The court did admit that "This relationship between Indian tribes and Indian children domiciled on the reservation finds no parallel in other ethnic cultures found in the United States,"[50] but then engaged in circular reasoning by citing the 1978 law itself as the reason for the anomaly.

In essence, Justice Brennan argued that once part of a native American tribe, always part of a native American tribe and so too one's offspring. Otherwise, wrote Brennan, "[A]doption by non-Indians weakens considerably the tribe's ability to assert its interest in its children."[51] The result of the U.S. Supreme Court decision was clear in its reasoning and results: If your parents were ever members of a reservation and/or lived on the same, its tribal government would forever have a claim on you until you were 18. The same claim would apply to your children, grandchildren, and progeny for time immemorial. It was a collective claim based upon one or two drops of shared ancestral blood, blood that would also trump all other ancestries you and your kin might possess.

Twenty-four years later, the U.S. Supreme Court reaffirmed this earlier court ruling in its 2013 Baby Veronica decision, which sent that case back to lower courts. While criticizing the South Carolina state court for wrongly applying the 1978 law, the high court nevertheless offered agreement with the section of the legislation that presumed, *a la* Abourezk, that "one hundred people" or more could count as extended family. This assumed institutionalized control over others and was based on blood. "The Indian Child Welfare Act was enacted to help preserve the cultural identity and heritage of Indian tribes,"[52] wrote Justice Alito for the majority.

In their 2013 decision, the Supreme Court thus sidestepped the issue of whether the original law that was intended to correct a previous injustice went too far in the other direction and was now creating new injustices. The high court also skipped over this salient point: How could insisting that a child's racial lineage be the dominant factor in where she should be raised for 18 years, be anything other than an illiberal surrender to the notion that human beings are the prior property of a collective? The court accepted that any native American ancestry was enough to activate the federal law with a preference for a permanent ethnic identity no matter how diluted, i.e., the barely one percent of Cherokee blood in baby Veronica over the 50% Hispanic. As Justice Alito wrote for the majority, "It is undisputed that Baby Girl [Baby Veronica] is an 'Indian child' as defined by the ICWA because she is an unmarried minor who 'is eligible for membership in an Indian tribe and is the biological child of a member of an Indian tribe.'"[53]

This combination of a focus on past victimization and a desire for purer, restored culture, but care of preferential policy anchored in race, reduces those alive today to a symbol, either of past harms or of present ideologies. It is why the 1.2% "Cherokee blood" in Baby Veronica could activate a custody fight and why Serenity lost her life: because the prior anti-individual treatment of aboriginals was replaced with newer anti-individual focus, one where girls and boys are again thought not as Serenity or Veronica, but as the property of a collective with the aim of cultural restoration. Both were objects of law and policy that were sincere-but-wrongheaded attempts to correct for past wrongs by repeating the same mistake in the present: refusing to look at Veronica and Serenity as individual children. Instead, Veronica and Serenity were assumed mere parts of a greater collective based in bloodlines.

But collectives always, eventually, demand a sacrifice.

CHAPTER 6

Civilization and its
Western discontents

---

*Nothing is more Western than hatred of the West—
that passion for cursing and lacerating ourselves.*

—PASCAL BUCKNER, *The Tyranny of Guilt*

Appropriating the British in Hong Kong

When I first visited Hong Kong in 2013, almost every politician, civil servant, and business leader I met emphasized three priorities they wanted the territory to retain vis-à-vis the regime in Beijing: 1) capitalism; 2) the rule of law, including the British legal code; and 3) Hong Kong's strong anti-corruption stance that dated from reforms in the 1970s.

I was in the territory on business for a think tank, to check on how Hong Kong planned to retain its lead in providing economic freedom to its citizens. For decades, the territory, whether under the British who left in 1997 or even under the Chinese government, was the premiere economic dynamo of East Asia. Hong Kong had prospered through a combination of good policy and benign neglect when the British were in charge. Successive governors and civil servants under the British chose the framework for capitalism; it was in contrast to the socialist drudge imposed in Great Britain in the postwar world until the government of Margaret Thatcher arrived in 1979. Luckily for those living in the territory, while the United Kingdom was enduring self-inflicted poverty, London seemed to neither notice nor interfere in the experiment in East Asia.

Hong Kong's prosperous rise is now legendary; but what struck me about the three priorities was how, in interactions with politicians and civil servants over two decades of policy work, their equivalents in Canada never mentioned those as priorities, much less articulated them as critical. Yet here was a Confucian-based culture, composed mostly of non-British and non-Europeans, who understood and valued the most consequential, positive aspects of the British legacy. Relevant to debates in the West over colonialism and ongoing allegations of imperial guilt, Hong Kong's leaders were uninterested in such sensitivities but the opposite: They wanted critical vestiges of past British colonialism and ideas strengthened, not abandoned. To wit, in 2019, when Hong Kong protesters rallied against even more interference from Beijing, protesters in Hong Kong raised a British flag.

In the West, to understate it, pro-"appropriation," pro-British, and pro-colonial sentiment is not popular among the chattering classes. From some college students to many in academia and a plethora of those in journalism, politics, and business and more than a few leaders in Canada's aboriginal community, Western civilization writ large is assumed to be the cause of multiple ills. Complaints range from American college students who rage about institutional racism (long outlawed) to the faulty cause-and-effect links for why remote reserves are poor and beset by tragic pathologies and from those who, along with the others, mistakenly see established Western norms and ideas as inimical to human flourishing.

This development has been in the pipeline for decades. In 1987, about 500 students at Stanford University famously chanted "Hey ho, hey ho, Western Culture's got to go." The chant was wrongly attributed to the Reverend Jesse Jackson; he joined the protest but when he heard the chant, his response offered a nuance not usually on offer today—Jackson objected to it, arguing that Western culture needed more voices but did not need to be replaced.[1] Since then the most radical and vocal students ignore Jackson's prudent counsel and instead engage in a narrative of utter blame. As an example, consider Massachusetts' Amherst College, where some of its students in their submission to the WeTheProtesters website chronicled previously, wanted their college president to apologize to "students, alumni and former students, faculty, administration and staff who have been victims of several injustices including but not limited to our institutional legacy of white supremacy, colonialism, anti-black racism, anti-Latin racism, anti-Native American racism, anti-Native/indigenous racism, anti-Asian racism, anti-Middle Eastern racism, heterosexism, cis-sexism, xenophobia, anti-Semitism, ableism, mental health stigma, and classism."[2]

In Canada, the authors of the 2015 truth and reconciliation report and the 2019 report into missing and murdered indigenous women and girls are in anti-Western civilizational sync with the 1987 Stanford University chant and the anti-Western college protest-culture. Both reports were clear that for any poor statistic and tragedy spotted among aboriginal peoples today, Western civilization and those who represent it, alive or dead, are to blame. In assigning responsibility for various enunciated ills, the truth and reconciliation report cited Europeans 65 times; "white" in 86 places; culture or cultural 403 times; education (as in examples of past harm or the need to re-educate Canadians) 498 times; and church, churches or Christianity in 633 instances.[3] Genocide was also referenced 31 times. The commissioners also demanded that the Pope apologize.[4] Similarly, in the 2019 report, "Christian" was mentioned in 52 spots, "European" in 82 references, "genocide" in 509 instances, and "colonization" or "colonial" 678 times. "Aboriginal men" or "indigenous men" were mentioned just 35 times, and then most often to argue they too were modern-day victims of colonialists.

The 2015 report was blunt that its central conclusion could be "summarized simply: *The main policy direction, pursued for more than 150 years, first by colonial then by Canadian governments, has been wrong.*"[5] Note that the argument was not that selected policies were wrong and racist but the "main policy direction" was—i.e., everything up to and including the present day. The various authors instead were convinced that Western civilization—ill-defined to conceivably include every variance from the British to the French, German, Spanish, Portuguese, and Dutch empires, which the British themselves would oppose—were all lumped together in one anti-Western narrative of blame.

The totality of anti-Western grievances is now obvious in our public squares. In Canada, statues of British historical figures have been removed with increasing regularity: The city of Halifax removed its founder's statue, of Edward Cornwallis in 2018,[6] after demands by local First Nations because Cornwallis, as was the brutal practice at the time by all sides, offered rewards for scalps.[a] In Victoria, in 2019, a statue of Canada's first prime minister, John A. MacDonald, near City Hall was removed, given his 19th-century views on race and for the promotion of residential schools[7] (though 70% of Canadians opposed the removal).[8] Five years earlier, Mayor-Elect Lisa Helps (the mayor who would later preside over Macdonald's removal) refused to swear allegiance to Queen Elizabeth II in a city itself named after another monarch in a province where the flag contains elements of the British flag.[9] In the United States, on the Columbus Day long weekend in 2017, New York City's finest were assigned to guard not the president, a visiting dignitary, nor a Hollywood celebrity but a statue—a seventy-six-foot-tall figure at the Manhattan traffic circle, named after the 15th-century Italian explorer, Christopher Columbus.[10] The reason for the on-guard order: vandalism of other Columbus statues in recent years. Those included one in Central Park with its hands painted red, symbolic of the assumed blood-guilt asserted by activists;[11] in Baltimore, where a Columbus statue was attacked with a sledgehammer; in Detroit, where a hatchet was sunk into Columbus's head.[12]

The attacks on MacDonald and Columbus and what they represent—the arrival of the British and Europeans—are surface examples of a now-familiar trend: the claim of victimhood due to a real or assumed historical wrong. Any nuance about clashing civilizations and not only the harm but useful, positive ideas and cultural transfers that can result—the Hong Kong example as a real-time exhibit—are lost in what is now a simplistic black-and-white, good-versus-evil caricature of human history.

The various victim cults today are aggrieved in a manner different than historic victim cults, profiled in subsequent chapters: 19th-century Germany, Yasser Arafat and his colleagues, and the pre-1994 Hutu leadership in Rwanda always directed their attacks at those seen as outside one's immediate nation, civilization, or tribe. For Germans, it was the French, 19th-century liberals,

---

[a] This was horrific, but as Peter Shawn Taylor wrote at the time of the statue's removal in 2017, "Recent academic research shows both French and British colonial governments paid for scalps long before Cornwallis landed in Halifax. And many Indigenous peoples were 'lifting the hairs' of their enemies for centuries before that." He further writes, "On his second voyage up the St. Lawrence River in 1535, Jacques Cartier noticed 'the skins of five men's heads stretched on hoops, like parchment' in native camps. Archaeological evidence also reveals tell-tale scoring on pre-Contact era skulls that could only come from stone knives." The point is not to defend Cornwallis's action but, as Taylor writes, to share the blame for a practice that occurred pre-and post-contact. As Taylor writes, "If scalping is Canada's original sin, then everyone's a sinner." (Peter Shawn Taylor, "One Canadian bears weight of nation's sins for scalping," National Post, August 24, 2017, https://bit.ly/2JkqR7X.)

and Jews; for Hutus, the Rwandan Tutsis; for Yasser Arafat and the leadership around him, Israelis and Jews. What has lately been added to the blame reflex is how the world's most prosperous and most liberating of all civilizations now has a class of people that self-loathe the very civilization, the very West—no matter any contrived claim to be separate from it—of which they are a part.

The problem is not Western self-criticism, which is a useful benefit of Western society; the problem is in the lack of distinction between that and pouring rhetorical acid on one's civilizational foundations when it was those pillars that allowed for expanded human freedom and flourishing. That is very different from critiquing a society where the founding ideas were illiberal to their core. It is thus one thing to be German and critical of one's own nation for what arose in the 19th century and which led to the atrocities in the first half of the next century; it is quite another to live in Canada and oppose the civilization of the Magna Carta, the Glorious Revolution, Adam Smith, Edmund Burke, Mary Wollstonecraft, William Wilberforce, and John Stuart Mill, among others, and ideas that ranged from suffrage for women, the rule of law, open societies, and civil rights. Those ideas and that civilization produced, as just one example, civil rights advocate John Diefenbaker. It was Diefenbaker, as prime minister in 1957, who began reversing discrimination against aboriginal Canadians and others. Diefenbaker was a product of 19th-century British liberalism. His actions came not in spite of that liberalism but because of it. It was that British influence and those 19th-century ideas that ultimately led to the 20th-century's flowering of freedom from institutional discrimination for everyone, regardless of their tribe.

The faults and omissions and harms inflicted in Anglo-Saxon countries before the mid-20th century were not the result of such ideas but in spite of them. The tragic wrong was that such civilizational ideals were not yet extended to all, including women, those of aboriginal ancestry, and ethnic and racial minorities. The key difference—let us be specific here to the Anglosphere—is that it long ago began to reform itself and did so successfully. Any falling short in liberty in the process was not due to faulty ideas and ideals, but in their very lack of implementation, the reversal of which is now a completed project. In contrast, many other societies suffered not from a lack of proper implementation of laudable ideas but from ideas that negated the individual from the start, ones that never posited the individual's civil rights as paramount at all but instead worshipped

- cultural and racial purity (Germany in the 19th century and until 1945);

- a classless society with radical enforced "equality" (communist countries in every era); or

- strict adherence to one religion and one dogmatic interpretation of it by the regime in power (Islamic fundamentalism in theocratic-ruled nations such as Iran and Saudi Arabia now).

All such societies did not offer up an ideal of ordered individual rights over the collective, and some still do not—instead yet crushing the individual.

In contrast to such regimes, the Anglosphere was where social reforms began centuries ago that led to the world we know today. The first nation with a court that ruled against domestic slavery in the last 500 years was England, in 1569,[13] followed by other anti-slavery judgments in 1772[14] and 1778.[15] Great Britain was also where the first organized, systematic effort to abolish slavery took root in the late-18th century and then soon after in Canada, with 19th-century abolition the result in the United Kingdom, in its colonies, and then, half a century later, the United States. While there are examples of other nations, France for one, that intermittently outlawed and revived slavery before outlawing it again in the mid-19th century, it was only the British navy that made the extermination of the trade a worldwide quest. Such efforts to end slavery should be compared with nations that did not abolish slavery until much later, with some as late as 1962 (Saudi Arabia and Yemen), Oman (1970),[16] and Mauritania (1981).[17]

Beyond such historic accomplishments, another way in which to place Western progress and anti-Western or anti-Anglo sentiment in proper perspective is to consider attitudes around the world on race and religion among populations. These also do not lend support to the reflexive critics of Western societies. In a 2013 World Values Survey of tolerance, including when citizens were asked if they would not want "people of another race" to be their neighbours, or "people of a different religion," the most tolerant countries were English-speaking and Latin American countries, such as Trinidad and Tobago, Australia, New Zealand, Argentina, Chile, Mexico, and, despite racial conflicts, the United States. (Canada was not surveyed.) The least tolerant responses were in the Middle East. For example, 44% of those in surveyed in the Palestinian territories did not want people of a different race as neighbours and 50% did not want to see someone of a different religion next door. The results in Europe were mixed. (Eight percent and three percent of the Dutch were uncomfortable with a different race/religion respectively while the figures for Romania were 23% and 19%, respectively.)[18] Racial tolerance was low in sub-Saharan countries and Asian nations, including India but higher, relatively, in Pakistan. On another issue, outside of Spain, Brazil, Mexico, the Anglosphere, and selected European countries, a significant percentage of respondents in the rest of the world did not want homosexuals as neighbours. The percentages were as high as 85% (Morocco and Turkey), 90% (Zimbabwe), and 94% (Azerbaijan); but, in much of the rest of the world, the proportion offering such a response was also often over 50%.[19]

In contrast to actual, sometimes brutal, threats to people across the globe today from governments or prejudice from neighbours, the West's newest victim cults still see historic sins and offences at home and everywhere. They see only the harms of history in the English-speaking world but not the leadership in moving the world away from humanity's worst practices. Instead of celebrating that civilization, the notion that the West is intrinsically flawed because of its own historic sins—obliterated institutionally now even if not in every beating heart—is to engage in victim thinking and advocacy of the most disingenuous and destructive sort.

The source of much anti-Western thought: Dead white European males

The newest victim narratives and anti-Western rhetoric have their origins in theorists that date back much earlier than white privilege theories from Peggy Mcintosh at a private women's liberal arts college in Wellesley, Massachusetts, or from Canadian commissions composed of anti-British, anti-European activists. Much of today's anti-Western critique has its origin in philosophers, social critics, and popular journalists, European and American, who have conceptualized Western norms and life as devilishly oppressive—irredeemably and structurally so. In the last century, obscure and public intellectuals alike wrote and propagandized that the West writ large is a bastion of racism, misogyny, discrimination, and prejudice. Proponents of this anti-Western civilization narrative include European and American thinkers from the 19th and 20th centuries.

For example, most anyone who has attended university has likely been exposed to the term "false consciousness." The term was first enunciated by Friedrich Engels in an 1893 letter to the German historian and politician, Franz Mehring.[20] In it, Engels argues that the "so-called thinker" who forms an ideology *believes* he did so from an examination of reality, the facts. However, Engels believed—Engels himself apparently excepted from this theory—that such thinkers hid their real motives even from themselves, from their own consciousness, thus the accusation of "false consciousness." Later European and American thinkers followed in Engels' tradition and rhetoric. One theorist widely assigned in undergraduate university courses is the Italian social critic, Antonio Gramsci (1891–1937). Born in Sardinia and who studied at the University of Turin, Gramsci's work has long been a core "must read" in political science classes. (I was assigned Gramsci in my undergraduate degree.) Gramsci, who majored in linguistics and helped found the Italian communist party, argued with his own fellow travellers who thought communism was scientific and propounded it on that basis. While most of his communist allies were busy arguing that their economic theories were what counted (thus the bias for a "scientific" Marxism), instead Gramsci thought ideas, action, and myths mattered more.

Gramsci argued that liberals (in the European and not American sense) were influential in Italy and elsewhere not because their views accorded with reality, which he thought was often constructed and not objective, but because they were merely better at convincing people through stories and analogies (e.g., "a rising tide lifts all boats"). In other words, Gramsci, in the language to which the 20th century's Marxists often resorted thought that the "bourgeoisie"—the middle class, shopkeepers, and the like—ruled merely because they were better propagandists. They influenced civil society's institutions (the churches, the media, unions, and politics) while communists were off debating how many workers could dance on the head of a Marxist-liberated pin. In order to battle the effectiveness of the liberals, Gramsci thought Marxists had to either act as they did in 1917 in Russia and take over a society and construct a new reality from the ashes of a revolution, or in western liberal democracies, left-wing propagandists needed to transform the "mass consciousness" of the population with propaganda. This notion—that liberal democracies and capitalists are merely better propagandists—is so widespread in academia as to be unremarkable.

The wretched of the West

Anyone at a Western university in the last 50 years has likely encountered versions of Engels' and Gramsci's theory and language. In addition, the other theorists who have followed in their intellectual footsteps and who have their own followers: the Martinique-born Frantz Fanon, whose *The Wretched of the Earth* became a classic anti-traditional educational tome since it was first published in 1963; France's Michel Foucault, whose works emphasized the notion that what people *thought* was reality was merely imaginary and constructed; Paulo Freire, the Brazilian educator, international bureaucrat, and philosopher who wrote *Pedagogy of the Oppressed* and argued that conventional education was a "practice of domination" by "oppressors." (Freire advised the "oppressed" to reject such assumed oppression in favour of "consciousness-raising.") Others who offer up varieties of this strand—that the masses in America had been victimized without even knowing it: MIT's famous linguist, Noam Chomsky, whose anti-Western screeds have been bestsellers among the university young for decades; radical 20th-century journalist Howard Zinn, whose book *The Twentieth Century: A People's History* portrayed American history as one long story of vice but never virtue; and Edward Said, the anti-Orientalist scholar who extrapolated from all of the above to make the case against the United States and the West in international affairs. Of note, Said did so while living in New York City, the very success of which, as a multi-ethnic, multi-racial, capitalist metropolis in a rules-based nation, by example, undercut Said's most vociferous anti-Western critiques at the very time he made them.

Theorists from Gramsci to Foucault stretched obvious points—language and action can shape *some things* such as an initial perception and impression—up to the stratosphere to give their observations more meaning than deserved. Such theories matter to pondering the rise of victim culture and Western self-loathing because, from Manchester to Turin and from San Paulo and Paris and then on to New York City and Cambridge, the work that originated courtesy with the more radical theorists in the 20th century now underlies much of the rhetoric today. Thus when,

- anti-capitalist professors choose to disdain financial success as merely "white," they echo the words of Freire: "One method of manipulation is to inoculate individuals with the bourgeois appetite for personal success."[21]

- a UCLA students' protest group claim that grammar is subjective and that correction and other criticism amount to a "larger institutionalized culture of racism on campus,"[22] they mimic Foucault's belief that reality is a mirage that can be rearranged by anyone, the assumption being that there are no hard facts beyond power-seeking of the privileged.

- students argue that cultural borrowing is appropriation and an injury, and some aboriginal leaders and activists compare the past intentional disparagement of native culture, wrong as it was, to genocide, they also dine in the company of Freire. It was he who first claimed that "cultural invasion... serves the ends of conquest."[23] He thus characterized cultural interchange as akin to actual, bloody conquistador conquests from centuries past. Freire: "Whether urbane or harsh, cultural invasion is thus always an act of violence against the persons of the invaded culture, who lose their originality or face the threat of losing it,"[24] wrote Freire in 1970.

- students speak of a larger, institutionalized culture of oppression— and that anyone pointing out that the West has progressively provided more opportunity, relative not to perfection but to history and to other nations today, must be trapped by false consciousness—such students mimic assertions from Marx, Gramsci, and Foucault.[25]

Gramsci et al. were wrong about most everything from oppression to capitalism: The drive to trade—from English shopkeepers to the late Steve Jobs—is anchored in how human beings have always behaved. It results from voluntary exchanges that have existed wherever human beings live in community and exercise peaceful choices. That reality of human activity combined with ordered liberty of the Anglo-Saxon variety allowed men and women to flourish in the last two centuries, and for ever-more nations outside of the Anglosphere in the postwar world, and this in a manner unknown in human history. In the past two centuries, real per-capita income rose more than eightfold worldwide.[26] As two Columbia University economists, Maxim Pinkovskiy and Xavier Sala-i-Martin have found, since just the 1970s, poverty rates around the world fell by 80% in the past four decades while global inequality also declined substantially.[27] Markets and liberty and their salutary effect upon living standards were not a result of propaganda victories but of recognizing how human beings thrive when given choice and necessary structure, i.e., freedom and responsible rules-based, limited government with divisions of power to prevent tyranny.

Relevant to today's debates, for such protagonists, much of the progress and also nuances are ignored. The story that Western nations are overwhelmingly and *structurally* racist, sexist, colonialist, and possessed by multiple other ills continues unabated. It is as if such critics have never travelled or bothered to inquire into the cultures, practices, and laws of other nations, or know any economic or civil rights history. Twenty-first-century students and others who use language of structure, oppression, consciousness, and myriad other grievance-assuming, victim-claiming jargon may not know—and here is *actual* false consciousness— the source of much of their language and assumptions: dead European white male social and cultural critics who thought much of life and human behaviour mere "constructs."

More generally, when last century's critical theorists and this century's victim cultists engage in bleak narratives, forever arguing that the reality of a much more tolerant and equal opportunity-anchored society today is an illusion, such critics and erstwhile victims live in an imagined Hades. They simply have not caught up with the demonstrable reality of a freer, more flourishing, prosperous world in the last 70 years, and where the exceptions today are not the nations in which they live, but societies whose regimes have traditionally opposed the Anglosphere and its ideas, ideals, and norms.

Hong Kong after 150 years of colonialism: On top

Escape from the anti-Western chattering classes in the West and instead wander around glittering, prosperous Hong Kong. You will yet stumble upon evidence of British rule from a previous era. What the British left behind includes geography named for colonial-era monarchs and military heroes (Victoria Harbour, Prince Edward Road, Wellington Street). Then there are the remnants of British architecture, ones that survived the onslaught of capital and cement that threw towers high into Hong Kong's harbour sky: St. John's Cathedral in early English Gothic style, built in 1849, which still functions as a place of Anglican worship; the old Edwardian-era Supreme

Court building (whose British architects designed the eastern façade of Buckingham Palace), later used for legislative purposes before reverting to a repository of things legal after the handover of Hong Kong to China. The Supreme Court building is emblematic of something else the British left behind in 1997, less obvious than architecture but more critical: the rule of law and political and civil institutions explicitly designed to both prevent abuse of rule and to encourage prosperity. The vestiges of empire that remain in Hong Kong, such as buildings, are interesting for tourists, but the elements of imperial rule that those in Hong Kong are now fighting to retain are the same as those communicated to me in 2013: The rule of law, capitalism, and anti-corruption efforts. Those who live in Hong Kong hold tightly to such concepts because they are close enough in history and geography to know how societies without such fundamental healthy rules and attitudes, colonial inheritances as they might be, function in their absence.

The results: Hong Kong's per-capita GDP was $3,466 in 1950, at a time when the equivalent figure in Great Britain was over triple that, at $10,846. By 1997, Hong Kong—a British colony for over 150 years—showed per-capita income of $29,941 while its colonial "mother," the United Kingdom, was more than $1,000 below that at $28,879. (Hong Kong already surpassed the U.K. five years before, in 1992.) By 2016, the territory, returned to China 19 years previous, recorded per-capita income of $48,330, or nearly 30% higher than its former imperial power, the United Kingdom, at $37,334.[28] Meanwhile, China in 2016 was still behind both with per-capita income at $12,569, barely one-quarter that of Hong Kong. More important than the numbers are the freedoms in Hong Kong that until recently were assumed but, as I write, now under attack: the dignity of the individual and her rights above that of the collective, freedom of the media, religion, the necessity of private property, the rule of law, independent courts, and relatively little corruption.

Hong Kong is an example of a territory and a population that avoided the siren song of a victim cult and instead continued to cling to the useful aspects of its British legacy that strengthened the territory, even today vis-à-vis a repressive regime in Beijing. Elsewhere, not everyone values that bequest or recognizes the inherent recklessness in continuously pursued grievance narratives. Examples of the latter are evident in the misery and wrecked societies to which we now turn, where victim narratives were cultivated for decades and civilizational tragedies resulted: the late Yasser Arafat and the Palestinians, pre-1990s Hutus in Rwanda, and Germans in the 19th century. The latter example is particularly instructive as that nation encapsulated every temptation common to victim cults and to an extreme: demands for perfection, a narcissistic romanticizing of culture, and extreme tribalism. In Germany, those elements metastasized in the 19th century and led to a victim cult that nearly ended civilization itself in the next one.

PART III

Civilization wreckers:
When victim cults metastasize

One of the most common justifications or
rationalizations for violence in human history is,
"Someone else hurt me, and now I'm going to hurt them."

—University of Alabama criminologist ADAM LANKFORD,
on Las Vegas shooter Stephen Maddock

CHAPTER 7

When victimhood goes viral: Germany's pre-Nazi narrative

―――――

Swiss historian Carl Burckhardt showed an acute understanding of the obsessions clouding the German mind in the first half of the twentieth century: A romantic interpretation of the past; a feeling of having been unjustly treated by history and of having suffered at the hands of inferior people....

—HANS KOHN, *The Mind of Germany*

Victim thinking before Adolf Hitler

If ever a nation could be characterized as possessing a collective personality disorder, Germany is it.

Germany, whether in its pre-unification parts or in its later unified whole, could, from the early-19th century and until the Second World War, be variously described as insecure, paranoid, and prone to pseudo-science and conspiracy theories. The country was also resolutely proud of learning little from others.

To understand the disaster that was Germany in the first half of the 20th century, one must grasp its collective disorder fashioned in the 19th. There, the various ingredients normally apparent in victim cults were present: pernicious ideas, "runaway" romantics, perfectionism, a too-narrow nationalism, and pathological blame of a minority. Unlike other grievance narratives, which might display only some of these elements, Germany possessed them all and intensely so.

Thus, Germans in the 19th century apportioned blame to real enemies

(France) and imagined ones (Jews). The pattern continued in the subsequent century, except that by then Germany's foes—much of Europe, Great Britain and the Commonwealth, the United States, and the Soviet Union— were of its own making. Make-believe antagonists again loomed large in Germany's collective psyche: Weimar-era politicians, the Treaty of Versailles, the assumed unfairness of reparations after the First World War, and of course Jews. Such real and made-up nemeses along with an existing cultural framework that defined outside influences as contaminants led Germany away from the relatively pleasant pastoral society of Bach and Beethoven to the genocidal concentration camps of Bergen-Belsen and Dachau. Germany's romanticized self-deception and victim narrative only ended with the country's own dismemberment and destruction in 1945. Here is how Germany's victim cult developed, was nourished, and then enveloped the world.

Germany's 19th-century nationalist symphony

Occupations often provoke a sense of victimization and nationalism; but, unlike other European states, the German variety was somnolent in the early Napoleonic era. At the end of the 18th century as nationalist impulses raged across Europe, it was not guaranteed that Germans would partake in such awakenings. As the German historian Hans Kohn has written, "Germany hardly knew any nationalism or political activity. The people lived peacefully, unmoved by French revolutionary appeals," with a rural population that was "strictly parochial " and "the rights of the many princes not questioned by their subjects."[1] Intellectuals were content to philosophize without needing or caring to test their ideas against reality; liberals only asked that they be left alone with freedom of mind and "the insulation of society from the state."[2]

A few tried to foment a robust German nationalism but met with little initial success. In 1793, the poet Johann Gottfried Herder observed Germany's divided state and warned it might suffer Poland's fate—a once-leading European power now dismembered twice that century (by Russia, Prussia, and Austria in 1772, and again in 1793 by Russia and Prussia)[3]: "Germany, are you slumbering on? Look what happens around you…. You still tarry to stand up like a man and wisely unite?"[4] August Wilhelm Schlegel, a poet and critic, complained of how the word "Fatherland has lost its magic power."[5] He was unhappy that all-encompassing familial and collective concept had been replaced by a general, "colder interest for mankind," e.g., the Enlightenment-era notion of liberalism attached to the individual.[6] Then there was Friedrich von Hardenberg, whose penname was Novalis; he wrote poetry glorifying the Middle Ages and his work was described by one historian as "filled with the infinite longing, the bereaved love, and the burning intensity of the complete romantic."[7] Another would-be town crier for German nationalism was Adam Müller. Born in Prussia, he later settled in Vienna and mythologized feudal society, which he believed to be closest to the will of God; Müller saw the liberal and enlightenment thinking popular in his own centuries as an aberration.[8]

Herder, Schlegel, Novalis, and Müller were unsuccessful, at least initially. The lack of nationalist fervour made little headway up against the still-dominant 18th-century German Enlightenment assumptions and thinkers of the non-romantic sort. For instance, writer and statesman Johann Wolfgang von Goethe despised romantics, who relentlessly pined for some ostensible golden age of German greatness. Such quixotic nationalists, wrote Goethe, forgot that under the French "We are living... in much greater liberty and without their narrow limitations." In 1799, Goethe argued against German nationalism for nationalism's sake. "At a time when everyone is busy creating new Fatherlands," he wrote, "the Fatherland of the man who thinks without prejudice and can rise above his time is nowhere and everywhere."[9]

Early nationalist appeals also floundered because with the French controlling parts of southern and western Germany, their initial reforms were often welcomed by some. That included Napoleon's legal alterations, the ending of monopolistic medieval-era guilds, and much-needed social and economic reforms.[10] Thus, some Germans preferred the French emperor—the "Prince of Peace" as some labelled Napoleon, over local rulers. The reference was to Napoleon's calming of the roiled French civil and political waters, this after the 1789 Revolution's and the Revolutionary Army's murderous excesses.[11] For instance, in 1802, Karl Theodor von Dalberg, the Imperial Elector of Mainz, wrote of Napoleon as "This extraordinary man, who brought order out of the anarchy in France... [who] has the greatness of soul that is needed to rise above being merely the benefactor of a single nation to become the benefactor of mankind."[12] The praise was philosopher-king, messiah-worship. But given the travails experienced by France and its neighbours after the Revolution, and the generally sensible Enlightenment-influenced reforms introduced by Napoleon, the praise was understandable if overly effusive and selective. In general, while the German states were in continual conflict between 1800 and 1815, the French-controlled areas were at least prosperous in the first decade.[13]

Making Germany great again

German quietude on nationalist matters would soon expire.[14] The end came partly because of the 1806 battle of Jena–Auerstedt where Prussian forces were soundly defeated.[15] That provoked a nationalist reaction in Prussia and in the rest of Germany; after that, the philosophers found a more receptive audience. One example of the brutality of the French occupation helps illuminate why: In an early November 1806 battle in the north German city of Lübeck, French soldiers stopped, stripped, and strangled Germans and plundered or ransacked most of the city's houses. One 18-year-old girl was raped by 22 soldiers and then thrown over the city wall; still alive and breathing but unable to move "in the reeds and mud of the pond's bank," the girl lay there for a few hours until "she breathed her last."[16] As historian Götz Aly writes, "Horrors like this happened in thousands of German communities during the French occupation."[17] It was thus a wonder that the sleepy nationalist sentiment had not been roused earlier. While some Germans benefited from French occupation, notably in the south and west, many other Germans lost out, with massive war contributions demanded from losing German states and with "blacksmiths, weavers, tailors, cobblers, tanners, furriers, and saddlemakers worked almost exclusively to meet the needs of the Grand Armée," and this "while soldiers plundered civilians, raped women, and burned down houses."[18] As Aly summarizes it, "For the vast majority of Germans, the French occupation was a time of executions and murders, inflation, and lasting economic devastation."[19]

The French presence and abuses did, finally, provide a spur to the nationalism long desired by the romantics and poets: a revived medieval-inspired Germany, courtesy of philosophical musing, past glories, and pagan mysticism. Thus in 1807 and 1808 in Berlin, Johann Gottlieb Fichte gave a series of speeches that provided the intellectual framework for Germany's awakening where he argued that Germans were an "original people" formed from natural and spiritual sources. For Fichte, this produced an exclusive German experience and understanding, a sort of "divine law"[20] of unique German culture. It was always and everywhere felt by all "true" Germans (but no one else) and was self-replicating. "Everywhere the higher culture was, and continued to be, the result of the interaction of the citizens of all German states," wrote Fichte, "and then this higher culture gradually worked its way down in this form to the people at large, which thus never ceased, broadly speaking, to educate itself by itself."[21] As the journalist and Third Reich chronicler William Shirer observed over a century later, such writings, coming as they did on the heels of Prussia's defeat by Napoleon, was "heady wine for a frustrated folk."[22] Or, as Hannah Arendt opined, Germans could now think of themselves as mystically tied together by a "blood relationship" related to "family ties, tribal unity and unmixed origin." This organic nationalism had great appeal for a people not yet tied together by *political* nationalism.[23]

Culture worship and collectives: The *volk*

The groundwork for this romantic nationalism was laid decades before. Herder had, in 1784, argued that true national culture springs from the *volk*—the people—and that such authentic culture is prior to the nation-state. In *Ideas on the Philosophy of the History of Mankind*, Herder theorized that the *volk* were connected to land and to the presumed native culture of that territory; the notion carried within it an assumed organic unity of people based on soil, blood, ethnicity, and religion. This pure and divine German-ness necessitated a nation uncontaminated by foreigners and outside influences, be they ideas or people. In Herder's day, the most obvious and immediate were the French who three decades later would finally be expelled from German territory. But over the 19th century, disdained and feared influences would include liberalism (seen as British), capitalism, cosmopolitanism—and Jews, viewed by the nationalists as a contaminated compendium of all of the foregoing.[24]

Another German philosopher, Georg Wilhelm Hegel, built on Herder's work but also on Fichte's belief that the nation was the supreme entity to be cherished and protected, not the individual or her happiness. Hegel "saw the essence of the state as its power over the individual citizen and as its ability to defend itself against other states," writes historian Kohn. "Hegel's prince was no longer the first servant of the state as the 18th century had understood him." Instead, he was "now the great man whom others obey even against their will."[25] This notion also assumed that the individual, if he mattered at all, mattered less than the organic whole. What counted was not the "cell" (the person) but the larger organism, the nation. The historian Heinrich von Treitschke, who concurred with Fichte, illustrated such thinking and summarized the servile Germanic mindset when he wrote, "It does not matter what you think, so long as you obey."[26] Friedrich Schlegel, brother to August Wilhelm Schlegel, who would lead German Romanticism in the university city of Jena, also signalled the diminished place for the individual in German *volk* thought when he wrote that "The concept of the nation requires that all its members should form, as it were, only one individual."[27]

For German thinkers and nationalists after Herder, the state and the leader were the bulwark against the outside world, one they often viewed as hostile. It was an understandable reaction to the recent French occupation but would soon become a dominant feature of German thought and contribute to a national paranoia about "contaminating" influences. Critically, in this conception of a nation-state, the individual was to subsume herself into that organic whole to not disrupt the unity of the larger organism; the individual was valued less, if at all, because of the romantic notion about collectivism as an assumed practical necessity. The collective, the German nation in this case, and the leader who directs it were seen as necessarily supreme. Power was likewise assumed to rightly flow down from the ruler to the population, and not from below, from citizens, to rulers.

This extreme notion of unity was opposite that of the classic English, liberal understanding of citizens and the state where inalienable rights begin with and are attached to individuals, rights which have been recognized and cemented over time. The German notion was in contradistinction to the core English presumption from the Magna Carta onward, that power is delegated from the people to their rulers and that citizens are the ultimate source of authority, not the monarch. The English notion assumed concentrated power was a danger, that individuals often need protection from the potential abuses of powerful entities *including* the state. Thus, divided power is necessary to preserve freedom. (The American founding fathers understood this. It was why they designed the institutions of state accordingly, with separate powers for the president, senate, house, and judiciary.) In this English conception and its later colonial expressions, a social contract exists between citizens and rulers and implies a two-way relationship, breakable only in extreme circumstances. It was opposite the romantic German notion of organic unity that was not to be disrupted and which smothered the individual. As to why such worked-out conceptions of the individual, citizens, the ruler, and nation mattered, that was soon to become clear to those in Germany who were seen as inauthentic, as foreign.

Intellectuals and students vs. "philistines" and Jews

An early example of how this 19th-century *volk* nationalism played out in everyday life came from Romantic poet Achim von Arnim, who founded the German Table Society in 1811. The society's aim was to strengthen Prussian and German nationalism vis-à-vis French rule under Napoleon (and which would soon end two years hence at the battle of Leipzig). The society was predicated on assumed German *volk* culture; the prejudices of it and the era were expressed through features of the club's social life including anti-Semitic poems, rhyming couplets and essays, and membership restrictions: Frenchmen, "philistines," women, and Jews (including converted Jews) were not admissible.[28] One friend of Arnim explained that the society's gestation resulted from the members' feeling that the Jews' desire for "curiosity and renewal" made them natural critics of existing orders. The society feared that Jews were trying to "slime, push and force" their way into German life and society.[29]

The nationalist, poet, and educator Ernest Moritz Arndt was also indicative of this revived German nationalism, a throwback to earlier centuries but popular for that same reason. In his lifetime, Arndt was seen as a hero for opposing serfdom and especially for opposing the French presence. However, as with other German nationalists of his era, Arndt defined his nationalism in "earthy" categories, which excluded foreigners from the possibility of ever becoming truly German. "The Germans have not been bastardized" remarked Arndt in 1815,[30] who preferred they stay that way. His focus on cultural purity led Arndt to assert that Jews were a "foreign plague and excretion."[31] Another nationalist, Friedrich Ludwig Jahn, founder of the gymnastics movement and who saw physical health as key to not only personal health but to a nation's, made comparisons between the physical laws that ruled animal and human life. Jahn thought he spotted similarities: "Animals of mixed stock have no real generative power," he wrote. "Similarly, hybrid peoples have no folk propagation of their own."[32] Jahn's claim was an early premonition of Social Darwinism before both Darwin and the subsequent pseudo-scientific twisting of his theory.

Still, Arnim, Arndt, and Jahn argued for the equality of people despite the differences they thought they spotted in each race. Jahn asserted humanity could only realize its full potential when such differences existed on the political terrain of equality. Arndt, though he believed animal characteristics could be extrapolated to explain racial differences between human beings, nevertheless asserted the functional and political equality of all peoples. Unlike later attempts to justify imperial domination, Arndt thought attempts to rule over other ostensibly unique races was wrong. (Hannah Arendt labelled this as "pre-racism," the notion that other races were equal but that "purity" yet demanded separate nations.[33]) Anyone who "would subjugate and rule foreign peoples" should be "cursed"[34] wrote Arndt, who later became a supporter of Italian and Polish nationalist movements on just this basis. But Arndt's nationalist sympathies were anchored in notions of purity and, later in life, Arndt again demanded that Germans "once and for all divorce what is foreign from what is native," i.e., presumed indigenous Germans from Jews.[35]

Ideas, student movements, and book burning

In 1814, one year after Napoleon's defeat at Leipzig and the forced exit of French forces from German territories, a nascent student movement arose preaching the virtue of this narrowly defined German identity. Taking up from where selected German philosophers left off, a students' nationalist fraternity, the first of its kind, was formed in Jena, in Thuringia, a region pregnant with nationalist touchstones: Martin Luther translated the New Testament into German at Wartburg Castle[36] and Napoleon's forces routed the Prussian army at Jena just eight years before. There was also this other inspiration in the local mountains, the life and legend of Frederick Barbarossa, the emperor responsible for Germanic unification in the 12th century: Credited for a conquering, expansionist phase into Italy, one Teutonic legend foretold of how Barbarossa would one day reawake to again save the Germans from their enemies. It had obvious resonance after the French occupation. Barbarossa would also be the name assigned to Adolf Hitler's eastern campaign, the German invasion of the Soviet Union, in 1941.

German history, the real and the romantic alike, merged with the musings of nationalist philosophers and the young to produce what often results from that mix, a self-righteous movement possessed by utopian visions who demand that the impure be expelled. The Jena fraternity's first item of business was a change in the bylaws of predecessor student organizations to make explicit that membership was restricted to Germans and Christians.[37] The first major gathering of such nationalist clubs for students took place at the Wartburg Castle on October 18, 1817. It was there, overlooking Eisenach in a festival akin to Woodstock but composed of young nationalists, that 450 students gathered to celebrate the four-year anniversary of Napoleon's defeat. For some, it was also a chance to dispose of "reactionary" literature and books blamed for "poisoning the Volk culture."[38] All such works and others were heaped onto bonfire stacks and burned. The philosopher Jahn, popular with students and a nationalist pied piper, was later found to have instigated the fires.[39]

The decline of religious anti-Semitism; the rise of an intellectual variety

Before considering other forces that shaped Germany's 19th-century grievance narrative, we should dismiss one lingering but fading influence, religious anti-Semitism. European Christianity had long possessed a disastrous, deep strain of anti-Jewish prejudice. The prime German example was the theologian and monk who split Western Christendom asunder, Martin Luther. As it happens, in Luther's early writing, ones largely forgotten due to his later ravings, the monk was initially *sympathetic* to Jews. As part of his early protest against a corrupt Rome, Luther included the Church's poor treatment of Jews as misplaced: "Popes, bishops, sophists and monks have hitherto dealt with the Jews in such a manner," wrote Luther, who with rare sympathy remarked, "that he who was a good Christian would rather have wished to become a Jew."[40] Nonetheless, Luther's initial empathy was the exception to his general anti-Semitic orientation. Twenty years after that anti-Rome missive, Luther's pamphlets possessed all the ramblings of one who today would be considered not only deeply prejudiced but possessed by conspiratorial beliefs and a lunatic.[41] In 1542, in "Concerning the Jews and Their Lies," Luther repeated false but commonly believed charges against Jews, which were a staple of anti-Semitism since at least the medieval age: The Talmud condoned Jewish deception; Jews poisoned wells, water, and springs; Jews would kill Christian children and use their blood in rituals; Jewish doctors poisoned Christians.[42] Protestantism's founder saw Jews as intruders in Christian lands and advised Germans to smash and burn their homes, shut down their schools and synagogues, destroy their prayer books, seize their property, and ban them from the roads and markets.[43] "We are even at fault for not striking them dead," he wrote.[44] And Luther's last bit of advice: Give Jews a choice between conversion to Christianity or having their tongues torn out.[45]

Over the centuries, Luther's influence mattered to European anti-Semitism and the Germany variety in particular, but by the 19th century it was residual in influence and not generative. That understanding matters to properly grasp the even more destructive German grievance culture that arrived later. To produce a paranoia about outsiders common to victim cultists, anti-Semitism needed to transcend its dying religious husk and be born anew. That occurred courtesy of intellectuals and pseudo-scientists in the 19th century. The clearest example of the transition from old anti-Jewish prejudice to a new strain is best demonstrated by Voltaire, the French philosopher most often referenced as an example of 18th-century tolerance and who influenced European thinking, including in Germany. Voltaire possessed "professional" and personal reasons for his dislike of Jews. He excoriated Christianity and Judaism alike because he saw Western civilization as originally Greek and Roman—pagan, in other words. Voltaire believed that Abrahamic faiths had "infected" Europe and made it feeble in contrast to the earlier stoic and Roman virtues he admired. Voltaire reserved special animus for the Jewish faith, given it was Christianity's antecedent. Thus in 1771, in his *Letters of Memmius to Cicero*, Voltaire serves as a ventriloquist for his character's anti-Jewish animus: "They are, all of them, born with raging fanaticism in their hearts.... I would not be in the least bit surprised if these people would not some day become deadly to the human race."[46] Similarly, the next year, in his essay "One Must Take Sides," and now in his own voice, Voltaire attacks all people of faith but reserves his most biting criticism for Jewish beliefs: "You have surpassed all nations in impertinent fables, in bad conduct and in barbarism," he wrote. "You deserve to be punished, for this is your destiny."[47]

Another part of Voltaire's antipathy, one common to intellectuals then and now: a disdain for capitalism, which he attributed to Jewish influence.[48] This twin hatred for the Jewish faith and commerce is evident throughout Voltaire's work.[a] In his 1756 *Dictionnaire Philsosophique*, Voltaire argues that European society was wrong to have taken its legal codes from the Jews and also offers a gratuitous swipe at Jewish commercial activity. In remarking on Jewish captivity in two of the ancient world's great centres of knowledge, Babylon and Alexandria, Voltaire castigates Jews as having squandered the opportunity to acquire knowledge and wisdom. Instead, he wrote, Jews focused only on money, "trained" as they were "only in the art of usury."[49] The French atheist did allow that Jews should "not be burned at the stake"[50] and also called on Christians to leave Jews alone.[51] That allowance would be little comfort to Abraham's children who long endured a strain of religious anti-Semitism only to see a new version arise courtesy of the French philosopher and other intellectuals. Others noted Voltaire's influence. One decade after the philosopher's death, a contemporary, Adolphe Thiéry, described Voltaire's influence in the new anti-Semitic strain: "The enemy of the Jews whose blows have hurt most is M. de Voltaire, who has prostituted his genius in order to enjoy the strange pleasure of degrading and condemning the Jews."[52] "Voltaire," as historian Arthur Hertzberg wrote, was "the major link in Western intellectual history between the anti-Semitism of classic paganism and the modern age."[53]

Critically, Voltaire's combination allowed for a more respectable Enlightenment-justified, anti-Semitism to emerge, one that allowed intellectuals to disdain both traditional Jews and those engaged in commerce. Others would follow Voltaire's lead, both on religion and stereotypes about Jews and money. The charge against capitalism and Jews was an easy prejudice to stir in the maelstrom of change thrown up by the Industrial Revolution and especially in the 19th century. It would only intensify with the arrival of Karl Marx. As an atheist, Marx despised religion and thought Jews had added one faith on top of another and the self-proclaimed philosopher-economist despised both. Marx savaged the commercial aspect of Jewish life, thus updating the anti-Semitic impulse and making it palatable for those suspicious

---

[a] Part of Voltaire's view was conditioned, perhaps, by his own losses. In 1726, Voltaire lost 20,000 francs due to an investment that went sour and was connected to a Jewish banker in London; Voltaire also made a questionable investment with a Jewish financier in Berlin and which led to a lawsuit.

of the successful, who just might happen to be Jews: "Let us consider the real Jew," he wrote, "Not the *Sabbath Jew*... but the *everyday Jew*," who asks and then answers his own rhetorical question: "What is the non-religious basis for Judaism? *Practical* need, *self-interest*... *huckstering* and the Jews' worldly god: *money*."[54] As historian Paul Johnson writes in his analysis of the above, the charge from Marx was that "Jews had gradually conveyed this 'practical' religion to all society."[55]

On-the-ground envy in Germany

The intellectual and economic scorn for Jews dovetailed with everyday life in Germany, undergoing significant disruption in the first half of the 19th century. At the time, agricultural reforms included peasant emancipation, but, also for some, expropriation. This, along with the secularization and takeover of church lands (upon which some peasants worked) resulted in a dramatic change in ownership and also employment, which plunged. As with elsewhere in industrializing Europe, as the size of farms increased and the number of people needed to work the land fell, dislocation became brutally common. In the first half of the century in Prussia alone, between 30,000 and 40,000 peasant farmsteads (and another 70,000 to 80,000 smaller parcels of land) were abandoned, lost, or incorporated into larger estates. This development was disastrous and produced widespread rural pauperism, exacerbated by harvest failures in the 1840s.[56]

Given the upheaval upending traditional economic life, the language of Marx would appeal to a mid-century German peasant: Jews were offered up as the archetype of the capitalism that the same farmer-peasant already despised. Given the wholesale disruption underway, it took little to arouse anti-Semitism courtesy of arguments from envy and, in the middle of the 19th century, the capitalist system itself was characterized by some Germans as "the victory of Jewish usury" within which Jews were characterized as "locusts."[57] The German population well knew its Old Testament, and the "locust" reference, from the Exodus story of wiped-out Egyptian crops as Jews left Egypt with Egyptian wealth, would have stuck in German minds. Except given their economic troubles, poorer Germans would identify with the ancient Egyptians and their losses, not the Jews embarking on their exodus to freedom.

Commercial prejudice

The philosophizing against commerce was reinforced with a predictable bias in any age: dislike of competition. The founder of the 1811 German Table Society, Achim von Arnim, is an example. Arnim's 1820 novel, *Primogeniture*, is filled with stories of Jewish deceit and greed, and he was also critical of the French Revolution that allowed Jews to pursue more trades and commerce than ever before: "Old aristocratic concessions were discontinued and the Jews freed from their narrow ghetto street," he laments. As with Voltaire, the personal history matters. Arnim inherited an estate with substantial debts and was never able to pay them back. Barely able to pay the interest on the debt and forced to release the family's only servant, Arnim also failed to provide his wife, Bettina, "with the appropriate aristocratic lifestyle."[58] Arnim's own failure was redirected at the Jews. As another example of the newer prejudice, the chairman of the Grandy Duchy of Posen objected to Jews not on religious grounds, he said, but due to their "disproportionate wealth and power."[59] Meanwhile, Cologne's Chamber of Commerce described Jews as "winding weeds that latch on everywhere."[60] In 1889, the anti-Semitic German Social Party wanted artisans, merchants, and farmers protected from the free market. It demanded that limits be placed on "those liberties benefitting Jewry because they drain the blood from and do great damage to productive, honest, working Christians."[61]

Anti-Jewish sentiment stemming from envy showed up elsewhere and was often noted by contemporaries. In 1831, Gabriel Riesser saw that age's anti-Semitism for what it was: "The true Jew haters of today envy the rich man his wealth, the busy man his employment and the beggar his rags." The latter was a reference to how some anti-Semites noticed how Jews cared well for their own poor when compared with Christians who did less for their religious compatriots.[62] In November 1880, after a petition with 220,000 signatures demanded limits on the trades that Jews were allowed to practice was submitted to the Prussian parliament, one deputy, a physician, Rudolf Virchow, argued that the notion Jews had inherent special, negative characteristics was motivated "primarily by envy."[63] Likewise, National Liberal Deputy Arthur Hobrecht argued that "a good portion of the ugly envy" directed at Jews stemmed from a "lamentable lack of self-confidence and energy" of German businessmen.[64] A *London Times* correspondent who covered parliamentary debates wrote of how hate and envy stemmed from the fact Germans were incompetent businessmen, whereas Jews were not.[65]

One Bavarian reformer summed up the source for the nationalism observed in Arnim and the other early 19th-century nationalists: It stemmed from their own failures. "Behind the mask of hypertrophic German-ness simmers the rage over the loss they feel they have suffered," argued Johann von Aretin.[66] Leo Pinsker, the Russian-Polish physician, and Theodor Herzl, both Zionists and who well knew of the older religious-based prejudice against Jews, also thought the latest version not a recycled religious strain but something new and with its own self-generating prejudice. The "contemporary version was held to be a new, secular and continuing phenomenon," wrote historian Hertzberg in reviewing Pinsker and Herzl's thoughts, who remarks that Germans freed themselves of the remains of medievalism only to latch on to "a contemporary reason for hating Jews."[67] Indeed, Voltaire, Marx, others, and garden-variety envy, allowed for an old prejudice to be modernized. Increasingly, Germans were less inclined to believe medieval claims that Jews would extract the blood of Christian children for use in Jewish religious ceremonies; now, Germans were more likely to believe that Jews busily extracted wealth out of a zero-sum German economy.

More fear of "contamination": The rise of Social Darwinism

Dangerous as were 19th-century nationalist musings, the anti-capitalist philosophers and on-the-ground envy, another strain in Germany's victim cult arrived mid-century, courtesy of a growing fascination with pseudo-scientific explanations. It would reinforce the German fear of foreign "contamination" only now with the ostensible justification of science. One early variant originated in France: Between 1853 and 1855, the French diplomat and author, Count Arthur de Gobineau, published his tome on assumed racial differences, the "Essay on the Inequalities of the Human Races." The nub of his four-volume work was that racial differences mattered and could explain the rise and fall of civilizations. His chosen racial division was threefold: Black, "yellow," and white, with the last category divided further into non-Aryan and Aryan. Some French, all the English and Irish, Scandinavians, those of the Low Countries and of Germany (but not everyone from Rhine and Hanover) were Aryan and "pure." Others—the southern races for Gobineau—were hopelessly mixed together and long ago diluted any cultural, national potency. For the French author, that explained why some nation-states were at their civilizational peak while others were in decline. With references to the Book of Genesis, linguistics, and anthropology, Gobineau argued that "The racial question dominates all the other problems of history." His theory, he argued, could explain "the whole unfolding destiny of peoples."[68]

Such pseudo-science had its pernicious effect. As Hannah Arendt would write a century later, "The inherent irresponsibility of romantic opinions received a new stimulant from Gobineau's mixture of races because this mixture showed an historical event of the past which could be traced in the depths of one's self."[69] In other words, the personal really did become political for 19th-century Germans. One's nation, earlier defined by culture and now also by race, would succeed or fail based on one's personal purity, the degree to which foreigners contaminated oneself and one's country. A more famous contribution came from Herbert Spencer, the British philosopher and scientist who coined the phrase "survival of the fittest." Spencer argued for what others would later characterize as "social Darwinism," the unwarranted leap from Charles Darwin's work (*On the Origin of Species* was published in 1859). Even before Darwin, but especially after, Spencer and others would extend the notion of natural selection, the evolutionary struggle, as also applicable to society and its groups and this via race. Spencer expounded on his own theory in a variety of works starting in 1857.[b] The clarity of his views is most starkly expressed in a late-19th-century letter to the Japanese statesman and diplomat, and later Justice Minister, Kanéko Kentarō. The Harvard-educated Japanese civil servant wrote Spencer for advice on the degree to which foreigners should be allowed to mingle with the Japanese, including questions of marriage. The response reveals both Spencer's consistency—he thought every race should be kept from intermingling and intermarrying—and also how he thought his views were grounded in science. "It is not at root a question of social philosophy [but]... is at root a question of biology," he writes.[70] Then, comparing humans to animals, Spencer insists that "There is abundant proof furnished by the intermarriage of human races and the

---

[b] Spencer's various works that touched on the matter included his 1857 essay, "*Progress: Its Law and Causes: First Principles of a New System of Philosophy*" (1862) and "*Principles of Biology*" (1864).

interbreeding of animals, that when the varieties mingled diverge beyond a certain slight degree *the result is inevitably a bad one in the long run.*"[71] The British scientist, then residing with an acquaintance whose work included that of inbreeding cattle, cited his conviction that such undesirability of mixed races was verified even with such experience.[72] Spencer then inveighed against allowing foreigners and Japanese to mix beyond simple economic activity and ends his letter with the advice sought by the justice minister: "No further privileges should be allowed," he writes, and as for foreigners and potential liaisons with the Japanese, including marriage, "It should be positively forbidden."[73]

Perfect English nonsense

Another example of mid-century pseudo-scientific pretense arrived in the form of a then-young Englishman, Houston Stewart Chamberlain. Born in Portsmouth, England, in 1855 and educated in France and Switzerland, Chamberlain eventually made his way to Germany. A mystic who preferred nature, the natural sciences, and astronomy, he became fluent in German and then a Reich citizen. After decades of an unfocused life, it was not until a nervous breakdown in 1896 (blamed on demons) that Chamberlain gained clarity and his life's mission. After his mental anguish led him to spend eight days shut up in a hotel room, Chamberlain synthesized his views and wrote the first draft of a book that encapsulated his one big idea: that race determined the fates of nations. The result, published three years later, was 1,200 pages long and a modest publishing success in Germany. *Foundations of the Nineteenth Century* theorized that the century then ending resulted from three inheritances: Greek philosophy and art, Roman legal codes, and Christ's personality. For Chamberlain, the only two pure races were Jews and Germans. (The Latins were a "chaos of peoples," he remarks.) As with Gobineau, Chamberlain gives "proof" of Aryan superiority by noting the Germanic conquering of Rome in the fifth century. It is there he thinks Teutonic destiny began, when German forces overwhelmed and controlled the legacy of antiquity, the Roman Empire.[74] In *Foundations*, Chamberlain is initially sympathetic to Jews, perhaps unsurprising given he identifies Jews as the only other pure race. He even condemns anti-Semitism as "stupid and revolting." He labels Jews as "different" but not "inferior" to the Teutonic race.

Yet, as William Shirer points out, Chamberlain then slips into the same anti-Semitism he condemns, creating a caricature of Jews and also denying Christ was a Jew, arguing instead that the Nazarene was an Aryan.[75]

The work of all three, Gobineau, Spencer, and Chamberlain, reinforced earlier-century dogma about assumed distinctions between pure Germans and everyone else, the presumed ethnic and cultural uniqueness that resulted from a mystical and mythical interaction of soil and culture. Their work was based on an unjustified leap from Darwin, but the pseudo-scientists anyway attracted much support for their conclusion: Races were to be kept separate for their own sake.

There was another late 19th-century addition to German notions about authentic culture and pure race—blood, of an aristocratic sort—from Julius Langbehn, an art historian and philosopher. In his 1890 book first published anonymously, *Rembrandt as Teacher*, Langbehn's nationalism was also racially exclusive but not for any and all Germans. Instead, Langbehn grouped together low Germans, the Dutch, many of the English, and even New Englanders as his preferred cohort. He excluded Prussians (already corrupted by the French, in his opinion) but also Russians and Jews. For Langbehn, Englishmen such as Oliver Cromwell, William of Orange, and William Shakespeare, along with Germans including Ludwig van Beethoven and Chancellor Otto von Bismarck were his archetypes, and also the Dutch artist, Rembrandt.[76] The low Germans and others had much in common because of their aristocratic nobility and pureness: "Blood is mightier than political nationality and mightier even than language," he wrote. "Blood affinity inescapably produces spiritual affinity."[77]

The art historian's work was a call for a new racial aristocracy, one opposed to fundamentally disruptive forces, be it capitalism, mechanization, and the barbarity of Prussian realism, which Langbehn thought chaotic and ugly. An aesthete but not a romantic, Langbehn instead saw refined heredity and aristocracy as key to a true nation. He imagined a unified, balanced, beautiful, and uncontaminated collective. *Rembrandt as Teacher* was an immediate success and a decades-long best-seller, with 13 printings in its first year. An expanded and revised version helped bring that total to 37 printings by the end of its second year. Then, after an interregnum of two decades, the book again soared in sales after 1918 and by 1945, *Rembrandt as Teacher* had been run through the printing presses 90 times.[78]

Nineteenth-century racial theories were spurious nonsense dressed in the language of science; but, unlike actual science, they lacked an empirical basis. Langbehn himself would abandon all such racial notions before his death in 1907, but the damage was done. The pseudo-scientific beliefs marched ahead. As William Shirer later wrote with reference to two pseudo-scientists, "both Gobineau and Chamberlain concocted racial doctrines so spurious that no people, not even their own, took them seriously with the single exception of the Germans."[79] Nonetheless, pamphlets and books about such topics as race and pure culture sold well in Germany. Gobineau's tome became the basis for clubs formed to discuss and promote his work, clubs named after him as one measure of his effect upon popular thinking. The English émigré, Chamberlain, was a member of one such society and it was there he received his initial inspiration and from which he reinvented Gobineau's racial theories for a new generation. Chamberlain's own book sold 60,000 copies within 10 years and multiples of that over the coming decades, especially when resurrected as policy by the National Socialists[c] in the 1920s and beyond.[80] As historian David Vital writes, such works allowed Germans to believe that "the principal determinants of men's inner moral nature, no less than their actual conduct, were inborn, carried down relentlessly from generation to generation."[81] From the notion of uniqueness, observed through the prism of race, a hierarchy could then be established, a mischievous notion pregnant with disaster, one soon to be a problem for Germany and then the world.

A self-reinforcing ecosystem of blame into the 20th century

Such pernicious notions soon spread into other aspects of German life and culture in the closing decades of the 19th century and then the early 20th. The German obsession for cultural and racial purity became ever-more evident in its paranoia about "infection." For example, orientalist and polymath Paul de Lagarde desired to replace Christianity and Judaism with something more authentically German. In the arts, Wilhelm Heinrich Riehl's 'Place and People' novels and Wilhelm von Polenz's *The Peasant* (1895) and Hermann Löns' *The*

---

[c] Chamberlain would die six years before the Nazis came to power, but not before meeting Adolf Hitler in Bayreuth in 1923. As William Shirer pointed out in *The Rise and Fall of the Third Reich*, Chamberlain was thrilled to meet Hitler. It renewed his hopes that his racial theory might influence a new German generation, and he joined the National Socialist Party soon thereafter.

Werewolf (1910) depicted Jews as grasping and immoral, as creatures who would steal land from virtuous peasants.[82] Composer Richard Wagner did for music what early 19th-century thinkers did for nationalism: suffused it full of romantic notions of an early, mythical Germany left pure and uncorrupted by others.[83] Even Germany's growing conservationist movement, the forerunner to modern Greens, rejected German Jews as not sufficiently German: Jews were too involved in industry and capitalism, too urban and cosmopolitan. With their deep attachment to a pure natural environment, the early Greens rejected industry and high finance (the latter synonymous with Jews such as the Rothschilds). Thus, urban centres such as Berlin and Vienna, full of landscape-disrupting commerce and industry, were despised by the greens as "Jew cities."[84]

The myth of Versailles victimhood

Germany's century-long simmering culture of purity, fear of foreign influences, and resentment was to run directly into the Great War, the war loss, and the subsequent Treaty of Versailles. The combination would exacerbate the narrative that outsiders were always at Germany's throat. As with many who think themselves victims, the notion that Germans might bear some responsibility for their world and anything wrong in it was often absent. Instead, others were to blame. After Germany's 1918 defeat, many Germans asserted the nation had been betrayed by its own Weimar government who agreed to an armistice in November 1918 and the subsequent Treaty of Versailles in 1919. The first was blamed on deceitful politicians accused of having "stabbed" the German military in the back; the second was attributed to the victorious allied powers.

Both additions to the German victim-cult were helped along, unwittingly, by the British. On the "stab in the back" accusation, the phrase originated not with Germans but a British general, Sir Neil Malcolm. Shortly after the armistice of November 11, 1918, General Malcolm dined with the German general, Erich Ludendorff, in Berlin. Over dinner, Ludendorff rolled out complaints against the German people (unworthy of the traditions of a fighting people, he argued) and against the Reich government (they failed to support the army and him personally). In response, the British general rhetorically crystallized Ludendorff's litany of grievances: "You mean, General Ludendorff," asked Sir

Malcolm, and with skepticism and not endorsing the notion according to one account, "that you were—*stabbed in the back*?" At this, the German general's eyes lit up in "fierce enthusiasm" and responded, "That's it exactly! We were stabbed in the back, *stabbed in the back!*"[85]

After the exchange, Ludendorff repeated the phrase over the new few months to family, friends, and acquaintances. It eventually became part of the official testimony of Field Marshall Paul Hindenburg, called to give evidence at a parliamentary inquiry into Germany's war loss in November 1919 to a government commission investigating the war loss. Hindenburg informed the assembled commission that "Our repeated request for the maintenance of stern discipline and the strict application of the law, met with no results."[86] He continued: "Our operations in consequence failed, as they were bound to, and the collapse became inevitable… As an English General has very truly said: *The German Army was stabbed in the back.*"[87] That was not actually General Malcolm's view, but it was too late. German victimhood was now officially expressed. Victimhood had gone viral.

It was a notion helped along by the premier economist of the age, John Maynard Keynes, the official representative of the British Treasury at the Paris Peace Conference until early June 1919. In Keynes' book, *The Economic Consequences of the Peace*,[88] first published in December 1919, the economist gives additional deadly ammunition to Germans already convinced that their own government had betrayed them. Keynes' charges against the treaty signed on June 28, 1919, were essentially threefold: First, Germany could not afford the amounts demanded and some were an exaggeration while other amounts demanded (pensions for British war widows and orphans) were unwarranted; second, attempts to enforce payments might ruin the economic interdependency of Europe and thus even the ability of Germany to repay lesser amounts; third, the costs of the damage done by German troops in France and Belgium had been exaggerated. All of it, in the view of Keynes, led him to believe the Treaty had been unfair to Germany.

This was a popular postwar theme, but mistaken. The treatment accorded to Germany was little different than past indemnities demanded by Germany when she had been victorious. France had paid reparations to Germany in 1815 and 1871.[89] Also, as historian Sally Marks points out in her 1978 work *The Myths of Reparations*, the evidence points in the opposite direction. Article

231, the "war guilt" clause as it is known, makes no actual mention of war guilt, and German allies such as Austria and Hungary never interpreted that clause as assigning guilt.[90] Other evidence hollows out the claim that Germany was treated unfairly. After the war, by August 1919, the allied powers delivered more than a million tons of food and "more than a hundred thousand tons of clothing, soap and medical supplies" to Germany, writes historian Lindley Fraser, "a larger total than went to any other country in the whole of Europe."[91] It was, in effect, a mini-Marshall Plan, akin to the post–Second World War rescue that aimed to reconstruct Europe rather than leave her bereft of industry and starving. Even the Keynes claim that Germany could not afford the demanded reparations was false. Germany kept its tax rates lower than those of the victors precisely to aid just that specious argument.[92]

The best postwar analysis of Germany, Versailles, and the allies came not from Keynes in 1919 but from a French critic, Étienne Mantoux, decades later. Educated at the London School of Economics and Oxford and Princeton Universities and who served in the Second World War,[d] Mantoux' book was written in the early 1940s and published posthumously. *The Carthaginian Peace—Or the Economic Consequences of Mr. Keynes*, is a reasoned rebuke to Keynes' exaggerated and often hysterical claims. Mantoux matches the earlier economist statistic for statistic. He also shreds some core Keynes' assumptions. One example: On Keynes' notion that Germany could not afford to pay the reparations, Mantoux notes that while Keynes thought he had demonstrated Germany could not be expected to pay £100 million per annum, "How then," asks Mantoux, "could she find many, many times as much to finance rearmament on a scale adequate to beat the combined forces of the Democracies?"[93] Nor, as Keynes also alleged, was Allied policy to blame for the hyperinflation that followed in Germany after Versailles. German leaders had already planned to deflate the mark precisely to avoid the actual costs of the reparations.[94] "The astronomic inflation which ensued was a result of German policy, not the occupation itself," wrote Marks. "The inflation enabled the German government to pay off its domestic debts, including its war debts, in worthless marks."[95]

---

[d] The reference is to the 1923 occupation of Germany's Ruhr coal mines by the French, who were attempting to force Germany to make good on treaty-promised deliveries of timber and coal to France. By January 1923, those had been withheld in part or wholly 34 of 36 times. The occupation would last until 1930. (Sally Marks, *"The Myths of Reparations," Central European History, September 1978, 11 (3), 252*).

Over the course of the 1920s, Germany would pay far less than anything discussed in 1919, decided on in 1921, and renegotiated on multiple occasions in the ensuing years. Germany would pay just 20 billion marks, far less than the 132 billion marks announced by the Reparation Committee in April 1921.[96] Even a portion of that was borrowed from foreign lenders, the debts later repudiated by Adolf Hitler once in power.[97] "Germany could have paid a good deal more if she had chosen to do so," wrote historian Marks, "but Germany saw no reason to pay and from start to finish deemed reparations a gratuitous insult."[98] Germans saw themselves as victims once again, only this time helped by the British and Lord Keynes in that complaint. As Mantoux more accurately diagnosed it, "there is not one single clause in the Treaty of Versailles that can be considered as an act of revenge."[99] That was not how Germans, steeped in the theology of victimhood and whose ritual blame of others, saw it.

And they would soon have a high priest to absolve them of responsibility altogether; an obscure German corporal would soon reinforce what aggrieved Germans already believed: The outside world was to blame—all of them—liberals, Bolsheviks, the British, Americans, and the Jews.

CHAPTER 8

Adolf Hitler:
(Self-professed) Victim

It was the fault of the 'entire social order'.

—KARL DIETRICH BRACHER, describing Hitler's 1906
reaction in Vienna to a losing lottery ticket,
in *The German Dictatorship*

The victim of Versailles

There was never a shortage of Germans willing to decry Versailles, but Adolf Hitler was the actualization of festering German insecurities, conceits, and grievances. He would adroitly exploit those and the Versailles Treaty on his path to the chancellorship. In his prison-written statement, *Mein Kampf*, published in two parts in 1925 and 1926, the future leader of the National Socialists and later German dictator wrote of how the Versailles Treaty was useful to remind Germans of their believed, beleaguered state: "What a use could be made of the Treaty of Versailles…!" he enthusiastically observed. "How each one of the points of that treaty could be branded in the minds and hearts of the German people until sixty million men and women find their souls aflame with a feeling of rage and shame…"[1]

Whether close to power or far away, Hitler relentlessly promulgated the accusation that Germany was unfairly treated. In September 1929, while the Nazis were yet a minor party in the Reichstag, with just 12 seats, Hitler teamed with the German Nationalist Party to draft the Law Against the Enslavement of the German People. The bill proposed to end reparations agreed to a decade earlier, to repudiate the Versailles-era admission by Germany that it was responsible for the war. He proposed to subject leading politicians to charges of high treason if the government agreed to new financial obligations.[2] Submitted to the Reichstag via a referendum, the bill barely garnered more than the required ten percent of the electorate if it was to be sent to the German parliament. It was anyway soon eviscerated by German lawmakers. Nonetheless, the draft law was a propaganda coup for Hitler; it gave him a platform on which to decry Germany's ostensible victimization.[3]

Hitler's anti-Versailles propaganda was effective because it manipulated German perceptions of the Great War and also German insecurities but also paralleled his own notion that he was a victim of others. After his failure in the 1923 Beer Hall Putsch, which led to his imprisonment, his initial reaction, one demonstrated throughout his life, was to blame others. As one biographer of Hitler, Ian Kershaw, writes, Hitler "had no trouble in assigning the blame to the mistakes, weakness, and lack of resolve of all the leading figures to whom he was at the time bound. They had betrayed him."[4] Nine years later, in a 1932 conversation in Dusseldorf, Hitler remarked that Germany's misfortunes were not really due to Versailles but stemmed from domestic weakness that allowed such onerous conditions to have been imposed in the first place. "We are not the victims of the treaties, but the treaties are the consequences of our own mistakes," he asserted. In other words, if only German citizens would reform their characters in a direction sought by the National Socialists, the nation would be less likely to commit such errors in the future.[5]

While using Versailles domestically to rouse support, Hitler also manipulated foreign sentiment. Aware that since John Maynard Keynes, many in Great Britain possessed large doses of war guilt, the potential to exploit it was rife. As historian Allan Bullock writes, remorse over Versailles allowed Hitler three propaganda advantages: It invoked sympathy for Germany as unfairly treated, it allowed Hitler to appear as the "representative of reason and justice," and the German leader could invoke the Wilsonian principle of self-determination against erstwhile naysayers of German nationalism.[6] "Nationalist resentment was an essential part of Hitler's stock-in trade," writes Bullock.[7] Thus, in a Reichstag address on May 17, 1933, and just before a disarmament conference in Geneva, Hitler portrayed Germany as a victim and played on both foreign sympathy and foreign guilt. In his "Peace Speech" Hitler portrayed Germany as unfairly treated if other countries, France in particular, did not soon follow Germany's mandated disarmament and remarked on the "injustice" of the dichotomy. With a view to Germany's forced disarmament, the German chancellor asked rhetorically how long it could continue to "be imposed on a great nation?" [8] Later that year, when the French made clear their policy was unchanged, Hitler announced Germany was withdrawing from the disarmament conference and also the League of Nations. "As a continually defamed people, it would be hard for us to stay within the League of Nations,"[9] remarked Hitler, in a threat before the actual withdrawal in October of 1933. Germany, Hitler protested, had suffered "an intolerable humiliation!"[10]

Hitler was a master at manipulating the guilt-feelings of others and especially the British. Four days after his Reichstag speech, Hitler repeated the humiliation charge to the British newspaper, the *Daily Mail*. The German chancellor told the *Mail* correspondent that given that almost all National Socialist leaders were combatants in the previous war, himself included, no one in his party desired "renewal of the horrors of those four and a half years."[11] Despite Hitler's nationalist views, ones that mimicked Herder and the other 19th-century philosophers who viewed citizens more as "cells" in the national body and less, if at all, as individuals, Hitler claimed that "Our youth constitutes our sole hope for the future." He asked the reporter rhetorically, "Do you imagine that we are bringing it up to be shot down on the battlefield?"[12] Sidestepping any German responsibility, Hitler informed British readers that whether Germany had been responsible for the Great War or not, his country bore the consequences. But that was the past and now it was "intolerable for us as a nation of sixty-five million [to be] repeatedly dishonoured and humiliated." Such "discrimination" against Germany, Hitler told the *Daily Mail*—and by extension Great Britain's public and politicians— must end. [13]

Hitler's insecurities combine with German neuroses

Hitler's belief that others conspired against Germany's greatness was calculated and effective at home and abroad. But it would be a mistake to think Hitler's bellicose airing of grievances were mere contrived scenes in multiple acts for a tyrant seeking power. It was that but never only that. For one, Germany's obsession with cultural and racial purity was also evident in Hitler's thinking, and the pair produced a toxic match. His reasons illustrate his own horrific, internal logic, ones that flowed from the stream of 19th-century German nationalism. This belief originated with Gobineau and Chamberlain, whom Hitler acknowledged as his inspiration. In conversations with the onetime Sturmabteilung (SA) head and then economic adviser, Otto Wagener, in June 1930, Hitler expounded on such influences: "The only people entitled to discuss racial questions are those who have read Gobineau and Chamberlain."[14] As Hitler continued in his conversation at the Bube Hotel in Bad Berneck, "Anyone who can't manage to summon up the time and understanding for such reading proves that he does not have the right to take part in debates on this deeply serious problem."[15] Thus, the pseudo-science that Hitler imbibed, as with the other Germans who subscribed to 19th-century racial theories, contributed to the German penchant for fear and paranoia about supposedly impure cultural and racial influences.

Germany's longstanding victim narrative twinned with Hitler's own resentments, which stemmed from his own insecurities: his lack of a university degree or even a high-school graduation certificate. Anxiety from that propelled Hitler's need to be seen as an intellectual. It is the reason why *Mein Kampf* was so verbose, ponderous, and dull. As historian Bullock observes, Hitler's "thwarted intellectual ambition, the desire to make people take him seriously as an original thinker," helps explain "the pretentiousness of the style, the use of long words... all the tricks of a half-educated man seeking to give weight to his words."[16] Describing Hitler's moods and vanities, Bullock remarks that,

> Resentment is so marked in Hitler's attitude as to suggest that it was from the earlier experiences of his Vienna and Munich days, before the war, that there sprang a compelling urge to revenge himself upon a world which had slighted and ignored him. Hatred, touchiness, vanity are characteristics upon which those who spent any time in his company constantly remark. Hatred intoxicated Hitler. Many of his speeches are long diatribes of hate—against the Jews, against the Marxists, against the Czechs, the Poles, and the French.[17]

A similar observation comes from another historian, Henry Ashby Turner Jr., who edited the memoirs of Otto Wagener, who had close ties to Hitler between 1929 until 1933. In Turner Jr.'s characterization of that work but also the memoirs of Albert Speer and others, he concludes the following about Hitler: "A half-educated, self-taught man laden with prejudices, with a preference for pseudo-science and a penchant for spinning out theories."[18]

Liberals, foreigners, and Jews: Hitler's narrative of blame

If Hitler had merely been a lazy, lightly educated, ill-tempered racist crank, he might have ended his life writing diatribes to German and Austrian newspapers decrying Jews and sharing those and other commonly held prejudices of his era but without much consequence, much in the way some 9/11 "truther" will obsessively post crackpot theories to the Internet today about who "really" was to blame for the collapse of the Twin Towers in New York City, or "birther" theories about where Barack Obama was *really* born. Fatefully, for Jews, Europe, and then the world, Hitler shared many Germans' entrenched, century-long paranoia for viewing others as *de facto* injurious to Germany. His spell-binding oratorical abilities also meant the population also had a champion to push back against Germany's ostensible mistreatment, a modern-day Barbarossa. In 1932, in explaining why he would never marry, Hitler told of how he possessed "another bride!—Germany!" and of how he was sworn to defend the good German *volk*, because of the "suffering, tormented by the accursed provisions of the Versailles Treaty, tyrannized by the enemy occupation and by foreign rule to the east and the west."[19] Germany was, as it had been since the early 19th century, the victim. It now had a long-awaited saviour in Adolf Hitler.

This combination of a century-long pathological fear of cultural, economic, and racial infection, and the second coming of a Barbarossa, only deepened Germany's pathology of blame. Hitler had a list of people, forces, and nations responsible for Germany's self-imagined, sorry state. One oft-forgotten target: Western liberalism and capitalism. Hitler saw all such influences as a scourge. They were, in his mind, inevitably connected with Jewish influence and control of others—the influence of 19th-century philosophers, pseudo- scientists, and anti-capitalists again influencing the Austrian corporal's thinking. Also, liberalism and an open economy allowed for individuals to flourish. That was opposite the German notion of the collective as necessarily supreme and which assumed a strong centralizing government (and all-powerful leader) not just in political affairs but also in economic and social matters. In the mid-

1930s, Hitler expounded on the problem as he saw it, on the need to replace the "egotistical spirit of profits of the individual with a communal striving directed to the interests of the entire community."[20] In language that could have been clipped from interviews with Occupy Wall Street protesters 80 years later, Hitler argues liberalism and open economies had betrayed all but the very rich. "The liberalism of the industrial states—their claim to freedom and independent control of property and jobs on the part of their employers—has been converted into its opposite!"[21] he exclaimed. "Nowadays, the only beneficiaries of liberalism are the elite; the masses... are the servants and slaves of the few. The quest for profit is supreme.... The owners of private capital, the great industrial magnates, the trusts control the state."[22]

Other countries and their perfidy were also accorded responsibility for German woes. In February 1938, the Austrian chancellor Kurt von Schuschnigg met with Hitler at his mountain retreat, Berghof, in the Bavarian Alps near Berchtesgaden. In response to the Austrian's request that the two countries' 1936 agreement remain the basis for the understanding between the two states, Hitler raged that "The whole history of Austria is just one uninterrupted act of high treason."[23] For the German chancellor, the larger power had suffered at the smaller entity's very suggestion of continued independent actions based on a treaty. Similarly, when planning for the invasion of Czechoslovakia and in his Nuremberg speech on September 12, 1938, Hitler decried what he saw as unforgivable actions by Czechoslovakia to preserve its territorial integrity. Hitler thundered to the Nuremberg rally that "You will understand, my comrades, that a Great Power cannot... suffer such an infamous encroachment upon its rights."[24] Thus, even as Hitler prepared to invade other countries, any resistance was met with the outrage of a narcissist denied his claim to the territories of others.

Germany's victimization becomes personal

During the Second World War, Hitler regularly portrayed Germany as the victim, maligned and molested by other nations. Hitler would even claim Germany had been forced into the destructive war against its will. On Germany's invasion of Poland in September 1939, Hitler said "It was in any case unavoidable; the enemies of German National Socialism forced it upon me as long ago as January 1933."[25] Hitler also assigned fault to the British for not siding with Hitler's tyranny, thus presumably avoiding war.[26] "If fate had granted to an ageing and enfeebled Britain a new Pitt instead of this Jew-ridden, half-American drunkard [Churchill]," groused Hitler, "the new Pitt would at once have recognized that Britain's traditional balance of power would now have to be applied… on a world-wide scale instead of maintaining European rivalries."[27] The United States and its leader were even tasked as responsible for the war that Hitler began. In a 1941 conversation with a Spanish diplomat, Hitler remarked that the American president Franklin D. Roosevelt was the "the arch-culprit for this war."[28]

Hitler also saw himself a victim because of his upbringing, and this in a comparison to Roosevelt. In reacting to the American entry into the war, in a speech on December 11, 1941, the German chancellor compared his upbringing with Roosevelt's: "[A] world-wide distance separates Roosevelt's ideas and mine," railed Hitler. "Roosevelt comes from a rich family and belongs to the class whose path is smoothed in democracies. I was only the child of a small, poor family and had to fight my way by work and industry."[29] This was an exaggeration. Hitler was the child of a middle-manager civil servant with a decent pension. He lacked for little and his own problem was that he disliked hard work. One teacher recalled Hitler as "cantankerous, wilful, arrogant, and bad-tempered," and one who lacked "self-discipline" and was "lazy."[30]

For Hitler, other forces were always at work in the background, by which he meant capitalism and Jews, indistinguishable in his mind. "In this war everything points to the fact that gold is fighting against work, Capitalism against peoples, and Reaction against the progress of humanity" asserted the German Fuehrer. "Even the support of the Jewish race will not avail the others."[31] Later, again remarking on Great Britain and Winston Churchill, Hitler was unable to conceive, as one might expect of a tyrant continually in denial and who was at this point (in early 1945) losing a war, that he faced a superior civilization: Great Britain, founded on vastly different assumptions than those prevalent in post–Enlightenment Germany, on the worth of individual as superior to that of the collective and state. Nor could Hitler grasp or admit that in Churchill he faced a worldly man of substantially more experience in battles, wars, politics, and life. Instead, Hitler retreated to his faulty, one-dimensional, conspiratorial understanding of forces and motives. For the German chancellor, the prime mover of democratic nations and the motivation of prime ministers and presidents was always the same: Jews.

The Fuehrer sacrifices the *volk*

This notion of Germany's victimization by others is a constant but of additional significance near the end of the war. Earlier, Hitler's ravings could be attributed to his penchant for propaganda and attempts to manipulate the public at home and the public, press, and politicians abroad. But as the German war machine neared the end, there was little value in such an approach. It is more likely that Hitler's expressed thoughts reflected his actual views. In February 1945, Hitler turns on allies and even his own population, the nation he once referred to as his "bride." Germany's southern European ally, Italy, was at fault: "Our Italian ally has been a source of embarrassment to us everywhere… we missed the bus thanks to our Italian allies."[32] The German public, in theory united with the ruler *a la* Herder's theory of an organic, collective state and which in practice was forcibly fused since 1933 with Adolf Hitler, were now failures with the Fuehrer, the aggrieved victim. In March 1945, in perhaps the most telling statement, Hitler orders Albert Speer to carry out the complete destruction of Germany. As Hitler and Speer argue over the order—that all material, bridges, trucks, communications, food supplies, anything in the path of oncoming allied forces were to be destroyed, and no matter the effect upon the German population—Hitler's contempt for his own people is undisguised. In arguing with Speer, Hitler makes it clear that the lives of the German people are dispensable: Hitler separates himself from Germany to stand alone but not to accept responsibility. He instead does so to damn others and collapse Germany akin to Samson's destruction of the pillars to which he was tied. In his final assignation of blame, Hitler makes clear who is at fault: "If the war is to be lost, the nation also will perish. This fate is inevitable," he tells Speer. Hitler then marks out the German people for denunciation and death: "The nation has proved itself weak."[33]

In the final week of life (Hitler and Eva Braun would together commit suicide on April 30, 1945), Hitler's belief in his own victimization is complete and rises to the surface one last time. After Herman Göring, the founder of the Gestapo, sent a wireless on April 23, 1945, to inform Hitler that he, Göring, was assuming the nation's command in accordance with a June 1941 decree (should Hitler be incommunicado or killed), Hitler lapses into raging self-pity before revoking permission and ordering Göring arrested: "An ultimatum! A crass ultimatum!" he protests. "Now nothing remains. Nothing is spared to me. No allegiances are kept, no honour lived up to, no disappointments that I have not had, no betrayals that I have not experienced—and now this above all else."[34]

In his will and in his testament, Hitler blames the war he began on Jews, capitalists, and the British. "It is untrue that I or anybody else in Germany wanted war in 1939," argues the German dictator soon to take his own life, and writes how "I have exhausted my time, my working energy, and my health in these three decades."[35] At the end, Hitler complains as if to give one last self-pitying howl into the hellish fires he alone lit: "Nothing remains. Every wrong has already been done to me."[36]

Adolf Hitler, who initiated and demanded a genocide and set the world ablaze with war, yet believed himself a victim.

CHAPTER 9

Rwanda's genocide and the Hutu grievance culture

*The ethnic ideology and policies of the Hutu-dominated
governments from the 1960s to 1994 [cast] the Hutu as the victim
and the Tutsi as the invader of Hutu land and the oppressor, thus
making him the scapegoat of the two Hutu governments' failures.*

—AMIABLE TWAGILIMANA, *The Debris of Ham*

Prelude to a massacre

As the Falcon 50 lifted off the tarmac at Dar es Salaam to leave behind the
sticky humidity of Tanzania's largest city, the airplane's VIP passenger,
Rwandan President Juvénal Habyarimana, was likely reassured in his selection
of seatmates. Back in Rwanda, his allies were increasingly erratic and their
loyalty in doubt. Some asserted the president had betrayed the Hutu cause;
so, perhaps as insurance, the president invited Elie Sagatwa along for the two-
hour flight.

Sagatwa, the president's brother-in-law, was part of the extreme Hutu
leadership, which had called for violent action against Rwanda's Tutsi
population; the Burundian president, another ally and also a Hutu, was also
on board. Surely the Rwandan president's political opponents would dare not
attack him while he travelled with fellow Hutus.

Before they left Dar es Salaam the three Hutu leaders had discussed the
Arusha accords, the peace treaty meant to bring a measure of calm to Rwanda.
The agreement was designed to end the country's on-again, off-again civil

war, the one that began in October 1990 with an invasion by the Rwandan Patriotic Front (RPF), a Tutsi-dominated militia based in neighbouring Uganda. Problematically, the deal gave radical Hutus in Rwanda a reason to believe the president had gone "soft" on the Tutsi minority.

It was an odd suspicion: In power since a 1973 coup he instigated as then-minister of defence, Habyarimana was part of Rwanda's ethnically charged problem. The president had long justified discrimination against Tutsis via ethnic quotas, and the president's inner circle was dominated by Hutu extremists. That included his wife, Agathe, who helped found a radical anti-Tutsi political party. And the president's own private guards were linked to death squads.[1] Besides, Habyarimana's own enthusiasm for the Arusha accords was underwhelming. In 1992 he derisively referred to the draft peace proposal as "pieces of paper." He continued to veto progress negotiated to and agreed to by his foreign minister. More recently the president had only agreed to negotiations with the opposition after pressure from abroad. Even after Habyarimana signed the peace agreement in early August 1993 he stalled on its implementation. The peace accord, meant to take effect 37 days later, was still orphaned by the spring of 1994.

Such anti-Tutsi rhetoric and action should have reassured the president's radical Hutu allies. Instead, that Habyarimana signed *any* deal with the opposition and the belief that his economic policies "favoured" the Tutsis were reason enough for the even more extreme Hutus to suspect he was no longer a soulmate in the extreme politics then enveloping Rwanda.[2] In a threat pregnant with foreshadowing, the head of the country's military intelligence agency warned that too many concessions would provoke a coup. He said the military itself would kill any Hutu politician responsible for such agreements.[3]

So, in the early evening of April 6, 1994, and while the president's pilot prepared for the final descent into Kanombe airport near Kigali, witnesses on the ground saw two surface-to-air missiles soar skyward. The first struck a wing and the second hit the plane's tail. The president's Falcon 50 burst into flames, spun out of control, and crashed into the garden of the presidential palace. It exploded on impact and splintered into a thousand bits of metal, fuselage, and flesh.

Rwanda's descent into 100 days of hell had just begun.

Africa's Switzerland

Before that antithesis of a spring when up to one million Rwandans were murdered by strangers and neighbours alike,[4,5] only African specialists and a few Germans and Belgians with an academic recollection of their countries' historic involvement could likely have conversed at length about "Africa's Switzerland." The reference was to the central African country's misty hills and green valleys. But if Rwanda had an un-African geographical description, it was also unique in that Rwanda was largely the legacy of a precolonial kingdom.[6] While many African nation-states resulted from colonial map-drawing, Rwandans were not an artificial entity dreamed up in Brussels, Berlin, London, or Paris. In centuries past, even Arab slave-traders had been unable to successfully invade Rwandan territory because much of the central and eastern parts of the country was centrally organized under a monarchy with militias who rebuffed most would-be invaders.[7] Instead, Rwanda for much of its history was a relatively independent success story that organically evolved with peoples and borders that resulted from local and not international events.

Given that history, a high degree of unity should have enveloped the country, as had happened with other, mostly undisturbed states. So why did this central African country end up known not for that history but for a genocide?[a] To answer that and before detailing how Rwanda's decades-long grievance culture descended into mass murder, consider other possible explanations including the country's pre-existing sometimes violent divisions and favouritism in the colonial era.

Ancestral animosity

One possible explanation for the 1994 genocide comes from Rwanda's own pre-colonial history, the assertion that Rwanda's three main ethnic groups—Hutu, Tutsi, Twa—were always destined to clash, this because of diverging early paths. Here some background is helpful: Hutus and Tutsis arrived in the region between the 10th and 15th centuries A.D. and lived off agriculture and cattle herding, respectively. (The latter occupation matters, as it allowed

---

[a] Pre-genocide, estimates pegged the Hutu population at between 84% and 90% of Rwanda's population, Tutsis between 9% and 15%, and the Twa at 1%.

Tutsis to garner more wealth, prestige, and then political power over the Hutu in subsequent centuries.) The smallest cohort in Rwanda was the hunter-gathering Twa; the most widely accepted accounts estimate their arrival in the Great Lakes region of central Africa in the eighth century B.C., so before either Hutu or Tutsis.[8,9,10] Divisions between all the groups were exacerbated later due to monarchical skirmishes and the creation of an army. For example, historian Jan Vansina points to a culture of violence in the 19th century that's rife with feuds, frequent betrayals, and assassinations among Rwanda's aristocracy where "everyone threatened everyone else."[11] The reign of Rwabugiri (1853–1895), a particularly vicious Tutsi king who believed any and every accusation and killed anyone who ostensibly threatened his reign, is a cogent example.[12] One entire lineage, a rival clan to Rwabugiri's, was wiped out in 1869. In 1870 the Queen Mother, Murorunk, blinded a pretender to the throne and massacred inhabitants in the Cyingogo region; she herself was murdered in 1876 with her assassins killed four years later and their female relatives later "persuaded" to commit suicide.[13] "The nearly permanent recourse to violence finally engendered so much tension and created such a climate of insecurity among the common people as well as among the elites," writes Vansina, "that it succeeded in dissolving the cohesion of even the most basic social groups. Everyone reacted by resorting to violence himself, hoping thereby to rid himself of one's enemies and to build up wealth so as to obtain more power."[14]

Other scholars point out that Rwanda's historical divisions were real but not rigid, that "Tutsi" initially applied to only a fraction of Rwandan herders and that early "Hutu" labels were short for rural boorishness or the loutish behaviour of the elite,[15] and that such labels only became distinct over time.[16] Historian David Moshman wrote of how "[t]he distinction between Hutu and Tutsi was a fluid one, "based on a combination of ancestry and socioeconomic status, including the ownership of cattle. Rwanda was a single society in which Hutu and Tutsi lived among each other, spoke the same language, shared religious beliefs, and intermarried."[17] Journalist André Sibomana, writing in 1999, agreed with such sentiments but thought the divisions starker because of what we might today call class differences: "The Twa tended to be hunters or potters, the Hutu were farmers and the Tutsi were cattle-keepers or traders—

and there was a hierarchy among them,"[18] wrote Sibomana.

Some ethnic hardening might have resulted from the formation of an army in the late 18th and early 19th centuries and where "Tutsi" applied to combatants and "Hutu" to non-combatants. Another change around 1870, a new system of agricultural exploitation, imposed tenant-like assumptions on families on arable lands, often Hutu. They were often forced to work two of every four days on property owned by provincial chiefs. That requirement was not imposed on the mainly Tutsi herders.[19] Those developments further calcified the Hutu-Tutsi categories and resentment. However, Vansina argues that when considering Rwanda's divisions—early migrations, economic activities, court service, warrior status, the army or chief/labourer divisions— "there is no doubt that present-day Rwandans really encompass three different biological 'populations' and that whatever scenario is adopted to account for this fact, the differences among the groups run so deep that they must extend back millennia rather than centuries."[20] Correlation does not equal causation, though, and 19th-century violence, an ethnic divide, and economic differences are not, on their own, proof of a definitive cause-and-effect "first mover" for genocide in the late-20th century. It would leave unexplained how other countries with deep ethnic, religious, or tribal cleavages did not produce genocidal catastrophes. Early violence and divisions in a society may make it easier for some to wreak havoc; but such events and facts are not sufficient to explain the leap to genocide.

European influence

Another possible explanation is found in German and then Belgian influence, as Rwanda's colonialists are sometimes advanced as a significant reason for the eventual deterioration and division in Rwandan civil life. In this account, German colonialists and missionaries who first arrived in Rwanda in 1897 came upon an already divided society and made it worse. They were followed up by the Belgians who scooped up Rwanda from the Germans, in 1916, during the First World War.[21] Relative to the Belgians, this argument is made by the Ugandan author Mahmood Mamdani, who argues that "It was not until Belgian colonialism that the local state structures were fully Tutsified, and that Tutsi hardened into a category signifying local privilege."[22] Others also assert that such colonialism and associated policies intensified the friction between Hutu and Tutsi.[23]

Both the Germans and Belgians did assume Tutsi superiority, that they were "destined to rule"[24] over Hutus. Under Belgian colonialism in particular and with the influence of the Roman Catholic Church, the pre-colonial ethnic divisions were arguably exacerbated. That was partly due to the church monopoly on education and also its involvement in Rwandan political life; both gave the institution significant power over intellectual development in the country and also real political influence. Thus, Tutsi favouritism was helped along by the local bishop who, along with others, advanced the Hamitic hypothesis, a popular racist theory that held that the minority Tutsi population were, class-wise, a step above others.[25] Said one Belgian Catholic cleric in the 1920s: "Generally speaking we have no chiefs who are better qualified, more intelligent... than the Tutsis."[26] Examples of special treatment followed: The first Catholic school for the sons of mostly Tutsi chiefs appeared in 1919 and in the 1920s five state schools were reserved exclusively for the sons of Tutsi chiefs.[27] Many Hutu chiefs were deliberately removed from power by the Belgians in 1926 and replaced with Tutsis—a "grave error," as one missionary later put it.[28] Perhaps not surprisingly, a few decades later, most Rwandan chiefs were Tutsis: "All the officials were Tutsi... in 1959, I think there were maybe two-sub chiefs were Hutu," recalled one colonial administrator.[29] Also, most often cited as evidence of European-entrenched ethnic division is how the Belgians introduced identity cards in 1931, this to identify able-bodied men and to count taxpayers but which listed ethnicities: Twa, Hutu, or Tutsi.[30]

On this basis, some blame Europeans for the calcification of Tutsi privileges and thereby creating the conditions for Hutu resentment and later revenge. Yet allegations of unrelenting favouritism for Tutsis during the Belgian colonial period are simplistic. As scholar Elisabeth King writes, "The variation and saliency of ethnicity does not mean the differences between Hutu, Tutsi and Twa were unimportant, or that they were inventions of colonial powers as some have later come to claim."[31] Or as Sibomana wrote in 1999, "It was not the whites who invented the words Hutu, Tutsi and Twa, nor did they invent the traditional ways of thinking. The whites conceptualized differences which they observed."[32] Also, in the early colonial period, most Catholic schools admitted far more Hutu than Tutsi students.[33] As one man who began his schooling in 1937 later recounted, there was just one school in Kigali and the school enrolled children of all varieties, Hutu, Twa, and Tutsi. That produced social cohesion, not division.[34] Rwandans interviewed after the genocide who attended school in the 1940s and 1950s recalled Hutu and Tutsi children at "school together in class seated on the same benches, playing together."[35] Teachers also recalled the ethnic-blind reality: "In schools, children were just children. We never wrote students' ethnicities on the forms," said one Belgian missionary.[36] By 1959, 250,000 Rwandan schoolchildren came from a rainbow of backgrounds.[37] Whatever errors attributed to the Germans and Belgians, to link colonialists to the 1994 genocide forgets that pre-existing ethnic divides were anyway present and that colonial influence ended two generations before the mass killings. Thus, the notion that early-20th-century colonial-era policy is a dominant factor in an end-of-century genocide also fails as a sufficient explanation.

The post-independence narrative of blame

Pre-colonial violence and imperial-era preferences mattered, but neither alone can explain the ensuing genocide; such elements also exist in other societies without ever descending into genocide. A more complete explanation needs to examine the state-sponsored grievance campaign—propaganda—that allowed for a psychological preference to form and made a unified and forward-looking Rwanda a much more unlikely outcome. Over three decades, the notion of Hutus as victims of the Tutsi minority became a constant in Rwandan public life because of the state's involvement in exacerbating that belief. Also, as with other propaganda campaigns, it helped that there were some statistical data and real instances of past discrimination to buttress the charge of past Hutu victimization by Tutsis and previous colonial powers. For example, the first Rwandan Hutu to graduate from university was Anastase Mukuza, in 1955, and after returning to Rwanda from Congo he was told his degree was not recognized. The young graduate was repeatedly rejected for public sector employment and ended up a typist and then an administrative assistant. Unsurprisingly, Mukuza was radicalized because of such treatment and became a leading figure in the post-independence government.[38]

In particular, as often drawn on in grievance narratives, the presence of statistical disparities between groups is taken as sure evidence of discrimination. Causal or not, the gaps in statistics are then used to justify new discrimination, this time against new individuals in the groups accused, in the past, of having benefited from the previous discrimination. In Rwanda, the new government run by Hutus after independence took steps to "correct" such statistics. They include how, in 1956, Tutsis represented 17% of the population but 32% of the enrollment in primary schools and also recorded greater proportions in higher education.[39] Politically, in 1959, the year of the social revolution (a violent Hutu uprising),[40] only 1 of 82 chiefs and 50 of 1,050 vice-chiefs were Hutu, with the rest Tutsi.[41] In 1962, in one town, in Butare, one researcher found that 46% of Tutsi children and only 13% of Hutu possessed more than five years of education.[42] In 1964, five years after the Social Revolution in which the Hutu rebellion against Tutsi and Belgian overrule began,[43] Tutsis made up almost half the country's administrative positions and over half of all secondary school teachers.[44] In the 1960s, on average annually, Tutsis made up 90% of the enrollment at the National University of Rwanda.[45]

The individual stories, statistics, and initial responses from the Tutsi leadership provided fodder for Hutu grievances, evident as the inevitability of decolonization approached. "The Hutu intelligentsia were experiencing acutely relative deprivation, of being excluded from power and resources in the postwar era,"[46] is how one academic described the social setting in the 1950s.

Meanwhile, Hutu nationalism arose not only from a frustrated Hutu counter-elite[47] but also from below, from the masses.[48] "Both traced economic problems among the poor to a 'racial' tension," i.e., vis-à-vis Tutsis.[49] "Suddenly [the Hutu] viewed the Tutsis not only as a race but as a foreign race, a race of conquerors who had imposed their domination over the Hutu and had to be driven out of the country," wrote Sibomana, referencing mid-century political life. Meanwhile, the Tutsi leadership was in denial about the magnitude of the problem and refused to address Hutu grievances until late in their rule.[50]

By the time of Rwanda's social revolution in 1959, it was clear that Rwanda's

Hutu leaders were intent on reversing Tutsi dominance with a blame narrative providing kinetic energy to that end. "The Hutu party viewed the Tutsi as a race of foreigners and colonizers who had exploited them...,"[51] noted one observer about the late 1950s. The previous approach to race inculcated by the Hamitic thesis—Tutsis were claimed to be distinct in origin, separate, and superior—now reversed: Hutu leaders portrayed the Tutsis as indeed separate, as outsiders intent on keeping Hutus down.[52] "It was the [Hutu's] turn to adopt the ideology which some Tutsi had used to justify their dominant position and to refuse all notion of power sharing,"[53] writes Sibomana. Gregoire Kiyabanda, soon to be Rwanda's first post-independence president, articulated just this position in a 1959 speech: "Our movement is for the Hutu, who have been insulted, humiliated, and scorned, by the Tutsi invader... We must ignite the masses; we are here to restore the country to its proprietors; this is the country of the Hutu."[54]

Reverse victimization, grievance propaganda, and social justice

A turnover of state-sponsored advantages from one cohort to another often invigorates those newly in power. However, the desire to overturn statistical advantages runs the risk of misinterpreting why those advantages accrued, and not necessarily always due to past discrimination. The political desire to ensure perfect statistical equality is also unhelpful for people that wish to move into a colour-, race-, and ethnicity-blind future. But in Rwanda, state policy after independence ramped up the grievance culture. Hutu leaders were obsessed with the past and with achieving statistical perfection in the present. That combination was evident early on.

In 1959, the opposition party, Parmehutu, soon to take power and composed mainly of Hutus, issued an education manifesto demanding that the racial identification of children in schools be recorded.[55] In 1960, Parmehutu's Tenth Congress passed a resolution in favour of "ethnic redistribution."[56] The rationale was that too many students in high school and college, as well as in the main teacher training school, were Tutsi.[57] According to one senior Hutu leader, such numerical tracking and rhetoric was justified because the Hutu had been disadvantaged for 400 years. The point of the 1959 social revolution, he asserted, "was to try and stop the injustice."[58] Similar to other African nations after independence, those deemed not indigenous were targeted: "Rwanda is the country of the Bahutu," declared the leadership of Parmehutu in 1960, "and all those, white or black, Tutsi, European or from other origins [must] let go their feudal and imperialist goals."[59] With the 1961 elections and independence from Belgium (effective in 1962), the now-Hutu government attempted to reverse numerical Tutsi advantages and effort began in earnest: Ethnic quotas were introduced for education beyond elementary school,[60] with Tutsi enrollment also to be limited in universities and government posts to reflect only the Tutsi proportion of the general population.[61] The policy was known as *iringaniza* or "social justice."[62] The government made clear to all, including one former missionary, that just as the Tutsi excluded Hutu that "[the Hutu] were going to do exactly the same thing."[63]

The Hutu government's obsessive counting of statistical Tutsi advantages would continue and was soon paired with a long-lasting propaganda campaign, and the drive to level out statistical differences between Hutus and Tutsis would end up with Orwellian descriptions: "Ethnic rebalancing," "clearing off," removing a Tutsi "surplus,"[64] and "ethnic equilibrium."[65] Also, in the early 1960s, the "cockroach" (*inyenzi*) slur first appeared. Those in government initially used the label against Rwanda's first independence party, the main opposition party, which was made up mainly of Tutsis. Over time, the "cockroach" tag was applied to all Tutsis. Along with another unflattering label, "snake," the language was another way to dehumanize Tutsis.[66] The epithets were pockmarked by violence and political killings. In 1962, Hutu mobs killed between 1,000 and 2,000 Tutsi in the region of Byumba.[67] In early 1963, the few Tutsi members of the national cabinet were fired and, after a show trial, executed for complicity with *inyenzi* terrorists." In December 1963, a Hutu politician in the Gikongoro prefecture called for assassination of the Tutsis and, in a foreshadowing of events three decades later, armed Hutu groups with spears, clubs, and machetes killed at least 5,000 children, women, and men. Other estimates put the figure as high as 8,000, about 20% of that prefecture's Tutsis. The violence spread with another 14,000 Tutsi killed in nearby regions.[68] The English philosopher Bertrand Russell labelled the organized killings as "the most horrible and systematic human massacre that we have witnessed since the extermination of the Jews by the Nazis."[69] It made no difference to the Hutu leadership. In 1964, in a Kigali speech, President Kayibanda warned that if Tutsi militias in the neighbouring border areas ever made it to Kigali, the total and sudden end of the Tutsi race would be the result.[70] In total between 1959 and 1967, as many as 20,000 Tutsis were killed while another 200,000 fled Rwanda.[71] After 1964, while Tutsis were still permitted, tenuously, to work in other occupations, politics was now decreed off-limits for any Tutsi who wished to live.[72]

The 1970s: An ongoing numbers obsession

By the early 1970s, impatience with the slow reversal of Tutsi advantages—they "still" accounted for half the enrollment at the post-secondary schools and universities—led to a student movement known as "Committees of Public Safety." In fact, the vigilante groups were under the direction of the country's security and intelligence agency and, in 1973, such committees led attempts to purge all Tutsis from secondary schools, teaching colleges, and universities.[73] Tutsi teachers were also targeted. "I remember, it was my grade five class," recounted one student. "The teacher was teaching, and when he saw a vehicle [from the Committee of Public Safety] pass, near class, he had to hide."[74]

With government backing and lists of Tutsis, the movement spread to government ministries and hospitals. The private sector was also pressed to dismiss Tutsis employed in banks, stores, and other businesses.[75] As with the early 1960s violence, the purges developed into pogroms. In the Gitarama and Kibuye prefectures, Tutsi houses were burned, the residents told to flee, and several hundred people were killed.[76] The 1973 assaults on Tutsis only stopped after Defence Minister Major-General Juvenal Habyarimana overthrew President Grégoire Kayibanda. He dissolved the constitution and turned Rwanda into a *de facto* single-party state and, for a time, concentrated on the economy.

Hatred history in Rwanda's schools: Indigenous vs. Tutsi

The political propaganda was accompanied by official educational polemics, which assumed Hutu victimization and the necessity of making modern-day Tutsis pay. For example, the post-1962 official history taught in Rwanda's schools included a romanticized notion of pre-Tutsi harmony in Rwanda, one where indigenous hunter-gatherer Twa were later joined by the Hutu who "cleared the forests and developed agriculture" and where both lived in harmony.[77] That was, until Tutsis were cast as late arrivals in this Hutu version of history, and who arrived as interlopers and villains.[b] Journalist Sibomana summarized this post-independence version of Rwandan history taught in the schools:

> The Tutsi came last… [and] cunningly seized power which until then had been in the hands of the Hutu. They imposed an oppressive, feudal system of monarchy and used the presence of Belgian settlers to consolidate their power. The situation lasted until the Hutu peasants were finally freed from serfdom, first by the social revolution of 1959 and the declaration of a republic and then by independence.[78]

This post-independence narrative where Hutus were superior because of indigenous innocence was thus no more satisfactory than the *pre*-independence version where Tutsis were presumed superior because of intelligence, but Hutu indoctrination produced its intended effect: the relentless propaganda that ethnicity soon had its intended divisive and deleterious effects on Rwanda's children. One Hutu, Émilie, recounted how children who did not know their ethnicity would be teased by other children.[79] Another, Jean-Marie, related the official educational history of the Hutu, Tutsi, and Twa: "[The teachers] wanted to show us how the Tutsi were bad… how the Tutsi mistreated the Hutu in years past."[80] Children were taught that "Rwanda was for Hutu. They are Rwandan. The others, it is for them to stay in Ethiopia."[81] Those in primary school lessons were warned that Tutsis wanted to "continue injustice and oppression," that Hutu were the long-time victims of Tutsi, all of whom were wealthy.[82] In reflecting on such propaganda post-genocide in 2002, Jean de Dieu Mucyo, who would later become the Rwandan minister of Justice,

---

[b] The Hutu claim to have arrived "first" in Rwanda deepened the country's divisions and also conflicted with another narrative, that Europeans were at fault for ethnic tensions because of past favouritism and Belgian-imposed identity cards. But the two claims could not both be accurate. If Europeans were to blame for the exacerbated divisions and on spurious grounds, i.e., that differences based on ethnicity were not conceived of before the Europeans arrived, and if that was the root cause of Rwanda's race problem, then the other attempt to isolate Tutsis by noting their later historical arrival should have made no difference to the Hutu radicals. Instead, all Rwandans, Tutsi or Hutu, should have been united in their opposition to the *ethnic label system introduced by the European colonialists*. Conversely, if the Hutu leadership was on solid ground to assert later arrivals to Rwanda, the Tutsis, did not have the same claim to true Rwandan citizenship, then later European "labelling" in Rwanda via the 1931 identity cards could make no difference. Interlopers are interlopers no matter the label applied, when, and by whom.

recalled his childhood education and how he was made aware of supposed Hutu-Tutsi differences:

> The teacher asked us [the class] to stand in two lines face to face. He asked if we looked the same. We laughed because we had the same life, traveled to the same school, wore the same clothes. The teacher told us we were not the same: he compared our heights and noses. Then our class was divided: long noses on one side, flat noses on the other. We had not been aware of our ethnic identity... but after this incident we no longer played together....[83]

One professor from Rwanda's National University later recalled that "Education rendered a disservice to generations," noting how students were forced to stand up and state their ethnicity.[84] By the 1970s and 1980s, even the educational material being produced by former Belgian and Catholic administrators flipped. Their previous promotion of Tutsis as superior flipped and were now "invaders from the north," who had conquered the indigenous Hutu inhabitants to "colonize" and "oppress" them.[85]

The education system's curriculum of victim-laden blame history was illustrative of the Hutu leadership's obsession with the past and victimization. As one interviewee noted after the 1994 massacres, history was not meant to be recounted as an objective, dispassionate chronicling of the past, but in the service of propaganda, this to reinforce the Hutu government's narrative of blame: "The way a teacher could teach history was not really history but 'hatred history'" recalled one student.[86] The result was a further entrenchment of grievances, with Hutu children trained to fear the Tutsis. Children were told Tutsis would one day wrench power back from Hutus.[87]

The young breathe in assumptions of which they are mostly unaware, and children from Rwanda's first post-independence generation, the ones subject to 1960s and 1970s educational propaganda, were no different. As scholar Elisabeth King concluded in her review of government education policy between 1962 and 1994, the education system contributed to "categorizing, collectivizing and stigmatizing Hutu and Tutsi into distinctive groups."[88] Tutsis were presented as "needing to bear collective responsibility for past Tutsi actions." The relentless propaganda romanticized the Hutu as indigenous, peaceful, and pure while Tutsis were invaders, conquerors, advantaged, and grasping for wealth. The result was an entire generation inculcated in a victim narrative and primed for the later political and media assault on Tutsis. State propaganda poisoned civil society.

Fear and loathing in pre-genocide Rwanda

By the 1990s, the decades-long, propaganda-instilled fear that Tutsis would reappear to kill Hutus was reinforced by events. In October 1990, after the Ugandan-based, Tutsi-led Rwandan Patriotic Front (RPF) invaded Rwanda and sparked the civil war, Juvénal Habyarimana's government framed the invasion and conflict as an "ethnic war."[89] The Hutu regime also staged a fake attack on itself, in Kigali, the day after the RPF's invasion. Akin to the Nazi burning of the Reichstag in 1933 blamed on Jews, the Hutu government attributed the Kigali attack to the opposition, to Tutsis.[90] It was a useful pretext for the regime to harass political opponents. After 13,000 Tutsis were rounded up in a mass arrest, Habyarimana called them "accomplices."[91] Rwanda's autocrats defended the extralegal actions and argued Rwanda needed ethnic communities "you can trust." [92] It was a clear message that Tutsis were, according to the regime in Kigali, treasonous.

One week after the initial October 1990 RPF invasion, the regime itself organized a massacre in a northern town that egged on the locals to kill Tutsis; 300 were murdered and 500 homes burnt. Similar regime-inspired killings took place over the next several months, usually where the RPF had been active.[93] In 1991, a government military commission identified the country's principal enemies as "Tutsi inside or outside the country" and accused them of not accepting the 1959 social revolution. The Commission warned Rwandans that Tutsis planned to take power "by any means necessary."[94] In 1992, after a leaflet announced 20 prominent Hutus as assassination targets, massacres were organized and hundreds of Tutsis and others in the opposition in the Bugesera region were murdered.[95] It was an omen of what was to come.

The media propaganda

Nearer to the 1994 genocide, inflammatory media rhetoric was added to decades' worth of educational indoctrination and political propaganda. The radical newspaper *Kangura,* financed by the Rwandan president's information bureau, called for ever-more educational quotas to benefit the Hutu majority and demanded exclusive Hutu representation in the military, political, and administrative positions of government. That same year, *Kangura* published its *Ten Commandments for Hutu* that synthesized hatred of Tutsis with misogyny. Commandment One decreed that every "Tutsi woman, whoever she is, works for the interest of her Tutsi ethnic group."[96] The newspaper denounced Hutu intermarriage to Tutsi as traitorous while other commandments instructed Hutu to avoid business partnerships with Tutsi, asserting all were dishonest and interested only in the supremacy of their ethnic group. "Hutus," advised *Kangura*, should "stop having mercy on the Tutsi."[97]

One widely circulated bit of propaganda included the claim that 85% of Tutsis had changed their identity, this to escape the quotas in education and government. With Hutu fears it was given a more sinister sheen: Tutsis were said to be faking their true identity in pursuit of murderous aims, with Hutus warned they would soon be killed *en masse* by Tutsis unless Hutus fought back.[98] *Kangura* claimed that the opposition RPF had prepared a war that would decimate the Hutus and leave no survivors.[99] "The enemy is always there, among us, and only waiting for the right moment to try and liquidate us," warned *Kangura* on another occasion.[100] One popular singer, Simon Bikindi, warned of how Tutsis wanted to restore their pre-1959 monarch, and that Hutu belief ancestors had been victimized by the Tutsi "whip" and "lash" and that they too might be subject to Tutsi domination unless stopped.[101] Human Rights Watch summed up the Hutu-backed strategy in this paraphrase of the narrative: "Tutsi posed a danger to Hutu, who were always the victims, whether of Tutsi military power or of Tutsi cunning… and so Hutu had a right and a duty to defend themselves."[102]

Radio broadcasts added to the incitement: In March 1992, one Radio Rwanda journalist claimed Tutsi women were planning to assassinate senior Hutu leaders; listeners were encouraged to attack the Tutsi-dominated opposition parties.[103] The station also broadcast a story that claimed the Tutsi planned to assassinate 20 prominent Hutu leaders.[104] Another station, RTLM, begun by President Habyarimana and his allies in 1993, delivered regular messages of provocation. Its ethnic propaganda was accompanied by music from popular singers with lyrics such that also encouraged animosity against Hutus who did not subscribe to the notion that Tutsis were subhuman: "I hate Hutus, I hate Hutus, I hate Hutus who think that Tutsis are not snakes."[105]

The radio station was described as "a snappy mix of upbeat music, colorful patter and bloodcurdling threats against the Tutsi, along with instructions on efficient ways to kill with homemade weapons."[106] Announcers openly called for the killing of moderate Hutus. In January 1994, the radio station also demanded that listeners target any Belgians still living in Rwanda.[107]

In February 1994, as efforts to install a coalition government faltered, killers, gangs, militias, and their battles became regular features of life in Kigali. One RTLM announcer exclaimed that "The grave is only half-full! Who will help us fill it?"[108] In early April, on Easter Sunday just before the genocide began, one announcer twice predicted that "a little something" was soon to occur and listeners were told Rwandans hate Tutsi "in unison and to the bottom of their hearts." Tutsis were asked to ponder how realistic it was to think they might escape.[109] RTLM then turned against President Habyarimana, warning that "if the citizens don't want him anymore, he couldn't get to his office. It's impossible."[110] The warning was broadcast just days before his plane was shot down, the event that would finally unleash the decades-long effect of propaganda and which led to panic.

Propaganda turns to murder

Past divisions, the reality of historical discrimination against Hutu, the Hutu leadership's obsession with statistical disparities, decades' worth of state-inculcated victim thinking in the education system, a civil war which gave plausible credence to Hutu fears that Tutsis might once oppress Hutus, and propaganda which stoked fears and mob behaviour—all of it set up conditions for a perfect firestorm of genocidal fury. It led to actions that defy the most cherished, positive notions human beings have about each other, that some actions are off-limits, even in a civil war. Once Rwanda tipped into the 20th century's newest killing field, the past propaganda against those labelled bacteria, cockroaches, and snakes allowed for taboo-breaking and mass killing of the sort previously observed in Germany under Adolf Hitler, China under Mao Tse-tung, and in Cambodia under Pol Pot. As with those genocides, euphemisms were also used in Rwanda: "Communal work" meant killings, "bush clearing" referred to chopping up men, while "pulling out the roots of bad weeds" referenced the slaughter of women and children.[111]

RTLM radio hosts read out the names and addresses of those to be murdered, and the killings multiplied as did the stories of horrors:[112] One priest recognized several Hutu killers as former parishioners, including a member who wore prayer beads for good luck in finding Tutsis.[113] One Hutu moderate, Prime Minister Madame Agathe Uwilingiyimana, was violated with a beer bottle and murdered with other colleagues; an RTLM announcer giggled that the moderates must have "resigned or simply wandered away."[114] One Hutu woman spent an entire day on a river bank methodically killing, with a hammer, women handed over to her. A father refused to let his young son accompany him to the roadblocks where captured Tutsi were identified and killed. "But at least I can kill a child of my own age!" wailed the boy."[115] Stefan, a Hutu who took part in killing Tutsis in Ruhengeri, was himself a close neighbour to the only Tutsi in his area. "The two had shared beers, conversations, and chores over the years" and "were like friends," he later recounted. Despite the shared experiences, Stefan broke the Fifth Commandment and murdered his neighbour.[116]

Sibomana wrote of how Rwanda's killers "took the time" to invent the worst type of cruelty," simply to intensify the suffering. "In complete indifference… they stood around drinking beer calmly, watching their former friends literally dying in agony at their feet."[117] Canada's Lieutenant-General Romeo Dallaire, who led an inadequately supplied United Nations force, provided multiple examples in his later book: hundreds of men, women, and children hacked to death in a church; a priest who assembled with 200 parishioners to protect them but who were murdered anyway; children between 10 and 12 years old who participated in the murders; mothers with babies on their backs who murdered other mothers with babies; one pack of killers that walked into a church, snatched 40 children and murdered them in full view of the United Nations Forces, just to demonstrate they could without consequences. Post-death, indignities were committed to the bodies. They included mutilation and cutting off the heads to 'prove' how Tutsi heads really were physically similar.[118]

Then there were the sexual crimes noted in graphic detail by Dallaire: "The legs bent apart. A broken bottle, a rough branch, even a knife between them. Where the bodies were fresh, we saw what must have been semen pooled on and near the dead women and girls," he wrote.[119] "There was always a lot of blood… many women and young girls had their breasts chopped off and their genitals crudely cut apart…. It was the expression on their dead faces that assaulted me the most, a freeze of shock, pain and humiliation."[120] Nature itself was mauled by Rwanda's genocide, the eastern rivers packed with bodies, the 40,000 bodies pulled from Lake Victoria, the corpse-eating dogs that also attacked the living, the rats that grew to the size of a terrier after having feasted on human flesh.[121] Twenty years after the genocide as *National Geographic* chronicled in 2014, the country was still "oddly devoid of dogs." The canines had developed a taste for human flesh during the genocide. All had to be exterminated.[122]

Lies, damn lies, and murderous statistics

When in the 1950s Hutu elites properly asserted that one sliver of Rwandan society did not have the right to rule over all and demanded equality, the problem was not in the demand for access, or education, government jobs, or the right to run for political office if by that one meant equality of opportunity-seeking as opposed to a statistical equality imposed via politics.[123] A demand for equality of opportunity on a go-forward basis is foundational for a liberal society where individuals are cemented at the centre of law, policy, and rights. But to succeed requires a certain forgetting, to not measure, count, and award education or employment by race and ethnicity on a go-forward basis, but to treat individuals *as* individuals, as distinct from their families and ancestors, regardless of how each individual supposedly arrived at their current state. To do anything else assumes an omniscience not given to man. It is to presume that all historical factors can be accounted for, that all effects upon progeny measured, and that the state and its employees can "correct" for millions of past choices and millions of past variables. It is an arrogant assumption that asserts deity-like awareness.

Hutu discrimination mimicked popular notions elsewhere in the world: Racial, ethnic, and gender quotas as a supposed corrective to past discrimination, this as if dealing with perpetrators of the past by handicapping their progeny in the present was a recipe for societal peace. Nonetheless, even some Western academics later tried to explain away such divisive Hutu policy. They saw it as simply a reversal of government-decreed injuries when Tutsis and colonialists ran the country. Thus, in her otherwise excellent look at Rwanda's education system between the 1960s and 1990s, even scholar Elisabeth King justifies reverse discrimination: "Considering the Tutsis were significantly advantaged in access to many schools in the colonial period, establishing quotas to improve horizontal equity is understandable. Indeed, many countries support affirmative action to redress past discrimination and to ameliorate equality of opportunities in education and employment."[124] King, as with others who look at the collective and not the individual in such analyses, overlooked the inherent danger in an obsession with measurements between groups. It is an invitation to deepened grievances and unrest, and individuals are inevitably sacrificed once again. Most statistical obsessions with disparities do not lead to violence and murder; they always lead to discrimination against individuals and merely because they are now part of the wrong tribe.

That Tutsis were often economically wealthier and more successful in education, business, and government was true. But it was not solely or even mainly because of past political and religious favouritism. Even past discrimination is not all there is to statistical differences. It rarely occurs to those entranced with their own victim narrative or even academics that individual and family choices, cultural presumptions, historical events beyond anyone's control, and multiple other factors can influence the outcomes of ethnic groups over time. Tutsis, historically engaged in cattle ownership, for that reason alone would have had a centuries-long financial advantage over the subsistence farming engaged in by the majority of the Hutu, or over pottery makers (the Twa). Time and certain occupations—helped by discriminatory laws or not, colonialist or not—can lead to statistical disparities. The differences continue up to and until a dramatic change in a local economy occurs, or until those in the comparatively less wealthy cohort begin to pursue other means of making a living.

What victimization propaganda wrought

However past economic differences are credited or blamed for the Hutu-Tutsi distinctions over centuries, they were not insurmountable. Nor was past discrimination a guarantor of later mass murder: South Africa's blacks were discriminated against for nigh a century. Post-apartheid, black South Africans did not unleash a killing spree against whites even though actual victimization in South Africa dated not in decades or generations back but in years, months, and days. Whatever else one posits as a possible cause for the Rwandan genocide, none alone or even in combination provide a complete causal explanation; those other factors also existed in other countries. Something else was needed: a state-sponsored grievance culture tied to statistical perfection, and never-ending, propagandizing blame of living Tutsis for whatever sins were ostensibly committed by their ancestors, or colonialists.

The Hutu belief in victimization and the assumption of Tutsi collective guilt added an extra emotional "kick." It allowed Hutu leaders and citizens to ignore any own-person or own-culture failure. Instead of thinking about how to peacefully, productively bring all Rwandans up, the focus on redistributive quotas and blame instead focused on bringing Tutsis down. In demands for statistical equality and anti-Tutsi propaganda, which relentlessly kept past wrongs alive as if they occurred yesterday, integration and societal peace became impossible. No Tutsi could ever be seen as an ally in post-independence Rwanda. After all, "they" had benefited even though groups are not persons and individuals are not their ancestors. Those who practise politics courtesy of surface similarities, as if people are mere cogs in a collective, inevitably create additional injustices and new victims. To those infused with the notion of data counting by group, as if doing so relieves past injustices, individual Rwandans became mere numbers in a data table. And society itself became a *tabula rasa* upon which statistical outcomes could be inscribed if only enough will, if enough force, was applied.

Requiem: A different path was possible

In Rwanda, as in other victim-narrative cultures, the story trapped those in it and led them away from even modest introspection and away from a realistic understanding of history. It allowed Hutus to ignore how something as banal as subsistence farming or herding cattle in centuries past could produce wide disparities later, ones unintentional, accidental, and no one's fault. It allowed the Hutu population to avoid the possibility that their ancestors or they themselves could have made different choices. For Hutus, the subterranean belief in victimization justified an attempt to refashion statistical outcomes and power relationships at any cost and through any method. It created an expectation that could never be satisfied. It linked some Hutus' present condition to the past and the choices of others; it absolved present Hutus of their own responsibility. The self-radicalized Hutu leadership with an inward-

and backward-looking orientation desired and demanded statistical human sacrifices be offered up for past wrongs. Moloch-like, they would end up with actual blood and flesh on their altar.

Rwanda's victim cult was primed, present, agitated, and eventually murderous. The continual targeting of Tutsis as the reason for Hutu problems was advanced by at least three entities: politicians and their extremist allies, selected media outlets, and educators. Looking back, Amiable Twagilimana notes how the 1959 Revolution, "which promised to end the feudalism and colonialism of the Hamitic race (the Tutsis)… instead sealed the lethal binary antagonism between the Hutu and the Tutsi." He argued that the political history of Rwanda's since the 1950s was one of "antagonistic radicalization between the elite of two ethnic groups whose thinking was grounded in a fallacious and racist histography."[125] Historian Scott Straus wrote that, "There is little question that the military and political hardliners who controlled Rwanda's state during the genocide instructed subordinates and the population to destroy the Tutsi population."[126] The same author, who mistakenly roped in imperialism as a distant causal explanation, yet admitted with reference to 1994 and previous mass killings in Rwanda that "The elites in power [were] responsible for the recurring massacres."[127] Indeed they were, but they were responsible long before that. It was those same Hutu elites that propagated a divisive grievance narrative in Rwanda's schools, universities, media, and government, the ones who piled up dry timber for decades that preceded the conflagration, the genocide. Post-independence, Rwanda's educators, media, and rulers all advanced the belief that the Hutu were victims of the "cunning" Tutsi.[128] That belief never abated as it might otherwise have in a state dedicated to equality of opportunity and not dividing a society yet again. Long before any Hutu picked up a machete that fateful Easter week to avenge that same presumed history, assumed Hutu helplessness and a belief in utter victimization was complete.

Rwandans were continually counted, divided, and herded by ethnicity and prodded and primed with propaganda and paranoia; all of it was cemented in a deep grudge furthered by those in power over decades. The president's plane crash was the last, incidental event that allowed for a state-sponsored grievance culture to explode.

"Rwandans," as Andre Sibomana wrote of the tragic events of 1994, "became the people they had been taught they were."[129]

CHAPTER 10

Yasser Arafat:
Palestine's eternal Peter Pan

He had a permanent chip on his shoulder, an angry undertone that seemed to insist: "We are weak, and you have injured us. We are thus entitled to do whatever we want. No one can judge us or stop us. And you, for your sins, must pay and pay forever."

—BARRY RUBIN AND JUDITH RUBIN, *Yasir Arafat: A Political Biography*

Olive branches and AK-47s

As the chairman strode to the podium amidst applause, he must have marvelled at his good fortune.

Only a few years previous, he was *persona non grata*. Expelled from Jordan after King Hussein tired of the existential threat the charismatic revolutionary posed to the country, and to Hussein's own throne, the Palestinian leader found only a half-hearted welcome in other Arab capitals. From Riyadh to Cairo, and no matter their publicly declared support, others had privately tired of his arrogant assumption they owed him for his frontline attacks against Israel and Jews.

Arab rulers would often pay him what amounted to protection money. That would at least divert his terror from their thrones to other targets. Everyone understood the *realpolitik* bargain: Interests of state and power and not camaraderie were in play.[1] More surprising was the gun-toting orator's luck in escaping opprobrium for his terror: Just two years previous, in 1972, Black September, the terrorist cell linked to the chairman murdered eleven Israeli—Jewish—athletes and a German security guard at the Munich Olympics.[2,3]

More recent was a May 1974 terror attack in the northern Israeli town of Ma'a lot. There, Palestinian gunmen killed 21 children and injured 65 more.[4]

In an age closer to our own, a revolutionary who so recently fomented terror attacks directly or through comrades would be hunted to his death. But this was the early 1970s and radicals and terrorism were still *chic*. For the starry-eyed, terrorists and tyrants from Che Guevara to Fidel Castro were the international political equivalents of 1960s flower children: They promised to right the world's wrongs through slogans and revolutionary acts. For some intellectuals, such men of action had the potential to actualize their belief that ostensible unjust societies could be razed and restarted anew. For the cynical, murderous revolutionaries were necessary for the end goal: a Palestinian state, the death of Jews, or both.

And so, Yasser Arafat, chairman of the Palestine Liberation Organization (PLO), arrived at the United Nations and spoke of peace. His "dream," he said, was to live in "one democratic State where Christian, Jew and Muslim live in justice, equality and fraternity."[5]

As Arafat would demonstrate over the ensuing decades, the PLO leader mastered the triple act of posing for peace, offering up the Palestinian experience as one of unrelenting victimization, while himself threatening, ordering, and carrying out terror. The peace-terror duplicity only occasionally cheapened his political currency, but it was never devalued enough to make him a pariah in the manner of Carlos the Jackal or, much later, Osama bin Laden. Barely two years after the PLO attack in Munich, six months after Ma'a lot, and as yet another terror attack was underway in northern Israel,[6] the 35-year-old Arafat with a pistol at his side spoke to the United Nations General Assembly and to the world.

Jews were the chairman's direct target, but Arafat needed support beyond those reflexively responsive to his narrow tribal call; the multiple references were meant to convince the world that Palestinians were not the only victims but so too many in his audience. The Palestinian issue was placed in a wider narrative, in the touchstone of imperialism that would resonate with UN delegates from the third world. In a tack used regularly by Palestinian leaders over subsequent decades, the Palestinian wretched of the earth were pressed upon, and not just because some other nationalists (Zionists) arose in numbers large enough to wrestle control of land away from Palestinians.

For Arafat, the Palestinians suffered because a broader force was at work, one that many in the audience might have encountered firsthand: Western colonialism. Arafat could thus widen the appeal of his cause and half-justify occasional terror by framing the issue in deeper, structural terms. The appeal even allowed the PLO chairman to express *faux* sympathy for selected Jews: "Just as colonialism heedlessly used the wretched, the poor, the exploited as mere inert matter with which to build and to carry out settler colonialism,"[7] Arafat told UN dignitaries, "so too were destitute, oppressed European Jews employed on behalf of world imperialism and of the Zionist leadership. European Jews were transformed into the instruments of aggression; they became the elements of settler colonialism intimately allied to racial discrimination."[8] As would become common in the decades since, real and alleged problems were blamed on colonialists, with "colonialist," "settler colonialists," and "imperialist" peppered throughout his speech dozens of times along with "Zionist" as routine as punctuation.

Narcissism *in extremis*

Arafat's twinning of the Palestinian victim-narrative with the sociocultural explanation for the third world's failure then popular—past or present colonialism was to blame—offered a clear, simple cause for Palestinian woes: Western imperialism. It also provided a common target for diverse peoples the world over: the West and its armies, institutions, and governments. Arafat could thus justify the subsequent, explicit threat attached to the ostensible peace offering, should the oppressive imperialists and their Middle East proxy not sue for peace on Arafat's terms: "Today I have come bearing an olive branch and a freedom fighter's gun," said Arafat, "Do not let the olive branch fall from my hand."[9]

But Arafat was about to over-reach, as when he informed delegates that their troubles ranked second to his revolution. "The highest tension exists in our part of the world,"[10] asserted Arafat to the assembled diplomats as he elevated the Palestinian cause to the premiere tragedy of the age. But an abundance of calamities were in evidence, and many surpassed the suffering of selected Palestinians in 1948 and in the decades since: the wars and civil wars in Rhodesia, Vietnam, and Eritrea; the ongoing Sino-Soviet tension; the 1971 war between India and Pakistan;[11] the various communist-capitalist conflicts in central and South America; an armed-to-the-teeth, divided Europe; and the Cold War, with its ever-present nuclear-tipped tension and the possibility of cataclysmic conflict between the two superpowers. Then there were the world's other, awful misfortunes. In the 1960s, the decade just before the PLO chairman became a familiar face on evening newscasts the world over, almost seventeen million people worldwide died of famine.[12] Between 1968 and 1970, the years that bracketed Arafat's first year as chief of the Palestinian Liberation Organization, one million people perished in a bloody internecine conflict in Nigeria. Then there were the floods of refugees: In the spring of 1971, after a West Pakistan crackdown on East Pakistan (modern Bangladesh) and with the killing of several thousand intelligentsias, ten million people fled to India's state of West Bengal from East Pakistan.[13]

Bloodied Palestinian "thorns"

By the time Arafat gave his 1974 speech to the United Nations, all such events had long been front-page, top-of-the-hour news. The PLO leader skipped over them and another reality: how Palestinians *and* Jews alike suffered in the wake of Israel's independence. Claims to unique Palestinian suffering also ignored the reason Israel was proclaimed as a state: Jews had their own historic claim to some of the land, and for which the Holocaust quite properly generated international sympathy. Arafat also ignored how, post-independence, Jews suffered as much as did Palestinians. All such realities should have weakened any special "pity" category that might then be applied to only Arabs in the Levant.

First, Palestinian suffering: In January 1948, in Jaffa, two members of the Jewish terrorist Stern Gang packed a truck with explosives hidden among oranges and then drank coffee at a café, waiting, until 20 Arabs in nearby coffee houses were killed in the ensuing explosion.[14] That same day, Jerusalem's Semiaramas Hotel was bombed by Haganah, another Jewish paramilitary unit. The hotel, used by an Arab military wing, also contained 11 Christian Arabs and the Spanish consular representative. All were killed.[15] Also in January, Yosef Weitz, director of the Lands Department for the Jewish National Fund, made it clear he wanted Arabs expelled from what soon became Israel. In his diary and with reference to Arab tenant farmers in two mostly Jewish villages in north Palestine, Weitz wrote, "Is it not now the time to be rid of them? Why continue to keep in our midst these thorns at a time when they pose a danger to us?"[16] In April, as the conflict deepened in advance of Israeli statehood, Weitz diarized that "Our army is steadily conquering Arab villages and their inhabitants are afraid and flee like mice." He had no illusions about the effect of the shelling: "If we continue on this course—and we shall certainly do so as our strength increases—then villages will empty of their inhabitants."[17]

One of the more infamous "emptying outs" occurred on April 9, 1948, when 250 Arab civilians, mainly women and children, were killed by Menachem Begin's paramilitary terrorist cell *Irgun* at the Arab village of Deir Yassan. Begin would later argue that advance warnings were given, that many villagers escaped in time. Israel's future prime minister claimed the remaining Arabs were inadvertently caught in the crossfire as Jewish and Araba militias clashed. The Arab recounting is different, that the massacre was deliberate. As historian Conor Cruise O'Brien pointed out in *The Siege*, that was also the recollection of many *Yishuv* (the Jews in Palestine before the state of Israel was established) "outside the ranks of Irgun."[18] The displacement of Arab populations was not always the result of Jewish military tactics. In April 1948, after several Arab commanders abandoned Haifa, Arab residents fled despite entreaties by local Jews to remain. The exodus was encouraged by the Damascus-based Arab Higher Committee, which made it clear it intended to shell Haifa.[19]

Still, exceptions such as Haifa aside, many Arab evacuations were forced and with tragic consequences. In one example, 50,000 Arabs from Ramle and Lydda (now Lod) were expelled from their towns by a Jewish brigade attempting to clear the road between Jerusalem and Tel Aviv. Details of the brigade's approach were revealed decades later by Yitzhak Rabin. In his 1979 account of the battles at Ramle and Lydda, originally intended for Rabin's autobiography (with that section censored by the Israeli government but leaked to the *New York Times*), Rabin recounted his command of the Harel brigade. Assigned to eliminate Arab Legion bases in militarily sensitive areas, Rabin was encouraged by David Ben Gurion to use force if the inhabitants refused to leave willingly, and Rabin and a colleague agreed the expulsion was necessary to prevent attacks on their supply route. Villagers were forced to march up to 15 miles where the expelled Arabs would then meet up with the Arab Legion.[20] The expulsion led to an unknown number of deaths of children and elderly due to the intense heat.[21]

Dead Jews

Those three towns, Deir Yassan, Ramle and Lydda, were one slice of an estimated 450 Palestinian towns and villages that disappeared from the new state of Israel after its founding,[22] some of them bulldozed from geographical history.[23] But Jews in the region also suffered in the lead-up to Israel's founding and for years afterwards. On the evening of December 2, 1947, a Muslim mob attacked the Jewish quarter in Aden, setting fire to Jewish shops and attacking residents. Ten Arabs beat the owner of a small sewing shop, Salam Ben Yichye Terem, senseless. The attack ended only with Terem thrown off a building, which killed him. After three days of riots in Aden, 82 Jews perished; a synagogue and 106 of 170 Jewish shops were destroyed along with Jewish schools and hundreds of Jewish homes; 38 Arab rioters were also dead.[24] In the months before Israel's establishment as a state, the violence intensified. On February 22, 1948, a car explosion on Jerusalem's Ben Yehuda Street killed 55 people, mainly Jews.[25] On April 14, 77 Jewish nurses, doctors, and patients were ambushed and murdered; they had been making their way to Hadassah Hospital on Mount Scopus.[26]

The grisly rough equality of Jewish and Palestinian suffering

The suffering at Israel's founding and during the Arab–Israel war did not end there. After the November 29, 1947, United Nations declaration in favour of a Jewish homeland and the subsequent 1948 creation of Israel, early Jewish flight from Arab countries was comparable to the woes of Arabs who fled or were expelled from Palestine/Israel. In Aleppo, Syria, where 17,000 Jews lived,[27] half emigrated after a December 1947 pogrom.[28] Two years on, the Syrian government froze Jewish bank accounts and confiscated all their assets.[29] In Egypt, in a measure reminiscent of 1930s-era restrictions on Germany's Jews, post-1947 laws prevented Jewish engineers, doctors, and teachers from practising their professions;[30] Jews were also the subject of pogroms and property confiscations. By the late 1950s, half of Egypt's Jews had left in a modern-day exodus. As with those in Iraq and Syria, Egypt's Jewish community had been prosperous with assets worth millions of dollars but, forced to uproot themselves, they lost everything. Bank accounts were blocked, private and commercial property confiscated, business firms liquidated, and Jewish employees fired. Department stores, banks, and other businesses owned by Jews were snatched by the Egyptian state, as were Jewish schools, youth centres, old-age homes, welfare institutions, hospitals, and synagogues.[31]

In Iraq, the country was home to 135,000 Jews, one of the largest and oldest Jewish populations in the Arab world, with 77,000 Jewish residents in Baghdad, one-quarter of the city's population. However, post-1948 legal changes in Iraq put Zionists in the same category as anarchists and communists, which meant their very association with an outlawed group made them libel to imprisonment or capital punishment.[32] In 1949, the Iraqi government took steps to bar Jews from schools, hospitals, and other public institutions. By the next year 110,000 Iraqi Jews had applied to leave the country.[33] They were allowed only 50 kilograms of luggage at their exit and, as in Egypt, all other property was confiscated without compensation.

In the first four years of Israel's independence, over one-third of the Jewish population in mainly Islamic countries would leave or be expelled.[34] In a telling contrast to the decline in Jewish populations in Islamic and Arab countries after Israel's founding, Israel's Arab population rose to 167,000 by 1950 from 156,000 two years previous.[35] Beyond that stark difference that demonstrated which minorities in which countries felt safe and who did not, the numbers of those affected on both sides of the divide over the years would have a grisly, rough equality to them. Between 711,000 and 726,000 Arabs fled or were expelled during and shortly after Israel's creation;[36] over time, 786,000 Jews[37] would leave Arab or mainly Muslim countries.[38] Jews suffered, at least numerically as much as Palestinians.

The tragedy of Palestinian Refugees Inc.

While some initial Arab refugee-flows resulted from the Israeli–Arab war and the selective-but-forced expulsions by Israeli forces, the creation of Palestinian émigrés was a joint effort by Israelis *and* Arabs alike. Arab countries were determined to ensure Israel was stillborn, and despite the postwar United Nations resolution that granted nationhood to two nationalities. That ensured additional Palestinian refugee flows and a permanent status as such, and the ongoing refusal of the Arab states to recognize Israel or to integrate Palestinian migrants ensured there would never be a shortage of Palestinian refugees. For many Arab leaders, permanent Palestinian victimhood was just good politics.

As Barry Rubin wrote in his 1994 book on the history of the PLO, almost everyone had a reason to keep the Palestinian refugee matter alive and as an ever-present tragedy. "There was something for everyone in maintaining the fiction that the Palestine question was the region's central, overwhelming issue, rather than internal conflicts and rivalries among and within Arab states."[39] After initial attempts to reclaim the West Bank, Jordan's King Hussein had little interest in allowing Palestinians to fully integrate and for a variety of reasons: an underperforming economy but also sectarian loyalties. For Egypt or Syria, operating in realpolitik time, it was politically advantageous to forever hang the spectre of refugees at Israel's doorstep. All three countries derived propaganda benefits, without which their own populations might more closely examine their own national, societal, and leadership failures, this while it was the United States that kept Palestinians alive and fed. (For example, in 1978, 40% of the aid budget for Palestinian refugees came from the United States.[40]) As for double standards, Qatar, Kuwait, and Syria denied citizenship to Palestinians while Saudi Arabia tried to keep Palestinians out entirely.[41]

By 1974, when Arafat spoke at the United Nations, 26 years had passed since Israel's birth. By then, the pattern of normal refugee flows should have resulted in a permanent resettlement of the Palestinians in other countries, as had occurred for some, but a full integration in nearby states was prevented by Arab governments. The unwillingness to absorb actual victims of the Israeli–Arab conflicts in a manner as did other countries meant that, half a century later, in 2007, the United Nations estimated that five million Palestinian "refugees" lived inside Jordan, Lebanon, Gaza, Syria, the West Bank, and East Jerusalem. Roughly one-third resided in what the United Nations labelled as refugee camps.[42] After 1948, the continuing intended victimization of Palestinians was the policy of most Arab governments and thus their permanent refugee status not the fault of Israel, the United States, or the assumed imperialist West. The claim to refugee status decades after Israel's founding was, in any historical context, a stretch. It was as if, in the early 21st century, émigrés who fled Hungary after the 1956 invasion by the Soviet Union, those who fled Vietnam in the later 1970s, or as if Cubans who left Fidel Castro's island gulag on a raft and settled in Florida were still labelled refugees decades later.

The notion of permanent Palestinian refugees was a construct, but a lasting one nonetheless. While the flows were substantial in 1947 and 1948, the Palestinian experience was not unique. It was comparatively dwarfed by other migrations in the 20th century. Between the early 1920s and into the 1930s, the Soviet Union shipped 1.7 million kulaks, mostly but not solely from then-Soviet Ukraine, to Siberian gulags.[43] During and after the Second World War, the flood of refugees forced to resettle outside their ancestral lands swamped the numbers later seen in the Levant. In 1939, the German and Soviet annexation of Poland meant one million Poles were forcibly deported from Poland by both powers.[44] Amidst the Second World War and its immediate aftermath, 12 million people, including Ukrainians, Poles, Belarussians, and others, were forcibly expelled or fled from the Soviet Union and Poland.[45] Post-war, it was the turn of Germans to suffer. With Stalin's plan to expel his enemies from his newly acquired spheres of influence, 12 million ethnic Germans were expelled from Eastern Europe by the Soviet Union and client governments between 1944 and 1950.[46] On the other side of the world, in 1947, 14 million refugees were on the move after the partition of India as Muslims fled India and Hindus escaped Pakistan.[47]

After 1948 and in subsequent Israeli–Arab conflicts, Jews increasingly migrated from Muslim-dominated countries and integrated elsewhere, some in Israel and some as far afield as Canada and Argentina. Despite their own roots in Arab and Persian societies that pre-dated Islam, Jewish populations moved *en masse* and gave up the notion, permanently, of ever returning to their homes in Egypt, Jordan, Syria, Iran, and Iraq. For Jews, there was no talk of permanent refugee status; compensation was also not forthcoming for those forced to abandon almost everything they owned, including ancestral homes. The Jewish refugees moved on, resettled, and created new lives in locales as diverse as Tel Aviv, Paris, Buenos Aires, New York, Montreal, and London, among others. The result and another telling contrast: By 2017, Arabs numbered over 1.8 million or nearly 21% of Israel's population.[48] But seven decades after Israel's creation, only 3,400 Jews yet resided in Arab countries in North Africa, with 2,200 of those in Morocco; in mainly Muslim countries such as Iran and Indonesia, there were just 8,500 and 100 Jews, respectively. The West Bank possessed the largest cohort of Jews in a mainly Muslim territory, with 393,000 out of a population of 2.9 million, or just over 13%.[49]

The Israel–Arab battles of 1948 and beyond produced tragic consequences for all and left real victims among both Arabs and Jews. They suffered in almost equal numbers, but only Palestinians were viewed as permanent refugees, in large measure because it suited the political agendas of Arab and Islamic leaders and international institutions such as the United Nations.

Colonialism, victim thinking, and the decline of the Palestinian economy

Arafat's 1974 UN speech intertwined his grievance and economic claims in a tight blame-Israel narrative. Arafat attacked not just Israel's initial 1948 establishment and boundaries and then its possession of territory captured in the 1967 Six Day War. He also excoriated Israel's economic success and Western capitalism, which he linked with colonialism and imperialism. Thus, Arafat demanded that the "plundering, the exploitation, the siphoning off of the wealth of impoverished peoples must be terminated forthwith."[50] For Arafat, any Israeli success came at the expense of Palestinians and was the cause of Palestinian poverty: "If we return now to the historical roots of our cause we do so because present at this very moment in our midst are those, who, while they occupy our homes as their cattle graze in our pastures, and as their hands pluck the fruit of our trees, claim at the same time that we are disembodied spirits, fictions without presence, without traditions or future," complained Arafat, who twinned a justification for intransigence with ongoing refugee status. "We speak of our roots also because until recently some people have regarded—and continued to regard—our problem as merely a problem of refugees."[51]

The image of Jews plucking fruit from Palestinian trees was powerful. It helped ensure the Palestinian diaspora would be less inclined to relinquish the claim to a right of return. It was compelling given that at the time of Arafat's speech in 1974 the establishment of Israel was a living memory for most Palestinians.[a] Arafat's economic assumption was flawed though he was not the first to assume a zero-sum approach to the economy in the Levant or anywhere else. The mid-20th-century left-wing journalist, I.F. Stone,

---

[a] Arafat's tree reference also possessed some little-noticed irony, given that the Jewish-majority state managed to make the desert bloom courtesy of the Jewish National Fund shortly after Israel's founding and then, later, via government policy. In all, 240 million trees would be planted over the decades. See: Israel Environment, Israeli Ministry of Foreign Affairs, https://bit.ly/2y9kAp1.

claimed conditions for the development of capitalism in Palestine were hardly ideal, noting what was available was a "tiny rim" that was "mostly desert, marsh and eroded hills."[52] Writing in 1948, Stone pointed out that costs were high and that Jewish immigration fuelled a speculation in property prices that drove costs even higher. He also remarked on the challenge given the environmentally damaging treatment of the land in the past: "The investment of capital, labor and devotion to restore a land that had been despoiled by centuries of ill treatment was too enormous to be profitable."[53] Except Israelis did just that, increasing per-capita GDP seven-fold to $31,701 by 2016 (from $4,192 in 1950),[54] and not because Israel's land was more fertile or more valuable compared with other plots of geography in the region; without oil, Israel's land was worth considerably less than nearby Middle Eastern states with which Israel was occasionally at war. Israel anyway managed to create a modern, functioning economy and a higher standard of living.

If Stone correctly identified the challenges to Israel's development, though blind to what the kibbutz model could initially accomplish and the significant, subsequent potential for capitalist development, Arafat's economic vision was one incapable of expansion at all until the politics of the Israel–Palestinian matter were settled to his satisfaction. Arafat's attribution of colonialism as the root of all economic evil had it backwards: In Israel, the land was transformed first by the kibbutz model and then by capitalism. Arafat wrongly assumed economic progress courtesy of labour and investment by others (Israelis of Jewish *or* Arab extraction) was exploitation instead of an improvement. As with his zero-sum view of peace—if Palestinians were perennially in a revolutionary phase it must mean Palestinians were constantly attacked—so too Arafat's economics: If Israel prospered, it must mean Palestinians had been robbed. (It was also consistent with Arafat's belief, also enunciated in his 1974 speech, that "a radical alteration of the world economic system" was necessary for third-world countries to develop.[55]) In this narrative, Palestinians were always the victim. Arafat could not or would not grasp other plausible explanations: first, that a permanent cessation of hostilities depended at least as much on the Palestinian leadership as Israel's; second, that prosperity might be an independent variable of modern capitalism and unrelated to 1948 and what land Jews did or did not take from Palestinians, that it mattered more what Arabs or Jews did *with* the land pre- and post-1948 and also their concurrent openness, or opposition, to capitalism.

For instance, the historical record rebukes Arafat's limited view that Palestinian control of the West bank and Gaza were necessary for prosperity. Israel's occupation after 1967 allowed for economic opportunities and not deprivation for Palestinians, regardless of Arafat's mistaken link between sovereignty and the economy. For the modern reader more familiar with post-2000 terror—and then barriers, walls, and highly restricted travel and trade between Israel and the West Bank and Gaza— contemporary accounts are startling. Writing in 1973 to commemorate the 25th anniversary of Israel, Walter Eytan wrote of how the Arab population in the West Bank and Gaza "is more prosperous and probably freer, than at any time before, bound by increasingly close economic and personal ties with Israelis. Something like 40,000 of these Palestinians work each day in Israel."[56] Eytan's comments could be seen as self-serving, an apologist for an occupying force, except that, in retrospect, the numbers back him up: Per person GDP in the West Bank/ Gaza rose from $1,607 in the Six Day War year of 1967 to $1,993 by 1973, and this adjusted for inflation, this while neighbouring Jordan's per-person GDP dropped from $6,294 to $4,915 in the same period.[57] Additionally startling for a 21st-century reader is the lessening of terrorism and the positive transformation of Gaza: "Where formerly unemployment was endemic and terrorism rife," wrote Eytan, "today every able-bodied person can find work either in Israel or the Gaza Strip itself (where in fact a labour shortage prevails at the present time) while terrorist action for the most part belongs to nightmare of the past." He continued: "Every Palestinian Arab has been able to see for himself the benefits of normal, constructive coexistence with Israel…"[58] Historian Martin Gilbert would later note what was obvious at the time Eytan wrote: That below the surface of increased Palestinian prosperity, Arabs resented the occupation and their own stunted national ambition. Eytan was nevertheless correct about the economic expansion in the territories in the early 1970s.

Enter the messiah leader-as-victim

Such economic progress was to be undone by Arafat and other Palestinian leaders who focused on the right of return, grievances, and terror, soon after Arafat and the Palestinian Authority were given control of the West Bank and Gaza in 1994. The grievance-inspired, non-economic focus led to an unnecessary negation of the West Bank and Gaza's unique geographical and economic advantages in the region, including access to Israel's much larger economy. At the beginning of the Second Intifada, in 2000, the economy of the Palestinian territories was just $4.3 billion; Jordan's was $8.5 billion, while Israel's GDP was $121 billion.[59] Palestinians needed Israel much more than Israelis needed workers from the West Bank and Gaza. Before the Palestinian Authority and Yasser Arafat assumed control in 1994, Israel employed 120,000 Palestinians in Israel proper, fully one-third of the Palestinian workforce in the West Bank and Gaza. By 1995, the number of Palestinians working in Israel dropped to 30,000 and then to near zero by 2000 as the Second Intifada began and terrorism again exploded into Israeli shops, buses, and hotels.[60]

After three decades of real growth in Palestinian incomes and after the most intense wave of suicide bombings, during which Israel secured her borders ever more tightly, the West Bank / Gaza per-person GDP dropped by one-third from an historic high of $4,471 in 1999 to just $3,005 in 2002 in the midst of the suicide bombings, and it would take until 2011 for the West Bank and Gaza Strip to recover to 1999 levels of GDP.[61] That it was the effect of the suicide bombings and Israel's just response to close off most access points to the West Bank / Gaza and not some other explanation, such as the 2001 recession, is clear from a look at neighbouring Jordan. There, per-person GDP had risen steadily from $8,493 in 1999 to $9,365 by 2002 and kept rising until the worldwide recession in 2009 by which time Jordan's per capita GDP was $11,938, nearly three times that of the Palestinian territories (at $4,191).[62]

In their continued focus on the right of return and one-sided grievance narrative, the Palestinian leadership thus sacrificed much of the existing West Bank–Israeli trade, jobs in Israel, and income for Palestinian families. Even then, even after all the suicide bombings and the takeover of Gaza by Hamas (in 2006), by 2011 Israel was still the main export market for the Palestinian territories with 86% of its goods destined for Israel. Comparatively, Jordan received only five percent and Saudi Arabia accounted for just one percent of the territories' exports.[63] The potential for greater Palestinian prosperity always existed. It was stifled by the unwillingness of the Palestinian leadership to practically, pragmatically deal with the reality that was Israel's existence. In this, Arafat was for once correct: The Palestinian matter was never just about refugees; it was also about the economy. In 2004, after one decade of rule by Arafat and his colleagues, per-person GDP in the West Bank and Gaza was lower than it had been when they took power in 1994.[64] The Palestinians were victims once again, this time courtesy of their own leadership.

Missed olive-branch opportunities

Beyond economic failure, Arafat consistently blunted offers to advance Palestinian interests and to contribute to a workable peace. In the late 1970s, Arafat was invited to participate in the Camp David accords that led to peace between Israel and Egypt. He eschewed cooperation and instead continued his role as the revolutionary *enfant terrible*.[65] Arafat's self-resuscitated grievances plus frustration at the stalled revolution produced surreal complaints. In 1982, after a decade in which the PLO used south Lebanon as a base from which to attack Israel, Israel invaded Lebanon to push back PLO forces. At the time, Beirut served as the PLO's fiefdom and headquarters and, as Israeli troops approached and shelled the city, and entered West Beirut, the PLO accepted an American offer for safe transit to Tripoli. Arafat was lucky but again believed he had been treated shoddily. Despite being ferreted out under the protection of 1,800 American troops,[66] the PLO leader blamed the "Zionist-U.S. invasion" for his plight.[67] Arafat was fortunate to have left Beirut in something other than a body bag. On August 30th, as the PLO prepared to leave for their exile in Tunisia, an Israeli sniper saw Arafat in his sights. But it was Israeli policy not to kill the PLO leader. Arafat lived.[68]

An American-led initiative from President Ronald Reagan in September that year, in response to the PLO's ejection from Lebanon, proposed a Palestinian state based on a merger of the West Bank, Gaza, and Jordan, with additional territory surrendered from Israel. But Arafat's allies rejected it. One PLO representative called it a "political bomb no different from the cluster bombs which our fighters confronted bravely in Beirut."[69] (The reference was to Israel's invasion of Lebanon, which had bottled up the PLO in the Lebanese capital, the one from which they had just fled.) Another derided the proposal as "an imperialist-Zionist plan."[70] Not every Arafat's compatriot saw it that way. The leading PLO moderate Isam Sartawi noted the positive aspects of the Reagan proposal. He urged consideration and was realistic about the just-completed escape from Lebanon after Israel's thrashing, arguing for an investigation into the cause of the PLO's Lebanon debacle. "Another victory such as this," joked Sartawi, "and the PLO will find itself in the Fiji Islands."[71] Sartawi's realism and black humor shortened his life; the PLO splinter faction led by Abu Nidal assassinated Sartawi in April 1983.[72]

The Arafat-constructed barriers to peace continued. In 1984, fearing Jordanian influence among Palestinians, the PLO rejected Jordan King Hussein's plan to work together on a Palestinian–Israeli peace settlement.[73] Two years later, Hussein ended his initiative and blamed Arafat for the dead-end: "We opened all the doors [for the PLO] but they continued to move in empty circles." King Hussein then closed PLO offices in Jordan and expelled its officials for the second time in two decades.[74] That same year, after more Arafat obfuscation, Morocco's King Hassan invited Israeli Prime Minister Shimon Peres to Morocco to discuss the Israeli–Palestinian issue; Hassan bypassed Arafat entirely out of frustration with the PLO leader's constant *refusenik* stance.[75] Meanwhile, Arafat's off-again, on-again terror attacks hindered the peace process and the goal of Palestinian statehood. In 1988 it appeared Arafat and the PLO would finally accept United Nations Resolution 242, which recognized Israel's right to exist. The PLO's acceptance of 242 was a precondition if Israel or the United States were to ever engage in direct talks with the terrorist group and, privately, the Palestinian leadership had offered hints to the U.S. State department that acceptance was forthcoming. A speech by Arafat was planned for a special United Nations session in Geneva in December and with already-agreed upon language to recognize Israel. The speech went ahead but absent recognition of Israel; instead, the General Assembly heard yet another polemical attack on Israel. The U.S. Secretary of State George Schultz, who on behalf of the White House was preparing to reverse American policy and recognize the PLO after the Arafat speech, instead cancelled his own announcement. The planned American press conference was deferred until Arafat made a mild backtrack several weeks later.[76]

Arafat's lasting failure

Arafat's most spectacular self-induced failure came when he rejected a proposed deal engineered by U.S. President Bill Clinton in 2000. The agreement, already acceded to by Israel, would have given the Palestinians all of Gaza and much of the West Bank without conditions. No strings were attached other than to continue negotiations in pursuit of a permanent two-state solution. The Palestinian side was offered 97% of the West Bank, all of Gaza, its capital in East Jerusalem, and control of the Temple Mount and of the Christian and Muslim quarters in the old city.[77] "The ball was now in Arafat's court," wrote President Clinton, who pointed out that other Arab leaders were impressed with Israel's acceptance. They thought Arafat should take the deal.[78] Even then, Arafat would not move from revolutionary to statesman. The failure was later recounted by President Clinton:

> By the end of the year I still hadn't heard from Arafat, so on New Year's Day 2001, I invited him to see me at the White House the next day. Before he came, he received Prince Bandar and the Egyptian ambassador at his hotel. One of Arafat's younger aides told me they had pushed him hard to say 'yes.' When Arafat came to see me, he asked a lot of questions about my proposal.... At times he seemed confused, not wholly in command of the facts. Most of the young people on Arafat's team wanted him to take the deal.... When he left, I still had no idea what he was going to do. His body language said 'no' but the deal was so good I couldn't believe anyone would be foolish enough to let it go.... Right before I left office, in one of our last conversations, Arafat thanked me for all my efforts and told me what a great man I was. 'Mr. Chairman,' I replied, 'I am not a great man; I am a failure and you have made me one.'"[79]

That Arafat blundered was widely understood at the time and Clinton characterized it as "an error of historic proportions."[80] Tunisian writer Lafif Lakhdar argued that the Clinton deal "may have been the best proposals any Palestinian could have been offered..."[81] *The Times* (London) characterized Arafat as the man who "threw away the best chance in a generation for an honorable settlement to the Middle East conflict."[82] In 2004, upon Arafat's death, the *New York Times* editorialized aloud about what tribute world leaders would instead have prepared if "in 2000, he had somehow found the courage to say yes to Ehud Barak and Bill Clinton." In its obituary titled "The Man Who Refused to Say Yes," the *Times* editorialized it was "not often in history that someone's legacy can come down to one single defining moment, to one single critical choice. But such is the story of Mr. Arafat's life, and it is almost unbearably disappointing."[83] The *New Yorker's* obituary writer opined that "rarely has a leader blundered more and left more ruin in his wake."[84] Writing in 2008 in London's Al-Sharq *Al-Awsat* newspaper, liberal Arab writer Dr. Mamoun Fandy condemned Arafat for refusing the 2000 deal. "Instead of declaring a state, [the Palestinian leadership] decided to declare a revolution… In other words, they reverted to the 'adolescence' of revolution," wrote Fandy. "Never again would the Egyptians, Americans, Europeans, and Israelis believe that the Palestinian leadership was truly capable of advancing from the 'adolescence' of revolution to the 'maturity' of state."[85]

The consequences of revolutionary victim *chic*

The failure in 2000 was the linear result of Arafat's ideological vision, which disdained compromise and would not relinquish the notion of permanent Palestinian victimization. Perhaps Arafat's obsession was also connected to his father's example (in Egypt where Arafat was born), who spent much of his life trying to reclaim property that the family lost 150 years before.[86] Whatever the source, Arafat's own vision of pushing Israel's Jews into the sea was a life-long obsession. In 1970, he proclaimed that the PLO's aim was to "liberate the land from the Mediterranean Sea to the Jordan River," and emphasized that "we are not concerned with what took place in June 1967…. The Palestinian revolution's basic concern is the uprooting of the Zionist entity from our land and liberating it."[87]

Arafat's overextended revolutionary *id* combined with his penchant for seeing himself as the victim would have been comical except for the continual terror trade in blood. Early on, he made clear his desire to turn the Middle East into a "second Vietnam."[88] Over the years, Arafat managed to approximate the casualties of a war though mainly for civilians in Israel and abroad. Between 1969 and 1985, PLO groups committed at least 8,000 acts of terror, mostly against Israel. In that 16-year period, Arafat's olive branch was rarely in view. The PLO and its terror franchises killed 650 Israelis and hundreds more from other countries.[89] Attacks from Palestinian terror groups were unrelenting and lauded no matter any Arafat rhetoric about peace. In 1989, the PLO leader praised a Gaza man who seized an Israeli bus and forced it into a ravine, killing 16 people and injuring 25. In 1990, the PLO applauded a Palestinian attack on Israelis vacationing in Egypt. The tour bus assault left nine dead and

17 injured. In 1994, after signing the Cairo Agreement (meant to build on the Oslo Accords the year previous), Arafat informed a Johannesburg audience just several days later that Palestinians would "continue their jihad until they had liberated Jerusalem."[90] Later, after Arafat turned down the Clinton deal, the attachment to terror was again explicit. In 2001, after a suicide bomber attacked an Israeli disco, Arafat comforted the family of the killer with the homily that he had "turned his body into a bomb [and was] the model of manhood and sacrifice for the sake of Allah and the homeland."[91] This was seven years *after* Arafat accepted the Nobel Prize for peace in Stockholm.[92]

None of this reassured Arab allies or Israeli moderates willing to work towards peace. Arafat's refusal to assent to an agreement frustrated Israelis sympathetic to a peace deal with the Palestinians. Yossi Sarad, leader of Israel's left-wing Meretz party told Arafat in 2001 that "Maybe it's time you stopped flitting around from one country to another. Settle down in Gaza and Ramallah and start bringing order, because this anarchy is going to bring a terrible disaster upon our people as well as on yours." Sarad told Arafat he should avoid making Israelis suspect that "you care more for an armed and violent struggle for a Palestinian state than the Palestinian state itself."[93]

The Peter Pan of revolutionaries

Arafat's choice to send the double signal of peace and terror poisoned the psychological disposition of moderates among the Palestinians and Israelis alike. Arafat himself was existentially stuck; he loved the Palestinian struggle more than the Palestinian state. He consistently handicapped the ability of others—Yitzhak Rabin, Hosni Mubarak, Jimmy Carter, Jordan's King Hussein, Bill Clinton—to arrange peace treaties between Palestinians and Israel.

Arafat's propensity to dash hopes for peace was not psychologically complex. He was a revolutionary, not a pragmatist, and few such ideologues successfully make the transition from the former to the latter. To cross that divide, the radical must sacrifice the enervating hope of utopia and forego the murderous thrill of power that accompanies directing terror, the ability to choose who lives and when enemies will die. Such revolutionaries must also begin the delicate task of downplaying past grievances, imagined or real, to minimize potential blowback and public fury from one's own side. For Arafat, the psychological effect of sacrificing revolution for peace would have been similar to what any politician in a normal state experiences once ejected from public office, a whiplash of inactivity after the previous daily enervating command of power. Democratic leaders find it emotionally difficult to relinquish such commanding power. To surrender to the mundane is doubly difficult for a revolutionary autocrat with the power to command the murders of enemies, one also beset by a stalled revolution. Arafat derived a deep sense of purpose connected both to his entrenched sense of victimhood and to his end goal, to reverse what he characterized as an historic humiliation, Israel's existence. None of that, the exchanging of bloodied intoxication for the bureaucratic career of a quasi-governor of a Palestine at peace, was tempting for Arafat. After a lifetime where prime ministers and presidents took his telephone calls and where Arafat chose the fates of others, the necessary but unexciting matters of a successful state—functioning institutions, working water pipes, paved roads and schools, trade with a former enemy—was not the "stuff" to excite a romantic revolutionary's imagination. It was additionally unattractive when Arafat believed he and Palestinians were due every inch of Israel.

Arafat's deep-seated attachment to grievances also revealed a psychological and a political immaturity and the impatient intensity of the revolutionary. He needed to redress past wrongs and aim at a national and political utopia no matter the cost to others. Indeed, Arafat's love of revolution and terror, of action and not plodding statecraft, led to suicide bombings, a country-long fence, walls, wars, and fewer economic opportunities for Palestinians. It all ended as it began, with no Palestinian state. To obtain that status would have required artful politics and compromise of the sort others from Northern Ireland to South Africa had already demonstrated in the 20th century. But peace with compromise was never on the table, including for the PLO chairman: "Our people cling to [their] land, holy Jerusalem and the holy places," said Arafat in 2001, "It will not surrender one grain of that soil of its homeland."[94] Though not alone in his absolutism (Hamas and the Muslim Brotherhood were even more intractable, or perhaps just more publicly honest about it) the gods gave Arafat decades to pursue peace with Israel. They did so while he was at the zenith of his power and possessed the ability to persuade compatriots with soft power or through some other, less pleasant means.

At best, had Arafat been capable of running a solid, results-oriented government, he might have turned the West Bank and Gaza into a Middle

East version of Hong Kong, or Dubai and Qatar, a not unwelcome outcome for Palestinians. At worst, had Arafat concluded a peace treaty with Israel and yet failed in governance, Palestine would at least resemble just another broken third-world collective, monotonous in its corruption, beset by petty politics and poverty, but at least at peace. But to govern a lightly populated, geographically small state with little economic, political, and military significance would have been an anticlimactic end to Arafat's career. The gods tasked the wrong man.

The terrorist-victim narrative

Late in life, Arafat argued that Palestinians would never have accepted the Clinton-brokered peace agreement with Israel. This is not exactly accurate. In 2000, at the time of negotiations, junior Palestinian negotiators told Israelis they were afraid to tell Arafat about concessions they suggested in preliminary negotiations in Stockholm.[95] While some Palestinians indeed opposed Arafat's peace efforts, just as some IRA members opposed Gerry Adams in his peace talks with Great Britain over Northern Ireland, Adams delivered in spite of any such opposition and his own terror associations, or more accurately, *because* of Adams' long-known attachment to terror to obtain his desired ends and, when necessary, even against fellow travellers.[b] Given his leadership in the Palestinian movement and his revolutionary credentials, akin to Gerry Adams and the IRA, Arafat's leadership and approval was necessary to any peace agreement, but his very existence always constituted a *de facto* veto. Arafat never used the costly, bloody capital he bought at a high price to others' lives. Unlike Adams, whose terror was a means to an end, Arafat's involvement in that dark art *was* the desired end, at least until Israel's assumed utter destruction. Arafat, when given any power, in negotiations and once ensconced in the West Bank in Ramallah, chose not

---

[b] See Ed Moloney, *A Secret History of the IRA*, published in 2002. In the book, Moloney, Northern editor for the Irish Times, chronicles the British attacks on and dismembering of select IRA cells. Moloney continually hints that the British prevention of select planned IRA attacks could have only taken place with inside information on such cells. Moloney never explicitly credits Gerry Adams or Martin McGuinness, another Provisional IRA leader, but he leaves little doubt in his writing that one or both men fed information to the British. If accurate, the motives of Adams and McGuinness would have been two-fold: to demonstrate that even more radical IRA members were not going to dictate to Adams or McGuinness when and what attacks were to be carried out, and also to save the peace process when that was the Adams–McGuinness priority.

to deliver the Palestinian side to a final peace deal. It was in contrast to Israel's leadership, which repeatedly demonstrated a willingness to compromise where a willing partner could be found. It was why Israel could negotiate a peace treaty with Egypt in 1977, which included a return of the Sinai. It was why Israel and Jordan could sign a peace treaty in 1994, returning conquered territory and creating mutually beneficial cultural, environmental, and commercial protocols.[96]

Palestinians also had an interest in peace but Arafat was unwilling, as per the example of Gerry Adams, to use his own bloodied capital to deliver it. Even had Arafat's claim of general Palestinian intransigence been accurate, Arafat deserved much of the blame: He was the prime Palestinian symbol since the 1960s. It was Arafat who ensured the image was that of an unbending revolutionary messiah, not that of a statesman who would take bold steps on a pragmatic path to peace. Arafat's refusal to accept the offered olive branch in 2000, the same one he proffered to Israel on the United Nations stage decades before, encapsulated his political life: revolutionary terrorism followed by opportunities to reform inevitably rejected and a return to shedding blood. Arafat's belief in the enduring unfairness of life for the Palestinians and himself vis-à-vis Israel, some other Arab leaders, the United States, and the West led him to play both his revolutionary and victim cards until the end. "Who but Arafat could launch a long terrorist campaign and then persuade the world to pity him as a victim?"[97] wrote Arafat biographers Barry and Judith Rubin shortly before Arafat's death.

"Peaceful settlements," Arafat once proclaimed, "can have only one meaning—surrender."[98] "I am a rebel and freedom is my cause," said Arafat to the United Nations in 1974.[99] Arafat was the perpetual perfectionist, political adolescent though of a deadly nihilistic sort, the Peter Pan of international politics who never matured. It was in keeping with Arafat's view of his life, and that of Palestinians as permanent victims of forces beyond their control, that upon his death in 2004, Palestinian children held signs aloft that blamed Arafat's passing on the Jews.[100]

The Arafat legacy: *Tora Bora* over Singapore

After the PLO leader's death in 2004 some Arab thinkers correctly identified the Palestinian problem even after Arafat as a continued fascination with revolutionary politics. Once the Palestinian terrorist faction, Hamas, took control of Gaza in 2006 elections, Dr. Fandy echoed his earlier criticism of the now-dead PLO leader. "Gaza's leaders were not," he wrote, "acting as someone faced with the task of [establishing] a state capable of managing its people's affairs."[101] He asked rhetorically when, after 60 years after the establishment of the state of Israel, "will the Palestinians advance from the 'adolescence' of revolution to the 'maturity' of statehood?" Fandy wrote that Gaza's potential, while small as a seaport, was similar to Singapore, which had long prospered: "Instead of adopting Singapore as a model," wrote the author, "the Palestinians have chosen the model of Tora Bora! They have transformed Gaza into part of Afghanistan, with its extremist Islamists, weapons, and missiles."[102]

Another author, the French-Tunisian writer Lafif Lakhdar, observed that the Palestinians suffered from a failure of leadership and a lack of self-criticism: "The first step in recovering from rejectionism is [applying] self-criticism: admitting that many Palestinians, Arabs, and Muslims are their own [worst] enemies," wrote Lakhdar, "and that they are the ones who bring disasters upon themselves— not the Zionists, Imperialists, Free Masons, Communists, or else globalization or the New World Order—as claimed by the discourse that presents the Arabs as victims and drives them back to the stage of childish whining."[103] One Israeli writer was more sympathetic but agreed with the diagnosis: "The Palestinians, of course, suffered most in the conflict," wrote Barry Rubin in 1994. "Losing their homeland brought great material deprivation and psychological trauma. It was not their fault they lived on ground claimed by another nationalist movement, Zionism. But their own leaders and choices repeated earlier mistakes, thus contributing to lengthening and deepening their plight."[104]

PART IV

Explanations, reality checks, and remedies

Forgetting—I would even go so far as to say historical error—is a crucial factor in the creation of a nation, which is why progress in historical studies often constitutes a danger for [the principle of] nationality. Indeed, historical enquiry brings to light deeds of violence which took place at the origin of all political formations, even of those whose consequences have been altogether beneficial.

—ERNEST RENAN, *What is a Nation?*

Only slowly could these men be guided back to the common truth that no one has the right to do wrong, not even if wrong has been done to them.

—Holocaust survivor VICTOR FRANKL, in *Man's Search for Meaning*, on fellow concentration camp prisoners after their release

CHAPTER 11

Common threads: Plato's perfectionists and Rousseau's romantics

We got to get ourselves back to the garden.

—CROSBY, STILLS, NASH AND YOUNG, *Woodstock*

Why two dead Greeks matter

As you jostle past the Vatican museum's crowds and into the hallways of Rome's most priceless collection of art, a side room near the entrance to the Sistine Chapel can almost be overlooked. There, visitors will find a fresco from the Renaissance artist, Raphael. Completed in 1510, *The School of Athens* contains figures from multiple centuries: the "weeping" and "laughing" philosophers Heraclitus and Democritus from ancient Greece; the medieval Muslim Spanish theologian, mathematician, and philosopher Averroes; even a contemporary figure thought to be Raphael himself. At its centre, the philosophers Plato and Aristotle are engaged in a Greek-style duel: a debate on how to best construct a just soul and a harmonious society. Their postures hint at how each philosopher saw the world and how men and women should rule themselves and each other. Their argument helps explain why some are attracted to grievance narratives and even more so why they are disastrous.

Plato is on the left with an upright hand motioning to the sky. As the classically educated Raphael well knew and as political philosophers explain in interpreting the two men's views, Plato's direction hints as if to say, "We must take our cue from something higher than ourselves to construct a just society." On the right, Aristotle, with palm open, motions to the ground.

He is often interpreted as asserting a position starkly different from Plato's, something akin to: "We must observe how men behave here, on the ground beneath our feet, and build our republic on that basis."

Raphael's positioning of the two philosophers accurately captures their opposite starting points. Plato is indeed inspired by otherworldly imaginings and Aristotle by down-to-earth practicality, by empiricism. To understand why their reflections matter many millennia later and how Plato's perfectionism animates grievance narratives, modern or historic, let us first grasp his thoughts and then move to Aristotle's objections. That, followed up with Rousseau's starry-eyed approach to history will place all victim cults in in their proper context: While modern victim cults in Western societies are animated in part by civilizational self-loathing, all grievance narratives, be they recent or ancient, draw from an even deeper well. It is one filled with perfectionist expectations and longings for a golden age.

Plato's vivid imagination

Plato believed in another, higher world from which men derive their inspiration and sense of justice. This was the world of the Forms, or Ideas. (Philosophers use both terms.) It was roughly akin to God for monotheistic religions, i.e., the notion some entity is eternal and precedes all else and anchors morality. Plato's Forms are similar though impersonal: They are universal and exist beyond our short, sharp human lives. As Plato would assert in *The Republic* through Socrates, if justice is merely what the rulers say it is, the result is a state and laws based on nothing more than the desires, opinion, and will of the strongest person. In that world, the weak easily suffer, and appeals to morality are useless because morality is only defined by those *in* power. Right and wrong, justice and injustice, are mere words defined entirely by rulers who may be kind or cruel. Similarly, in a democracy absent any notion of some otherworldly standard, what the majority deem to be right or wrong, *is*. Morality, in such a view, is entirely culture-dependent. That view existed in *The Republic* in the character of Thrasymachus, who argues exactly this position, that justice is merely a self-enclosed loop from men in power and back again: There is no appeal to some universal morality. Everything else is just so much chatter and pretend-justice.

In opposition to such moral relativism, Plato, via the character of Socrates, argues that if justice is to mean anything, something more than a thinly veiled cloak for the ruler's preferences, justice must exist outside of us. But here a problem arises: Where would we find it? For Plato, proof is found in our imaginations, where we often apprehend a notion. For example, when someone speaks of a beautiful woman, different women come to mind: for some, a Rubenesque figure with dark hair; for others, a slender red-head with freckles. Critically, the very notion of beauty exists apart from us. Plato labels that concept grasped by our minds the *universal*, while some woman we know and think of is the *particular* manifestation of it. The fact that we can imagine beauty and also have specific examples in our world means the first precedes the second. The universal exists apart from any earth-bound, culture-bound, or even personal interpretation of it.

For Plato, this is proof that justice exists beyond us: Our minds apprehend morality on some higher plane of existence, and where justice is uncontaminated by our own limited perception. For those who believe in the Forms, or God, this independent idea of justice allows for reform and for the protest of the unjust. As the late *New York Times* columnist William Safire argued in *The First Dissident*, his book about the biblical character of Job, men and women can even spar with the Deity on that basis.[1] For Plato, because justice exists in this otherworldly place untouched by human imperfection, it is why we should strive to "unpack" that universal for our world. As further proof, consider that we often imagine an object and then later create it from that initial bit of inspiration. We imagine a chair and then craft one out of wood, nails, and varnish. For Plato, if we can imagine it, we can build it. It is the same with justice, including attempts to be just within ourselves or in Athens. We should begin with our imagination and its intuitive grasp of that universal notion of justice.

There is some sense in Plato's approach. After all, without imagination to improve our world, we would be little different from unreasoning animals who act only according to instinct and never from inspiration. Absent our imagination, we would be doomed to a perfunctory, merely biological life: There would be no art, architecture, or music, or at least none with creativity and flourish; any beauty would be accidental. Why not dream of a better world and set out to refashion our own? One might argue, did not Martin Luther

King, Jr., do just this in his "I have a dream" speech at the Lincoln Memorial on August 28, 1963?[2] King appealed to a higher morality, one that put his fellow citizens and politicians in the dock and with a vision that has largely triumphed in the decades since. For Plato, this higher plane and vision must inform how we live and the governments we create so as to maximize justice in ourselves and in our society.[a] *A la* King, why *not* work towards perfection in our souls and in society instead of meekly accepting the flawed one around us as inevitable?

Why Plato's thinking intensifies the victim cult: Our own imagined perfection as the end goal

Enter the empiricist, Aristotle, to spoil Plato's musings. For Aristotle, some ethereal imagining of where perfection exists apart from our world is one, but only one, problem with Plato's theory of how to arrive at justice: That other world may exist but if it does, we cannot observe it. If you cannot see, touch, and handle something, how then can you imitate it? It is akin to waking up and thinking that because in your dream you landed on a distant planet, it makes sense once you wake up to set out for the Milky Way with a two-engine airplane: The means are insufficient to the desired end. The other problem: The imagined planet may not even exist.

And there is yet another problem: Our world includes billions of other people with their own, very *different* imaginings of what constitutes perfection and the good life; they also have their own interests, which will inevitably collide with ours. The best example of this is when the character of Socrates recommends an early form of communism. His vision includes children, spouses, and possessions shared in common for the ruling and warrior classes in the republic. (Plato recommends three classes in his imagined city-state: Rulers, soldiers, and workers, with the first two in "cahoots" to control the latter.) The aim of sharing everything and everyone is to avoid having people think that anyone, even children, or any property, is theirs. If everyone and everything is shared and if the parentage of the children in Athens is

---

[a] For Plato and Aristotle, justice was more comprehensive than how we use the term, a reference to laws and government and arguments over morality. For the Greeks, justice was closer to the notion of what we think of self-actualization in a psychological sense, each person fulfilling a role best suited to their nature and, in society, for each person to fulfill a role that coincides with their aptitude, ability, and talent.

unknown, the theory is that attachment is less likely, or impossible. Thus jealousy, envy, and hatred will be absent among rulers and soldiers and that will lead to harmony. That was the theory.

For Aristotle, this following after ethereal, esthetic perfection—today we might label it "ivory tower" thinking—is the sign of a mind untethered from reality. Plato's imagined republic is not how real men and women behave. "There are two things above all that which make human beings cherish and feel affection," he writes in reference to possessions and family, "what is one's own and what is dear."[3] Aristotle thus draws the obvious conclusion: While we may voluntarily and occasionally share some possessions, we are unlikely to invite every neighbour to use our lawnmower, to use a modern example. Or we may be fine with a brother-in-law who stays for one night but not six months. More critically, we never "lend" out our spouses and children. If someone attempts to "share" those dearest to us, we will be jealously protective to the point of rage and murder.

For Aristotle, contra Plato's imagined city, there is nothing just about forcing flesh-and-blood men and women to conform to an imaginary world and its perfect Forms that has no relation to our world. It asks (or forces) men to pretend they care not for their lover and their own children if someone else takes them. For Aristotle, such attempts ignore human nature and other realities and are doomed to failure. Forced stratifications and communal living are, in fact, what will lead to disharmony in the republic. It is why, even in 20th-century communist societies, tyrants could never quite kill off the nuclear family, because families *are* a possession in every sense. We will not be torn from them or they from us without a bloody fight. Instead of Plato's imagining, Aristotle asks us to create a better society out of the actual clay around us, not out of the imagined nebulae we cannot touch, but from observing men and women first and offering a plan second. If we want actual harmonious societies, we must first take into account what people think and feel, how they behave, and the choices they make.

This is why Aristotle asks us to investigate why men behave the way they do. "It is how things develop naturally from the beginning that one may best study them," he writes in *The Politics*.[4] We must first see men as they are if we are to create a city-state such as ancient Athens, or a nation today, that actually works, including if we are to offer practical remedies to injustice.[5]

This is also the proper way to understand Martin Luther King's call to justice. King did call men to a higher standard, and out of his imagination. He was a minister and believed in his faith and in justice as God-given. He appealed to an otherworldly standard and acted as modern-day Jeremiah or John the Baptist, calling men to account. Critically, while King's call to justice for American blacks did originate in his mind and in his faith, in his belief that God and justice exist, it was also anchored in what is best characterized as actionable possibilities.

King's vision was in part successful because he demanded a cessation of existing behaviour and unjust laws; he did not call for perfect outcomes.[b] He grounded his calls in observable reality and practical possibilities. No politician was forced to retain racist laws based upon long-discredited race theories; no southern restaurant owner was compelled to continue to ignore African Americans at the lunch counter. On the latter point in particular, all people had to do was *stop*. In contrast, had King demanded that the federal government abolish racism in the human heart, he would have over-reached. While that end is also desirable, legislators are not normally capable of changing hearts; that change happens due to other influences that range from personal interactions and religious and cultural shifts that spur reform among other reasons. Legislators are capable—albeit in very limited ways—of affecting behaviour through the law. Men and women can also cease their own harmful actions. Neither reform is akin to an attempt to create a utopia. In demanding changes to discriminatory laws and prejudicial behaviour, King called on Americans and their leaders to act as free moral agents in the public square and in their places of work. King was not asking his fellow citizens to board a rickety plane on a trajectory to an unknown planet. He was asking for his fellow Americans to ignore skin colour, to treat others as equal, and simply serve lunch.

---

[b] It is akin to the difference between negative rights and positive rights. Negative rights are traditional civil liberties, such as freedom from torture, freedom of speech, association, and religion, among others. Those are relatively easy for a state to deliver, as all the state need do is to not infringe upon expression, one's person, associations, and religious practices. In contrast, positive rights such as a "right" to welfare cannot be guaranteed. Governments can try and deliver such goods but, for example, in the event of a collapse in the economy and government revenues, a welfare right would be unlikely to continue, at least at previous levels. In contrast, even a relatively poor state can deliver negative rights: It can simply leave citizens alone by not repressing their speech, or interfering in their religious practice.

Unlike King, Plato's imaginings started with the imagined ideal as *the* ideal and is never referenced to behaviour on the ground. For Aristotle, this is the danger and the distinction: Men and women are not clay, capable of endless molding and manipulation into whatever behaviour some dreamer thinks desirable. And therein lies the seed of tyranny including grievance narratives that then demand an action. Perfectionist utopian fantasies tempt adherents to leave the world of real men and think that the only barrier between men and paradise is *effort* or *will* and usually that of others. That is potentially fatal to the rest of us because of its corollary: Those who resist are lazy, uncomprehending, or "disobedient" to the "laws of history" or someone's notion of justice or the divine. It is then alleged that the rest of us deliberately conspire against necessary reform. It is why, in 20th-century communist states, those who did not meet quotas were "re-educated" or murdered. It is why theocratic tyrannies such as Iran's punish those who fail to strictly adhere to a theocrat's perfectionist morality. The mere inability to meet perfectionist ends makes such citizens assumed enemies of the state. In the view of the Platonic perfectionist, it is not that citizens *cannot* physically produce the quota demanded by a central planner or follow the theocrat's vision of God's will; it is that they *will* not. For the perfectionist, failure to produce or to obey is always a failure of will, never of capabilities.

This is why Plato's perfectionism leads to another error, his one-sided view of threats to a community. Plato assumes that the worst outcome is disharmony, including civil war. But another danger is equally injurious and can be worse than division: tyranny, imposed in the name of perfection, of utopia, or just because one person or group holds all the power. Some of America's founding fathers well understood this human reality. Most famously, James Madison in The Federalist Papers No. 10, wrote that while factions could tear a society apart, the remedy to that was not to aim for unity of opinion or belief as the cure—forced behaviour through tyranny was worse than the disease. Nor was installing some philosopher-king workable because, as Madison wrote, "Enlightened statesmen will not always be at the helm."[6] Instead, Madison advised for a separation of powers, this to ensure no one faction had permanent control of the institutions of state, i.e., no one faction would have all the power.[7] That is evident in the design of the American republic: the legislative, executive, and judicial.

Plato thinks extreme unity, a guardian class, and shared people and possessions, all animated by another-worldly notion of apprehended justice, is the ideal, and the ideal means to a peaceful harmonious society. Aristotle and Madison think that originates in an imagined perfection and not in a realistic appraisal of men. Ignore how men behave and the end will always be tyranny. A perfectly imagined republic is a perfectly tyrannical project. It cannot be otherwise. It is why starting not just with inspiration—but with perfection as *the* inspiration—is the core problem in Plato's philosophy. Plato places a burden on men that they cannot carry and which will lead to their destruction.

Victim cults and Rousseau's romanticism

Whatever else one may think of Plato's attempt to create a utopia, he as with other utopians imagined a future idyllic world. In contrast, the 18th-century French philosopher Jean-Jacques Rousseau imagined that man could be educated back to his natural impulses, ones that Rousseau considered good and authentic. In other words, he looked back and saw perfection, paradise there. "Before art fashioned our manners and taught our passions to speak an obliging language," wrote Rousseau in his 1750 essay "Discourse on the Arts and Sciences,"[8] "our morals were rustic but natural." Or this from Émile in 1762: "The first impulses of nature are always right"[9] and "God makes all things good; man meddles with them and they become evil," wrote the philosopher.[10]

For Rousseau, who also considered man perfectible,[11] civilization was the problem: Man had been seduced by the world then emerging, with the alluring but cheap trinkets of commerce and artificial civilization and all its noisy, cacophonic activity. That led to an abandonment of his natural inclinations including the passions, compassion, and a desire for authentic connections with his neighbours. It was a hollowing-out of natural man further abetted by the French salon. To grasp what Rousseau was on about, think of 18th-century France and its powdered wigs, peacock-like dresses, the put-upon manners practised by European upper classes, and the inevitable class snobbery. For the sensitive philosopher, all such activity interfered with authentic feelings between people because they began to look at each other as competitors in the race to vanities and riches: slave or master, worker or boss, buyer or shopkeeper, and strutting "peacock" contests between French nobility. "No more sincere friendships, no more real esteem, no more well-founded trust," wrote Rousseau in 1750 in the "First Discourses," but instead "suspicions, resentments, fears, coldness, reserve, hatred, and betrayal...."[12]

This is why Rousseau thought men were only authentic and good prior to civilization. Compare the fakery and foppery to barefoot children running through mountain pastures without a care, playfully teasing each other without malice. Few would prefer the salons to such an idyllic life, and this is Rousseau's vision. It is why, as applied to formal education—where part of the process is to train the young to be still, patient, learn from adults, and acquire the capability to suppress the passions in pursuit of knowledge—Rousseau argued that "Our passions are the chief means of self-preservation; to try and destroy them is therefore as absurd as it is useless," and to do so would be to "overcome nature, to reshape God's handiwork."[13] For Rousseau, himself often forbidden to play outside when young, such a natural life was preferable to the existence of society and the grinding work in school, butcher shops and bakeries, and fake sentiments at French parties, or as we might illustrate today, to the monotonous work in factories, office cubicles, and barista bars, and to deadly boring conversation at cocktail parties. "Man would have nothing as nature made it,"[14] he wrote in his book on education, *Émile*, in 1762.

The effect of Rousseau: Tilling the historical grievance garden

Rousseau was consequential and in the context of an industrializing Europe and his call to return to nature held understandable appeal. Émile has served as a *de facto* sacred writ for romantic progressives and varying back-to-nature movements ever since, a sentiment to which we should be partly sympathetic insofar as the topic is the natural world and in how we approach the environment. We might also identify with Rousseau's irritation with cocktail chatter as opposed to authentic relationships, or be dismayed at the anti-human elements in modern architecture—two specific exasperations of mine, I confess. The latter, for example, with its banal and severe steel, glass, and concrete creations, treat men and women as stage props or factory robots and not as living creatures who might like fresh air, sunshine, and aesthetic beauty in their everyday work and homes.

Beyond such sympathies for Rousseau as applied to nature and our natures in specific instances, the early-20th-century psychoanalyst Sigmund Freud rightly objected to Rousseau's idea that civilization was largely responsible for our misery. Freud thought such a notion astonishing.[15] After all, Freud reasoned, civilization allowed for man to distinguish himself from our animal ancestors and served two purposes: To protect men from the vagaries of nature and to adjust their mutual relations,[16] by which Freud meant that men and women can better shield themselves from the arbitrariness of the natural world when in community and also learn to live with others. For example, we can work together in useful ways to build dikes and dams to prevent floods; we can also give our neighbour food when they are hungry if we live in a community.

Rousseau never actually thought that men and women could escape civilization and return to the state of nature; even Rousseau was more conscious of his romanticism than that. But his romantic longing for a perfect, past world that never existed was unhelpful because it led to anti-civilizational impulses predicated on the notion that cultural authenticity was equal to a kindler, gentler life. That belief ignores how pre-industrial, pre-Enlightenment life was miserable compared to that which existed even in Rousseau's time, to say nothing of ours. This was even truer of those who lived off the land, as did most of humanity before urbanization. We have some sense of that world from historian William Manchester, who describes elements of early medieval life: A serf's basic agricultural tools were "picks, forks, spades, rakes, scythes, and balanced sickles but very little iron, no wheeled plowshares with moldboards," which meant serfs in northern Europe with heavy soils had to turn it over by hand.[17] As for a pleasant pastoral life before industrialization and urbanization, it was a fiction. Homicides occurred at a rate twice that of accidents, and only one out of every 100 murderers were brought to justice according to English coroner's records. As of A.D. 1500, the best roads on the continent were still those built by the Romans a millennium or more before. "Peasants labored harder, sweated more, and collapsed from exhaustion more often than their animals," wrote Manchester.[18]

We know from other sources that life was short: One thousand years ago, the average infant could expect to live just 24 years, with one-third of infants perishing in their first year of life. In contrast, by 2000, the average infant, using a worldwide average, could expect to live 66 years (and longer in

Europe, North America, and East Asia). By the year 2000, infant mortality also dropped to 7 per 1,000 births in Europe.[19] It matters not if we approve of how some of this progress occurred—conquest, trade, and capital movements—as all three led to our world.[20] Only a romantic ideologue would recommend the impossible, a reversal.

Nevertheless, the romantic longings of Rousseau combined with Plato's perfectionist impulses are both embedded in victim thinking, where adherents fixate on a more authentic and harmonious past free from civilization's crosscurrents. They then see others as contaminants of whatever tribe with whom they choose to identify. It is why some today are extremely sensitive to notions of purity. Somewhere deep inside they have latched on to a perfectionist notion supplemented by romantic longing for its protection or fulfillment. It is why romantic perfectionists always find some element (culture, skin colour, race, ethnicity, nationalism, or a specific economic outcome) to fetishize. They do so not just to guard the practical wisdom built up over the centuries—that much is defensible—but to instead wrap themselves in an isolated cocoon of their own imagination. They are terrified of cross-cultural or cross-racial "contamination." They worship a perfect past.

Rousseau as the victim cult's philosopher

The combination of perfectionism and romanticism has always been a formula for deepened and never-ending grievances. There is no end to the possible mutations of complaints once a perfectionist Platonic standard is created out of imagination and then sacralised by Rousseau's romanticism, uninterested in practicalities. It is why Rousseau is the perfect philosopher of the victim cult, financially dependent on others for most of his life yet possessed by the belief he deserved much more, be it fame, money, or pity. He ignored his own choices, hated responsibility, and was completely blind to his own faults, or simply did not care.[21] Rousseau treated women poorly and ignored his own five children. He never provided support and instead let them languish in orphanages. Tellingly, Rousseau justified this with reference to Plato: "I thought I was performing the act of a citizen and a father and I looked upon myself as a member of Plato's Republic."[22]

Rousseau often would claim he was the victim. It was evident in his blind narcissism to the suffering of others, as when Rousseau once wrote a letter to a recent widow but instead of consoling her, wrote of "How much more I am to be pitied than you."[23] In another missive where compassion was due, he argued with his correspondent: "What could your miseries have in common with mine?"[24] For Rousseau, the world was always at fault and never himself, once posting a list of complaints against others on his front door in Paris. His grievances included complaints against "priests, fashionable intellectuals, the common people, women, the Swiss."[25] Despite his own attitudes and actions, alternately insulting and demanding, Rousseau thought himself the victim of a worldwide conspiracy,[26] including ones he thought organized by philosopher David Hume and another by the French foreign minister, Duc de Choiseul.[27]

Late in life Rousseau wrote of how "[n]ature has shaped me for suffering"[28] and how "I have borne unhappiness."[29] As historian Paul Johnson has opined, "Rousseau was one of the greatest grumblers in the history of literature [insisting]… that his life had been one of misery and persecution."[30] Tellingly, Rousseau defended Plato when he wrote, "In popular estimation [Plato's system of thought] stands for all that is fanciful and unreal," and described Plato as one who "only sought to purge man's heart."[31] It was a paean to perfectionism to which Rousseau also aspired. But such fastidiousness was the cause of his own deep suffering: He expected life to cater to him, and for those nearby and for his civilization to be flawless. It is a common temptation to all who nurture victim stories: Life is not perfect but it once was and, until Eden is restored, I am a victim of civilization, of others, of you.

CHAPTER 12

Everyone's (ancestor was) a victim

Socrates taught us: "Know thyself."

—ALEXANDER SOLZHENITSYN, *The Gulag Archipelago*

Slavery in the time of Shakespeare

In July 1625, on the south coast of England, reports began to filter into villages about the arrival of corsairs (Barbary pirate ships) and which lurked near the shores.[a] In one hamlet, the vice admiral of Cornwall was told at least "twentye sayle upon this coast."[1] The reference was to a fleet of corsairs in search of villagers near the English shore who could be easily captured and later sold into slavery in North Africa. As it happened, the early warnings were prescient. One village at Mount's Bay was attacked while its villagers were at communal prayer; 60 women, men, and children were dragged from the church back to the ships.[2] That same summer, another Cornish settlement, Looe, was attacked: 80 mariners and fishermen were bound and taken to the corsairs, and into a life of slavery. More would have been captured but the villagers were warned and fled to the surrounding hills. In revenge, the invaders torched the town.[3] Meanwhile, a second fleet of Barbary vessels had been spotted off the north Cornish coast; it captured Lundy Island in the Bristol channel, made it their base, raised the standard of Islam, and seized and sacked villages along the Cornish coast all summer. By one estimate, from the mayor of Plymouth,

---

[a] "Barbary" originated with the name given to native Berber tribes-herdsmen and mountain-dwellers in North Africa by others, including Romans and subsequent conquerors who considered them less sophisticated and "barbarians."

1,000 English boats (skiffs) were destroyed that season with an equivalent number of English villagers captured and transported off to slavery in North Africa.[4]

The Duke of Buckingham ordered a defence against the corsairs to be led by Francis Stuart; but the Duke was realistic about the odds, noting that "they [the corsairs] are better pirates than the English ships."[5] The attacks that summer were not unique. Fifteen years previous, one historical estimate placed the number of white Europeans (here used broadly to include those from the British Isles) already enslaved in North Africa at between 25,000 and 80,000.[6] Thus, even before the attack on Cornwall, traffickers in human flesh had hunted for slaves among English and European coastal towns and villages for years.[7] By the time inhabitants of Mount Bay were rounded up and into Barbary corsairs, the threat of such attacks were already long a recurring threat for those in the British Isles and for coastal Europeans.[8]

Between 1609 and 1616, one official report notes at least 466 English ships were captured and their crews thrown into slavery, often with ex-English-sailor assistance to the corsairs.[9] Elsewhere, the pirates and slave-traders attacked the Portuguese archipelago of Madeira in 1617 and captured at least 1,200 people.[10] One decade later, 800 captives, mostly women and children, were snatched in Reykjavik and other Icelandic towns by Barbary forces.[11] In 1631, the Dutch traitor Morat Rais raided the Irish town of Baltimore[12] and carried off 20 men, 89 women, and some additional human cargo—children.[13] One account notes all of Baltimore's inhabitants had been seized.[14] Ceriale, Italy, was raided in 1637 by Algerian and Tunisian sailors, with "64 men, 94 children, and 125 women" taken;[15] also in 1637, Algerians raided Calpe in Spain and left with a bounty of 315 captives, mostly women and children.[16] In 1645, a nighttime raid on Cornwall by a Cornish renegade and their Barbary companions resulted in "goods and prisoners, including about 200 women, some of them ladies of rank and fortune," according to the contemporary account.[17]

By the mid-17th century, attacks upon European shipping and populations from Iceland in the north to Sicily in the south had already been ongoing for eight centuries.[18] But that the English and Irish coasts once served up human cargo is mostly forgotten in the mists of time. The image of North Atlantic English villages raided by North African pirates and slave-traders seems at odds with the perceived power relationships of that era, for instance, the strengthening of England under Queen Elizabeth in the late-16th century and the seafaring power for which that country would later become known. But in the early-17th century, England was not yet the master of the waves and its coastline was still a source of vulnerability. There is another reason why the image of pleasant English villages near to the Elizabethan and Shakespearean eras accosted by slave-traders is forgotten:[b] because the trade in "white flesh," while substantial in its own time, was understandably eclipsed in our collective, historical memory by the later, much larger trans-Atlantic trade in black Africans. In the context of today's grievance narratives, the worldwide history of slavery including the forgotten captured from the shores of England and Europe—and soon also to be recounted, aboriginal-on-aboriginal slavery in the Pacific Northwest—are useful to recount to make this point: Any sensible person alive today should rather "break bread" with almost anyone in any country now rather than over-celebrate one's ancestors, given almost everyone's ancestral tree has the awful mark of slavery on it, or worse. And a secondary point: It was only the colonial-era British who were determined to wipe slavery from humanity's list of acceptable practices. That matters in an age where victim narratives are driven by a focus on the sins of Western nations but rarely those of other civilizations. Just as rarely do the critics consider what the world might look like had the West and its ideas and actions, including its positive contributions such as the abolitionist movement, been absent. Everyone's ancestors, at some point, made everyone else's life as per Thomas Hobbes's description: solitary, poor, nasty, brutish, and short. It helps to recall that truth, lest modern victim-cults continue to be enamoured with long-dead tribes.

The historic trade in human flesh

The mid-20th-century historian Will Durant argued that the rise of slavery was linked to the rise of agriculture. Previously, in hunter-gatherer societies, slavery was little sought as hunters' wives and children would suffice for the work necessary to the survival of a tribe.[19] The rise of agriculture necessitated extra labourers and gave early farmers an incentive to enslave others to

---

[b] Queen Elizabeth I died in 1603 and Shakespeare perished in 1616.

develop their land. Also, the nexus of farming and commerce also changed the nature of warfare; rather than kill a captured opponent and thus forego an opportunity for "free" labour, enemy warriors were instead kept alive as slaves to perform unpleasant tasks.[20]

Examples of slavery abound in antiquity. In Judea, hundreds of thousands of slaves were used to cut timber and transport material for public works projects, including Solomon's Temple and palace.[21] In Babylon, during Nebuchadnezzar's reign, contracts of sale often concerned slavery. There, as elsewhere, slaves resulted from captives taken in battle, from slave mothers giving birth to future slaves, and also from slave raids and which included attacks and raids from foreign, marauding Bedouins."[22] In Sumer (modern-day southern Iraq), slavery was highly developed with slaves considered a form of property, an economic right.[23] In ancient Egypt, many workers in agriculture were slaves and were elsewhere captured in war or domestically enslaved after they were unable to repay debts.[24] The Assyrians and Phoenicians practised slavery, and their supply of other human beings came from similar sources as other ancient cultures, i.e., war and conquest.[25] In Rome, slavery was notable for its "inhuman economy," as one author characterizes it.[26] On large estates, slaves were imprisoned, treated akin to animals, and, when their efficiency dropped, sold to state mines where conditions were even more severe. This led to "bargain" markets where such slaves were cheap to purchase.[27] The conditions of slaves improved, somewhat and only comparatively, after the Severan period in the early-third century A.D., this after the suppression of piracy and a decline in civil wars led to fewer slaves, which made existing slaves more valuable. The practice of manumission (freeing of a slave) and the influence of Stoicism, which preached the brotherhood of man, also helped, and contributed to a relatively better existence, where the distinction between slave and freeman weakened.[28]

Religion was agnostic on slavery until recently

Until the abolitionist movements of the 18th and 19th centuries, faith made little difference to the practice of slavery over the ages. After the rise of Christianity, scripture was added to Roman practices and assumptions to justify slavery, or at least, to not challenge it, though scripture was also later quoted in defence of abolishing the practice.[29] In Christianity's first century,

Saint Paul encouraged slaves to be obedient to their masters and sent back the slave Onesimus to his owner Philemon.[30] Christianity's earliest evangelist did at least encourage Philemon to look upon the slave as a "brother in Christ" rather than as a slave,[31] and in another letter, also encouraged slave-owners to regard slaves as their spiritual equals.[32] In Islam, in what the West calls the medieval era and what Islam regards as its golden era, slaves were at the bottom of the social structure with blacks, Berbers, Greek, Turks, Spaniards, Kurds, and Armenians. Ruling Arab Muslims were at the zenith of the societal pinnacle. They were followed by non-Arab Muslims and then "people of the book" (Christians, Jews, Zoroastrians, pagan Berbers, and Hindus).[33] Islamic societies in that age, as with European ones in a later era, profited greatly from slavery. In Islam, slavery was additionally consequential, given the institutions of concubinage, the harem, and how individual slaves might gain power as personal favourites, bodyguards, and even as quasi-rulers in selected instances.[34]

In theory, both Christianity and Islam prohibited enslaving those in their own faiths. In practice, the tragedy of slavery cut across cultures and religions. The money to be made was of some incentive here, and the definition of an adherent was fluid; the practice occurred even with clearly defined believers. That Christians enslaved each other is evident from one high-profile example: In 1379, Pope Clement V proclaimed that the Venetians captured in war could be sold as slaves.[35] In Islam, Muslims could pledge their own children as collateral, which then would lead to slavery in the case of default. Muslims also offered fellow Muslims as slaves to Christians in Iberia (Spain).[36] Race prejudice was part of it: Slavery often involved the sale of black Muslims by white Muslims on the northwest coast of Africa, for example.[37]

Europeans in chains

Developments in the Middle Ages created the conditions for the enslavement of Europeans. Saracens, Moors, and others of the crescent conquered the Levant, North Africa, and selected territories in southern and central Europe, victories that were the rule and not the exception for a faith and a culture on the ascendancy in the European medieval age, and which often included enslaving the conquered. Islam's rise and subsequent military successes in the Mediterranean and southern Europe included Arabian ships from the

Caliph of Moawiya (A.D. 641–668) which invaded Byzantine waters and occupied the islands of Cyprus and Rhodes and advanced upon Crete and Sicily.[38] Successive territories in Spain were conquered by the Moors by 712 and in 720; in 732, Islamic armies were stopped 100 miles from Paris when defeated by Charles Martel at the Battle of Tours.[39] In 737, Muslims laid siege to Toulouse and captured Avignon. Further south, Pantellaria fell in 806; in 813, Moors ravaged Corsica (which they had previously occupied but then had been driven out of in 807), as well as Sardinia, Nice, and Civita Vecchia; in Sicily, Palermo was conquered in 831; Syracuse succumbed to Islamic forces in 878. Closer to Rome, the Pope was forced to fend off attacks and buy protection with annual payments in silver.[40]

By the early-9th century, with the capture of North Africa, Spain, and with their reach into Frankish territory and Asia, the Islamic presence extended to what turned out to be its greatest geographical grasp. But it was hardly the end of battles, wars, and conquests by Islamic armies, and, prior to the Crusades, the opportunity to enslave Europeans was one after-affect that followed in the train of conquering armies. The conquests allowed Moors, Saracens, and Musselmans[c] to capture slaves in locales as far afield as Italy in the south, Russia and Iceland in the north, Gaul, and the British Isles.[41] Individual examples abound: When the Saracens seized the Italian island of Pantellaria in 806, the marauders sold the monks there into slavery in Spain; in Venice, in the ninth century, local merchants sold Christian slaves to the Musselmans; the Belgian historian Henri Pirenne labelled this trade the "most important branch of Venetian commerce at the time and this despite attempts to outlaw it."[42] The trade in slaves in what is now France was also regularly outlawed, in 779, 781, and in 845; but, as with many profitable and outlawed trades, the practice continued. In the ninth century, an escaped captive who fled to Lyons told of his slavery in Cordova. In the 10th century, the only trade mentioned in historic accounts between prosperous Moorish Spain and Gaul was that of trafficked slaves that came from the latter.[43] The Iberian Peninsula was the locus for the trade in Christian slaves. During the reign of al-Mansūr (Almanzor, A.D. 938–1002) and in one campaign alone, against

---

[c] Muslim conquerors were known by a variety of names depending on their origins and the century. Saracen, in its original Roman-era meaning, referred to nomadic desert tribes who lived on the Syrian border of the Roman Empire. It later referred to Arabs in general, and during the crusades referred to Muslims in general.

the Kingdom of Léon, 30,000 Christians were captured and enslaved.[44] In an age where medieval Europe was backwards, poor, and divided relative to civilizational accomplishments in Moorish Spain and to the Islamic world in general, a structurally weaker Christendom provided human fodder for a more technically advanced society. In the Middle Ages, slaves were about the only property worth anything that medieval Europe could offer to the Islamic world. "The men, women, and children were led across the Alps and the Mediterranean were then the most valuable commodities underdeveloped Europe could offer to Islamic Africa and Asia," writes the American historian and sociologist Seymour Drescher.[45]

The Reconquista and unintended consequences

Even after the medieval age waned, Europe suffered additional Barbary attacks upon its coasts, in part because of an action of extreme religious intolerance that would haunt the country that unleashed it. When Christian Spain conquered the last remnants of Moorish Spain, in Granada in November 1491, Granada's Muslims were, for a period, allowed to retain their religion, rituals, property, dress, and even tax levels.[46] But eight years later, Queen Isabella issued a decree that Spain's Moors must convert to Christianity or leave. An exodus of even those who had nominally converted to Christianity, known as "Moriscos," set in motion the societal equivalent of the law of unintended consequences. An estimated three million people left Spain in the subsequent century, some of whom had intimate knowledge of Spanish coasts.[47] Many who settled in North Africa also maintained links with their Spanish compatriots. That proved useful for espionage and slaving. Indistinguishable from Spain's local Christian population in language, dress, and habits, Moriscos could reside with friends and family and melt into the local population, in some cases, to raid and capture fishermen, priests or merchants, or women working in vineyards; the Moriscos returned with captured human cargo to North Africa.[48] One of the more enterprising expelled émigré clusters turned out to be 4,000 men and women known as the Hornacheros, after the Spanish Andalusian village where they lived prior to Spain's expulsion. Hornacheros rebuilt the then-ruined settlement of Rabat (directly across the estuary from Salé in modern-day Morocco) and named it New Salé. Possessed with a deep resentment against Spain, they aligned with pirates from Algiers and

Tunis, who had already attacked European merchant shipping for a century. As one example, the Hornacheros from Rabat-Sale played a significant role, including in the 1618 attack on Lanzorate, part of the Spanish Canary Islands chain, when 6,500 corsairs ravaged the island in 1618.[49]

The period between the late-16th century and to the end of the 17th century was a vulnerable time for those in the Mediterranean and along the north Atlantic. As Drescher writes, "Corsairs raided the Atlantic coasts of Portugal, Spain, France, England, and Iceland. Occasionally they roamed as far as Brazilian and North American coastal waters. Over the course of three centuries, Icelanders, Irish, Scottish, Welsh, English, French, German, and Scandinavian captives flowing from western Europe would be joined by Greeks, Albanians, Armenians, Hungarians, Poles and Russians from the eastern parts of Europe."[50] The conquering and accompanying slave trade are why even Edward Said, often critical of how Western writers, scholars, and others interpreted Islam and the Arab world, nevertheless wrote that, "Not for nothing did Islam come to symbolize terror, devastation, the demonic hordes of hated barbarians."[51] Said was describing medieval Islamic armies that engaged in scorched-earth tactics and enslavement, among other horrors. "For Europe, Islam was a lasting trauma,"[52] writes Said, explaining the millennial-long clashes between Christendom and Islam until the Ottoman defeat at Vienna in 1683.

The all-civilizational horror

Early capturing and slaving of Europeans and those in the North Atlantic predated the rise and much larger trafficking in African slaves; but in its era, the numbers captured were already significant. Estimates of enslaved Europeans and others vary depending on the period examined. By one estimate, the numbers of English and Irish captured between 1600 and 1750 amounted to at least 20,000 men, women, and children.[53] Robert Davis estimates the number of Europeans enslaved between 1530 and 1780 at between 1 million and 1.25 million.[54] From the middle of the 15th century until the middle of the next one, more Europeans were enslaved in North Africa than all the African slaves in Europe, the Americas, and Atlantic isles combined.[55] Seymour Drescher estimates that between 1500 and 1680, three million Europeans (and one million black Africans) would be enslaved and sent to North Africa in those centuries. That would contrast with one-and-a-half million black Africans carried to the New World into slavery during that same period, except that the white-on-black slave trade was just beginning.[56]

Regardless of the exact number of Europeans and those from the British Isles enslaved from the beginning of the Renaissance until the conquering of Algeria by French forces in 1830—which ended Algerian piracy, the last remnant of the problem—the trade had already peaked in the 16th and 17th centuries, this before diminishing in real numbers. The trade in white flesh was also already small compared to trafficked Africans. After 1680, the British, Europeans, and Americans would transport five times as many African slaves to the Americas as were ever delivered to Muslim North Africa and to Asia.[57] In total, between the 16th and 19th centuries, 12 million enslaved Africans would end up in the Americas (with another one million bound for coastal Atlantic islands and to points in the Indian Ocean basin).[58] Another 12 million Africans would die *en route*.[59] The trade in slaves from Europe and the north Atlantic was substantial in its own right; but it was a relative fraction of the slave trade in Africa that would finally and properly be attacked by abolitionists.

Slavery in the Pacific Northwest

A world away, in the lush rainforests of the upper and isolated inlets and interior of the Pacific Northwest, the moral stain common to the rest of humanity was also present. "Slavery was a permanent status in all Northwest Coast societies," wrote anthropologist Leland Donald in his 1997 book, *Aboriginal Slavery on the Northwest Coast of North America*.[60] Slaves could end up in that predicament for any number of reasons: captured as part of inter-tribal warfare, after inter-tribal raids, born to an existing slave, or if they were an orphan (which could lead to enslavement even in one's own tribe, as occurred among the Clayoquot, Lummi, Chinook, and Puyalup-Nisqually). A wife could be sold and enslaved through a deliberate attempt by her husband at humiliation (recorded among the Haida, for example). One could even end up in slavery voluntarily, this to pay off one's debts, a practice that occurred in other societies where slavery was present.[61]

As with slavery elsewhere in the world, captives in the Pacific Northwest were considered property. They were sometimes given as gifts, including at potlatches; on other occasions slaves substituted as payment for fees due to shamans.[62] In recounting one potlatch ceremony near Victoria, British Columbia, in 1863 with local Salish people and others from nearby Nanaimo and Washington state territory, a list of gifts reveals how slaves were another form of property: "Ten costly coppers, ten large canoes, fourscore and ten slaves, elk skins, twenty score of sea-otter garments, marten garments, dancing blankets, and many horn spoons and horn dippers and many costly abalone shells, and earrings of killer whale teeth and many boxes of grease and crab apples...."[63] Donald notes this as the only reported case of slaves given away in the southern region of what later became British Columbia, but the practice was more common further north. Examples include a feast distribution among the Nakwaktak, where four slaves were presented to the chiefs of Nakwaktak offshoots; in 1832, a Kaigani man gave 10 blankets and a slave as compensation for the accidental killing of a Henya; in Sitka in the 1850s a slave was awarded in compensation for the death of a local woman.[64] On a much bigger scale, the Haida "made a successful large-scale attack on the Gispakloats during which they killed a large number and took many women and children captive," with a later peace settlement leading to an exchange of slaves by both sides.[65]

Slavery in the Pacific Northwest developed at some point between 500 B.C. and A.D. 500, long before European contact,[66] and at contact, slaves were clearly set apart from the existing tribal ranking system and prestige-seeking in the region.[67] Early indigenous peoples also possessed other practices that predated contact with the British and Europeans: cannibalism and the killing of slaves, the latter of which also occurred and for a variety of reasons: funeral feasts, the building of a new home, a new title, the erection of a totem pole, or as part of the ceremony at potlatches.[68] A Russian Orthodox priest recounted how in one Sitka ceremony where a new clan chief was appointed, four slaves were strangled as part of the ritual.[69] On another occasion, among both the Mowachaht and the Clayoquot, a slave was killed to celebrate the first whale kill of the season.[70] In Tlinglit folklore, a memorial potlatch was necessary so fellow spirits in the village of the dead would not despise the newly deceased.[71] The memorial included the murder of a slave.[72] Among the Nuu-cah-nulth, a wolf dance also occasioned the taking of a slave's life.[73] Lastly, in one account of a ceremony at Fort Rupert, British Columbia, two female slaves were burnt as part of a ceremonial display, though they volunteered in the belief they would be resurrected four days hence.[74]

The regional slave trade was numerically smaller in absolute terms, though similar as a proportion of some local populations,[75] ranging from almost nil to as high as 40%; the average was 15% of the local population.[76] One reviewer of Donald's book disagreed with some estimates as to the extent of the trade but not the reality of the trade and attached practices: "Everyone will agree that there were slaves in pre- and post-contact Native Northwest Coast communities. Few will discount the possibility of at least some ritual cannibalism connected with warfare or other ceremonies,"[77] wrote Christopher Archer in his 1998 review of Leland Donald's work.

The slave trade in the worldwide context, and early British abolitionists

Familiarity with slaves captured from the coasts of the British Isles, elsewhere in Europe, or in the Pacific Northwest is mostly absent in our collective memory today, in part because colonial-era governance is often presumed as the worst encounter that could happen between diverse peoples and civilizations. Also, slavery elsewhere in the world was comparatively massive, industrial, and obvious. Ships docked and sailed from ports on both sides of the Atlantic with slaves loaded and unloaded as mere cargo. To note other examples of slavery makes the transatlantic slave-trade no less horrific: The useful observation is that slavery was nearly ubiquitous and with people over the centuries from a multiple colours, creeds, and ethnicities having both practised it and suffered from it, depending on the era.

Moreover, some societies prolonged the trade long after Great Britain and selected European countries ended it.[d] In specific, the United Kingdom was among the first nations and empires to consistently and systematically rule against slavery at home, legislate against the trade, and then abolish it abroad. The first known instance of a clear English declaration against slavery occurred in 1569, when a Russian slave was brought to England and flogged by his English owner, Cartwright (no first name is known). With most details

---

[d] Selected countries abolished slavery, or tried to, before Great Britain. In 1315, France's Louis X issued a decree to abolish slavery on French soil, but it did not apply to French colonies. In 1794, the revolutionary government under Robespierre decreed slavery abolished in the colonies as well, but the practice was re-established by Napoleon in 1802. France finally abolished slavery in its empire in 1848.

lost, we do know that that act of transportation placed the slave-owner in the crosshairs of an English court, where the justice ruled that English law did not recognize slavery. "England was too pure an air for slaves to breathe in,"[78] wrote the justice. It is unclear what happened to the Russian slave.

Two centuries later, in a better-documented case, Somerset v. Stewart in 1772, the status of slavery in England was definitively clarified. The case involved James Somerset, a slave brought to England by a Boston customs official, Charles Stewart. Somerset escaped two years after arriving but was later recaptured. The Court of King's Bench justice was to rule on whether the recapture was lawful under English common law. An affirmative decision would have meant that slavery on English soil was permitted even if the act of buying or selling of a slave occurred elsewhere. Justice Mansfield, who also cited the 1569 case, ruled in favour of Somerset: "The state of slavery is of such a nature that it is incapable of being introduced on any reasons, moral or political, but only by positive law, which preserves its force long after the reasons, occasions, and time itself from whence it was created, is erased from memory," wrote Mansfield. He then gave his objection to the practice and his decision: "It is so odious, that.... Whatever inconveniences, therefore, may follow from a decision, I cannot say this case is allowed or approved by the law of England; and therefore the black must be discharged."[79] In another, similar case, of Knight v. Wedderburn in 1778, a Scottish court ruled that Joseph Knight, a slave brought to Scotland from Jamaica by John Wedderburn, and who left slavery, was entitled to do so just that as slavery was not recognized in Scotland. (Wedderburn had initiated the lawsuit, seeking Knight's return.)[80]

The rarity of slavery in the British Isles was pointed to by the advocate for James Somerset, a lawyer by the name of Hargrave, who gave English historical records as proof. Only "villains," i.e., convicted criminals, could be pressed into slavery, and only in the towns in which they were convicted. There was no general practice of slavery in England, either of other Englishmen or of foreigners.[81] In fact, as far back as 1593, even few of the villains ended up as slaves, with Sir Thomas Smith observing that there, "be so few that it is almost not worth the speaking."[82] This was also the practice elsewhere in northwest Europe, where the presumption of individual rights and thus freedom from slavery was also already clear in northwest Europe. "Chattel slavery had largely disappeared within most of the region north and west of the Alps,"[83] notes Seymour Drescher, with reference to mid-16th-century practice.

Beyond helpful court decisions, anti-slavery advocacy and animus in the United Kingdom was driven by evangelical Christian anti-slavery societies, whose religious objections to slavery was grounded in their view of men as made in the image of God regardless of race and equal in his eyes. Such abolitionists also found a political champion in William Wilberforce, the British parliamentarian whose decades-long efforts to abolish slavery were inspired by his own evangelical faith. Wilberforce's first known act of opposition to the slave trade occurred in 1773, when he was 14 years old, in a letter to a York newspaper where he wrote "in condemnation of the odious traffic in human flesh."[84] Seven years later, Wilberforce was elected as a member of parliament. Wilberforce's early convictions showed publicly in his first major assault on slavery in 1789 with his May 12 speech in parliament on the matter. In it, Wilberforce condemns not the slave-holders first but instead takes responsibility himself and also for his nation: "I mean not to accuse any one, but to take the shame upon myself in common with the whole Parliament of Great Britain for having suffered this horrid trade to be carried on under our authority," said Wilberforce. It was a long, eloquent, and even charitable speech meant to persuade slaveholders and their parliamentary supporters with reason and an appeal to conscience. Wilberforce then moved 12 resolutions including an early plea for abolition, though that and the others failed.[85] The independent member of parliament followed up with anti-slavery bills in 1791, 1792, 1793, 1797, 1798, 1799, 1804, 1805, 1806, and 1807.[86] Due to his efforts and others, in one month alone (in 1807), parliament received 800 separate petitions calling for an end to slavery, with 700,000 signatures.[87] At the time, the population of Great Britain was just 10.9 million.[88]

Wilberforce would expend his entire parliamentary career and ultimately his life to effect abolition. One of Wilberforce's first abolition bills, in 1793, fell short by just eight votes, but successes included the Foreign Slave Trade Bill (in 1806) and the Abolition of the Slave Trade Act (in the House of Lords, in 1807). While the trade was outlawed in 1807, slavery in the empire was still allowed until 1833, when the government finally introduced the Slavery Abolition Act, which abolished slavery and freed slaves across the British Empire effective the following year. That was eight years after Wilberforce left parliament due to ill health. Gravely ill in 1833, when the Whig government introduced the compromises necessary to obtain passage of the Slavery Abolition Act, Wilberforce was informed of the government's plans, and in what seems to have been a self-induced will to live until his cause reached fulfillment, Wilberforce would die just two days later on July 29, 1833, at the age of 73.

Canadian abolitionist actions

Canada's colonial governors and justices took their lead from London and from Wilberforce. John Graves Simcoe, the governor of Upper Canada between 1791 and 1796, was himself inspired by Wilberforce and pledged from the start of his governorship that any laws and policies in his domain that provided a framework and supported slavery were henceforth under attack. Thus, two years after his arrival, Simcoe introduced a "frontal assault" on slavery within the province, which made the importation of any more slaves illegal, a first step often used by abolitionists to erode slavery as an institution.[89] While that act did not free existing slaves—there were yet businessmen and others who held slaves and supported the practice—Simcoe's action set in motion slavery's decline in Upper Canada, including placing slave-owners on the moral defensive. Concurrently, the courts were allies in limiting the slave trade in provinces where it had not yet been outlawed: Lower Canada and Nova Scotia, for example. In the latter, two successive chief justices (who served between 1791 and 1833) "dedicated themselves to 'wearing out' slavery by waging a judicial war of attrition on slave-owners," wrote historian R. Winks in his 1971 book on the history of black Canadians.[90]

The result of political and judicial action from the 1790s under Simcoe and then his judicial allies forward was a steady decline in slavery in Upper Canada after Simcoe's bill and into the next century. Evidence for this is clear in that by the time of the Slavery Abolition Act of 1833, the practice had already effectively been ended by Canadian judges a decade earlier, by the 1820s. That included abolition in the holdout provinces of New Brunswick, Nova Scotia, and Lower Canada, where slavery still retained "sufficient public support."[91] Telling was the amount set aside by London for compensation to slave-owners at the time of the 1833 Imperial Act: None was provided for British North America given, as Winks notes, the imperial government considered it already effectively abolished. With nearly 800,000 slaves freed across the empire, the number may have been fewer than 50 slaves in central and eastern Canada by the time abolition took effect on July 1, 1834.[92]

Abolitionist efforts in the Pacific Northwest

On the other side of the country, it was the British along with Americans who would end slavery in the region, though given the remoteness, the practice would continue for another six decades before it was fully abolished. As one example, in British Columbia, in 1840, six years after the Slavery Abolition Act took effect (it was passed in 1833 and effective in 1834), James Douglas, later a governor of Vancouver Island but then commanding Fort Vancouver, wrote of how the Taku Tlingit prized slaves above all other property, slaves being "the most saleable commodity here."[93] He noted that in the case of the Haida, many predatory raids for slaves were undertaken not to revenge past battles, "but simply with a sordid view to the profits that may arise from the sale of the captives taken."[94]

Douglas was opposed to slavery in words but also action though his approach differed depending on the slaveholders. Writing the colonial office in London, he pointed to how, with "Indian" communities, "I have hitherto endeavoured to discourage the practice by the exertion of moral influence alone," but "Against our own people I took a more active part, and denounced slavery as a state contrary to law; tendering to all unfortunate persons held as slaves, by British subjects, the fullest protection in the enjoyment of their natural rights."[95] The differing treatment was due to his realism: Stamping out slavery in remote aboriginal communities was difficult to enforce.

On occasion though, with First Nations, Douglas did more than just exert moral influence. In 1849, Douglas ransomed a slave by buying his freedom for 14 shillings.[96] Beyond such individual acts, his ability to stamp out the trade in a lightly populated colony in the mid-19th century were few: Douglas called the slave trade "detestable traffic" and noted the evils to which the trade gave rise, but said he knew of "no remedy within our power."[97] That this was so is evident from the earliest available population count in British Columbia, in 1871, the year the colony joined Confederation. The total population of the province was 33,586, with over two-thirds of aboriginal ancestry (23,000) and "other" including British and American settlers numbering just 10,586.[98]

The numbers thus made it nearly impossible to enforce the British Empire's ban on slavery. In British Columbia, slaves would be freed when their status was made known to colonial administrators; but the colonial government and missionaries "seem to have accepted they were in a weak position to enforce their authority."[99]

Decades later, Great Britain's edict was finally matched in the United States by President Abraham Lincoln's 1863 Emancipation Proclamation. Even then, slavery was slower to disappear from the Pacific Northwest, in part because the trade in an isolated corner of North America barely registered in public consciousness, though some recorded its continuing existence.[100] In western Washington State, a treaty between the Makah and the United States government obligated the Makah to end slavery. In 1869, the section of the treaty on slavery was not yet enforced, although it apparently led to better treatment of slaves. The chronicler, James Swan, was optimistic slavery would soon end: "It is to be hoped that, in a few years, under the judicious plan of the treaty, slavery will be gradually abolished, or exist only in a still milder form."[101] In 1878, Hall Young, a missionary, freed some slaves from the Stikine but noted that their owners objected, and in some cases only pretended to liberate slaves. Writing in 1888, United States Admiral Alfred P. Niblack wrote of how the Russians had, when they controlled Alaska, made some effort to ameliorate "the hardships of this wretched [slave] class in the vicinity of the Sitka."[102] Of note, slavery in Alaska was still ongoing at the time of the 1867 purchase by the Americans, and only after would it receive "its deathblow among the Indians,"[103] with reports of slavery in Alaska continuing until the 1890s.[104] The remote nature of the Pacific Northwest helps explain the slow death of slavery in the region, though the combination of the British and American presence, pressure, and agreements led slavery to finally disappear from the region by 1900.[105]

Slavery touched nearly every corner of our world, and until very recently. Two centuries ago, few desired its elimination and even fewer were willing to fight that assumption. The modern bias against the colonial British is often one-sided, tallying up colonial ills but not benefits. That makes history incomplete: That nation and imperial power was the first to even attempt to remove a longstanding scourge of mankind *from* mankind and over the objections of rulers and populations in much of the rest of the world, who only recognized such civil rights later. It is also why romanticizing our own tribes is often faulty and folly: We too easily ignore the benefits another tribe introduced into ours. The earliest abolitionists, British and imperial, helped rescue all of humanity's tribes—be they European, those in the Americas, in Africa, and in the Arab world—from humanity's most enduring sin and from their own contemporaries who practised it. It was a significant accomplishment. It is also why those of us alive today should prefer the company of each other, over too-easy identification with those of an earlier era, merely because they share some family bloodline, ethnicity, or national heritage. It is preferable to identify specific, heroic people in any society in any era and identify with them; after all, many of our ancestors were ignoble in comparison.

CHAPTER 13

Five arguments for a statute of limitations against the past

---

*In the lives of the saints, there is the story of the hermit who
saw in his dream a monk who had died long ago, and who had been
rather weak in his life. The monk was in an especially lovely and honored
part of paradise. The hermit asked, 'How were you granted this place
with all your weaknesses?' and the monk answered it was because
he had never blamed, not a single person, in his life.*

—LEO TOLSTOY

The clash

In the short history of our species on earth—50,000 years and 113 billion human beings born with 7.5 billion sharing the planet today[1]— human beings have defined and divided each other in every possible way: by ethnicity, class, and religion; by first arrivals from newcomers; by nationalities and ideologies; whether one's clan is young or old, educated or self-made; from the highlands or the lowlands; whether rural or urban; whether a farmer or rancher; whether gay or straight; and by race, gender, and colour, among multiple possibilities for definitions and divisions.

Such divisions are not always undesirable or harmful, but specifics matter. The 18th-century philosopher and parliamentarian Edmund Burke thought "little platoons"—our families, clubs, churches, coffee houses, pub friends, and other small "tribes"—were the organic cells of healthy societies. Today we might add online groups, hiking clubs, or neighbourhood associations devoted to keeping a nearby river bank clean. Those divisions are natural and voluntary; they form because we need community and gravitate to those with whom we are familiar. We cannot love seven billion people; we can love our spouse, children, brothers, sisters, parents, and friends, and we can care for those in our neighbourhood. We more easily feel kinship with those with whom we share a common culture expressed through beliefs, traditions, and priorities. It is also why we marry one person and not 20 and become attached to our home, city, and causes. Such desires and peaceful tribal behaviour are more than defensible; they are desirable.

Still, divisions can be toxic when born out of hatred or fear, or when people or the state exclude others based on unchangeable characteristics, skin colour, and ethnicity, the obvious examples. Given both the positive and harmful reasons people divide and the potential consequences of either, it helps to think of humanity as one long experiment in attempts to reach peace, prosperity, and freedom from tyranny. With billions who share the same blue planet, clashes are inevitable, and that produces real victims with lists of injustices and harms immeasurable.

To analyze each harm, hurt, and evil in history, and then the claims—true or false or some shade of grey—is an impossible task. To this point, a sampling has been chronicled: Some university 20-somethings who believe themselves injured by words, looks, grammar, and "microaggressions"; some of indigenous heritage or whose skin colour is not "pale" who can accurately point to historical injustices; others who simplistically attribute one grievous human sin—prejudice, for example—as all-causal; and the reflexive anti-Western theorists at the back of much of the foregoing. Then there are the last two centuries' murderous victim cults where the perfectionism-utopianism, tribalism-nationalism, and romanticism present in all victim narratives were constantly propounded over decades until a spark or a demagogue multiplied the mark of Cain by millions.

To encapsulate all such cults and the infinities of others is to try and grasp every star in the universe. Instead, let us return to the grounded approach of Aristotle: How can we create an actual, just world, not from our imaginations but from what is in front of us, and then ask: How should we proceed? To do just that, return to one example in more detail: the argument for reparations for slavery from American essayist Ta-Nehisi Coates. Then ponder another claim, cross-country and cross-cultural, from India vis-à-vis the British from

Indian Member of Parliament Dr. Shashi Tharoor, in a speech on what Great Britain owes India for imperialism. Both claims can help us think through the more compelling, real grievances; the issues involved; when to offer restitution; and when to declare a statute of limitations on the past's claim against the present.

The claim for reparations

In his 2014 essay, *The Case for Reparations,* Coates offered examples for why Americans should not only recall the historic treatment of black Americans, but why slavery, the Jim Crow era, and multiple other evils might at least partly explain some present-day social and economic problems within black communities. In his essay, Coates chronicled the prejudice and links to subsequent harms: the evils and horrors of slavery; the parting of black families; the antebellum-era stealing of land and other property from southern blacks; the terrorizing and lynching of African Americans in the deep south; the discriminatory housing-policy that cut many black Americans out of the legitimate mortgage market between the 1930s and 1960s (widespread in the north in cities such as Chicago); other business-directed segregation; and the injustice of postwar treatment of blacks who returned from war to find much of the country unwilling to acknowledge their sacrifices and instead were again harassed, redlined, terrorized, and murdered.[2]

The essay set off a new round of calls for reparations, and Coates argued America could never be whole until his fellow Americans dealt with the "compounding moral debts"[3] from 250 years of slavery, 90 years of Jim Crow, 60 years of "separate but equal," and 35 years of racist housing-policy. For Coates, the differences between black and white America result from the effect of that unpaid balance, with "interest accruing daily, are all around us."[4] He asserted that reparations would at least seek to close that gap and act as a sort of moral disinfectant for the republic: "Reparations—by which I mean the full acceptance of our collective biography and its consequences," he writes, "is the price we must pay to see ourselves squarely."[5]

For Coates, the way forward is intimately tied to reparations, for the "healing of the American psyche and the banishment of white guilt."[6] Coates offered up a partial economic argument about slavery and other past evils and the claimed effect upon modern-day black Americans: "It is as though we have run up a credit-card bill," he writes, "and having pledged to charge no more, remain befuddled that the balance does not disappear."[7] Using a 1973 figure of the difference between black and white per-capita income, $34 billion that year, Coates argues that "Perhaps no statistic better illustrates the enduring legacy of our country's shameful history of treating black people as sub-citizens, sub-Americans, and sub-humans than the wealth gap," and muses that "reparations would seek to close this chasm."[8]

International claims for cosmic justice

Domestic assertions that link past injustices to present ills and press for reparations are not alone. Similar demands are now made between nations. In a 2015 Oxford Union debate, Dr. Shashi Tharoor, a lawyer and member of parliament for India's opposition Congress Party, argued that the two-centuries- long presence of the British in India was responsible for multiple ills. Similar to Coates's reasoning for compensation, Tharoor's call encompassed the economic, social, and moral. For instance, Tharoor argued that 200 years of Britain's economic rise was due entirely to "depredations in India" and that Britain's industrial revolution occurred due to a de-industrialized India. Tharoor also attempted to quantify the social and moral costs of imperialism: how tens of thousands of Indian lives were lost in two world wars along with billions in unrepaid loans; the "massive psychological damage" from British imperialism—including undermined social traditions, property rights, and authority structures and the lingering effect of colonialism—which, for Tharoor, encompassed racial, ethnic, and religious tensions. As a summary of a statistic, Tharoor offers how when Great Britain arrived in India, the latter country's share of the world economy was 23%; when they left, in 1947, it was just four percent. Thus, argued Tharoor, the United Kingdom should pay India reparations for that gap, presumably due to the British imperial-era presence.[9] As with Coates, for Tharoor, the quantifications are converted into an overarching moral principle: It is the acknowledgment of the evils of the British Empire that is most necessary. It is why reparations could even be symbolic: "Personally, I will be quite happy," remarked the Indian M.P. at the end of his Oxford debate, "if it was one pound a year for the next 200 years after the last 200 years of Britain in India."[10]

Pondering fair claims

The economic arguments from both Coates and Tharoor are inadequate to the hoped-for end. With any reparation and compensation claims, one first must deconstruct that math and then plunge into the deeper assertion in grievance narratives which animate them, the question of justice. However, on the first element, the $34-billion statistic from Coates is akin to arguments in Canada that compensation is owed to native Canadians for past harm. The claim suffers from the same flaw: the assumption that direct links can be made to incomes and wealth today—not just harm that occurred two decades ago—but 200 years previous. That ignores how continual waves of immigrants and those already present in a country added to its growth in spite of prejudice, while those who engaged in deadly harm in ages past are dead. But economies, even ones where discrimination has occurred, are not static. It is why at the end of the Civil War, United States GDP was $119 billion in 1865 and $18.7 trillion in 2018 or $3,394 per capita in 1865 and $56,922 per person in 2016 (with inflation factored in).[11] As per the Canadian example of economic growth since the 19th century examined in chapter three, every American generation since the Civil War, native-born or immigrant; black or white; Asian-American, Hungarian, or Hispanic, contributed to that growth. The economic tides long ago removed any direct cause-and-effect link between the distant past and outcomes now and where nearer choices and events are the plausible and actual explanations, as we previously saw with Thomas Sowell's work on economic outcomes.[12]

Another argument for reparations is that slavery led to the modern capitalist economy, but that too is also unsupportable. As Sowell notes in his analysis of the slave trade for Great Britain, "...if all the profits from slavery had been invested in British industry, this would have come to less than 2 percent of Britain's domestic investment during that era,"[13] and that when such profits are tallied against later British efforts to suppress and end the slave trade, i.e., the pounds spent on its navy and military to such an end, such expenditures are comparable to the earlier profits. Similarly, in the United States, the cost of the Civil War was over $60 billion (in 2008 dollars), according to the U.S. Navy Department, with three-quarters of that cost, $45 billion, borne by the anti-slavery Union.[14] As Sowell writes, the cost of the Civil War that ended slavery might also be comparable to its previous profits: "Appalling as it may be to think of untold millions of human beings sacrificed for no larger purpose than the transient aggrandizement of others, that is what the historical record suggests."[15] As with any attempt to tabulate the wrongdoing of the past as a justification for restitution roughly a century or two later, every ledger has two sides, and if we are to engage in the grisly math of such calculations, the blood and treasure dedicated to ending slavery must also be weighed on the scale of intergenerational "IOUs."

On Tharoor's assertion of economic damage from the British, he was correct that India under colonialism saw a decline in the domestic market for Indian handicrafts, ones previously in demand by pre-British Moghul rulers. The result was economic damage in that specific instance to India by the British presence and its preferential policies.[16] However, the Indian member of parliament and lawyer was overly broad in attributing the drop in India's share of the world economy as due mainly to the British presence. Tharoor obtained his statistic from the work of the late British economist, Angus Maddison. Maddison, who died in 2010, would not have agreed with Tharoor's overly general claim. Maddison himself encountered similar sentiments in his career and wrote that to reject the broad claim was not to deny colonial exploitation. In 1971 Maddison pointed out that there was "a good deal of truth in the deindustrialization argument," but that "oversimplified explanations... exaggerate the role of British commercial policy and ignore the role of changes in demand and technology."[17]

The shrinking share of GDP also has to be placed in a worldwide context and with a view to Western strength and Asian weaknesses at the time interactions occurred. That includes the withdrawal of China from an active role in Asian trade in the 15th century; the closing off of Japan in subsequent ones; and concurrent developments in Europe that favoured economic growth, such as the rise of religious tolerance.[18] All of that translated into a growing world economy, especially after 1820 when it entered a dramatic expansion and, in part, because of British policy, influence, and reach around world. Not all nations shared in such growth equally. Nonetheless, per-capita income rose in India, and the rest of Asia (minus China) and Africa in real terms, by more than one-quarter between 1870 and 1913, until the First World War ended an era of growing prosperity for everyone.[19] By 2000, worldwide, per-capita GDP was eight and a half times that of 1820.[20] In other words, the world economy expanded and India's shrinking *share* was in part due to earlier British harm to the textile sector, but more so due to faster growing economies elsewhere.

When might compensation be due? The responsibility nexus

Beyond specific charges that can be asserted as true, debated, or dismissed as false, it is a mistake to ignore the charges from the past against the present on the grounds that historical wrongs happen but "winners win" and "losers lose," so that should be the end of it. Liberal democracies do, internally, attempt to redress individual injustices by means of restoration—of property, for example—and other forms of restitution. The issues of apologies, compensation, and reconciliation are legitimate to not only ponder but, on occasion, to act upon.

That some past harmful acts can affect subsequent generations is properly acknowledged. It was just to compensate those who were physically and sexually abused in residential schools by those whom the state charged with educating and protecting children.[21] Likewise, Coates's example of denied mortgages based on race and fraudulent lending when tied back to specific institutions and persons directly affected, and possibly their children and grandchildren, are also examples of clear cause-and-effect links with the perpetrator clearly in view. Also, when a state steals a family's property, never to be returned, that family's life is all the more challenging in the subsequent decades, as it was for those of Japanese ancestry in Canada and the United States. It was why those who saw their homes, fishing boats, and other property confiscated and themselves interned deserved restitution, even though the compensation that did arrive was only partial.[22] While accepted by Japanese associations in both countries as final, the claimants always deserved full redress, and this because there was no ambiguity about the loss: homes and other private property stolen by two governments in each country. Lastly, when Germany under the National Socialists sought to exterminate Jewry in Europe and removed grandparents, parents, spouses, children, and friends from the human canvas, Holocaust survivors had a just demand. In the case of the Holocaust, nearly unique even among genocides, it also was proper for one nation, Germany, to pay another, Israel, given that the eradication of entire lineages meant that only the Jewish state could properly receive compensation.[a]

In such examples, the link between state injustice and compensation soon after, or even decades afterwards, is tight, straightforward, and provable. When a direct link exists between past prejudicial actions or, even worse, harms, and to a person or family still alive today, a useful case can be made for restitution. However, the case weakens the older the example both because of the difficulty of sorting through guilt and innocence as if all of history was a courtroom but also because of the preponderance of *other*, closer prime-movers that disrupt any facile, assumed, easy calculations: the rural location of a reserve and the lack of private property with which to build wealth; the social breakdown of the family in the later-20th century for black American families; technological changes; and wars which harm everyone of every creed and colour and also render most any claim of permanent victimhood and calculations of harm nearly meaningless. At some point, too many waves really have crashed into the shore of our collective histories and retreated, and any effect from deeds committed long ago removed with the receding tide.

Opponents of the present

Clear cause-effect links that tie a recent generation or two to near harms and restitution soon after is a more feasible project. Unlike that, attempts to attribute collective guilt between the long-dead and those alive is historically questionable, incalculable, and a sign of a victim cult unsatisfied with the arrival (at least in the West) of a liberal society, where individuals are finally treated as just that in law and policy and not as members of a collective. To continue the grievance narrative beyond such reasonable limits leads to attempts to manipulate outcomes in the present and on the same flawed basis: Fellow citizens are treated not as equal individuals but as mere cogs in a collective assigned by others. That leads to new, actual victims, as we saw in the example from Harvard University where those of East Asian ancestry were discriminated against because they are the "wrong" minority. Harvard's intention is more noble than when Harvard discriminated against Jews in the 1920s—because they were Jews—as the university's present justification is to

---

[a] Likewise, Eli Wiesenthal's lifelong devotion to hunt Nazis to bring them to justice tied actual people to clear crimes, and, with the goal of specific, contemporary justice.

ensure more African Americans receive a college degree at Harvard. But the effect is the same: individuals sacrificed to the collective and for reasons of race or ethnicity. Instead of such Sisyphean attempts to create intergenerational justice, consider five arguments for a "statute of limitations" against the past in favour of attitudes and policies that instead aim at future, flourishing society.

One: Charging all negates moral agency for those actually responsible

Grievance narratives that reach back beyond clear links to recent harms and instead include those committed against the long-dead blur the distinction between those who committed historical injustices and those who fought such evils in the same generation. Just as harmful: Such victim narratives excuse present-day perpetrators by blaming those who long since returned to the dust. The 2019 inquiry into murdered aboriginal women was particularly egregious on this point: blaming Europeans, the British, and the West writ large for the tragedies among aboriginal women but not those who took their lives—their spouses, other family members, boyfriends, and acquaintances who knew the women.

More broadly, to demand compensation in the present for distant wrongs traps those who in their own era fought evil into the same intergenerational notion of collective guilt. For example, Coates quotes scripture in support of his case for compensation from Deuteronomy, that when a slave was set free, they were also to be liberally given support: "And when thou sendest him out free from thee, thou shalt not let him go away empty: thou shalt furnish him liberally out of thy flock, and out of thy floor, and out of thy winepress."[23] But another scripture is also relevant, this from Ezekiel: "The son will not share the guilt of the father, nor will the father share the guilt of the son; the righteousness of the righteous man will be credited to him, and wickedness of the wicked will be charged against him."[24] Coates's own examples are illustrative because they undermine his argument for general reparation payments from today's generation for the sins of centuries past: payments in 1782 from Quakers to their own 78 freed slaves (350 acres, a school, and provision for their education) and in 1783, by order of the Massachusetts legislature and out of the estate of Colonel Isaac Royall (15 pounds and 12 shillings). In neither case did compensation come from the public at large.

Where a government or institution did pay—Coates's examples include West German reparations to Israel in 1952 ($7 billion), the Bank of America and Wells Fargo in their settled discrimination suits ($355 million and $175 million, respectively)[25]—some victims were still alive. In such cases, it was the same entity directly responsible for the harms, the slave-owners or their estates, the (West) German government, and banks, who made reparations within living memory of the most egregious acts. Here is what is also obvious, even from the Coates's examples used to justify compensation: Other banks not guilty of redlining and religious institutions not involved in slaveholding did *not* provide reparations. Critically, *nor should they have been expected to, given how others in that same era fought slavery*. To offer a general indictment of a generation is inaccurate, politicized history. It makes no moral distinction between those who fought for reforms and those who *fought* reforms. The notion that governments today that represent the public should be tasked to compensate for slaveholders' evil of two centuries ago also assigns guilt to the very people who fought such evils, the abolitionists. Such present-day judgments are a slur because they are issued in general terms against the very people that gave their own lives to dismantle prejudice, racism, and slavery.

Two: The Anglo-Saxon West attacked such evils before any other civilization

This is obvious and evident in the fight against slavery, which only one culture and imperial power took seriously. After Great Britain's abolition of slavery in its empire and subsequent 19th-century use of its navy to interdict and halt the slave trade worldwide, slavery still had deep roots in the African, Arab, American, and Indian worlds for decades to come. When, in March 1844, the English abolitionist James Richardson presented himself to the governor of Magador in Morocco, there to petition the emperor to end slavery, the governor replied that he could not even accept and pass on the petition to the emperor lest his tongue be cut out. The Moroccan told Richardson his mission was against his religion and contrary to the "rights of Men and the Laws of God."[26] In the 1860s, the slave trade also continued uninterrupted elsewhere. The "import and export" of slaves through Egypt, and excluding the internal trade, rose from an average of 11,000 annually in the 1850s to 25,000 annually in the 1860s.[27] The peak of the slave trade across the Sahara desert and Indian

Ocean rose from 9,000 annually in the 18th century to 43,000 on average in the 19th century.[28]

There was better progress in abolishing slavery elsewhere, but after the British example: By 1900, the list of nations and territories that had already banned slavery, in addition to Wilberforce's United Kingdom, included Haiti, the Netherlands, Portugal, Spain, France, Hawaii, Peru, Chile, Mexico, Sweden, Norway, Uruguay, Bolivia, Brazil, Greece, Serbia, Denmark, Venezuela, Paraguay, India, Moldavia, Granada, Ecuador, Argentina, Moldavia, Russia, Cuba, the United States, the Ottoman Empire, Zanzibar, Madagascar, Cambodia, Italy, Korea, and Egypt. In the first half of the 20th century, Guam, Kenya, Cameroon, China, Zambia, Siam, Malaysia, Tanzania, Morocco, Afghanistan, Iraq, Sudan, Turkey, Nepal, Burma, Sierra Leone, Ethiopia, Nigeria, Botswana, Bahrain, and Kuwait would all also abolish slavery, at least in law although not always in practice. Some nations, though, were very late to abolition. It would take until the second half of the 20th century to add the following to the list: Qatar, Bhutan, Niger, Saudi Arabia, and Yemen. The last two countries to ban the ownership of other human beings were Oman and Mauritania, which abolished slavery in 1970 and 1981, respectively, or 197 years and 208 years after 14-year-old William Wilberforce wrote his first letter decrying slavery.

Three: History is rarely about obvious moral choices

Actual victims in any age deserve our sympathy. But charging and convicting the past via the present ignores what should in most cases be a difficult conundrum: Apart from rare, clear evil-and-good divides in history—slavery and freedom, German National Socialists and Jews, Josef Stalin's starvation of Kulaks—in most other histories, people in one age may reasonably believe they acted justly; those in later decades or centuries may conclude the opposite. For example, University of Northern British Columbia history professor Ted Binnema, in a review of mid-19th-century archival documents, argues that pre-Confederation politicians in Canada first defined the term "Indian" in law in 1850 (and which served as the basis for later iterations and also who could live on reserve), in response to advocacy from indigenous communities in Lower Canada. That advocacy resulted from the problem of whites trying to acquire "Indian" land illegitimately or for low prices. That initial attempt and

1850 definition was, Binnema argues, "intended to conform to the 'ancient customs and traditions' of these Indigenous communities," and attempt to protect such land from whites.[29] One hundred and seventy years later, it is assumed that mid-19th-century colonialists were trying to define "Indian" for nefarious purposes; Binnema argues the opposite motivation was in play. It is an example of why it is risky to pretend most historical interactions were all a series of binary bad/good choices with future consequences obvious to those alive at the time.

Another example: The late University of Chicago philosopher Allan Bloom would ask his students this question: If you were a British administrator in India, would you ban the cultural practice of *suttee*, where an Indian widow throws herself on her husband's funeral pyre? To answer, as some of Bloom's students did, that the British should never have been in India is not the response of an adult attuned to real-world choices. Any insistence on historical guilt or innocence must account for choices available to those alive at the time, not pretend-options imagined decades or centuries later. One should grapple with actual history. That brings us back to Shashi Tharoor, who in his Oxford debate implicitly defined freedom as a *nation's* freedom from a foreign power. Shashi assumes that a nation's freedom from foreign dominance is the pinnacle of all possible freedoms. Except that other liberties also matter and are on occasion given life by someone other than an indigenous ruler: The British presence in India was one such case where a widow about to be burnt, or infanticide, was prevented. One can try to weigh British imperial interference in India on the intergenerational scales of justice, but that also requires an accounting of the empire's benefits: fewer children killed due to infanticide and fewer widows burnt due to *suttee*. The British presence allowed for such questioning of norms, a defiance of the same, and at least some saved children and widows. Tharoor's claim posits one set of rulers as morally preferable because they are native to a territory. That omits who wins and who loses under various regimes, local or colonial, and such persons are not always the same people. This is not an argument for restarting colonialism in India. It is an argument for dispensing with simplistic, one-sided historical accounts that portray all outside influences, as always harmful with indigenous rulers and norms as always moral, or off-limits when attempts at guilt calculations are made but which place weights only on one side of the scale.

Four: Straight lines from the past to the present do not exist

The assumptions behind the various victim claims anchored in ancestral harm is that clear lines of responsibility can be traced from the dead past to the present day. It assumes guilt or innocence can be declared by sorting through ancient actions and injuries by armies, rulers, and states, as if all such events can be scooped up and analyzed for independent variables as if a scientific experiment. The attempt and the assumption ignore colliding interests, actions, and passions in history, including interpretations of the same. Consider: It is difficult enough to obtain justice in a 21st-century courtroom where conflicting accounts, faulty memories, evidence, or lack thereof all collide. That justice errand becomes a fool's mission when the creation of intergenerational scales of justice is attempted. One gamely tries to weigh the deeds done long ago by dead men every bit as imperfect—and not less so—than those alive today, with pretend efforts to calculate how past acts impacted the fortunes of those now living.

Ponder an example from notions about the Crusades. One popular view expressed today is that the Christian pilgrims and soldiers, who pillaged parts of Europe and the Levant to win Jerusalem for their religion and deity, bear some responsibility for actions and reactions in the Arab and Muslim world vis-à-vis the West one millennium later. For example, in 2001, shortly after the 9/11 attacks, President Bill Clinton, in a Georgetown University speech, referenced the Crusades, including massacres in Jerusalem of Jews and Muslims, telling his audience that such stories are yet "told today in the Middle East, and we are still paying for it."[30] Clinton claimed a straight line exists between those events and modern antagonism in the Islamic world vis-à-vis the West. The accounts of such slaughter are true but the cause-and-effect claim is not. As Thomas Madden, the chair of the department of history at St. Louis University later wrote, scholars of the Crusades have long known that, after "1291, [when] Muslim armies removed the last vestiges of the Crusader Kingdom from Palestine, the Crusades largely dropped out of Muslim memory."[31] Madden, himself a scholar of the Crusades and citing others including Jonathan Riley-Smith and Carole Hillenbrand, notes it was actually 19th-century Europeans, some critical of colonialism and others supportive of it, who reintroduced the Crusades into the popular imagination in the Islamic world. "Europeans, who had bound the Crusades to imperialism, brought the story to the Middle East during the 19th century and reintroduced it to the Muslims,"[32] writes Madden. From there, Arab nationalists would later use the Crusades as an example of the first attempt by the West to colonize the region.

That many in the Islamic world today sincerely believe the Crusades are why they should be angry at the West, including the late Osama bin Laden, is not in dispute, but the notion the Crusades were forever a grievance narrative in the Islamic world and the cause of modern terrorism is incorrect. The blame of the Crusades illustrates how any event, no matter how ancient, can be resurrected in service of a grievance and a cause. More generally, the conquests of the Levant and Europe by invading Islamic armies occurred long before any Roman pontiff thought of a crusade to win back Jerusalem and environs; they predate the Crusades by four centuries, beginning early in the seventh.

Here is a competing example, from historian Will Durant, one with a much tighter causal link: actions that predate the Crusades by mere decades. It was the caliph Al-Hakim bi-Amr Allah (996–1021) of the Fatimid dynasty who, "half-mad with wealth and power,"[33] persecuted Christians and Jews including burning their temples and churches. It was Al-Hakim, writes Durant, who "ordered the demolition of Church of the Holy Sepulchre in Jerusalem; the execution of this order was a contributory cause of the Crusades."[34] That is a much clearer cause-and-effect link than the one offered up by President Clinton and others with an interregnum of 1,000 years.

Beyond the obvious hindrance Al-Hakim's actions pose to the notion that ancient Crusaders were the first movers with no prior actions in play, the reality is that armies of Christendom and the Islamic world both possessed forces that clashed before, during, and after the Crusades with centuries of terror and horror imposed on multiple populations. Any attempt to account for all of that, to weigh assumed guilt on the scales of intergenerational justice, and to try to balance which side can claim the preponderance of victimization or moral superiority, is folly. It presumes a mathematical, legal, and moralistic accounting, which is impossible. (Even the image of scales is a simplification, as it presumes two constant "sides" in a dispute instead of continually shifting regimes and alliances.) To try to account for historical injustices—if that is how we are to see the clashes by armies a millennium previous—is a utopian project. It assumes the ability to assign proportions of blood-guilt and blame in moral contests and battles between ancients.

As per the example of English imperialism in India, exactly how would one calculate such matters—the outlawing of infanticide, saving of widows— versus the economic damage to the textile industry and the infringed pride of the subcontinent's hundreds of millions? Or specific to North America: If one is native to the continent—or rather whose ancestors were here since the Bering Plains migration—one can wish that Spanish, French, English, and Scottish invaders and settlers never arrived. But those who suffered in battles and conquests 500 and 150 years ago are long dead. Meanwhile, those of us alive today, no matter our ancestry, are better off than our ancestors. We *all* are because of the technological and economic advances: any "Brit" when compared with her ancestors when the Romans invaded in A.D. 43; so too Europeans who benefited from the introduction of Arabic numerals and the revival of ancient philosophers, and this courtesy of Arab invaders a millennium ago. The examples of cross-cultural "contamination" and benefits, no matter how introduced, are legion.

Still, calculate if one must, whether in-country or between civilizations: Rome's conquering of pagan Britain; Germans against the empire of Rome; Muslim conquests of Spain and the destruction of holy sites in the eighth century; the Crusades in the early part of the next millennium and tit-for-tat destruction in return; 1776 Americans who suffered at the end of British muskets; United Empire Loyalists in New York and Boston who were tarred and feathered and who lost their properties and were chased north to the raw, harsh forests of British North America; Englishmen in India and their prejudice against the population; local Indian caste-prejudice against each other; slavery in the American south; African victims of European slave traders; then add Arab slave traders with a million European slaves in the middle of the last millennia and 12 million Africans enslaved by Europeans and Americans after that. Weigh: indeterminable number of pre-Columbian battles in the Americas; slavery in the Pacific Northwest; Aztec sacrifices and cannibalism; the ongoing raids and wars between the indigenous in the Americas before, during, and after Columbus and other Italians, Spaniards, Russians, Portuguese, English, Scottish, and others arrived to further add extra bricks on the historical scales of cosmic justice; East Asians against the Dutch, Portuguese, British, Japanese, and Chinese; Latin Americans with historical grievances against Americans; central and eastern Europeans against Russians and Germans and all of Europe's nations against each other; Turkey's genocide of Armenians; and Jews who have been treated horrifically by just about every kingdom, nation, and empire.

If we are to continually recall and add up actual, previous victimization for the purpose of modern-day weighing on intergenerational scales of justice, it will be a momentous task. It is an accounting that will inevitably end in incompleteness, exhaustion, and failure. It is an exercise in historical hubris.

Five: Individuals feel pain, not the collective

Most critically, the siren song that justice must be done for the long-dead imposes a collective "fine" on the present. It repeats the mistake of ages past where what mattered was not your own character or ideas, but your colour, ethnicity, or some chosen attribute, such as religion. But that means treatment today by the state, its agencies, a university, or workplace, is partly contingent on one's ancestors.

Aside from contrary causal explanations for economic and statistical results observed, the reason such historical accounting is problematic and why such grievance narratives should be dampened is because, to put it plainly, we are not our ancestors. Collectives, cultures, societies, faiths, and countries are never victimized even though we often use language that suggests otherwise. The collective, however identified, is not the entity that haemorrhages. It is children, women, and men who suffer, bleed, and die: a Frankish soldier who responded to Pope Urban II's call to crusade in 1095 only to later lose his life *en route* to the Holy Land; a battle-hardened servant of Saladin who perished in the retaking of Jerusalem in 1187; the wife and children of a Scottish tribal warrior who died in 1719 in the battle with the English in the Scottish Lowlands; the teenage African chained and taken captive and shipped to the American South; the French employee whose factory in Alsace was bombed into rubble by the Germans in the Great War; the American, Brit, Canadian, Australian, New Zealander, and Indian who perished fighting Nazis in the next one; Jews who met the death of God and their own at Auschwitz. Let us be entirely lucid: *They* felt the pain, not us. It is *those* flesh-and-blood people who suffered. So too anyone close to them who knew and felt their anguish.

But here is who did not: their progeny and others generations or centuries later who merely share the same family tree, skin colour, or nationality but nothing else. Expressed another way: The dead do not need our sympathy or our justice and cannot benefit from it. Instead, those of us alive today do. And this is especially true in an age where tribalism is again resurgent. All of us, whether born in New York City, Mumbai, on a First Nations reserve, Shanghai, or Vancouver have much more in common with our modern-day neighbours than with our ancestors or the born-again tribalists of the narrow and nasty variety that exist in every age. That matters to a proper understanding of history and to avoiding tragedies in the future.

The folly of intergenerational calculations

Beyond clear lines of theft to thief, slaveholder to slave, or murderers to those who perished, entire countries and their populations alive today would be caught in impossible calculations if the working assumption for justice is that an act from the distant past can be partly remedied with compensation today, or even that it should serve as the basis for active discrimination between groups today. If one wishes to begin to calculate intergenerational guilt, one cannot stop only at misdeeds and worse; the laudable actions of individuals, families, organizations, and governments in ages past must also be added to the intergenerational balancing act. All of it is why the further one travels down historical paths long overgrown by the thickets of newer generations, peoples, immigrants, and other possible causes for today's observed effects, the more impossible it is to begin, never mind finish, such calculations. Beyond tight provable links between harm and harmed in recent generations and decades, it is otherwise preferable to avoid the impossible calculations that seek cosmic justice from the dead. Let them—and us—rest in peace.

Grievance claims that stretch back further than the living or their children assume an ability to see the entirety of history with unblinking, omniscient knowledge. Inevitably, by dragging moderns into ancient events in a vain attempt to create just societies today, or for some other less noble purpose, victim cultists pit one tribe against another as if peace was not already a difficult enough project without adding historical baggage to humanity's weak back. Such attempts set the present against the past with the consequence that the past is where victim cultists stay stuck, mired in the muck of old injuries and renewed tribal thinking.

They thus miss a better and more useful quest, to answer this query: What contributes to peace and prosperity in and between peoples, cultures, and nations *today*? And to which the proper response is: to treat individuals as individuals with all their own desires, foibles, and potential.

And then stop.

CHAPTER 14

Asian Americans and the challenge of the early republic

We go boasting of our democracy, and our superiority, and our strength. The flag bears the stars of hope to all nations. A hundred thousand Chinese land in California and everything is changed... The self-evident truth becomes a self-evident lie.

—MASSACHUSETTS REPUBLICAN SENATOR GEORGE FRISBIE HOAR, opposing an 1881 bill to ban Chinese immigration to the United states for twenty years.

Japanese Americans and Manzanar

They came for Jeanne's father first.

With hot Santa Ana winds from the east and cool ocean breezes from the west, Terminal Island was normally pleasant, and, as it happened, seven-year-old Jeanne, her siblings, and her parents were there to spend a few holiday hours with Jeanne's brother, Woody, and his wife, Chizu.[1]

Most everyone else in the family lived in Ocean Park, in Santa Monica. It was there in a rented home that Jeanne's parents made a reasonable living courtesy of the Pacific Ocean. Her parents owned two fishing boats and just two weeks previous put a down payment on a Studebaker, a purchase of which Ko Wakastuki was particularly proud. One block from the beach, the combination immigrant and American-born family of Japanese ethnicity was a world away from other Japanese, and Ko liked it that way, preferring integration into America over old-world expectations that often came with new-world immigrant communities.

In 1941, Terminal Island in Los Angeles harbour was home to a commercial fishing industry in which the local Japanese prospered. With a population of nearly 4,000, more than half were of Japanese ancestry.[2] It was also home to a naval base, quarantine station, prison, and shipbuilding port. The island's naval base made it a red zone for an agitated federal agency, and why the family's visit to Terminal Island just after Christmas 1941 (three weeks after Japan bombed Pearl Harbor) was interrupted by Federal Bureau of Investigation agents who arrived to pick through the belongings of the local Japanese to remove any items—and persons—deemed suspicious. Two agents knocked on Woody's door, "FBI men in trench coats and fedora hats—like out of a thirties movie," Jeanne would later write. As they left, "Papa was between them. He didn't struggle."[3] For Jeanne's mother, Riku, it would be two months before she received a letter from her husband, postmarked at Bismarck, North Dakota. Ko Wakatsuki was being held at Fort Lincoln, an all-male camp for "enemy aliens," where he would soon suffer severe frostbite.[4]

The attack on Asian Americans

By August 1942, 110,000 Japanese Americans were transported to internment camps. The egregious attack on civil liberties was hardly the first instance of government cruelty. From its beginning, the American republic had long engaged in a circuitous route to implement its founding ideals of liberty and justice for all. Slavery was the most obvious and wickedest exception to the American ideal that all men were created equal.

With that caveat, the stories of those Americans with Pacific ancestry matter for that reason and because in contrast to theories that past prejudice is reflexively deterministic upon future success, by the 21-first century, the "Pacific class" (as I will refer to early arrivals from East Asia), demonstrated the most remarkable turnaround, perhaps in history: One century ago and more, to be Asian in a country mostly white and black was to be denied the right to become a naturalized citizen. It was, even if American-born, to be subject to petty and profound discrimination because it was your ethnicity that mattered, not your character, mind, and achievements. It was to face a wall of discrimination from the start. One brick came courtesy of labour unions, another from politicians, and yet another from judges, and all in the milieu of a large white population with ingrained prejudice albeit with a few notable exceptions. In the main, Asian Americans were banned from membership in unions, some churches and movie theatres, bowling alleys, and swimming pools. To be of Japanese or Chinese background was to experience a quasi-forced ghetto in major cities and a lifelong isolating experience almost everywhere else.

That early discrimination makes the later success of Asian Americans all the more remarkable. By the second decade of our century, those with family roots in East Asia had long ago risen to be among America's most educated class, the least likely to be involved in crime, those with the most stable family dynamics, and among the most financially successful of all Americans.[a] Critically, the earliest immigrants from East Asia and their progeny fought hard to integrate into American life; they little wished to voluntarily extend the isolation and silos in which others, the racists, would have them stay. Instead, their stories reveal a chosen path that contradicts the unhealthy obsession of today's *cultural* victim-cultists intent on carving peoples into ever-smaller tribes bound together by grievances. For those relentlessly focused on the past and its tragedies, the ideal of the melting pot seems frozen. In contrast to that negative vision, the history of Americans with roots in East Asia provides an example of an approach that undermined the pillars or prejudice and, in the meantime, laid the foundation for the future success of Asian Americans. It includes the constructive power of not only stubbornness in the best sense, but how targeted actions, ideas, and a desire for integration eventually propelled Asian Americans to the top rungs of American life. Chinese and Japanese immigrants and their native-born progeny dismantled obstructions on their own terms. In so doing, the earliest Chinese and Japanese immigrants forced America to live up to her ideals. That turned out to be positive for all. But first a glimpse at the struggle of early immigrants to the United States, illustrated by those whose origins were in China and Japan.

P.T. Barnum and Afong Moy

Initial curiosities before they became objects of prejudice-laced contempt, the first East Asian immigrants to arrive in the United States were almost ethereal:

---

[a] Given that Chinese and Japanese arrivals to America were the first from Asia to arrive in substantial numbers, and the data available on the same, this chapter will focus on those two cohorts. There are similar travails and success stories in the United States (and Canada) from other immigrant communities from every country in Asia.

Three stranded Chinese crewmen accidentally landed at Baltimore in 1785 and remained for a month after their captain left his ship to marry and never returned. Slightly more permanent arrivals followed: In 1818, five Chinese students studied at the Foreign Missions School at Cornwall, Connecticut, while in the 1830s, Chinese sailors and traders were observed in New York.

The new arrivals, if they stayed for more than a fortnight, quickly became a cultural curiosity, the mildest way to describe how others saw and used them. In 1834, 16-year-old Afong Moy was a literal living museum piece, part of an exhibition. Moy was displayed in museums in New York and Brooklyn going about her day-to-day life, wearing a silk gown, slippers, and eating; museum patrons could watch her use chopsticks and an abacus.[5] She attracted 20,000 spectators over six days. Later, Moy, along with Chang and Eng Bunker, the original Siamese twins, were featured in expositions around the United States, courtesy of circus maestro P.T. Barnum.[6]

A more permanent wave of Chinese immigrants to the United States arrived in the late 1840s, in California, and from two spurs that often create mass migration: trouble at home and opportunity abroad. In 1847, a credit crisis arose in China's Guangdong province after British banks cut off funding to warehouses along the Pearl River delta. That created tens of thousands of suddenly unemployed labourers,[7] after which many Chinese emigrants struck out for Southeast Asia while others crossed the Pacific to participate in the California gold rush. They were part of the boom that saw San Francisco's population sprout from a 500-person village in 1848 to a small city of 30,000 people by 1850, making it roughly as populous as Chicago. In all, during the California Gold Rush more than 100,000 Chinese would make their way to California,[8] but the earliest arrivals would soon hit the mid-19th-century fence of personal and institutional prejudice, which decades later would become a fortified wall.

In the summer of 1849, California artisans, merchants, mule dealers, and teamsters joined white miners to protest the relatively few Chinese labourers then in the country and who worked for less than whites.[9] That same summer, on July 7, a miners' meeting at the MokeIumne River called on "foreign taskmasters [and] men in their employ to leave the mines."[10] In 1850, political action followed popular prejudice. A California Foreign Miners' Tax was imposed on the Chinese at $20 per head, per month. The tax was designed to reserve the jobs, mines, and profits for white Americans and white-owned companies. It also held a pecuniary attraction for the state government, accounting for between 25% and 50% of state revenues, depending on the year.[11] The tax also exposed the Chinese community to bureaucratic harassment, corruption, and occasional mortal danger: Tax collectors often gave fake receipts to the Chinese miners so as to extort even more money later; some early tax bureaucrats even tortured and killed miners for their goods and gold.

The 1850s were a continual challenge for the Chinese in America. In 1852, the California state legislature enacted another impost on those attempting to reach the golden state: a $500 bond[b] for each foreign passenger who disembarked from an incoming vessel.[12] Meanwhile, the political harassment of the Chinese diaspora was regularly backfilled with judicial blessings. In 1853, in Nevada County, California, George Hall and two other whites were indicted for murdering Ling Sing, a Chinese miner who tried to defend another miner whom Hall attempted to rob.[13] The next year, Hall was found guilty and given a death sentence. His lawyer appealed on the grounds that the same law which prohibited testimony from blacks, mulatto, and Indians against whites also applied to Asians. Twenty-nine-year-old Chief Justice Hugh Murray of the California Supreme Court agreed, asserting that similarities existed between "American Indian, Mongolian and Asiatic peoples." Chinese testimony was disallowed. "The judgement is reversed and the cause remanded,"[14] wrote Murray. Ling Sing's murderer went free.[15]

Anti-Chinese prejudice later went viral, and national. After 75 Chinese labourers were hired away from California to break a strike by Irish women at a steam laundry in Belleville, New Jersey, in 1870, one writer, the Scottish-born John Swinton, editorialized in the *New York Tribune* about the strike and Chinese labour. In an essay one historian describes as "part anti-capitalist diatribe, three parts racist rant,"[16] Swinton railed against "capitalists" and the labour imported that would make them "absolute dictators of labour in America." Swinton combined racism and protectionism in his demand that Chinese emigration stop. He asserted more Chinese would result in dangerous

---

[b] The fee could be cancelled if a permanent fee ranging from five to fifty dollars was paid instead. Most ship captains paid the cheaper but non-refundable fee and just added it to the already hefty fare that America-bound passengers paid up front or later, to sponsors who always made sure such immigrants repaid such loaned fares in full.

"race-mixing." Swinton argued "Mongolian blood is a depraved and debased blood" and that "the Mongolian type of humanity is an inferior type," the continued introduction of which would produce a "half-breed" and "permit the transfusion into the national veins of a blood more debased than any we have known."[17]

As the numbers of those with Chinese ancestry in the United States rose (1870 census records show 63,199 persons of Chinese origin in the United States with four-fifths of those in California,[18]) efforts to integrate into the American fabric were met with more such rhetoric and ever-harsher political resistance. As early as 1790, Congress decreed that only white immigrants could become naturalized citizens, but that was not enough for the exclusionists.[19] In 1881, John F. Miller, a California senator known for his anti-Chinese views, introduced one more brick in the wall, a bill in Congress that aimed to stop Chinese immigration dead, for 20 years, the rest of the 19th century.

As with the commotion over the 1870 New Jersey strike-breaking by Chinese workers, prejudice again matched up with an economic interest in the 1881 legislation. Miller justified his proposed exclusion on the grounds that the Chinese worked too hard, were "machine like" and were "little affected by heat or cold, wiry, sinewy, with muscles of iron." "They are," he said, "automatic engines of flesh and blood... patient, stolid, unemotional..."[20] Miller's views originated in a combination of protectionist labour sentiment and the assumed superiority of his own colour, culture, and race. He excoriated those from Asia as a "degraded and inferior race, and the progenitors of an inferior sort of men." The senator urged his colleagues to protect "Anglo-American civilization without contamination or adulteration [from]... the gangrene of oriental civilization."[21]

Some who opposed Miller, such as Massachusetts Senator George Frisbie Hoar, identified the bill's transparent racial animus. "The last of human delusions to be overcome," said Hoar, as he referenced the Declaration of Independence and the recent Civil War as touchstones. In the 1850s, Hoar had been a member of Free Soil Party, a short-lived entity whose sole purpose was to fight the expansion of slavery into free states, and Hoar later joined the anti-slavery Republican Party. In 1881 debates over Miller's proposed legislation, Hoar reminded his audience, just 16 years after the end of the Civil War, how race had already "left its hideous and ineradicable stains in our history."[22] The president, Chester A. Arthur, argued a 20-year ban on Chinese immigration was unreasonably long. He noted the contributions of Chinese émigrés in building the transcontinental railroad and to the nation's agricultural base and industry; President Arthur then applied his veto pen to the congressional legislation. But Hoar and Arthur were in the minority among both elite and popular opinion: *The New York Times* editorialized against Hoar's appeal to the Declaration of Independence, arguing that "It is idle to reason with stupidity like this."[23] The public response: President Arthur's image was burned and his effigy hanged.

The veto victory was anyway temporary. California representative Horace Page soon introduced a second attempt to ban Chinese immigration, a compromise bill of sorts. The legislation shortened the immigration ban to 10 years with exceptions for students, teachers, merchants, and household servants. However, it removed the possibility for someone of Chinese ancestry to ever become a citizen. The House passed the Page Bill 202 to 37 (34 Republicans and three Democrats opposed the bill),[24] and it sailed through the Senate with 32 in favour and 15 opposed (all Republican).[25] This time, President Arthur signed it into law on May 6 in 1882, and the Chinese Exclusion Act[26] soon had its intended effect: While 10,000 Chinese entered the United States on average annually between 1852 and 1882,[27] the annual numbers plunged to 8,031 in 1883, 277 in 1884, and just 10 in 1887.[28] Only the 1868 Fourteenth Amendment, which automatically granted citizenship to anyone born in the United States, saved those with Chinese ancestry but American-born from the same politically determined fate as immigrants: exclusion.[29]

Anti-Asian sentiment finds a new target: The Japanese

While anti-immigrant activists and organized labour busily inflamed and shored up such anti-Chinese prejudice and then locked it down with legislation from supportive politicians, the Japanese had, concurrently, just begun to arrive in the United States. The first families settled at Gold Hill, near Sacramento, in 1869.[30] Japanese immigration was initially a trickle, with national census figures showing just 55 people of Japanese ancestry in the United States in 1870. But after Japan lifted its own ban on permanent emigration in 1886, the numbers arriving at the American west coast soared, with 85,716 Japanese in America by 1900 and 152,745 as of 1910, the census year in which those of Japanese origin would surpass those of Chinese ancestry[c].[31]

That increase made the Japanese the newest target for prejudice and protectionist sentiment, especially for labour unions. Big labour and its organizing muscle had long worked to transform popular prejudice into hard legal walls, and the American Federation of Labor was at the forefront of such efforts. For example, at its 1893 conference the AFL stated its opposition to Chinese immigration to the United States in stark, racist terms. The umbrella organization for American labour unions asserted the Chinese were "a degraded people, and bring with them nothing but filth, vice and disease."[32] After having the Chinese effectively banned from entering the United States, in 1882, the AFL turned its attention to opposing Japanese, Korean, East Indian, and Filipino immigration.[33] In 1901, the AFL adopted its first anti-Japanese resolution, calling on the federal government to amend the Immigration Act to include all others with Asian heritage. With reference to the now-banned Chinese, AFL delegates voted for a motion that described the Chinese Exclusion Act as having been "succeeded by an evil similar in general character, but much more threatening... large and increasing numbers of Japanese and Korean laborers."[34] Thus, when the Chinese Exclusion Act came up for congressional renewal in 1902, the AFL was enthusiastically supportive; meanwhile, the now-passed legislation made the ban on Chinese immigration permanent, effective in 1904.[35] American Federation of Labor president, Samuel Gompers, made clear why the Japanese should be excluded from the American labour market—fear of competition for jobs, especially from those with a different colour or culture: "The Caucasians are not going to let their standard of living be destroyed by negroes, Chinamen, Japs or any others,"[36] said Gompers. At the turn of the century, this was the voice of organized labour: paranoid about competition for jobs and animated by racism.

America's anti-Asian low point

For Asian Americans in search of citizenship and equal treatment before the law, the 20th century started out little better than the previous one. The next

---

[c] Those recording Chinese as their ancestry fell to 94,414 in 1910 from 118,746 in 1900.

four decades would turn out, institutionally at least, worse: Politicians made ever-more attempts to ban additional Japanese immigration and attempted to restrict the possibility for naturalization for those already in the United States. While some Japanese immigrants "slipped" through legal loopholes to become naturalized American citizens, in 1906 the U.S. Attorney General ordered federal courts to cease issuing applications to the Japanese. In 1911 the U.S. Bureau of Immigration and Naturalization Service reinforced that decree with a reminder that only whites and blacks could apply for naturalization.[37] Federal harassment also continued into the 1920s. One senator attempted to strip second-generation (i.e., American-born) Japanese of their citizenship if their parents had been ineligible. That attempt failed, but Congress considered the same bill again one year later, without passing it. Instead, a 1922 Act did strip *Nisei* women (second-generation Japanese-Americans) of their citizenship if they married an "alien," a male born in Japan.[38]

Federal barriers were accompanied by additional harassment at the state level, California being a relentless example. In 1909 the California legislature alone passed 17 anti-Japanese resolutions. One gave "aliens" five years to become citizens. Otherwise, their machinery and land were confiscated, sold, and the money paid to them, but now with little prospect of earning a living in the manner previously known.[39] Of course, given that the federal government barred first-generation Asian immigrants from becoming citizens, the Japanese were caught in an intentional, discriminatory legal "no man's land" between the California and federal laws.[40] More was to come: In an effort to shut down any "loopholes," California voters passed an initiative by a margin of two to one in 1920 that prevented non-citizens from owning stocks in agricultural landholding companies, selling or transferring property to each other, or acting as guardians and holding trust land or shares for others. The referendum was aimed at the same first-generation Japanese who, in their attempt to maneuver around the previous ban on farm ownership, set up stockholding companies that could allow themselves, or their American-born children or others, to hold property in trust.[41]

The courts provided little help in all this and were most often an additional hindrance. By the 1920s, a long-running test case with the potential to allow naturalized citizenship for those of East Asian origin reached the United States Supreme Court. Takao Ozawa, born in Kanagawa prefecture in 1875, moved to California as a teenager and was the perfect candidate to argue that laws banning naturalized citizenship for those of Asian heritage were unconstitutional. Ozawa was a Christian with American-born children who spoke only English; he was also dismissive of Japan's claim that all its emigrants were yet Japanese citizens. Ozawa fulfilled every technical requirement for naturalization according to the law in effect when he applied for citizenship: A 28-year resident of the United States when only 20 years were required, and possessed of high character and impeccable English, Ozawa also noted how he was unlike the traitor General Benedict Arnold. The infamous revolutionary traitor was "an American, but at heart he was a traitor... [while] in name, I am not American, but at heart I am a true American,"[42] testified Ozawa.

None of it mattered. By the time Ozawa's case made it to the U.S. Supreme Court, in 1922, the justices concurred with a Hawaii court-ruling six years previous. That judgment decreed Ozawa's "Mongolian race" to have prevented naturalization due to the racial exclusion clause in the 1906 Immigration Act. "Of course," the justice wrote, "there is not implied—either in the legislation or in our interpretation of it—any suggestion of individual unworthiness or racial inferiority."[43]

The Ozawa ruling and the 1922 legislation were not yet the legal nadir for Asian Americans. That came two years later, when the U.S. Congress added a *coup de grace* to any hopes for equal opportunity and equal treatment for anyone of Asian heritage. The Immigration Act of 1924[44] allowed for only an additional two percent of each nationality's 1890 U.S. population to enter the United States each year; it excluded Asian immigrants from even that trifling allowance.[45] That Congress passed the Act during the Roaring Twenties was proof that even a prosperous decade was no safeguard against the combination of labour protectionism and public prejudice. Even more was to come 20 years hence when the internment of America's Japanese would become the latest and most injurious federal government action against the Pacific class in the 20th century.

What the victim cultists would have predicted...

Consider what all such discrimination, the harassment, and petty and profound prejudice against the earliest Chinese and Japanese *should* have meant. According to proponents of the notion that past egregious actions and unfairness pose an almost eternal barrier to success, the result should have been failure: in education, family, economic outcomes, and in the broader communities. After all, the original 1882 ban on Chinese immigration to America was, in various forms, not lifted until the Second World War, in 1943.[d] For the Japanese, who endured multiple reversals in what meager rights they did possess, it was not until June 1952 that Congress passed Public Law 414, which gave those of Japanese ancestry, "aliens," the right to become U.S. American citizens.[46] Moreover, Chinese and Japanese Americans continued to experience informal discrimination for years after formal, legal equality was granted.

Those two communities *should* have foundered on the hard rocks of prejudice and discrimination. That was the theory. Reality would turn out very different.

---

[d] It took sympathy for China as a wartime ally vis-à-vis America's then enemy, Japan, and a 1942 visit by Chinese nationalist leader Chang Kai-Shek and his wife Madame Chang Kai-Shek to lead to a (1943) revocation of the 1882 Act and for those of Chinese ancestry to finally become American citizens. See: Iris Chang, *The Chinese in America: A Narrative History* (New York: Viking, 2003), 227.

CHAPTER 15

Living well is the best revenge:
The rise of America's Pacific class

The Chinese brought distinctive cultural traits to America—such as reverence for education, hard work, thriftiness, entrepreneurship and family loyalty— which helped many achieve rapid success in their adopted country.

—IRIS CHANG, *The Chinese in America*

Trumping prejudice

By the middle decade of the 21st century, Asian Americans had trumped prejudice and triumphed. Per-person income for those whose ethnic ancestry was Korean, Chinese, Japanese, and Taiwanese trumped that of white Americans, who in 2014 earned $31,752; Korean Americans earned slightly more than white Americans ($31,970), with those of (non-Taiwan) Chinese and Japanese roots higher, as much as 42% more for those who traced their roots to Taiwan ($45,084). The comparable figure for black Americans was $19,297.[1]

For some, such figures might point to discrimination against African Americans. In fact, they point to the critical need for higher education and the difference it makes to incomes, as the two are strongly correlated: While 53% of black Americans reported at least some college or higher in 2014, the comparable figures for others were 61% (whites), 68% (Chinese), 75% and 76% (Korean and Japanese, respectively) compared to 87% of those with ancestral origins in Taiwan. On the flipside, while 48% of blacks and 39% of whites recorded only a high-school education or less, just 13% of Taiwanese Americans were in such a category.[2]

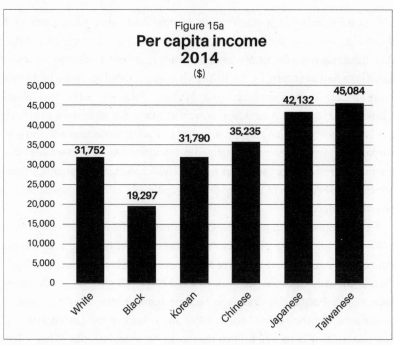

Source: "American Community Survey, 2014, 1-year estimates," S0201, U.S. Census Bureau.

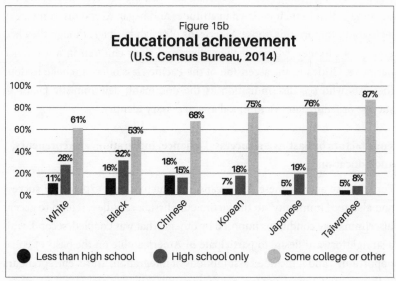

Source: "American Community Survey, 2014, 1-year estimates," S0201, U.S. Census Bureau.

Education has always mattered to income and other barometers of a flourishing life, and the higher income and education numbers for Asian Americans are not a recent development. They have been evident to observers for at least half a century. By the 1970s, when such advantages were becoming more widely discussed, sociologist William Petersen noted this about Chinese and Japanese Americans: how "these two minorities broke through the barriers of prejudice and, by such key indices as education and income, surpassed the average levels of native-born whites."[3] As he also wrote, "This anomalous record, like the earlier one of Jews, challenges the premises from which other etiologies of poverty, crime illegitimacy, and other social ills are typically deduced."[4]

A closer examination of the rise of America's Pacific class shows that long before even mid-century legal reforms to the status of Japanese and Chinese Americans, Asian Americans were already recording higher education levels than white Americans as far back as the 1920s. Whether on education or income, the Pacific class long ago became not only the most educated of Americans, but they earned the most of any cohort in the United States. It is a pattern that is so well known now as to be unremarkable. What is less known is how such success was obtained and how early such successes were occurring—long before politicians in Washington D.C. and California began to soften in their anti-Asian attitudes and began to end discriminatory legislation. Importantly, those Americans of Asian heritage, though they had every right to, never trapped themselves and their children in a grievance narrative. Critically, the ascension of the Pacific class offers a rebuke to dour theorists who see discrimination as the dominant, deterministic factor in success or failure, and victimhood as a necessary identity.

Four factors in East Asian success: Defiance, integration, entrepreneurs, and education

For Chinese and Japanese Americans, four factors help explain the success and also the "immunity" to the victim cult: first, a relentless refusal to accept discriminatory conditions imposed by others. That was coupled, second, with a straightforward desire to participate in American life on the basis of equal opportunity, and it included assumptions of integration. Third, entrepreneurs in the various Chinese and Japanese communities made a real-world difference to their own lives, their children, and their communities. The fourth reason was the relentless emphasis on education, and here the pattern is consistent as far back as the data goes, for an entire century. All of it helped blunt the effect of the discrimination from others. These four factors helped Asian Americans carve out their place in the American experiment and the American dream.

Factor one in undermining prejudice and victimization: Consistent defiance

Casual as it may seem, sanguine "grit" was one critical factor in overcoming multiple public, union, political, and judicial barriers with attempts to counter discrimination and attacks against the Chinese and Japanese communities. There was an identifiable, consistent, and often well-organized refusal to allow others to cement Chinese and Japanese Americans as something other than people in control of their own fates. This stance was critical in forcing the nation to live up to its ideals of a land of opportunity for all, to provide a frank accounting when politicians, judges, and the public failed such ideals.

The earliest immigrant experiences provide examples. In 1852, after California Governor John Bigler called on the state legislature to "check the tide" of Asian immigration, Norman Asing (Sang Yuen), a naturalized citizen, Christian, and merchant in San Francisco, wrote to the governor to express his constitutional disgust in this, the land of liberty: "You argue that this is a republic of a particular race—that the Constitution of the United States admits of no asylum to any other than the pale face. This proposition is false in the extreme, and you know it."[5] In 1853, when a California court ruled a Chinese person could not testify against whites on the basis that Chinese were akin to blacks and native Americans—groups that were also (obviously in the case of black Americans) barred from participation in mainstream American life—the Chinese community refused to "acquiesce easily to white efforts to relegate them into a permanent underclass."[6] In the South, where no such laws were in effect, several local Chinese sued their employer after a skirmish with a supervisor left one Chinese person dead and two others wounded. The judge allowed the Chinese to testify on an equal basis against the whites;[a] he

---

[a] The ruling demonstrated that a refusal to accept white-assigned status could, on occasion, bear fruit, though the era's racial pecking-order meant the ruling was obviously of no comfort to black Americans.

also provided for court testimony in Chinese and eventually ruled in favour of the plaintiffs.[7]

In yet another example of pushback, in 1885, the San Francisco board of supervisors refused an operating licence to Yick Wo, a Chinese laundryman, even after his fire and health inspections permits had been granted. Such denials were a trick employed since at least 1873, and the Chinese laundry guild filed a class-action lawsuit, alleging many of the city's building ordinances between 1873 and 1884 had been targeted at the Chinese. The U.S. Supreme Court later ruled in favour of the plaintiffs, remarking that, while the ordinance had the surface appearance of impartiality, "its enforcement was not."[8]

In 1894, Wong Kim Ark provided yet another example of an unwillingness to accept injustice. Born in San Francisco, Wong left the United States to visit his parents in China; but when the 21-one-year-old returned the following year, he was denied re-entry. Wong launched a lawsuit that eventually ended at the United State Supreme Court. In 1898, the court found that the Fourteenth Amendment, which granted citizenship to everyone born on U.S. soil, of course, *did* apply to Wong. "The fact… that acts of Congress or treaties have not permitted Chinese persons born out of this country to become citizens by naturalization," wrote Justice Horace Gray, "cannot exclude Chinese persons born in this country from the operation of the broad and clear words of the Constitution."[9] It was a rare victory for those of Chinese ethnicity.

Perhaps the most dramatic example of pushback was Wong Chin Foo. The child of an elderly destitute father in China who gave him up at age 13 to be raised by missionaries in Shandong, Wong arrived in the United States in 1867 to complete his education. Wong, who converted to Christianity in China and to Confucianism in America, would later describe himself as the "first Confucian missionary to the United States."[10] A journalist, raconteur, and polemicist, Wong founded the first Chinese language newspaper east of the Rockies, in 1883, in New York City (*The Chinese American*).[11] Wong also lectured and debated, arguing against stereotypes and perhaps only in the manner that someone who, for that age, had seen more of the world than most others in the 19th century ever could.

Wong was focused, brave, and a contrarian; he was happy to "muck it up" with the reflexively prejudiced of his era. That included the immigrant Irish, who produced their own share of bigots while yet decrying prejudice against their own cohort. One example: Dennis Kearney, a San Francisco labour leader, who helped found the Workingmen's Party of California. Pro-socialist, the party regularly bashed the Chinese community as having undercut the wages of white working men. Kearney, born in Ireland in 1847 and who arrived in the United States, at San Francisco 21 years later, was elected secretary at the party's formation in 1877. He was a talented demagogue. That meant trouble for the moneyed class and the Chinese; he led mass rallies such as one at San Francisco's Nob Hill with 2,000 men where he threated to lynch "railroad magnates, thieving millionaires, and scoundrelly officials."[12]

Kearney's party was mostly an electoral failure, but it did pressure officials in California into preventing the Chinese from voting; the party was also instrumental in excluding the Chinese from work at selected companies in the state and from public work projects.[13] But it was in 1883, when Kearney's star power had dimmed, and when he showed up in New York City to try to rouse locals, where Wong's tenacity and acid-tipped pen were in evidence. After Kearney refused to debate Wong on the recently passed 1882 Immigration Act that banned most Chinese immigration, Wong wrote that Kearney was a "disappointed demagogue" who had only planned on "stirring up the prejudices of your ignorant but well-meaning brother Irishmen."[14] Kearney attacked Wong's English abilities, risky for a man whose own English was heavily accented. He nevertheless criticized Wong as one who "writes like a blackguard" and "cannot write English anyhow."[15]

Wong responded with a handwritten letter that excoriated the labour leader: "I write this letter to you entirely in my own handwriting, so as to give your cowardly evasiveness no fuller opportunity."[16] Wong then challenged Kearney on the possibility he might be illiterate: "I have no chance to decide whether you can write at all, for your caution prevents you from putting your penmanship and your spelling upon record," wrote Wong, who added, "The law against challenging to a duel protects you from being called to account elsewhere for your insults to my people; but should it be possible for you to waive that protection, I should not shrink from meeting you with your own weapons. Contemptuously, Wong Chin Foo, Editor, *Chinese American*."[17]

At the end of the contest of wits, many east-coast newspapers landed on Wong's side. One example: *The New York Tribune*: "The joke of all this is that Kearney finds a Chinaman quite equal to his own style of warfare, and actually threatening to drive him out of New York. Wong Chin Foo succeeds at least in making the sand-lots agitator look ridiculous." Or as a southern newspaper, the *Arkansas Gazette,* editorialized: "Wong Chin Foo is a very clever chap, both as a writer and speaker, and although he is a sensationalist, always hunting for something that will make an effect, he is a 'bigger man than old Kearney.'" [18]

Factor two: The early demand for integration over continued isolation

If first- and second-generation Chinese Americans provide examples of tenacity in the face of discrimination, the Japanese community also boxed back against old and new acts of prejudice with determined opposition. As with those of Chinese ancestry, progress was never straightforward but pockmarked with success and failure. Unlike early-21st-century activists who routinely argue particular cultures are sacred, that to imitate or borrow from other cultures constitutes "appropriation," activists one century previous took a very different view: They sought integration and opportunity in the wider culture. They did not seek continued isolation. That was exactly what the prejudiced gatekeepers in the late-19th and first half of the 20th century would have preferred.

An early example is Takano Fusatarō, who immigrated to the United States in 1886. He was relentless in attempts to pry open American labour-union membership to Japanese workers. He helped found The Friends of Labor, a collective of Japanese labourers that tried to act as co-belligerents with the American trade-union movement. Fusatarō, a jack-of-all-trades worker and thinker, also wrote essays in American labour journals and corresponded with the head of the American Federation of Labor (to whom he offered suggestions on how best Japanese workers might be organized). Over the years he persisted, despite relatively little success in persuading the AFL and others to drop their racist bans on Japanese-American participation. [19]

Another example of a pro-integrationist was Kanzaki Kiichi during the First World War. As one of the few University of California Japanese graduates, he highlighted how Japanese associations encouraged Japanese immigrants to donate to the American Red Cross and buy Liberty Bonds and War Savings Stamps, that they were utterly committed to the American war effort. In his appearance before the House Committee on Immigration and Naturalization, in 1920, Kiichi also argued that first-generation immigrants were at least "fifty per cent American in spite of the many obstacles put in their way" and that native-born Japanese Americans were "one hundred per cent American."[20] He argued the barriers to integration rarely came from the Japanese community, but from those opposed to their full participation in American life. He cited racial prejudice, alien land laws, residential segregation, and especially the denial of naturalization rights, which prevented just such participation. Asserted Kiichi, "the question of assimilation can never be solved permanently unless equality of races and equality of opportunity are established, unless all the barriers [to] assimilation are melted away."[21]

A Japanese immigrant, Yamato Ichihashi, also pushed back and in favour of integration. Ichihashi had arrived in the United States at age 16 and attended public schools in San Francisco, obtained two economics degrees from Stanford and a Ph.D. from Harvard (in 1913). While at the Stanford economics department he was also appointed a special agent for the United States Immigration Commission. In that role he studied Japanese immigrants and reported on the same over two decades. Ichihashi regularly reassured other Americans that, contrary to a stereotype that combined disdain for unskilled labour and antipathy to those of Asian origin, the Japanese in the United States were not the "scum" of Japan. Instead, Ichihashi pointed out how Japanese immigrants brought as much capital to the country as did recent European immigrants, how they strove to learn English, and that they were among the most literate of all immigrants, including those from Europe. He would regularly remind his audiences that far from an economic "drag" on the economy, Japanese immigrants were net contributors.[22] Those from Honshu, Kyushu, Shikoku, Hokkaido, and Okinawa desired full participation in American society and were every bit as able and qualified to participate and give back to the United States, as were immigrants from Holland, Germany, Great Britain, and France.

The campaign for integration was evident in other ways in the early decades of the 20th century. Japanese individuals, associations, temples, churches, and their leaders were, for example, at the forefront of anti-gambling and anti-prostitution efforts in their communities. They attempted to wipe out vices for which such communities were accused of having incubated. Anti-gambling drives in particular were "held in virtually every Japanese settlement," writes Yuki Ichioka. Moral crusaders, often working with the Salvation Army, posted warnings of "deleterious moral effects" in Japanese-operated restaurants, stores, hotels, poolhalls, bars, bathhouses, and boarding-houses."[23] Community leaders also monitored gambling houses to dissuade Japanese gamblers from entering. Because many of the latter were run by Chinese, opposition could bring with it a high price: Takeba Teikichi, a member of the Stockton Anti-Gambling Committee, was murdered by gangsters in 1920.[24]

Such efforts to integrate were not always matched with good-faith responses by the dominant white community in California. Discrimination continued into the 1920s and 1930s, albeit apparently with some lessening. At the time, prejudice was still a regular feature of California social life, where one could still see "Whites Only" signs in the state. Depending on the establishment, the Japanese were intermittently forbidden entry to movie theatres, swimming pools, and even mountain lakes. As Erika Lee writes about a young girl whose ethnicity was Japanese, "Yoshiko Uchida and her sister never considered themselves anything other than American while growing up in Berkeley." They soon discovered, in adolescence, that not all Americans saw her the same way. Uchida was forced to call clothing stores, theatres, salons, and swimming pools in advance to inquire if Japanese were welcome. "Can we come swim in the pool? We're Japanese... Will you rent us a house? Will the neighbours object?"[25] Even without outright bans, the Japanese could still be shunted to side rows or balconies, the equivalent of racist treatment of blacks.[26] In 1934, the California Japanese newspaper *Kashu Mainichi* noted that some of this treatment had abated over the previous decade—"it is a vastly changed California from a decade ago, a far more civilized tolerant state," wrote the editors. Yet, there were exceptions. In Glendale, where an anti-Japanese campaign had arisen, the newspaper encouraged the Japanese American Citizens League to work with people of goodwill to work towards the "eventual obliteration of this shame."[27]

It was similar on the east coast, though, with an example of resistance from the Chinese community. In New York City, in 1933, one city alderman proposed that laundries be allowed to operate only if the owner were a citizen, and with high licence fees and security bonds on top. The measures were meant to shut Chinese-owned laundries out of the market. In response,

Chinese owners formed the Chinese Hand Laundry Alliance to fight the proposal. "Tens of thousands of Chinese laundry men would be stranded in this country...."[28] noted the Alliance in public statements. That angle perhaps cleverly played on white American prejudice, but the group also appealed on another level: "... and our wives and children back home would be starved to death."[29] The proposed fees were reduced and the citizenship requirement waived, and the organization grew to 3,200 members by the next year.[30]

Thus, whether in the Chinese community in the 1850s and 1880s or in 1930s New York and California, a critical component of equality-reaching attempts included relentless battles against institutionalized and informal discrimination. Critically, it assumed a proactive attempt to integrate into mainstream society as the examples of Fusatarō, Kiichi, and Ichihashi demonstrate.

Factor three in avoiding victimhood: Entrepreneurs

With a relentless pushback against the discriminatory intentions of others and the assumption that integration was desirable, the emerging Pacific class was already preparing the foundation from which future generations would catapult into the highest reaches of American life. Yet one more factor must be credited with Asian American success: entrepreneurs. In any society, the entrepreneurial ethic is a potentially society-transforming value: Entrepreneurs have to be optimistic and believe in future success; otherwise risk-taking is psychologically impossible. It also contributes to an ethic of possible abundance instead of fighting over a stagnant pool of wealth; thus, a commercial culture contributes to a wider-opportunity ethos in communities.

Immigrants who resettle in another, utterly foreign land are by that action already risk-takers and, for early Chinese and Japanese immigrants, the orientation for entrepreneurial activity sprang from multiple influences, including cultural attitudes inculcated over time and which later percolated abroad. In the case of the Japanese, for example, urban historian Joel Kotkin observes that despite the self-enforced isolation of Japan during the Tokugawa era (1603–1867), it was during this period that an emerging class of commercially oriented outsiders was created, one which set the mold for Japan's economic culture[31] that would later serve the country well after Japan opened up after the Meiji Restoration in 1868, and which began the process of modernization of Japan. That same culture also assisted those Japanese who ventured abroad after that same opening, i.e., the earliest Japanese immigrants to the United States.

In China, the situation was somewhat different. With a look at the 16th to 18th centuries, China's educated elite over-focused on "trying to attain the status and prestige of the official scholar-class," writes historian Benson Tong. The result was a stunted domestic Chinese commercial culture and which sidelined endeavours that might have led to economic change. Tong also notes "heavy government extractions... also dampened the spirit of entrepreneurship."[32] This loss to China, however, was the rest of the world's gain, including America's. The effect of domestic Chinese policy was to drive the entrepreneurially inclined and those simply in need of work elsewhere but who took their entrepreneurial ethos along with them, as early as 1849 in the case of the United States. Tong writes that many were thus primed to succeed upon their arrival in the United States: "Forward looking, rather than past-oriented, emigrants hoped in the long run to control and improve their lives."[33] One example: Many Chinese initially arrived from Xinning, "the [Chinese] county that supplied most of the experienced wage laborers for that sub-region's market-oriented economy."[34] When such immigrants arrived on America's Pacific shores, their existing entrepreneurial drives primed them for potential success in their adopted country. Historian Jack Chen points to the cultural values imported into the United States by early Chinese immigrants: "They shared with the best of Americans the work ethic, an ingrained respect for work, the idea that work is noble and elevating and that a job worth doing is worth doing well," and also an elevated sense of craftsmanship.[35]

An example comes from Chicago with the influence of the Chinese in the late-19th century, and courtesy of one ex-labourer with an entrepreneurial bent, Moy Dong Chow. While in California, he already fixed his eye on Chicago and the opportunities of a city at the crossroads of a river, lake, and commerce. Moy subsequently wrote to Chinese compatriots in San Francisco, encouraging them to come to Chicago; some did, and so too over the next decade did 40 of Moy's extended family from Taishan county, in Guangdong.[36] The result of Moy's risk-taking led to Chinese entrepreneurs not only in Chinatown but in black and white neighbourhoods, where small businesses opened up and included grocery stores, restaurants, laundries, and cigar shops.[37] From one person of Chinese ancestry in 1870 in Chicago to 584 by 1890 and 1,179 in 1900, the start of that city's Chinese community had much to do with Moy, whom contemporaries described as known for his "stubbornness, resourcefulness and shrewdness."[38]

To be sure, the rise of the East Asian entrepreneur-class was also an imperative, connected to a lack of other career choices.[39] In California, as late as 1938, Chinese Americans were still barred from many professions, including law, dentistry, veterinary science, medicine, architecture, financial administration, and even the realtor's profession; most unions also barred Chinese and other Asian Americans during those decades.[40] Government and societal discrimination left enterprising individuals and families with few options *but* to strike out on their own. The result was a channelling of labour into service work or railway construction, or into starting a business. Early Chinese immigrants and second- and third-generation Americans were often forced to carve out niche business opportunities in their communities and, where possible, in the broader population because of the limitations in other fields.[41] The Japanese story was similar, with discrimination and banishment from many professions the norm. That left most Japanese Americans little choice but careers in service, agriculture, fishing, and small merchant activities. In the first 40 years of the 20th century, a higher-than-average proportion of Japanese relative to the general population were small-scale entrepreneurs, operating grocery stores, laundries, restaurants, shoe shops, and other businesses.[42] Nevertheless, as author Iris Chang summarizes the phenomenon of the Chinese communities in this fashion: The "reverence for education, hard work, thriftiness, entrepreneurship, and family loyalty... helped many achieve rapid success in their adopted country."[43] For both the Chinese and Japanese communities and at the time discrimination was most intense, both anyway charted a course to success and for a share in the American Dream based on a desire for equal opportunity. Entrepreneurs and capitalism broadly understood were part of the reason why they brought "old country" habits and ethics with them, refined even in the furnace of prejudice and anti-Asian policies in the new world.

Factor four: Education

Perhaps the most consequential factor in the eventual rise of the Pacific class in America was another element that contributed to success in the coming decades: Education. It was a critical factor in sidestepping a victim cult among East Asian immigrants and their progeny, and the importance of education was already evident in the same era that discrimination against Chinese and Japanese communities was most intense, in the early decades of the 20th century. It was then that education, noted and remarked on much later by mainstream America in the second half of the 20th century, was already relentlessly pursued in both Chinese and Japanese families. In the Chinese community, it resulted in part from the historic Confucian emphasis on "book learning as a worthy goal,"[44] but also for entirely practical reasons: Chinese immigrant parents desired a better life for their children. Given that career choices were often limited by legally enforced discrimination, by unofficial prejudice-laced barriers, by poor English skills, or by the need for capital to start a business, immigrant parents, as one historian writes, emphasized medicine and engineering, which were also "lucrative, prestigious and stable."[45]

Beating the system: The college track circa 1920

This education priority is clear in the early-20th century, where school and college attendance among Asian Americans was already significant as a proportion of school-age children, relative to whites.[46] In 1910, the proportion of Chinese and Japanese children in attendance at school was significantly below that of whites. However, by 1920, students of Japanese and Chinese ancestry at most ages matched or surpassed white children in school enrollment. The trend was even more pronounced by 1930.

Higher-than-white enrollment at the primary and high-school levels was soon matched by similar statistics at college, and it is more evidence of this anti-victim phenomenon: East Asian Americans never waited for long-deserved equal opportunity in American laws and institutions before carving out their future and their children's opportunities whenever possible—in this case, via education. It was all the more remarkable given that the years between 1924 and the Second World War were among the worst decades for institutionalized racist discrimination against Asian Americans.

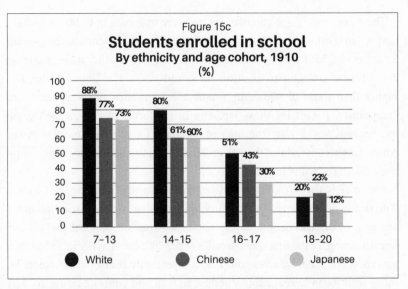

Source: Charles Hirschmann and Morrison G. Wong, "The Extraordinary Educational Attainment of Asian Americans: A Search For Historical Evidence and Explanations," Social Forces, Vol. 65:1, September 1986 using U.S. Census Bureau data from 1933, 1963, and 1970.

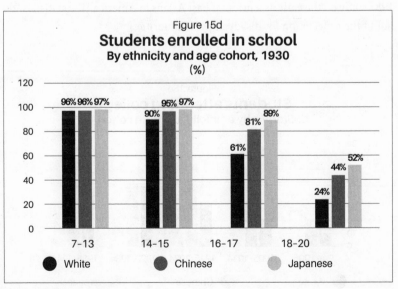

Source: Hirschmann and Wong.

These positive college attendance rates were true even in California where anti-Asian sentiment was most potent. While attendance rates in the Golden State were higher for *every* ethnicity when compared to other states, Japanese and Chinese college participation there and across the United States was higher than those of whites in almost every instance and with only rare exceptions.[47] Except for those Japanese in California of college age during the Second World War (the internment years for the Japanese), as Asian Americans became adults, they recorded college-attendance rates consistently higher than the white population.

Remarkably, the cascading educational achievement of Japanese and Chinese Americans in the early-20th century was not due to any institutionalized *lessening* of discrimination, as the opposite—growing political prejudice—was occurring. In the first three decades of the 20th century, organized labour, governments, their agencies, and courts relentlessly shut down attempts by those with Asian heritage to naturalize, to own and cultivate farms, to start a business, and even to integrate. However, "The patterns for educational attainment among America's Japanese and Chinese showed evidence of early success," wrote Charles Hirschmann and Morrison Wong in their landmark 1986 study on the early ascension of East Asians in America. The statistics "do not fit the expectation for disadvantaged minorities."[48]

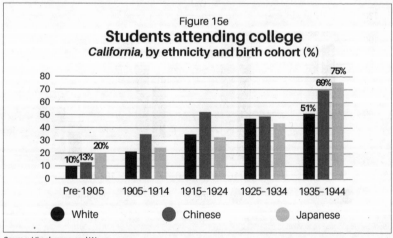

Figure 15e
Students attending college
California, by ethnicity and birth cohort (%)

Source: Hirschmann and Wong.

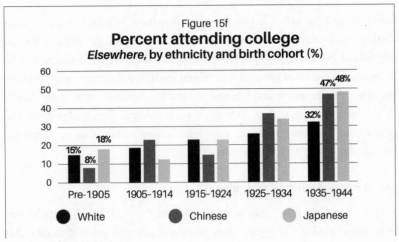

Figure 15f
Percent attending college
Elsewhere, by ethnicity and birth cohort (%)

● White ● Chinese ● Japanese

Source: Hirschmann and Wong.

Undermined prejudice

The reality of significant achievement by the two communities *should* call into question the assumption and then the expectation that discrimination is always and everywhere a deterministic factor in education, income, and life achievement. It is a popular notion but often incorrect. The record of the Japanese and Chinese communities serves as a hopeful reminder that the prejudice of others need not permanently snare all who encounter it. "It appears that the societal discrimination of the first half of the 20th century, although extensive, did not diminish the ability of Japanese- and Chinese-American families to support the education of their American-born children at levels comparable to that or above that of the majority population," remarked Hirschmann and Wong.[49]

Indeed, early-20th-century discrimination was met by a parental class and culture that focused on education as one way, perhaps the *only* way given other barriers, of ensuring their children might have a better chance at future success. Such parents, and the children themselves, invested their lives in education. They did so despite the lack of any guarantee that such dedication might be worth much in a nation intent on restricting their economic flourishing and their integration into American life. But Chinese and Japanese Americans persisted, and even progressed, against the reality of early-20th-century prejudice and barriers. Education, most often driven by family, turned out to be a key factor in emancipation, in helping to undermine the legal and political barriers. After all, it was increasingly difficult for the prejudiced, by the 1920s and 1930s to say nothing of later decades, to take seriously the claims of protectionist labour leaders, politicians, or others with prejudice that Japanese and Chinese Americans posed some sort of "threat" to the nation's way of life, not when such cohorts already demonstrated educational success and soon, economic achievements, that trumped the average American on such measures.[50]

The non-inevitability of victimhood

When the earliest East Asian immigrants from the Pearl River Delta arrived in search of gold in California, there was never any guarantee of those riches or of *any* success in the then-barely-80-year-old republic. When the earliest Japanese settled at Gold Hill, there was likely no conception of how their struggles would, one day, contribute to the American narrative of life, liberty, and the pursuit of happiness. But such a contribution and transformation did transpire despite the willful brick walls constructed by others. In the same decades as state legislatures, Congress, courts, and presidents regularly prevented East Asian access and integration to mainstream American life, Japanese and Chinese Americans already carved out a critical foundation for their progeny's eventual breaching of those same fortifications. Early immigrants and their sons and daughters were consistent in their attempts to challenge legal and institutional discrimination, to emphasize integration over isolation, to expect educational attainment by their children, and to start their own businesses, whether out of necessity or from sheer entrepreneurial "zest." The combination eventually resulted in progress and prosperity. It occurred in an America that, at the time, was willfully blind and deaf to the part that Asian Americans were playing in furthering and expanding the American Dream.

Proponents of the notion that past prejudice has a deterministic effect on our futures invariably focus on historic ills because of their assumption: It is only through attention to ancient wrongs and presumably "corrective action" by a government today that people might finally prosper. The early-20th-century Japanese and Chinese communities demonstrate something very different: A rebuke to the notion that even intended marginalization means surrender to a status assigned by others, that of a permanent victim.

"That discrimination is evil in itself is beyond question," wrote William Petersen in his 1978 work on the prejudicial history against Chinese and Japanese Americans. "The question is whether even the most debilitating discrimination need incapacitate a people if it is not reinforced by other pressures."[51] As the Chinese and Japanese communities in America demonstrated, that need not be anyone's permanent, assigned-by-others' fate, at least not in a country that posited an ideal of liberty. Or, as Jeanne Wakatsuki Houston noted in her biography, "The fact that America had accused us, or excluded us, or imprisoned us, or whatever it might be called, did not change the kind of world we wanted."[52] As it happened, with tenacity in the face of prejudice, a desire for integration and not isolation, along with entrepreneurship and education, the Pacific class won out over prejudice and helped carved out a new and better America.

Self-selection is not the explanation

Some theorize that the early-20th-century educational achievement of Japanese and Chinese Americans resulted from the type of immigrant still permitted to enter the United States after the 1882 Chinese Exclusion Act, such as teachers, merchants, and others who were still allowed to arrive during the subsequent restrictive decades. The theory is that self-selection accounts for the higher proportions of Asian children enrolled in school, because of educated parents.

But much of the immigrant "stock" from Asia in either the 19th century and the first half of the 20th resembled earlier immigrants in their work. In 1900, seven of ten Chinese worked in agriculture or domestic and personal services (the stereotypical Chinese laundry, note Hirschmann and Wong), with two-thirds of Japanese workers in agriculture that year. Similarly, most of both cohorts continued to work in low-paid and low-status jobs as of 1930.[53] That reality was soon to change. Journalist Tajiri, writing in 1934, noted that "long has the Oriental taken it on the chin, taken it standing up. But the times have changed and the immigrant Oriental with the mark of soil and of lowly service upon him is passing, and in his stead are thousands of young men and women, educated, raised under American conditions and in an American environment."[54]

Still, at the time, the parents and grandparents of later highly degreed Asian Americans were, in the first three decades of the 20th century, in work that was overwhelmingly manual and not degreed. Even those involved in non-manual labour were mostly in occupations that also did not require college (i.e., real estate or insurance). This is why Hirschman and Wong concluded it was "difficult to argue that these changes in the occupational distributions represent an upgrading in the social class of Asian Americans."[55] So, the explanation cannot be that most Asian immigrants, including the relatively few admitted between 1882 and the Second World War, had a predilection to higher education. Most did not, or, at least, whatever education they did possess was not reflected in their occupations in the United States in the first three decades of the 20th century. Yet their children and grandchildren would soon match and then surpass immigrants from Europe, first in educational attainment, and then in incomes.

CHAPTER 16

Two wars and two families: A personal reflection

A person who broods on revenge only worsens his wounds.
His injuries would heal if he would refrain.

—Francis Bacon

Central Europe 1914

In the early summer of 1914, Lydia, then three years old, would have looked around to see a simple home: a two-room house, one with a board floor over the cellar and with whitewashed walls. Most of the furniture was basic and handmade, "a long wooden table, several chairs and benches, and a cradle," as relatives would later describe it in a family history booklet. It was a typical farm house of its era, late-19th-century vintage: A log house connected to the barn by a central area with a dirt floor at its entrance; a loft covered the entire building. The house and barn were enclosed by a thatched roof made of rye straw. Inside the home, white cotton curtains would flap when the windows were open in the heat of summer; a large brick baking-oven and another brick oven both served the dual purpose of keeping the home warm in winter and to prepare food. Julianna, the mother, would make "huge batches of ten or eleven loaves of bread every week to feed her large family," shaping them into "round loaves" and setting them "to rise on the thick feather blankets on the beds," according to the same account.[a] The round loaves were slid into

---

[a] In this chapter, I avoid endnotes. The recounted family history comes from Dot Ruff and Lena Pawloske, The Story of Nickolaus and Julianna Busenius, September 1982, and from a family tree compiled by Harvey Milke, for descendants of Johann Milke. I have also drawn on conversations with relatives and my late grandparents. This story is from the paternal side of my family. If I recounted family history on my maternal side, it would be an equally interesting tale. At present, the memory I most cherish on that side is my maternal grandmother's constant kindness and cheerfulness, despite challenges. Those are also traits possessed in abundance by my mother.

the fired-up oven with a large wooden paddle. Rudimentary shelves stored utensils and supplies in the kitchen.

The home and barn stood on a narrow, 15-acre farmyard; plowing was performed with a single-furrowed walking plow pulled by two horses over ground where wheat and flax would eventually rise. The barn was home to those horses along with seven cows and calves and between 15 and 20 chickens, depending on the day. The two-room house and loft were home to 15 children over the years (not all lived to adulthood). There were eight boys and seven girls, one of whom was my grandmother, Lydia. Her early childhood home was in Ludmilovka, 12 miles from the district capital of Zhytomyr, in Ukraine. The climate was mild and the family farm had trees with apples, pears and plums, the taste of which Lydia even at three would have remembered at harvest time.

Lydia's parents always wanted to move to Canada and at one point were sent money by Edmonton relatives to make the journey. In July 1914, the family packed up all the belongings they could carry and made their way to the port of Libau, in Latvia. Before embarking, a medical examination found treatable eye disease in most of the family. That necessitated a two-week delay, by which time the ill wind of fate intervened: War broke out in Europe. With soldiers in the streets and ships burning in the harbour, the family returned to their home town.

Events would again conspire, and not in their favour: As the German army advanced on Ukraine in July 1915, my paternal grandmother's entire family was on the move, expelled from Ludmilovka along with other Germans on the assumption their ethnic tribe would inevitably be disloyal to Ukraine. Over a two-year refugee journey, my grandmother, her siblings, and her parents migrated over thousands of miles via wagons, caravans, and freight cars through Central Europe and Russia in search of work, food, and shelter. They eventually ended their journey in Siberia in 1917 and found work on a farm, along with seven other families, near Marionovka. It was owned by a Mennonite German farmer whose last name was Fast and whose first name is unknown to us.

Their stay was short-lived. The Bolsheviks took power in Russia in the November 1917 Revolution, but they took three years to cross the Volga. By 1920, the revolution's foot soldiers reached Omsk and then the Fast farm and soon confiscated it for the new regime and for themselves. The best horses and wagons were taken, as was grain, food, clothing, and anything else of value desired by the revolutionaries. Fast and other landowners were taken prisoner, never to be seen again. Lydia, along with the rest of her family, soon migrated back west, this time to Minsk and then, much later, finally, in early 1927 to Canada. They endured a 13-year disruption to their plans. There, a few years later, my grandmother would meet my grandfather, Adolph Milke. He was also of German stock, having left the then-German region in west Poland and his village, arriving at the port of Halifax in 1929 and from there making his way to the wilds of western Canada. Adolph and Lydia would meet in Edmonton and marry in 1933; Adolph was 26 and Lydia was 22.

In the 1930s, my grandfather regularly urged his own family to emigrate to Canada. My great-grandmother refused, apparently writing to my grandfather a variation of the following sentiment, which I paraphrase: "My parents lived and died on this farm; my grandparents worked, lived, and died on this farm; I will live, work, and die on this farm too." Fate again intervened and had its own course to set for my great-grandmother's future. The Germans invaded Poland in September 1939, and three of my grandfather's brothers were either drafted into the German war machine or, as is possible given German infatuation with pure culture and pure race and for a German empire, signed up for service. All three would die during the war: Ludwig II was killed during the German Army's siege of Stalingrad on November 5, 1942; Erich, for whom my father was named, died either on August 24 or 25, 1943, in Sudabschnitt in the Soviet Union; and Johann III died at Brest-Litovsk in March 1945. My great-grandfather passed away during the war, in 1942, in Kozy, the north-central village in Poland where his wife, my great-grandmother, was born and insisted on staying. Postwar, with Poland overrun by the Soviet Union, German farms were confiscated for the Poles and at some point, my great-grandmother made her way to Edmonton where she lived until her death in 1966. After the war, my grandfather, never a bitter man, did express sorrow to his mother. If only had she had listened to him and moved the family to Canada as he always urged in the 1930s, her sons—his three brothers—might still be alive.

I recount the stories because in 2002 my brother and father travelled to the old family farm in Kozy, 250 kilometres due south of modern-day Gdansk, in Poland. They first wandered around the village, peeked into the Lutheran church where my grandfather was baptized, and then found their way to the family farm. Upon arriving and introducing themselves, the Polish family who now lived there seemed nervous. Perhaps they wondered if the visit was a precursor to a property claim for the land and farm confiscated from my great-grandmother a half-century previous.

That action was never envisioned by any of us. After the ejection of communism from Poland in 1989, there was modest compensation to some Milkes somewhere in Germany for the family farm. It is not clear whether, if the farm had been wholly returned, a marginal portion of it would have made any substantial difference to anyone in our family tree, my grandparents included.[b] For one, property divided among multiple progeny in inheritances is usually inconsequential to building wealth unless one's surname is Rockefeller. In addition, subsequent economic booms and busts often make such inheritances inconsequential by the second or third generation anyway. It is why stories of subsequent generations who bankrupt the family business are legion. It is more likely that time and the continual tide of events would have washed over and obscured any such inheritance.

My grandfather's choices, as with everyone's, were more determinative. He initially eked out a living on a farm near Edmonton. When that enterprise hit a rough patch, he moved the family to Kelowna in the 1950s. There he made a decent living building modest houses between that decade and the 1970s. Coincidentally, with history in the rearview mirror, my grandparents did own land in Kelowna where Okanagan College now exists, a central location not far from Lake Okanagan. Had they held part of that land, they might have become wealthy. The property my grandparents once owned is now dotted by that college, a high school, apartments, and single-family homes. My grandfather sold off that land in parcels in his earliest years in the city because he earned his living pounding nails and erecting homes to sell; he never thought, or desired, to hold property beyond its immediate use. He was a cautious man with no burning desire to be rich. He was happy with the modest income he derived from building and selling homes in what was then a small, ordinary town in the British Columbia interior, where most people

---

[b] The Ludmilovka, Ukraine, farm where my grandmother grew up was never owned by the family. It was apparently owned by rich Russian royals, with rent due twice a year.

had modest incomes and similar ambitions. An example of his values: My grandfather once told me he priced his homes slightly below their actual value so the next owner would have a little bit of potential profit himself. He thought that was prudent if one wanted to sell a house rather than have money tied up in the hopes of squeezing another dime or dollar out of a sale. I think he was right to live that way.

In the first 20 years of life, before I left Kelowna, my grandparents were alive that entire time. Growing up, I never heard them complain about anything: Not my grandmother's multiple years in central and Eastern Europe and Russia as a child refugee, where two of her sisters, one younger (Alvina) and one older (Olga), would die in those early years; or missed opportunities. In all the years of shuttling around before, during, and after wars, she could never go to school; as a result, she never learned to read or write. For the rest of her life, my grandmother marked legal documents with an "X." Nor did I ever hear my grandfather complain of his family's loss, not the farm or even his brothers, though he must have missed them terribly. He never mentioned that he once held land that could have made him rich. I only heard that story later from an uncle.

When I think about their lives, my grandparents were victims—of others, of two wars, and people and events over which they had no control—but they never thought of themselves that way. They thus also avoided the temptation of Cain: bitterness. My memory of my grandfather is of one who expressed continual gratitude at what a wonderful country he lived in; how grateful he was for Canada.

I am sure my grandmother felt the same way. I suspect she must have missed the siblings she lost, perhaps also the farm she knew as a child. All I know for sure is that my grandmother made a new life. If she looked back at all, it was to bring the best, not the worst, from the past into the present. My grandparents always kept a decorative and a working garden until very late in life. Their yard was full of red roses, and plants and vines full of potatoes, peas, rhubarb, and beans. They also had trees with apples, pears, and plums. Perhaps that fruit was a reminder of the best memories from Lydia's early life in Ukraine.

That makes sense to me, as my grandmother never lived as a victim.

ACKNOWLEDGEMENTS
AND THE SPUR FOR *THE VICTIM CULT*

The initial genesis for this book came from my ongoing work over the years on aboriginal issues and frustration with the same. Without detouring into a rabbit trail of examples, I watched as some indigenous leaders (and plenty of non-aboriginal) repeat and recommend the same policy mistakes and thus fulfill the definition of insanity: repeating the same thing over and over and expecting different results.

It also became clear that too many, with notable exceptions, anchored their ideas and policy in multiple grievances, some contrived and some deadly accurate, but with the result that their own potentially positive future instead became trapped in victim narratives. This book began with that observation as a spur. In eight years of research, it soon became clear that victim cults, as I came to label them, are a recurring problem in human history and for all the reasons explained in the book.

Given how *The Victim Cult* was conceived, it is a fortunate coincidence that I met Ellis Ross in the spring of 2019, as I was completing the book. Ross is a former elected chief councillor for the Haisla First Nation on the coast of British Columbia. As I heard Ross speak at an event in Calgary, and in discussions afterward, it became clear that he saw the same problem I did: how people, communities, and entire nations can, if not vigilant, become stuck in the past. That guarantees a miserable future.

The topic of First Nations in Canada, analyzed in various ways in *The Victim Cult*, is a difficult issue, one with potential "landmines" in policy and public life. That is why even the grievances, misguided or correct, placed in proper context or used for some other end, should be openly but critically discussed. This is especially useful for those whose ancestors 20,000 years ago crossed the Bering Plains to become the first settlers in the Americas. Sincere but error-prone policy and an over-focus on grievances damage First Nations more than anyone else. Thus, given the spur for this book, there is fortuitous irony that Ellis Ross agreed to write the foreword, and my first "thank you" is to Ellis.

In addition, others who were very helpful include Patrick Donnelly, Faith Farthing, Tom Flanagan, Philip Cross, Livio Di Matteo, Ian Brodie, Nancy Wise, Joel Emes, Tricia Radison, Louise Fairley, my book agent Sam Hiyate, and Diane Terrana at The Rights Factory. One friend, Mark Mitchell, alerted me to how the enslavement of those living in the north Atlantic and Europe was once a reality, history of which I was unaware. I would also like to thank Pat Trottier and Gwyn Morgan for their generous support for this book.

My siblings, Tim, Lois, and Sharon also provided some advice and feedback, and I am grateful to them as well. Tim in particular read over chapters during his summer holiday and provided "fresh eye" feedback. Milan Szabo, as usual, provided a superb cover and interior book design.

Thank you to all of you.

ENDNOTES

Chapter 1: From Cain and Abel to Donald Trump: A journey through blame

1. Genesis 4:10, *The New Student Bible, New International Version* (Grand Rapids: Zondervan, 1992), 31.
2. Ibid.
3. Genesis 4:6–7, 31.
4. Ibid.
5. Genesis 4:9.
6. Genesis 4:10.
7. John Chrysostom, "Against the Jews," Homily 4, https://bit.ly/2O284T0.
8. Will Durant, *The Age of Faith (The Story of Civilization, Volume IV)* (New York: Simon & Schuster, 1950), 282–83.
9. Chrysostom.
10. Harry Jaffa, *A New Birth of Freedom: Abraham Lincoln and the Coming of the Civil War* (Oxford: Rowman & Littlefield, 2000), 231–232.
11. Dred Scott v. Sandford, 60 U.S. 393 (1856), https://bit.ly/2WfCwJv.
12. Melvin I. Urofsky, "Dred Scott decision," *Encyclopaedia Britannica*, last modified August 1, 2019, https://bit.ly/2xUDNJb.
13. Paul Quigley, *Shifting Grounds: Nationalism and the American South, 1848–1865* (Oxford: Oxford Scholarship, 2012), 30.
14. Jaffa, 170.
15. Quigley, 29.
16. Carol Anderson, *White Rage: The Unspoken Truth of Our Racial Divide* (New York: Bloomsbury, 2017), 46.
17. Karl Marx, *Economic and Philosophic Manuscripts of 1844* (Moscow: Progress Publishers, 1977), 36.
18. Ibid., 109.
19. Stéphane Courtois, Nicolas Werth, Jean-Louis Panné et al, T*he Black Book of Communism*, translated by Jonathan Murphy and Mark Kramer (Cambridge and London: Harvard University Press, 1999), 59.
20. Ibid., 46.
21. Nicolas Werth in Courtois, Werth, Panné et al., 470.
22. Mao Tse-tung, *Report on the Peasant Movement in the Human* (1927), https://bit.ly/2YQtfJ1.
23. Werth, 582–593.
24. Robert Conquest, *Reflections on a Ravaged Century* (London: John Murray, 1999), 48–49.
25. Werth, 568–569, 572–573.
26. "Oklahoma City Bombing: 20 Years Later," Federal Bureau of Investigation, April 16, 2015, 1–31, https://bit.ly/2qr7jUj.
27. Tracy McVeigh, "The McVeigh Letters: Why I Bombed Oklahoma," *The Observer*, May 6, 2001, https://bit.ly/2gQwSNC.
28. James Hider and Philippe Naughton, "Fort Hood Gunman Major Nidal Hasan Had Being [sic] Trying to Leave 'Anti Muslim' Army," *The Times*, November 6, 2009, https://bit.ly/2Lky8H4.
29. Christopher Diamond, "Fort Hood Shooter Goes on Hunger Strike," *Army Times*, April 4, 2017, https://bit.ly/2NUkSuL.
30. Reuters, "Factbox: Excerpts From 1,500-Page Norway Killer Manifesto," July 24, 2011, https://reut.rs/2JF3ia5.
31. Ibid.
32. Edward Said, *Orientalism* (New York: Vintage Books, 1994), xix.
33. Ibid., xv.
34. Quigley, 29.
35. Zeke Miller, "Trump Blasts 'Nasty,' 'Unfair' Debate Questions," *Time*, August 15, 2015, https://bit.ly/2Lq1fJd.
36. Hank Berrien, "7 Times Donald Trump Whined Life Was Unfair," *The Daily Wire*, March 28, 2016, https://bit.ly/2JAQCje.

37. Callum Borchers, "Did a Debate Moderator Just Get Donald Trump to Back Down? Yes, He Did." *Washington Post*, December 16, 2015, https://wapo.st/2YMMO4U.

38. Jesse Byrnes, "NY Tabloids Mock Trump over Iowa Loss," *The Hill*, February 2, 2016, https://bit.ly/2Y13kRs.

39. "Trump Slams 'Unfair' Media Coverage of Iowa Caucus Loss," *Fox News*, February 2, 2016, https://bit.ly/30FoUZJ.

40. Jesse Byrnes, "Trump: Contested Convention Would Be 'Pretty Unfair,'" *The Hill*, March 8, 2016, https://bit.ly/2G6h2sf.

41. John Frank, "Angry Donald Trump Blasts Colorado GOP Results as 'Totally Unfair,'" *Denver Post*, April 20, 2016, https://dpo.st/30tEYNS.

42. Hank Berrien, "7 Times Donald Trump Whined Life Was Unfair," *The Daily Wire*, March 28, 2016, https://bit.ly/2JAQCje.

43. Theodore Schleifer, "Trump Defends Criticism of Judge with Mexican Heritage," *CNN*, June 5, 2016, https://cnn.it/2LPpM9R.

44. "Donald Trump Blasts Media for Dishonest, Unfair Coverage," *Fox News*, June 27, 2016, https://bit.ly/2NTWiKF.

45. Christopher Brennan, "Donald Trump Compares Himself to Victims of Police Shootings, Rejects Invitation to Speak at NAACP," *New York Daily News*, July 13, 2016, https://bit.ly/29xdDQw.

46. Rory Carroll, "Top Trump Adviser: News Corp Bashes Him Due to Commercial Interest in China," *The Guardian*, July 18, 2016, https://bit.ly/30upJnV.

47. Berrien.

48. Peter W. Stevenson, "18 Times Donald Trump Complained about Being Treated Unfairly" *Washington Post*, April 29, 2016, https://bit.ly/30upJnV.

49. Jason Schwartz, "55 Years Ago—'The Last Press Conference,'" don Foundation, November 14, 2017, https://bit.ly/2YPE0v2.

50. Jeremy Diamond, "Donald Trump: 'I Keep Whining and Whining Until I Win,'" *CNN*, August 11, 2015, https://cnn.it/2Y6uZjU.

Chapter 2: The fake victimhood of 20-something totalitarians

1. "UCLA Call 2 Action," Care2 Petitions, accessed August 4, 2019, https://bit.ly/2Y14UTF.

2. Ibid.

3. Ibid.

4. "Val Rust," UCLA Graduate School of Education & Information Studies, https://bit.ly/2YVDnjC.

5. Sam Hoff, "Students Defend Professor after Sit-In over Racial Climate," Daily Bruin, November 20, 2013, https://bit.ly/1ppJd8d.

6. Colleen Flaherty, "In-Class Sit-in," *Inside Higher Ed*, November 25, 2013, https://bit.ly/2LWfHba.

7. Ibid.

8. Ibid.

9. Ibid.

10. Heather MacDonald, "The Microaggression Farce," *City Journal*, Autumn 2014, https://bit.ly/2Z03tC0.

11. Carlos Moreno, "Independent Investigative Report on Acts of Bias and Discrimination Involving Faculty at the University of California, Los Angeles," October 5, 2013, 10–14, https://bit.ly/2xkYyQ7.

12. MacDonald.

13. Colleen Flaherty, "Adding Faculty After Sit-In," *Inside Higher Ed*, December 9, 2013, https://bit.ly/2GgCwmp.

14. Kathryn Hinderaker, "The Assault on Academic Freedom at UCLA," *The College Fix*, October 23, 2017, https://bit.ly/2JDZWEl.

15. Flaherty.

16. MacDonald.

17. Stephanie Kim, "Moore Hall Sit-In Addressing Discrimination Lacked Open, Tolerant Spirit," *Daily Bruin*, November 20, 2013, https://bit.ly/2YXc2O3.

18. UCLA Call 2 Action.

19. MacDonald.

20. "Kenjus T. Watson," Rankin & Associates Consulting, accessed August 4, 2019, https://bit.ly/2YSjREB.

21. "Kenjus Watson," University of California Los Angeles, accessed August 4, 2019, http://ucla.academia.edu/KenjusWatson.

22. "Email from The Intercultural Affairs Committee – Yale University," Foundation for Individual Rights in Education, October 27, 2015, https://bit.ly/1Ql615e.

23. Erika Christakis: "Dressing Yourselves," email to Silliman College (Yale) Students on Halloween costumes, October 30, 2015, https://bit.ly/1HBXDad.

24. Monica Wang and Victor Wang, "Salovey, Holloway affirm support for Christakises," *YaleNews*, November 18, 2015, https://bit.ly/2Y8Sfhb.

25. Jamie Kirchik, "Reflections on the Revolution at Yale," *Quillette*, September 9, 2018, https://bit.ly/2YXF5Rz.

26. "Yale Halloween Costume Controversy," recorded video, Foundation for Individual Rights in Education, last updated November 6, 2015, https://bit.ly/1NNozdL.

27. Ibid.

28. Wang and Wang.

29. David Shimey and Victor Wang, "Students Submit New Demands to Salovey," *YaleNews*, November 13, 2015, https://bit.ly/2XMsOmt.

30. Shimey and Wang.

31. Peter Salovey, "Statement from President Salovey: Toward a Better Yale," *YaleNews*, November 17, 2015, https://bit.ly/2Y7COWK.

32. Nico Perrino, "Yale Faculty Resign from Residential College Roles; Concerns about Free Speech Remain," Foundation for Individual Rights in Education, May 26, 2016, https://bit.ly/2XT16iV.

33. Blake Neff, "Meet the Privileged Yale Student Who Shrieked at her Professor," *The Daily Caller*, November 9, 2015, https://bit.ly/30AEQfx.

34. Wang and Wang.

35. Ibid.

36. Ibid.

37. Perrino.

38. Chloe Marina Manchester, "Day of Absence Changes Form," *The Cooper Point Journal*, April 10, 2017, https://bit.ly/2XO3fBh.

39. Bari Weiss, "When the Left Turns on Its Own," *New York Times*, June 1, 2017, https://nyti.ms/2rqnKRq.

40. Bret Weinstein, "The Campus Mob Came for Me—and You, Professor, Could Be Next," *Wall Street Journal*, May 30, 2017, https://on.wsj.com/2rUD1fO.

41. Manchester.

42. Gamewatch, unedited, "Bret Weinstein Tries to Reason with Angry Student Mob as They Call for His Resignation," May 27, 2017, https://bit.ly/2NYaa6p.

43. Ibid.

44. Ibid.

45. Steve Bremner, "Bret Weinstein and the Cowardice of College Leaders," *Spiked Online*, May 30, 2017, https://bit.ly/2LZdtYG.

46. Ibid.

47. "Racism", Merrriam-Webster, https://bit.ly/2gA53Hm.

48. Iris Chang, *The Chinese in America: A Narrative History* (New York: Viking, 2003), 178.

49. United States District Court, District of Massachusetts, Boston Division, Students for Fair Admissions Inc. v. President and Fellows of Harvard College, 14–18 (July 30, 2018), https://bit.ly/2JG4R6c.

50. Shelby Steele, *Shame: How America's Past Sins Have Polarized Our Country* (New York: Basic Books, 2015), 41–47.

51. Phyl Newbeck and Brendan Wolfe, "Loving v. Virginia," *Encyclopedia Virginia*, accessed August 4, 2019, https://bit.ly/2rikpaa.

52. Government of Tennessee, "Anti-Miscegenation Laws by State," accessed August 4, 2019, https://bit.ly/2YcWRmw.

53. Frank Newport, "In U.S., 87% Approve of Black-White Marriage, vs. 4% in 1958," Gallup, July 25, 2013, https://bit.ly/2QPyXqD.

54. Leslie Ashburn-Nardo, "The Confronting Prejudiced Responses (CPR) Model: Applying CPR in Organizations," Academy of Management Learning & Education, 2008, Vol. 7, No. 3, 332–342.

55. Ibid., 335.

56. United Stated District Court.

57. "College Salary Report: Best Universities and Colleges by Salary Potential," PayScale.com, undated, https://bit.ly/30Ce725.

58. WeTheProtesters, The Demands, https://bit.ly/2LsdwN8.

59. WeTheProtesters, The Demands, Campus Demands, https://bit.ly/30wdd7s.

60. Shimey and Wang.

61. Bremner.

62. George Bridges, "George Bridges Statement in Response to Student Demands," *The Cooper Point Journal*, May 26, 2017, https://bit.ly/2rmaCg8.

63. Theodore J. Kaczynski, "The Unabomber Manifesto: Industrial Society and Its Future," *Washington Post*, September 19, 1995, https://wapo.st/2NhoUMl.

Chapter 3: Blinded by Blame

1. "A Timeline of Official Apologies from the Federal Government," *Canadian Press*, May 23, 2019, https://bit.ly/2LbnimD.

2. Jessica Murphy, "Does Justin Trudeau Apologise Too Much?" *BBC News*, March 28, 2018, https://bbc.in/2JqDUVw.

3. Catherine McIntyre, "Read Justin Trudeau's Apology to Residential School Survivors in Newfoundland," *Maclean's*, November 24, 2017 Statistics Canada, https://bit.ly/2WAb9hc.

4. Ibid.

5. Amy Smart, "Trudeau Apologizes to Tsilhqot'in Community Members for 1864 Hanging of Chiefs," *CBC News*, November 3, 2018, https://bit.ly/2FZ4MK3.

6. "A Timeline of Official Apologies from the Federal Government."

7. "Remarks by Prime Minister Justin Trudeau to Apologize to LGBTQ2 Canadians," Justin Trudeau, Prime Minister of Canada, November 28, 2017, https://bit.ly/2HmDHTN.

8. "A Timeline of Official Apologies from the Federal Government."

9. Jason Warrick, "Trudeau Exonerates Chief Poundmaker, Apologizes for Treason Conviction," CBC News, May 23, 2019, https://bit.ly/2S55NVK.

10. "A Timeline of Official Apologies from the Federal Government."

11. Murphy.

12. Tristin Hopper, "What Really Happened in the Chilcotin War, the 1864 Conflict that Just Prompted an Exoneration from Trudeau?" National Post, March 27, 2018, https://bit.ly/2G27jmM.

13. Ibid.

14. Stephen Hume. "Canada 150: 'Hanging Judge' Matthew Begbie Protected Minorities, Brought Justice to Rural B.C.," Vancouver Sun, April 1, 2017, https://bit.ly/2Xx4HDg.

15. Randy Boswell, "Historian Slams Pardon of Executed Soldiers," *Vancouver Sun*, August 17, 2006.

16. Nelson Bennett, "Tsilhqot'in Turn Back Taseko Mines Workers in Block," *Business in Vancouver*, July 2 2019, https://bit.ly/2LxavLA.

17. "Highlights from the Report of the Royal Commission on Aboriginal Peoples," Government of Canada, https://bit.ly/2d4gsvz. 1996.

18. "Aboriginal Population Profile, 2016 Census," Statistics Canada, last modified July 18, 2018, Catalogue no. 98-510-X2016001. https://bit.ly/2V69XBf.

19. Government of Canada, "Highlights."

20. Ibid.

21. "Honouring the Truth, Reconciling for the Future," Truth and Reconciliation Commission of Canada, 2015, https://bit.ly/1OHGnsC.

22. Wally T. Oppal, "Forsaken: The Report of the Missing Women Commission of Inquiry," British Columbia, https://bit.ly/2Y6WbPT.

23. "Reclaiming Power and Place: The Final Report," The National Inquiry into Missing and Murdered Indigenous Women and Girls, Vol. 1a, 178, https://bit.ly/2XICCgv.

24. Ibid., 225.

25. Ibid., 243.

26. Ibid., Vol. 1b, 111, https://bit.ly/2NPMm4X.

27. "Honouring the Truth, Reconciling for the Future," https://bit.ly/1OHGnsC, 8.

28. "Reclaiming Power and Place," Vol. 1a, 5.

29. "A Legal Analysis of Genocide," The National Inquiry into Missing and Murdered Indigenous Women and Girls, Supplementary Report, 2019, 9, https://bit.ly/2XxjD4U, 9.

30. Ibid.

31. Thomas Sowell, Conquests and Cultures: *An International History* (New York: Basic Books, 1998), 254–255.

32. Mark Milke, "Ever-Higher: Government Spending on Canada's Aboriginals Since 1947," Fraser Institute, 2013, 9–22, https://bit.ly/2XQk92h.

33. Ravina Bains and Kayla Ishkanian, "Government Spending on Aboriginals," Fraser Institute, 2015, 10, https://bit.ly/2M5etdE, 10.

34. Milke.

35. Calvin Helin, *Dances with Dependency, Out of Poverty through Self-Reliance* (Vancouver: Orca Spirit, 2006), 26.

36. Ibid.

37. "Figure 1.1: Distribution of the Aboriginal Population by Population Centre Size, Canada, 2016," Statistics Canada, https://bit.ly/2Xxr3cM.

38. "Population and Dwelling Count Highlight Tables, 2016 Census," Statistics Canada, https://bit.ly/2xFJT1G.

39. "Education in Canada: Key Results from the 2016 Census," Statistics Canada, November 29, 2017, https://bit.ly/2VrFkly.

40. "Attawapiskat Chief Worried about the Future after Mine Closure," CBC News, March 7, 2019, https://bit.ly/2YcLg6Y.

41. Ibid.

42. Haisla Nation, The Meaning of Reconciliation: Haisla Nation History, undated, https://bit.ly/2NSO4SZ.

43. "Aboriginal Peoples in Canada: Key Results from the 2016 Census," Statistics Canada, October 25, 2017, https://bit.ly/2o9Zpye.

44. "Aboriginal Population Profile for Indian Band and Tribal Council Areas," Statistics Canada, 2016 Census.

45. "Statistics Canada – 2016 Census," Catalogue number 98-400-X2016178, https://bit.ly/2KvBEg3.

46. "Aboriginal Population Profile for Indian Band and Tribal Council Areas."

47. "Reclaiming Power and Place," Vol. 1a, 508.

48. Ibid., 519.

49. "Missing and Murdered Indigenous Women and Girls," *JustFacts*, Department of Justice, July 2017, https://bit.ly/2IfmM31.

50. "Missing and Murdered Aboriginal Women: 2015 Update to the National Operational Review," Royal Canadian Mounted Police, 14, https://bit.ly/2lZH0RC.

51. "Reclaiming Power and Place," Vol. 1b, 249–258.

52. Sara Bernard, "Rape Culture in the Alaskan Wilderness," *Atlantic*, September 11, 2014, https://bit.ly/2dQ92iF.

53. "Table 2: Self-Reported Sexual Assault, by Sex of Victim and Socioeconomic Characteristics, Canada, 2014," Statistics Canada, https://bit.ly/2JKBOyC.

54. "Stop Sexual Abuse on Reserves," *Toronto Star*, editorial, November 7, 2016, https://bit.ly/2fDZZQ7.

55. "'Their Souls Killed as Children': Indigenous Women and Self-Destruction as a Result of Sexual Abuse," *CBC Radio*, August 8, 2016, https://bit.ly/2SjiKvg.

56. Kristy Kirkup and Sheryl Ubelacker, "Open Secret: Sexual Abuse Haunts Children in Indigenous Communities," *Toronto Star*, November 6, 2016, https://bit.ly/2r1NwKq.

57. "Registered Indian Population, by Type of Residence, Age Groups and Sex," Statistics Canada, December 31, 2016,https://bit.ly/30oUJWi.

Chapter 4: Victims of identities and arguments over privilege

1. Thomas Sowell, *Economic Facts and Fallacies* (New York: Basic Books, 2011), 178–179, 182–183, 192–193.
2. The Global Slavery Index 2018, Mauritania, https://bit.ly/2LWImNh.
3. "Mauritania ignores slavery, but jails those who protest against it," *The Economist*, July 21, 2018, https://econ.st/2uxeduC.
4. Peggy Mcintosh, "White Privilege: Unpacking the Invisible Knapsack" and "Some Notes for Facilitators," originally in *Peace and Freedom Magazine*, July/August 1989, https://bit.ly/2jSNfcn, 10–12.
5. Melanie Moriss, "Becoming Trustworthy White Allies," University of Yale, Yale Divinity School, 2013, https://bit.ly/2xOyb4Y.
6. Eden King and Kristen Jones, "Why Subtle Bias is Often Worse than Blatant Discrimination," *Harvard Business Review*, July 13, 2016, https://bit.ly/29HAnkY.
7. Imani Perry, "'Identity Politics' Address Real Problems of Discrimination," *New York Times*, November 23, 2016. https://nyti.ms/2Lk672b.
8. Wikipedia, "White Privilege," https://bit.ly/1KRFegR.
9. Catherine Kim, "A White Woman from Ohio Asked Gillibrand about White Privilege," *Vox*, July 12, 2019, https://bit.ly/2Y4xT8X.
10. Ibid.
11. "What is White Privilege? Ryerson University, undated," https://bit.ly/2xJODDG.
12. Josh Schlossberg, "Getting Triggered at a White Privilege Conference," *Areo Magazine*, https://bit.ly/30xP2W3.
13. "Employment Equity in Federally Regulated Workplaces," Government of Canada, undated, https://bit.ly/2YTm6aD.
14. Sowell, 183.
15. Thomas Sowell, *Black Rednecks and White Liberals* (New York: Encounter Books, 2005), 204.
16. Ibid.
17. Ibid., 179.
18. Ibid., 242.
19. Sowell, 2011, 192–193.
20. Thomas Sowell, editor, "Three Black Histories," *Essays and Data on American Ethnic Groups* (Washington D.C.: Urban Institute, 1978), 39.
21. Sowell, 2011, 178–179, 182–183, 192–193.
22. Daniel Patrick Moynihan, "The Negro Family: The Case for National Action," U.S. Department of Labor: Policy, Planning and Research, https://stanford.io/32qQSKk, 5.
23. Ibid., 5–6.
24. Francis Fukuyama, *Trust: The Social Virtues and the Creation of Prosperity* (New York: Penguin Putnam, 1995).
25. Francis Fukuyama, *The Great Disruption: Human Nature and the Reconstitution of Social Order* (New York: Free Press, 1999).
26. Robert Putnam, *Bowling Alone: The Collapse and Revival of American Community* (New York: Simon & Schuster, 2000).
27. Deirdre McCloskey, *Bourgeois Dignity: Why Economics Can't Explain the Modern World* (Chicago: University of Chicago Press, 2000).
28. Deirdre McCloskey, *Bourgeois Equality: How Ideas, Not Capital or Institutions, Enriched the World* (Chicago: University of Chicago Press, 2016).
29. Charles Murray, *Coming Apart: The State of White America, 1960–2010* (New York: Crown, 2012).
30. J.D. Vance, *Hillbilly Elegy: A Memoir of a Family and Culture in Crisis* (London: Williams Collins, 2016), 60.
31. Ibid., 194.
32. Ibid., 60.
33. William Ryan, *Blaming the Victim* (New York: Vintage Books, 1976), xii.
34. Ryan, xiii–xiv.
35. Sowell, 2011, 182–183.

36.   Thomas Sowell, *Conquest and Cultures: An International History* (New York, Basic Books, 1998), 327.

37.   "America Community Survey, 2014, 1-Year Estimates," U.S. Census Bureau, S0201.

38.   Ibid.

39.   Sowell, 1978, 41–45.

40.   Ibid.

41.   Ibid., 45.

42.   Pew Research Center, Statistical Portrait of the U.S. Black Immigrant Population, April 9, 2015, https://pewrsr.ch/2Sh3cYW.

43.   Canada. Human Resources and Skills Development Canada. Report of the Commission on Equality in Employment / Judge Rosalie Silberman Abella, commissioner. 1984. https://bit.ly/2Y4Hi0g.

44.   Martin Loney, *The Pursuit of Division: Race, Gender and Preferential Hiring in Canada* (Montreal and Kingston: McGill– Queen's University Press, 1998), 7.

45.   Ibid.

46.   Lois W. Moorcroft, "Correcting Wrongs: When Is It Government's Responsibility?" Canadian Parliamentary Review, 1998, https://bit.ly/2Y25a0w.

47.   Judge Rosalie Silberman Abella, Commissioner, *Report of the Commission on Equality in Employment,* Human Resources and Skills Development Canada, 1984, Vol. 1, https://bit.ly/2JVQlYv, 62.

48.   Ibid., 85.

49.   Ibid., 87.

50.   Ibid., 88.

51.   Ibid., 92–94.

52.   Ibid., 89.

53.   Howard Palmer and Leo Driedger, "Prejudice and Discrimination in Canada," *Canadian Encyclopedia,* March 4, 2015, https://bit.ly/2NRYUrf.

54.   "Figure 28, Proportion of Foreign-Born Population By Continent of Birth," Statistics Canada, 1981 to 2031, https://bit.ly/30yh3g9, 34.

55.   Conrad Winn, "Affirmative Action and Visible Minorities: Eight Premises in Quest of Evidence," *Canadian Public Policy,* Vol. 11, No. 4 (Dec., 1985), 689.

56.   Ibid., 694.

57.   "Ethnic Origin, Ages 15 and Over," Table 98-400-X2016189, Census of Population 2016 (Canada).

58.   Ibid.

59.   Ibid.

60.   "Immigration and Ethnocultural Diversity Highlight Tables," 2016 Census, 2017, catalogue no. 98-402-X2016007.

61.   Hannah Ellis-Petersen, "Racial Identity Is a Biological Nonsense, Says Reith Lecturer," *The Guardian,* October 18, 2016, https://bit.ly/2ehv2zR.

62.   Hannah Ellis-Petersen.

63.   Megan Gannon, "Race Is a Social Construct, Scientists Argue," *Scientific American,* February 5, 2016, https://bit.ly/2dU78vg.

64.   "A Bit of History," Ontario Human Rights Commission, undated, https://bit.ly/2JE7Hc4.

65.   Shelby Steele, Shame: How America's Past Sins Have Polarized Our Country (New York: Basic Books, 2015), 2.

66.   Ibid., 2–3.

67.   Ibid., 6–7.

Chapter 5: New victims and the false lure of pure culture

1.   Allyson Bird, "Decades-Old Federal Act Removes 2-Year-Old Girl from Only Family She's Known, But Was That The Law's Intent?" *The Post and Courier,* January 7, 2012, https://bit.ly/2MCVcAL.

2.   Cornell Law School, 25 U.S. Code Chapter 21, 1978, Indian Child Welfare Act, https://bit.ly/2MFxO5t.

3.   NIOCWA, undated, Indian Child Welfare Act of 1978, https://bit.ly/1W2kSFS.

4.   Adoptive Couple v. Baby Girl, 570 U.S. Supreme Court, 2013, https://bit.ly/2LZkkCb.

5.   Melissa Gray, "Birth Father Arrested In 'Baby Veronica' Adoption Fight," CNN, August 13, 2013, https://cnn.it/2LYqp1L.

6. "Baby Veronica" Handed Over to Adoptive Parents, Cherokee Nation Confirms," *CBS News*, September 24, 2013, https://cbsn.ws/2LYs3QN.

7. Bird.

8. Mississippi Band of Choctaw Indians v. Holyfield, 490 U.S. Supreme Court, 30 (1989), https://bit.ly/2T4hmwJ, 35.

9. Ibid., 33.

10. Cornell Law School.

11. Mississippi Band of Choctaw Indians v. Holyfield, 35.

12. Ibid., 54.

13. *Four-Year-Old Marie: An Investigative Review*, Office of the Child Youth Advocate Alberta, October 2016, https://bit.ly/2yCvKTK, 9.

14. Ibid., 17.

15. Child, Youth and Family Enhancement Act, Government of Alberta, 2017, https://bit.ly/2YIG7zH, 24-25, 32.

16. Policy Directive in the Adoption of First Nation Children, Alberta Children's Services, 1997.

17. Jeannine Carriere and Sandra Scarth, "Aboriginal Children: Maintaining Connections in Adoption," chapter 10 in *Putting a Human Face on Child Welfare: Voices from the Prairie* (Prairie Child Welfare Consortium, 2007), https://bit.ly/2GNyvWO, 208.

18. *Four-Year-Old Marie*, 16.

19. *Practice Strategies for Lifelong Connections*, Government of Alberta, 2014, https://bit.ly/2Rc829q.

20. *Walking as One: Ministerial Panel on Child Intervention's Final Recommendations to the Minister of Children's Services*, Government of Alberta, 2018a, https://bit.ly/2IbhKFO.

21. *A Stronger, Safer Tomorrow: A Public Action Plan for the Ministerial Panel on Child Intervention's Final Recommendations*, Government of Alberta, 2018b, https://bit.ly/2XGmecV.

22. *Four-Year-Old Marie*, 10.

23. Ibid., 16.

24. Ibid.

25. Heather Boetto, "Kinship Care: A Review of Issues," *Family Matters*, No. 85, September 2010, https://bit.ly/2YKo9AU, 60-67.

26. Mississippi Band of Choctaw Indians v. Holyfield, U.S. Supreme Court, 34.

27. Ibid., 54.

28. Patrick Johnston, "Revisiting the 'Sixties Scoop' of Indigenous Children," Institute for Public Policy, Policy Options, July 26, 2016, https://bit.ly/2ZwPcgi.

29. Ibid.

30. Ibid.

31. Ibid.

32. *Highlights from the Report of the Royal Commission on Aboriginal Peoples*, Government of Canada, 1996, https://bit.ly/2d4gsvz.

33. Ibid.

34. Ibid.

35. Ibid.

36. *Truth and Reconciliation Commission of Canada: Calls to Action*, 2015, https://bit.ly/2YxyDAO, 5.

37. "Indigenous Children and the Child Welfare System in Canada," National Collaborating Centre for Aboriginal Health, undated, https://bit.ly/31dSci7, 2.

38. Ed John, *A Report on Indigenous Child Welfare in British Columbia: Final Report of Special Advisor Grand Chief Ed John: Summary of Recommendation*, 2016, https://bit.ly/2Kf4hy1, 6.

39. Ibid., 176.

40. Ibid.

41. Ian Mulgrew, "Girls 'Want To Stay' with Family: Court Case Centres on Role of Culture in Child Rearing," *Vancouver Sun*, October 24, 2003, B1.

42. Ibid.

43. Ibid.

44. Bird.

45. Mississippi Band of Choctaw Indians v. Holyfield.

46. Ibid., 46.
47. Ibid., 40.
48. Ibid., 52.
49. Ibid.
50. Ibid.
51. Ibid.
52. Adoptive Couple v. Baby Girl, 570 U.S. Supreme Court, 2013, https://supreme.justia.com/cases/federal/us/570/12-399/, sec. IV.
53. Ibid., footnote 1.

Chapter 6: Civilization and its Western discontents

1. Jon Reider, letter to the editor, "Jesse Jackson Didn't Lead Chant Against Western Culture," *Chronicle of Higher Education*, November 21, 2016, https://bit.ly/30KVaKI.
2. WeTheProtesters, The Demands, Campus Demands, https://bit.ly/30wdd7s.
3. *Honouring the Truth: Reconciling for the Future, Summary of the Final Report*, Truth and Reconciliation Commission of Canada, https://bit.ly/1OHGnsC.
4. Ibid., 330.
5. "Highlights from the Report of the Royal Commission on Aboriginal Peoples," Government of Canada, 1996, https://bit.ly/2d4gsvz.
6. Anjuli Patil, "Cornwallis Rally in Halifax Celebrates Statue's Removal," *CBC News*, February 4, 2018, https://bit.ly/2JhfqOd.
7. "Statue of John A. MacDonald Removed from Victoria City Hall in Act of Reconciliation," *National Post*, August 11, 2018, https://bit.ly/2NDzO04.
8. Stuart Thomson, "Even Liberals Agree with Tories that Sir John-A's Statue Shouldn't Have Been Removed, Poll Finds," *National Post*, September 6, 2018, https://bit.ly/2Xy0QFS.
9. Amy Smart, "Victoria's New Mayor Swears Allegiance, Just Not to the Queen," *Victoria Times Colonist*, December 4, 2014, https://bit.ly/2FXZpee.
10. Steve Hendrix, "The Columbus Day Holiday is Under Attack, and So Are Statues Honoring the Famed Explorer," *Washington Post*, October 9, 2017, https://wapo.st/2L65skP.
11. Ibid.
12. Pamela Wood, "Christopher Columbus Monument Vandalized in Baltimore," *Baltimore Sun*," August 21, 2017, https://bit.ly/2whV7dK.
13. Krista J. Kesselring, "Slavery and Cartwright's Case before Somerset," Legal History Miscellany, October 10, 2018, *https://bit.ly/2LG5Mr2.*
14. Somerset v. Stewart (1772), Court of King's Bench, https://bit.ly/2Od33qW, 510.
15. Ibid., 500.
16. David Brion Davis, *Slavery and Human Progress* (New York: Oxford University Press, 1984), 379.
17. "Mauritania," The Global Slavery Index 2018, https://bit.ly/2LWImNh.
18. Inglehart, R., C. Haerpfer, A. Moreno, C. Welzel, K. Kizilova, J. Diez-Medrano, M. Lagos, P. Norris, E. Ponarin & B. Puranen et al., editors, 2014. World Values Survey: Round Six - Country-Pooled Datafile Version: www.worldvaluessurvey.org/WVSDocumentationWV6.jsp. Madrid: JD Systems Institute, 68–69, 76–77.
19. Inglehart, et al., 74–75.
20. "Engels to Franz Mehring," *Marx-Engels Correspondence* (International Publishers: 1968) July 14, 1893, https://bit.ly/2LjJXgF.
21. Paulo Freire, *Pedagogy of the Oppressed* (New York: Penguin Books, 1970), 130.
22. Colleen Flaherty, "In-Class Sit-in," *Inside Higher Ed*, 2013, https://bit.ly/2LWfHba.
23. Freire, 133.
24. Ibid.
25. Michel Foucault, *Power/Knowledge; Selected Interviews and Other Writings*, 1972-1977 (New York: Pantheon Press, 1980).
26. Angus Maddison, *The World Economy: A Millennial Perspective* (Paris: OECD, 2001), 27.

27. Maxim Pinkovskiy and Xavier Sala-i-Martin, "Parametric Estimations of the World Distribution of Income," NBER Working Paper No. 15433, October 2009, National Bureau of Economic Research, https://bit.ly/2yAkRSt, 2.

28. Jutta Bolt et al., Maddison Project Working Paper 10, 2018, Maddison Project Database, https://bit.ly/2pkn3bQ.

Chapter 7: When victimhood goes viral: Germany's pre-Nazi narrative

1. Hans Kohn, *The Mind of Germany: The Education of a Nation* (New York: Harper & Row, 1960), 69.
2. Ibid.
3. Glenn E. Curtis, Poland: *A Country Study* (Washington: The Library of Congress, 1992), https://bit.ly/2YhTPcS.
4. Kohn, 70.
5. Ibid., 52.
6. Ibid.
7. Marshall Dill Jr., *Germany: A Modern History* (Ann Arbor: University of Michigan Press, 1970), 96.
8. Ibid., 97.
9. Kohn, 36.
10. John Breuilly, "Urbanization and Social Transformation, 1800-1914" in Sheilagh Ogilvie and Ricard Overy, editors, *Germany: A New Social and Economic History*, Vol III: Since 1800 (New York: Oxford University Press, 2003), 201.
11. Kohn, 73.
12. Ibid.
13. Breuilly.
14. Kohn, 73.
15. Frank B. Tipton, "Government and Economy in the Nineteenth Century" in Sheilagh Ogilvie and Ricard Overy, editors, *Germany: A New Social and Economic History, Vol III: Since 1800* (New York: Oxford University Press, 2003), 113.
16. Götz Aly, *Why the Germans? Why the Jews? Envy, Race Hatred and the Prehistory of the Holocaust* (New York: Metropolitan Books, 2014), 45.
17. Ibid.
18. Ibid., 43.
19. Ibid.
20. Johann Gottlieb Fichte, *Addresses to the German Nation*, 1807 and 1808, https://bit.ly/2YfDLZd, 5–6.
21. Ibid., 12.
22. William L. Shirer, *The Rise and Fall of the Third Reich: A History of Nazi Germany* (New York: Simon & Schuster, 1960), 98.
23. Hannah Arendt, *The Origins of Totalitarianism* (New York Harcourt, 1976), 166.
24. Shirer, 98.
25. Kohn, 72.
26. Shirer, 99.
27. Kohn, 59–60.
28. Aly, 48.
29. Ibid., 49–50.
30. Kohn, 76.
31. Aly, 52.
32. Arendt, 166–67.
33. Ibid., 166.
34. Ibid., 167.
35. Aly, 52.
36. Kohn, 59.
37. Aly, 51.

38. Steven Michael Press, "False Fire: The Wartburg Book-Burning of 1817," *Central European History*, Vol. 42, No. 4 (December 2009), 633–637.

39. Ibid., 636–637.

40. H.I. Bach, *The German Jew: A Synthesis of Judaism and Western Civilization* (Oxford: Oxford University Press, 1984), 34.

41. Ibid., 34.

42. Will Durant, *The Story of Civilization, Part VI: The Reformation—A History of European Civilization from Wycliffe to Calvin: 1300-1564* (New York: Simon and Schuster, 1957), 727.

43. Paul Johnson, *A History of the Jews* (New York: Harper and Row, 1987), 242.

44. Alex Ross, "Bach's Holy Dread," *The New Yorker*, January 2, 2017, https://bit.ly/2iAxOFB.

45. Durant, 727.

46. Arthur Hertzberg, *The French Enlightenment and the Jews: The Origins of Modern Anti-Semitism* (New York: Schocken Books, 1968,) 300.

47. Ibid., 300–301.

48. Ibid., 283

49. Johnson, 308–309.

50. Ibid.

51. Hertzberg, 281.

52. Ibid., 298.

53. Ibid., 10.

54. Johnson, 351.

55. Ibid.

56. Jonathan Osmond, "Land, Peasant and Lord in German Agriculture Since 1800" in Sheilagh Ogilvie and Ricard Overy, editors, *Germany: A New Social and Economic History, Vol III: Since 1800* (New York: Oxford University Press, 2012), 82.

57. Bach, 128.

58. Aly, 50–51.

59. Ibid., 36.

60. Ibid., 34.

61. Ibid., 81.

62. Ibid., 227.

63. Ibid., 78.

64. Ibid., 80.

65. Ibid., 81.

66. Ibid., 51.

67. Hertzberg, 5.

68. Shirer, 104.

69. Arendt, 175.

70. Lafcadio Hearn, *Japan: An Attempt at Interpretation* (New York: Grossett and Dunlap, 1904) https://bit.ly/2ycZQwA, 531 and 529.

71. Ibid., 530–531.

72. Ibid.

73. Ibid.

74. Shirer, 106.

75. Ibid., 106–107.

76. Kohn, 273.

77. Ibid.

78. Kohn, 272–275.

79. Shirer, 103.

80. Ibid., 106–107.

81. David Vital, *A People Apart, The Jews in Europe: 1789-1939* (Oxford: Oxford University Press, 1999), 806.

82. Johnson, 393.

83. Ibid., 392–93.

84. Ibid., 393.

85. Lindsey Fraser, *Germany Between Two Wars: A Study of Propaganda and War-Guilt* (London: Oxford University Press, 1944), 16.

86. Ibid.

87. Ibid.

88. John Maynard Keynes, *The Economic Consequences of the Peace* (London: MacMillan and Co., 1924).

89. Margaret MacMillan, *Paris 1919: Six Months That Changed the World* (New York: Random House, 2001), 191.

90. Sally Marks, "The Myths of Reparations," Central European History, September 1978, 11 (3): 233, 237.

91. Fraser, 35.

92. Reparation Commission Letter to February 11, 1922, translated by K.D. Frankenstein, Federal Reserve Bank of St. Louis. March 24, 1922, https://bit.ly/2Z6OBSw, 63–71.

93. Etienne Mantoux, *The Carthaginian Peace, or The Economic Consequences of Mr. Keynes* (New York: Charles Scribner's Sons, 1952), 15.

94. Reparation Commission Letter, 63–71.

95. Marks, 245.

96. Ibid., 236.

97. Ibid., 254.

98. Ibid., 255.

99. Mantoux, 96–97.

Chapter 8: Adolf Hitler: (Self-professed) Victim

1. Allan Bullock, *Hitler: A Study in Tyranny* (New York: Konecky & Konecky, 1962), 314.

2. Marshall Dill Jr., *Germany: A Modern History* (Ann Arbor: University of Michigan Press, 1970), 19.

3. Bullock, 148.

4. Ian Kershaw, *Hitler 1889-1936: Hubris* (London: Allen Lane/Penguin, Press,) 251.

5. Bullock, 314.

6. Ibid., 321.

7. Ibid., 122.

8. Ibid., 322.

9. Kershaw, 492.

10. Bullock, 322.

11. Ibid.

12. Ibid., 323.

13. Ibid.

14. Henry Ashby Turner Jr., ed., *Hitler—Memoirs of a Confidante*, translated by Ruth Hein (New Haven and London: Yale, 1985) 204.

15. Turner Jr., 204.

16. Bullock, 122.

17. Ibid., 383.

18. Turner Jr., xxiv.

19. Ibid., 32.

20. Ibid., 238.

21. Ibid.

22. Ibid.,168.

23. Bullock, 423.

24. Ibid., 453.

25. Ibid., 769.

26. Ibid., 633.
27. Ibid., 771–772.
28. John Keegan, *The Second World War* (London: Penguin Books, 2005), 537.
29. Bullock, 663.
30. Ibid., 27.
31. Ibid., 632.
32. Ibid., 771.
33. Ibid., 775.
34. Ibid., 787–789.
35. Adolf Hitler, "Last Political Testament," April 29, 1945, https://bit.ly/2Yjo17v.
36. Bullock, 787–789.

Chapter 9: Rwanda's genocide and the Hutu grievance culture

1. Arthur Kay Klinghoffer, *The International Dimension of Genocide in* Rwanda (New York: New York University Press, 1998), 22. See also Roméo Dallaire, *Shake Hands with the Devil: The Failure of Humanity in Rwanda* (Toronto: Vintage Canada, 2004), 149.

2. Lean Ann Fuji, *Killing Neighbours* (London: Cornell University Press, 2009), 46.

3. "The Rwandan Genocide: How It Was Prepared," Human Rights Watch, 2006, https://bit.ly/2Yec5nq, 7–8.

4. "International Conference on Genocide, Impunity, and Accountability: Final Report," Rwanda, Office of the President, 1995, https://bit.ly/2MdzHGh, 7.

5. Mahmood Mamdani, *When Victims Become Killers: Colonialism, Nativism and Genocide in Rwanda* (Princeton: Princeton University Press, 2001), 5.

6. Scott Straus, *The Order of Genocide: Race, Power and War in Rwanda* (London: Cornell University Press, 2006), 207.

7. Christopher C. Taylor, *Sacrifice as Terror: The Rwandan Genocide of 1994* (New York: Oxford, 1999), 37.

8. Marie Béatrice Umutesi, *Journal of International Affairs*, Fall/Winter 2006, Vol. 60, Issue 1, 157–171.

9. Learthen Dorsey, *Historical Dictionary of Rwanda: African Historical Dictionaries* (London: The Scarecrow Press, 1994), 251.

10. Scott Straus, *The Order of Genocide: Race, Power and War in Rwanda* (London: Cornell University Press, 2006), 19.

11. Jan Vansina, *Antecedents to Modern Rwanda: The Nyiginya* Kingdom, translated by the author (Madison: University of Wisconsin, 2004), 180–81.

12. Emmanuel Viret, *Rwanda–A Chronology (1867-1994),* Online Encyclopedia of Mass Violence, 2010, https://bit.ly/2KxfwSI, 6–7.

13. Ibid., 7.

14. Vansina, 180–81.

15. Ibid., 134–135.

16. Ibid.

17. David Moshman, "Identity, History, and Education in Rwanda: Reflections on the 2014 Nobel Peace Prize," *Child Abuse & Neglect,* June 1, 2015, Volume 44, 1.

18. André Sibomana, *Hope for Rwanda: Conversations with Laure Gilbert and Herve Deguine* (London: Pluto Press, 1999), 85–86.

19. Vansina, 134–135.

20. Ibid., 37–38.

21. Emmanuel Viret, 8–10.

22. Mahmood Mamdani, 229.

23. "The Rwandan Genocide: How It Was Prepared."

24. Elisabeth King, *From Classrooms to Conflict in Rwanda* (Cambridge: Cambridge University Press, 2013), 41.

25. Viret, 2010, 10–11.

26. King, 43.
27. Ibid., 53.
28. Ibid., 41.
29. Ibid., 45.
30. Dominique Franche, *Rwanda: Généalogie d un genocide* (Paris: Mille et une Nuits, 1997), 45.
31. King, 39.
32. Sibomana, André, *Hope for Rwanda: Conversations with Laure Gilbert and Herve Deguine* (London: Pluto Press, 1999), 85.
33. King, 53.
34. Ibid.
35. King, 55–56
36. Ibid., 53.
37. Ibid.
38. Mamdani, 112.
39. King, 55.
40. "Rwanda: A Brief History of the Country," undated, United Nations, https://bit.ly/1eMpxbx.
41. Viret, 2010, 11.
42. King, 55.
43. Viret, 17.
44. Dorsey, 91.
45. King, 83.
46. Rachel van der Meeren, "Three Decades in Exile: Rwandan Refugees 1960–1990," *Journal of Refugee Studies*, Vol. 9, No. 3, 256.
47. Viret, 14.
48. Mamdani, 117.
49. Ibid.
50. Aimable Twagilimana, *The Debris of Ham: Ethnicity, Regionalism, and the 1994 Rwandan Genocide* (Lanham: University Press of America, 2003), 70.
51. Ibid.
52. Taylor, 77.
53. Sibomana, 84.
54. Straus, 58.
55. King, 78.
56. Twagilimana, 76.
57. Ibid.
58. King, 89.
59. Twagilimana, 73.
60. King, 78.
61. Anna Obura, *Never Again: Educational Reconstruction in Rwanda* (Paris: UNESCO, 2003), https://bit.ly/2GrUrX2, 43.
62. King, 72.
63. Ibid.
64. Straus, 190.
65. Taylor, 45–46.
66. René Lemarchand, *Rwanda and Burundi* (London: Pall Mall Press, 1970), 198.
67. Viret, 22.
68. Online Encyclopedia of Mass Violence, 23.
69. Twagilimana, 75.
70. Viret, 20.
71. There are a range of estimates on the numbers killed in 1994. See Online Encyclopedia of Mass Violence, 21, and Mahmood Mamdani, 130.

72. Mamdani, 134.
73. Twagilimana, 76.
74. King, 73.
75. Online Encyclopedia of Mass Violence, 189–190.
76. Online Encyclopedia of Mass Violence, 24.
77. Sibomana, 80.
78. Ibid.
79. The Kinyarwandan term for ethnicity is *ubwoko*, which with reference to a person's clan eventually came to mean ethnicity, Fuji, 105.
80. Fuji, 108.
81. Moshman, 2.
82. King, 105.
83. Maria Hodgkin, "Reconciliation in Rwanda: education, history and the state." *Journal of International Affairs,* 2006, 60.1, 201.
84. King, 84.
85. Taylor, 82.
86. King, 71.
87. Sibomana, 84.
88. King, 71.
89. Jordane Bertrand, *Rwanda : Le piège de l'histoire* (Paris : Karthala, 2000), 99.
90. Fuji, 50.
91. Straus, 25.
92. Fuji, 52.
93. Ibid., 51.
94. Straus, 25.
95. Online Encyclopedia of Mass Violence, undated, 36.
96. John A. Berry and Carol Pott Berry (eds.), *Genocide in Rwanda: A Collective Memory* (Washington, D.C.: Howard University Press, 1999), 113–115.
97. Ibid.
98. Twagilimana, 97.
99. "The Rwandan Genocide: How It Was Prepared," 6–7.
100. Quoted in Nigel Eltingham, *Accounting for Horror: Post-Genocide Debates in Rwanda* (London: Pluto Press, 2004), 23.
101. Twagilimana, 96.
102. "The Rwandan Genocide: How It Was Prepared."
103. Sibomana, 49.
104. Dorsey, 145.
105. Dallaire, 261.
106. Stephen Kinzer, *A Thousand Hills: Rwanda's Rebirth and the Man Who Dreamed It* (Hoboken: John Wiley & Sons Inc. 2008), 109–10.
107. Online Encyclopedia of Mass Violence, 32.
108. Kinzer, 131.
109. Ibid., 132–33.
110. Ibid., 133.
111. Mamdani, 194.
112. Dallaire, 272.
113. Sibomana, 71.
114. Kinzer, 141.
115. Sibomana, 103.
116. Fuji, 152.
117. Sibomana, 69.

118. Fuji, 181.

119. Dallaire, 279, 314, 420, 430.

120. Ibid.

121. Dallaire, 379, 336.

122. Peter Gwin, "Rwanda: The Art of Remembering and Forgetting," *National Geographic,* April 8, 2014, https://bit.ly/1oGRPHR.

123. Online Encyclopedia of Mass Violence, 14.

124. King, 89.

125. Twagilimana, 73.

126. Straus, 22.

127. Obura, 100.

128. Sibomana, 85–86.

129. Ibid.

Chapter 10: Yasser Arafat: Palestine's eternal Peter Pan

1. Barry Rubin and Judith Rubin, *Yasir Arafat: A Political Biography* (Oxford: Oxford University Press, 2003), 43.

2. Barry Rubin, *Revolution Until Victory? The Politics and History of the PLO* (Cambridge: Harvard University Press, 1994), 155.

3. Rubin and Rubin, 2003, 60–62.

4. Rubin, 1994, 48.

5. Yasser Arafat, Speech to the UN General Assembly, October 13, 1974, https://bit.ly/2njOuDu.

6. Rubin, 1994, 48.

7. Yasser Arafat.

8. Ibid.

9. Ibid.

10. Ibid.

11. Sumit Ganguly, "Wars Without End: The Indo-Pakistani Conflict," *Annals of the American Academy of Political Science,* September 1995, Vol. 54, 174.

12. Stephen Devereux, "Famine in the Twentieth Century," Institute of Development Studies (IDS) Working Paper No. 105, 2000. https://bit.ly/2LFsTlx, 9.

13. Ganguly, 174.

14. Martin Gilbert, *Israel: A History* (revised) (Toronto: Key Porter, 2008), 159.

15. Ibid.

16. Ibid.

17. Ibid., 174.

18. Conor Cruise O'Brien, *The Siege* (London: Weidenfeld and Nicolson, 1986), 281–282.

19. Gilbert, 172–173.

20. David Shipler, "Israel Bars Rabin from Relating '48 Eviction of Arabs," *New York Times,* October 23, 1979, https://nyti.ms/32QyKJP.

21. Larry Collins and Dominique Lapierre, *O Jerusalem* (New York: Simon and Schuster, 2007 edition), 551.

22. Rubin, 1994, 4.

23. Gilbert, 271.

24. Martin Gilbert, *In Ishmael's House* (Toronto: McClelland & Stewart, 2010), 210.

25. O'Brien, 281.

26. Gilbert, 2008, 170.

27. Ada Aharoni, "The Forced Migration of Jews from Arab Countries," *Peace Review: A Journal of Social Justice,* 2003, 15:1, 58.

28. Colin Shindler, *A History of Modern Israel* (Cambridge University Press, 2008), 63–64.

29. Aharoni.

30. Ibid., 57.

31. Ibid., 56–57.

32. Shindler, 63–64.

33. Aharoni, 55–56.

34. Shindler, 63–64.

35. "Final Report of the United Nations Economic Survey Mission for the Middle East," Part 1, United Nations, 28 December 1949, https://bit.ly/2KiGBa0, 15, 26, 30, 31.

36. Ibid.

37. Almost concurrently, nearly 400,000 Jews left mainly Arab or Muslim countries for Israel between 1948 and 1951 and 586,000 Jews in total that would eventually make such a journey. Another 200,000 Jews would eventually immigrate to countries other than Israel. See Ada Aharoni, 54–55.

38. Aharoni, 54–55.

39. Rubin, 1994, 126.

40. Barry Rubin, 1994, 129.

41. Rubin, 1994, 131.

42. "The United Nations and Palestinian Refugees," 2007, United Nations and UNWRA, https://bit.ly/2r3UUak, 6.

43. Timothy Snyder, *Bloodlands: Europe between Hitler and Stalin* (New York: Basic Books, 2010), 27.

44. Snyder, 153.

45. Snyder, 332.

46. Steffen Prauser and Arfon Rees, "The Expulsion of 'German' Communities from Eastern Europe at the End of the Second World War, European University Institute, Florence, HEC No. 2004/1, https://bit.ly/2OmtPxn, 4.

47. "The State of the World's Refugees, 2000," Chapter 3, United Nations High Commission on Refugees, 2000, https://bit.ly/2JYxoWg.

48. "Population by Population Group," Table 2, Israel, Annual Data 2018, Central Bureau of Statistics, https://bit.ly/32Rml8x.

49. Sergio DellaPergola, "World Jewish Population 2017," https://bit.ly/2JgF4CL, 60–62.

50. Arafat.

51. Ibid.

52. I.F. Stone, *This is Israel* (New York: Boni and Gaer, 1948), 63.

53. Ibid.

54. Jutta Bolt, Robert Inklaar, Herman de Jong and Jan Luiten van Zanden, Inflation-Adjusted 1990 International Geary-Khamis Dollars, from version 2018, Angus Maddison Project Database, 2018. Maddison Project Working Paper 10, https://bit.ly/2pkn3bQ.

55. Arafat.

56. Gilbert, 422–423.

57. Bolt, et al.

58. Gilbert, 422.

59. Current U.S. Dollars, World Bank, Data for the West Bank and Gaza, Jordan and Israel, https://bit.ly/2LJ3do4.

60. Rubin and Rubin, 2003, 153.

61. Bolt, et al.

62. Ibid.

63. *World Statistics Pocketbook*, 2013 edition, United Nations, 2013, https://bit.ly/32SiXdC.

64. Bolt, et al.

65. Barry Rubin and Judith Rubin, 2003, 80–82.

66. "Yasser Arafat," Israel and Jerusalem Studies, undated, https://bit.ly/2YAGJvC.

67. Rubin and Rubin, 2003, 90.

68. Martin Gilbert, *Israel: A History* (revised) (London: Black Swan, 2008), 508.

69. Rubin, 1994, 59.

70. Ibid., 59–60.

71. Aver Yaniv, "Phoenix or Phantom? The PLO After Beirut," *Terrorism*, Vol. 7. No. 3, 1994.

72. Yaniv.

73. Rubin, 69–70.

74. Ibid., 79.

75. Mark Tesler, *A History of the Israeli-Palestinian Conflict* (Bloomington: Indiana University Press, 1994), 667.

76. Rubin, 109–111.

77. "2000: The Jerusalem Intifada," The Telegraph, May 1, 2002, https://bit.ly/2Gyycit.

78. Bill Clinton, *My Life* (New York: Alfred A. Knopf, 2004), excerpt from Jewish Virtual Library, https://bit.ly/2SI8tsA.

79. Ibid.

80. Ibid.

81. Lafif Lakhdar, MEMRI Dispatch # 2713, January 4, 2009, https://bit.ly/2MjfKhu.

82. Barry Rubin, "The Reason There is No Palestinian State Today: Arafat," Jerusalem Post, November 14, 2010, https://bit.ly/2SHaoxL.

83. "The Man Who Refused to Say Yes," *New York Times*, editorial, November 6, 2004, https://nyti.ms/2JVX8CC.

84. David Remnick, "The Old Man," *The New Yorker*, November 22, 2004 https://bit.ly/2YnjErV.

85. Mamoun Fandy, MEMRI Special Dispatch # 1952, June 8, 2008, https://bit.ly/2OoaThJ.

86. David Brooks, "A Brief History of Yasir Arafat," *The Atlantic*, July/August 2002, https://bit.ly/2Y6BnbP.

87. Gilbert, 2008, 418.

88. Rubin, 1994, 34.

89. Ibid., 25.

90. Gilbert, 2008. *Israel*, 571.

91. Remnick.

92. Ibid.

93. Rubin and Rubin, 261.

94. Jonathan Halevi, "Understanding Arafat Before His Attempted Rehabilitation," Jerusalem Center for Public Affairs, August 16, 2004, https://bit.ly/2JYjbbI.

95. Rubin and Rubin, 2003, 188.

96. The Hashemite Kingdom of Jordan and the State of Israel, Treaty of Peace, October 26, 1994, https://bit.ly/2gA047M.

97. Ibid., 219.

98. Rubin, 1994, 34.

99. Arafat.

100. Zach Pintz, "Palestinian Film Shows Palestinian Children Blaming Arafat's Death on Israelis, Jews," *The Algemeiner,* November 11, 2012, https://bit.ly/2Y9FBzu.

101. Fandy.

102. Ibid.

103. Lakhdar.

104. Rubin, 1994, 149.

Chapter 11: Common threads: Plato's perfectionists and Rousseau's romantics

1. William Safire, *The First Dissident: The Book of Job in Today's Politics* (New York: Random House, 1992), 7–8.

2. Martin Luther King, Jr., "I Have a Dream," August 28, 1963, The Martin Luther King, Jr. Research and Education Institute, https://stanford.io/1FqpWGi.

3. Aristotle *The Politics*, translated by Carnes Lord (Chicago: University of Chicago Press, 1984), 59.

4. Ibid., 35.

5. Ibid., 149.

6. James Madison, *Federalist* No. 10, *The Federalist Papers*, https://bit.ly/2ynC7u2.

7. Ibid.

8. Jean-Jacques Rousseau, *Discourse on the Arts and Sciences, 1750*, originally published in 1762, translated by Ian Johnston (Vancouver Island University, 2018), https://bit.ly/2XUJqIK.

9. Jean-Jacques Rousseau, *Émile* (London: Everyman, 1993), xxxii. Originally published in 1762.

10. Ibid., 6.

11. Frederick Copleston, *A History of Philosophy*, Book Two, Vol. VI (New York: Doubleday, 1985), 67.

12. Rousseau, 2018, 62.

13. Copleston, 7.

14. Rousseau, 1993, 6.

15. Sigmund Freud, *Civilization and its Discontents*, translated By James Strachey, original German edition 1930 (New York: W.W. Norton and Co., 1966), 33.

16. Ibid., 36.

17. William Manchester, *A World Lit Only by Fire: The Medieval Mind and the Renaissance* (Boston: Little, Brown and Company, 1992), 5–7.

18. Ibid., 6.

19. Angus Maddison, *The World Economy: A Millennial Perspective* (Paris: OECD, 2001), 17, 29, 34.

20. Ibid., 18–35.

21. Johan Huizinga, *The Making of a Saint: The Tragi-Comedy of Jean-Jacques Rousseau* (London: Hamish Hamilton Ltd.), 73.

22. Paul Johnson, *Intellectuals* (London: Weidenfeld and Nicolson, 1988), 23.

23. Huizinga, 208.

24. Johnson, 10.

25. Ibid., 15.

26. Huizinga, 183.

27. Johnson, 15.

28. Huizinga, 17.

29. Ibid., 75.

30. Johnson, 9.

31. Rousseau, 1993, 9.

Chapter 12: Everyone's (ancestor was) a victim

1. Giles Milton, *White Gold: The Extraordinary Story of Thomas Pelow and Islam's One Million White Slaves* (New York: Farras, Straus and Giroux, 2004), 11.

2. Ibid., 12.

3. Ibid., 12–13.

4. Ibid.

5. Ibid.

6. Untitled, *New York Times*, editorial, August 6, 1882, 6.

7. Milton, 13.

8. Michael B. Oren, *Power, Faith and Fantasy: America in the Middle East 1776 to the Present* (New York: W.W. Norton, 2007), 19.

9. Stephen Clissold, *The Barbary Slaves* (New York: Barnes & Noble Books, 1977), 136.

10. Khalid Bekkaoui, *White Women Captives in North Africa: Narratives of Enslavement, 1735-1830* (New York: Palgrave Macmillan, 2010), 2.

11. Clissold, 1977, 54.

12. Clissold, 1977, 140.

13. Bekkaoui, 2.

14. Roy Caroll, "New Book Reopens Old Arguments about Slave Raids on Europe," *The Guardian*, March 11, 2004, https://bit.ly/2ynmIde.

15. Bekkaoui, 2.

16. Ibid.

17. Ibid.

18. Oren, 8.

19. Will Durant, *The Story of Civilization, Part 1. Our Oriental Heritage* (New York: Simon and Schuster, 1954), 19–20.

20. Seymour Drescher, *Abolition: A History of Slavery and Anti-Slavery* (Cambridge: Cambridge University Press, 2009), 6.

21. Durant, 337–338.

22. Ibid., 229.

23. Ibid., 125.

24. Ibid., 157.

25. Ibid., 292–293.

26. John A. Garraty and Peter Gay, *The Columbia History of the World* (New York: Harper & Row Publishers, 1972), 195.

27. Ibid.

28. Garraty and Gay, 215 and 363.

29. John R. McKivigan and Mitchell Snay, editors, *Religion and the Antebellum Debate over Slavery* (Athens: University of Georgia Press, 1998).

30. *The New Student Bible*, Ephesians 6:5–8, New International Version (Grand Rapids: Zondervan, 1992), 1282.

31. Ibid., Philemon 1:8–15, 1321.

32. Ibid., Galatians 3:28, 1271.

33. Garraty and Gay, 271.

34. Ibid.

35. Drescher, 13.

36. Ibid., 12.

37. Ibid., 22.

38. Henri Pirenne, *Mohammed and Charlemagne,* translated by Bernard Miall; originally published in 1935 (New York: Barnes & Noble Books, 1992), 153.

39. Garraty and Gay, 270.

40. Pirenne, 156, 159-162.

41. Pirenne, 86, 97, 159, 250.

42. Ibid., 159, 179.

43. Ibid., 250, 259.

44. Clissold, 1977, 7.

45. Drescher, 4.

46. Will Durant, *The Story of Civilization Part VI. The Reformation: A History of European Civilization from Wycliffe to Calvin: 1300-1564* (New York: Simon and Schuster, 1957), 203.

47. Ibid., 220.

48. Stephen Clissold, "The expulsion of the Moriscos, 1609–1614," *History Today*, Volume 28, Issue 12, 1978, 821.

49. Mar Jonsson, "The Expulsion of the Moriscos from Spain in 1609–1614: The Destruction of an Islamic Periphery," *Journal of Global History*, Vol. 2, Issue 02, July 2007, 211.

50. Drescher, 27.

51. Edward Saìd, *Orientalism* (New York: Vintage Books, 2003), 59; originally published in 1979.

52. Ibid.

53. Drescher, 28.

54. Caroll.

55. Drescher, 29.

56. Ibid.

57. Drescher, 29–30.

58. Ibid., 36.

59. Samuel Flagg Bemis, *John Quincy Adams and the Foundations of American Foreign Policy* (New York: Alfred A. Knopf, 1949), 412.

60. Leland Donald, *Aboriginal Slavery on the Northwest Coast of North America* (Berkeley and Los Angeles: University of California Press, 1997), 177.

61. Ibid., 103–120.

62. Ibid., 163–164.

63. Ibid., 163.

64. Ibid., 162.

65. Ibid., 162–163.

66. Ibid., 309 and 311.

67. Ibid.

68. Ibid., 169–171.

69. Ibid., 166.

70. Ibid., 172.

71. Wendell H. Oswalt and Sharlotte Neely, *This Land Was Theirs: A Study of Native Americans* (New York: Mayfield Publishing Company, 1999), 274–276.

72. Aurel Krause, *The Tlingit Indians: Results of a Trip to the Northwest Coast of America and the Bering Straits.* (Seattle: University of Washington Press, 1956), 155–161.

73. Donald, 172.

74. Ibid., 173.

75. Ibid., 194.

76. Ibid., 194–195.

77. Christon I. Archer, "Review: Aboriginal Slavery on the Northwest Coast of North America," BC Studies, 119, Autumn 1998, 108.

78. *Krista J. Kesselring, "Legal History Miscellany,* Slavery and Cartwright's Case before Somerset,"*October 10, 2018,* https://bit.ly/2LG5Mr2.

79. *Somerset v. Stewart, 1772, Court of King's Bench,* https://bit.ly/2Od33qW, 510.

80. Knight v. Wedderburn upheld, African American Registry, undated, https://bit.ly/2SA6qqB.

81. *Somerset v Stewart,* 500.

82. Drescher, 22.

83. Ibid.

84. R. Coupland, *Wilberforce: A Narrative* (Oxford; Clarendon Press, 1923), 89.

85. Ibid., 119–130.

86. Alexander C.R. Hammond, "Heroes of Progress, Pt. 8: William Wilberforce," HumanProgress, December 28, 2018, https://bit.ly/2SslypX.

87. James Walvin, "The Public Campaign in England Against Slavery 1787-1834," 68. Quoted in Thomas Sowell, *Race and Culture: A Worldview* (New York: Basic Books, 1994), 211.

88. Online historical population reports, Enumeration abstract, 1801, University of Essex, https://bit.ly/2LLEzm1, 4.

89. R. Winks, *The Blacks in Canada* (Montreal: McGill-Queen's University Press, 1971), 97.

90. Ibid., 102.

91. Ibid., 110–111.

92. Ibid., 111.

93. Donald, 226.

94. Ibid.

95. "Sir James Douglas," *Dictionary of Canadian Biography,* undated, https://bit.ly/2KjofWX.

96. Ibid.

97. Ibid.

98. Censuses of Canada 1665 to 1871, Statistics Canada, https://bit.ly/2YPk1QY.

99. Donald, 243–245.

100. Ibid., 243.

101. Ibid.

102. Ibid.
103. Ibid.
104. Donald, 243–245.
105. Ibid.

Chapter 13: Five arguments for a statute of limitations against the past

1. Toshika Kaneda, "How Many People Have Ever Lived On Earth?" Population Reference Bureau, March 9, 2018, https://bit.ly/2GfEwcc.
2. Ta-Nehisi Coates, "The Case for Reparations," *The Atlantic*, June 2014, https://bit.ly/1KC95mS.
3. Ibid.
4. Ibid.
5. Ibid.
6. Ibid.
7. Ibid.
8. Ibid.
9. Shashi Tharoor, "This House Believes Britain Owes Reparations to her Former Colonies Speaking for the Motion –Sr. Shashi Tharoor," Oxford Union, May 28, 2015, https://bit.ly/2Y46Z21.
10. Ibid.
11. "What Was the U.S. GDP Then?" Measuring Worth.com, undated, https://bit.ly/2YmvJ5K. (All figures adjusted for inflation to 2012 dollars.)
12. Thomas Sowell, *Black Rednecks and White Liberals* (New York: Encounter Books, 2006).
13. Thomas Sowell, *Race and Culture: A Worldview* (New York, Basic Books, 1994), 215.
14. Stephen Daggett, Costs of Major US Wars: Congressional Research Service Report for Congress (RS22926), July 24, 2008, https://bit.ly/2MgP7Kb.
15. Sowell, 1994, 215.
16. Angus Maddison, *The World Economy: A Millennial Perspective* (Paris: OECD, 2001), 109, 115.
17. Angus Maddison, "Class Structure and Economic Growth: India & Pakistan since the Moghuls, 1971," chapter three online edition, https://bit.ly/2K1AY0z, 13.
18. Maddison, 2001, 47, 66, 70, 80.
19. Ibid., 100.
20. Ibid., 27.
21. "Indian Residential Schools," Indigenous and Northern Affairs Canada, undated, https://bit.ly/2ewlzby.
22. See CBC, "1988: Government Apologizes to Japanese Canadians," September 22, 1998, https://bit.ly/2XZP5x5; Thomas Sowell, editor, "Three Black Histories," *Essays and Data on American Ethnic Groups* (Washington D.C.: Urban Institute, 1978), 84; and "Compensation and Reparations for the Evacuation, Relocation, and Internment Index (Redress Case Files), United States government, undated, https://bit.ly/2JMa9P7. The settlement in Canada in the 1980s included $300 million, including $21,000 each for 13,000 survivors, and additional money for other purposes, out of 22,000 interned. In the United States, compensation arrived in two programs, one in the 1950s and one in the 1990s. Post-war, the Federal Reserve Bank estimated the lost property was worth $400 million or $3.7 billion in today's dollars. But the first 1950s-era program was worth just $37 million for 26,650 claims, about 10% of what was owed. A later program initiated under Ronald Reagan as president would pay over $1.6 billion to 82,219 claimants, or about $20,000 each, and thus was still short.
23. Coates.
24. *The New Student Bible*, Ezekiel 18:20, New International Version, (Grand Rapids: Zondervan, 1992), 900.
25. Coates.
26. Seymour Drescher, *Abolition: A History of Slavery and Anti-Slavery* (Cambridge: Cambridge University Press, 2009), 3.
27. Ibid., 372-373.
28. Ibid.
29. Ted Binnema, "Protecting Indian Lands by Defining Indian: 1850-76," *Journal of Canadian Studies*, Vol. 48, No. 2, Spring 2014, 5–39.
30. Thomas F. Madden, "Inventing the Crusades," *First Things*, June 2009, https://bit.ly/1KwzYZC.

31. Ibid.
32. Ibid.
33. Will Durant, *The Story of Civilization, IV. The Age of Faith* (New York: Simon and Schuster, 1950), 285
34. Durant.

Chapter 14: Asian Americans and the challenge of the early republic

1. Jeanne Wakatsuki Houston and James D. Houston, *Farewell to Manzanar* (Boston: Houghton Mifflin, 1973), 7.
2. Leonard Broom and Ruth Riemer, *Removal and Return: The Socio-Economic Effects of the War on Japanese Americans* (Los Angeles: University of California Press, 1949), 158.
3. Houston and Houston.
4. Ibid., 51.
5. Iris Chang, *The Chinese in America: A Narrative History* (New York: Viking, 2003), 26.
6. Judy Yung et al., editors, *Chinese American Voices: From the Gold Rush to the Present* (Berkeley and Los Angeles: University of California Press, 2006), 429.
7. Chang, 17.
8. Ibid., viii.
9. Gunter Barth, *Bitter Strength: A History of the Chinese in the United States, 1850-1870* (Cambridge: Harvard University Press, 1964), 135.
10. Barth, 134.
11. Ibid.
12. Chang, 43.
13. Jean Pfaelzer, *Driven Out: The Forgotten War Against Chinese Americans* (Los Angeles, University of California Press, 2008), 39.
14. William L. Tung, *The Chinese in America: 1820-1973* (New York: Oceana Publications, 1974), 97.
15. Chang, 43-44.
16. Scott D. Seligman, *The First Chinese American: The Remarkable Life of Wong Chin Foo* (Hong Kong: Hong Kong University Press, 2013), 56.
17. Seligman, 56.
18. Chang, 93.
19. Jana Evans Braziel, *History of Migration and Immigration Laws in the United States* (Amherst: Department of Comparative Literature at the University of Massachusetts, 2000), https://bit.ly/1nZmdcl.
20. Chang, 130.
21. Ibid.
22. Ibid., 131.
23. Ibid., 130-131.
24. "House Resolution 5804," Government Track, April 17, 1882, undated, https://bit.ly/2YhzqcA.
25. Ibid.
26. "Chinese Exclusion Act," 1882, Harvard University Open Collections Program, https://bit.ly/1oTCilr.
27. Yung et al., 10.
28. Chang, 144.
29. Chang, 95.
30. Houston and Houston, xi.
31. David O' Brien and Stephen Fugita, *The Japanese American Experience* (Bloomington: Indiana University Press, 1991), 137, Appendix 1.
32. Yuki Ichioka, *The Issei: The World of the First Generation Immigrants, 1885-1924* (New York: The Free Press,1988), 99.
33. Ibid., 91-92.
34. Ibid., 100.
35. Harvard University Open Collections Program.
36. Ichioka, 102.
37. Houston and Houston, xi.

38. Ichioka, 252–253.

39. Yamato Ichihashi, *Japanese in the United States: A Critical Study of the Problems of the Japanese Immigrants and Their Children* (Stanford: Stanford University Press, 1932), 261.

40. Ichioka, 153.

41. Ibid., 224–225.

42. Ibid., 219.

43. Takao Ozawa v. U.S. (1922), https://bit.ly/2ywWrJf.

44. Ichihashi, 298–318.

45. "The Immigration Act of 1924 (The Johnson-Reed Act)," U.S. Department of State: Office of the Historian, https://bit.ly/1mENzqr.

46. Houston and Houston, xii.

Chapter 15: Living well is the best revenge: The rise of America's Pacific class

1. "American Community Survey, 2014, 1-year estimates," S0201, U.S. Census Bureau. (Median measurements are for "alone" i.e., a single race or ethnic identity that is not combined with another.)

2. Ibid.

3. William Petersen, "Chinese Americans and Japanese Americans," in Thomas Sowell, editor, *Essays and Data on American Ethnic Groups* (New York: The Urban Institute, 1978), 66.

4. Ibid.

5. Judy Yung et al., editors, *Chinese American Voices: From the Gold Rush to the Present* (Los Angeles: University of California Press, 2006), 10.

6. Iris Chang, *The Chinese in America: A Narrative History* (New York: Viking, 2003), 94.

7. 98.

8. Yick Wo v. Sherriff Hopkins, 1886, Supreme Court of the United States, https://bit.ly/335OAAs.

9. Chang, 138.

10. Scott D. Seligman, *The First Chinese American: The Remarkable Life of Wong Chin Foo* (Hong Kong: Hong Kong University Press, 2013), 113.

11. Ibid., 89.

12. Ibid., 112.

13. Ibid.

14. Ibid.

15. Ibid.

16. Ibid., 115–116.

17. Ibid.

18. Ibid.

19. Yuki Ichioka, *The Issei: The World of the First Generation Immigrants, 1885-1924*, (New York: The Free Press, 1988), 91–102.

20. Ibid., 195–196.

21. Ibid.

22. Ibid., 194–195.

23. Ibid., 178–179.

24. Ibid.

25. Erika Lee, *The Making of Asian America: A History* (New York: Simon & Schuster, 2015), 120.

26. Larry Tajiri and Guyo Tajiri, *Japanese American Journalism in the World War II Era* (Urbane: University of Chicago Press, 2012), 10.

27. Ibid.

28. Chang, 203.

29. Ibid.

30. Ibid.

31. Joel Kotkin. *Tribes: How Race, Religion and Identity Determine Success in the New Global Economy* (New York: Random House, 1992), 129–130.

32. Benson Tong, *The Chinese of America* (Westport: Greenwood Press, 2000), 22.

33. Ibid., 24–25.

34. Ibid.

35. Jack Chen, *The Chinese of America* (Cambridge: Harper & Row, 1980), 117–118.

36. Huping Ling, "The New Trends in American Chinatowns" in Bernard P. Wong and Chee-Beng Tan, *Chinatowns Around the World: Gilded Ghetto, Ethnopolis, and Cultural Diaspora* (Boston: Brill, 2013), 56–58.

37. Ling, 57.

38. Ibid.

39. Bernard P. Wong and Chee-Beng Tan, *Chinatowns Around the World: Gilded Ghetto, Ethnopolis, and Cultural Diaspora* Boston: Brill, 2013), 66.

40. Tong, 67.

41. Shehong Chen, *Being Chinese; Becoming Chinese American* (Chicago: University of Illinois Press, 2002) 11. See also Wong and Tan.

42. Yamato Ichihashi, 118.

43. Chang, 2003, p. X.

44. Ibid., 175.

45. Ibid.

46. Charles Hirschmann and Morrison G. Wong, "The Extraordinary Educational Attainment of Asian Americans: A Search For Historical Evidence and Explanations," Social Forces, Vol. 65:1, September 1986, https://bit.ly/3196D70, 3.

47. Ibid., 15.

48. Ibid., 13.

49. Ibid., 16.

50. Eric Walz, *Nikkei in the Interior West: Japanese Immigration and Community Building, 1882–1945* (Tucson: University of Arizona Press, 2012), 101.

51. Petersen, 66.

52. Jeanne Wakatsuki Houston and James D. Houston, *Farewell to Manzanar* (Boston: Houghton Mifflin, 1973), 85.

53. Hirschmann and Wong, 17.

54. Tajiri and Tajiri, 10.

55. Hirschmann and Wong, 17.

INDEX

A note about currency and language

Readers should assume that currencies are local, i.e., that when I refer to American income statistics, such figures are in American dollars. I've also adjusted most dollar statistics for inflation and flagged them as such in the text or endnotes. International comparisons referenced to Angus Maddison are in Geary-Khamis dollars, a hypothetical unit of currency that allows for purchasing-power-parity comparisons between countries and also real—i.e., inflation-adjusted—comparisons over centuries.

On language, I have followed George Orwell's preference in "Politics and the English Language" to avoid euphemisms and also to break rules where necessary. In this book, especially as applied to aboriginal issues, I use "aboriginal," "native," "First Nations," "tribe," "Indian," and "indigenous." I do so because, depending on the locale, some readers will be more familiar with one term or another. For example, in the United States, "tribal government" and "tribes" are in common usage; whereas in Canada, "First Nations" refers both to governments on reserve and also to those once labelled for statistical purposes as a "status Indian." "First Nations" is thus distinct from the more general category of "indigenous" or "Aboriginal," which can include Métis or Inuit or others. There are also historical, legal, judicial, and constitutional references that necessitate using some term or another. Hopefully the context makes clear the reason for the usage. Part of my choices in words also involves not falling into the trap of using language others use, *a la* Orwell's caution, for political ends. Some aboriginal activists use "indigenous" to assert residency in the Americas from time immemorial, except that is akin to the Genesis creation narrative. We all have ancestral roots in Africa. On other matters, I use "men," "women," and "man" instead of "human" or "humankind." The latter two terms have all the warmth of concrete. I default to using terms that create images of real people, even if used in generic ways on occasion, i.e., "man." Lastly, a variety of terms are simply more interesting for the reader when 100,000 words are to be read.

ABOUT THE AUTHOR

Mark Milke is a public policy analyst, keynote speaker, author, and columnist with six books and dozens of studies published across Canada and internationally in the last two decades. Mark's work has been published by think tanks in Canada, the United States, and Europe, including the Fraser Institute, the Montreal Economic Institute, American Enterprise Institute, Heritage Foundation, and Brussels-based Centre for European Studies. A regular columnist, his commentaries have appeared in the *Globe and Mail, National Post*, and *Maclean's*.

Mark is president of the Sir Winston Churchill Society of Calgary and a past-president of Civitas. In his doctoral dissertation on international relations and political philosophy, Mark analyzed the rhetoric of anti-Americanism in Canada, while his master's thesis chronicled the double standard on human rights in East Asia. Born and raised in Kelowna, British Columbia, Mark lives in Calgary and is an active hiker, skier, and runner with an interest in architecture, photography, cities, and history. His website is www.markmilke.com.

Additional copies of *The Victim Cult*

The Victim Cult is available in bookstores and through online retailers. Volume discounts for *The Victim Cult* are available by contacting the author directly though his website at
www.markmilke.com or **mark@markmilke.com**.